PEDIATRIC T·R·A·U·M·A NURSING

Edited by

Connie Joy, R.N., M.S.N., C.E.N.
Director of Emergency, Trauma, and
Maternal/Child Health
Director, Sky FlightCare
Aeromedical Helicopter Program
Brandywine Hospital and Trauma Center
Caln, Pennsylvania

AN ASPEN PUBLICATION®
Aspen Publishers, Inc.   1989   Rockville, Maryland
                                                                  Royal Tunbridge Wells

Library of Congress Cataloging-in-Publication Data

Pediatric trauma nursing/edited by Connie Joy.
p. cm.
Includes bibliographies and index.
ISBN: 0-8342-0040-6
1. Children—Wounds and injuries—Nursing. 2. Pediatric Emergencies.
3. Emergency nursing. I. Joy, Connie, RN.
[DNLM: 1. Emergencies—in infancy & childhood. 2. Emergencies—nursing.
3. Wounds and injuries—in infancy & childhood.
4. Wounds and injuries—nursing. WO 700 P3712]
RD93.5.C4P45   1989   617'.1'0088054—dc19
DNLM/DLC
for Library of Congress
88-7738
CIP

Copyright © 1989 by Aspen Publishers, Inc.
All rights reserved.

Aspen Publishers, Inc., grants permission for photocopying for personal or internal use, or for the personal or internal use of specific clients registered with the Copyright Clearance Center (CCC). This consent is given on the condition that the copier pay a $1.00 fee plus $.12 per page for each photocopy through the CCC for photocopying beyond that permitted by the U.S. Copyright Law. The fee should be paid directly to the CCC, 21 Congress St., Salem, Massachusetts 01970.
0-8342-0040-6/89 $1.00 + .12.

This consent does not extend to other kinds of copying, such as copying for general distribution, for advertising or promotional purposes, for creating new collective works, or for resale. For information, address Aspen Publishers, Inc., 1600 Research Boulevard, Rockville, Maryland 20850.

> The authors have made every effort to ensure the accuracy of the information herein, particularly with regard to drug selection and dose. However, appropriate information sources should be consulted, especially for new or unfamiliar procedures. It is the responsibility of every practitioner to evaluate the appropriateness of a particular opinion in the context of actual clinical situations and with due consideration to new developments. Authors, editors, and the publisher cannot be held responsible for any typographical or other errors found in this book.

Editorial Services: Marsha Davies

Library of Congress Catalog Card Number: 88-7738
ISBN: 0-8342-0040-6

Printed in the United States of America

1 2 3 4 5

*To all nurses who care for injured children
and their families*

and

*To my husband, Rick, for his encouragement, support,
and honest belief that nurses are the true heroes
of health care.*

Table of Contents

Contributors xi

Preface xiii

Acknowledgments xv

Chapter 1—Regionalization of Pediatric Trauma Care 1
    Connie Joy

    The Problem of Pediatric Trauma 1
    Rationale for a Regionalized Approach to
        Pediatric Trauma Care 2
    Essential Elements of a Regional Pediatric
        Trauma Care System 3
    Improving Pediatric Trauma Care 7

**Chapter 2—Initial Assessment and Stabilization of the
        Critically Injured Child** 9
    Heidi Zwick

    Unique Aspects of the Child 9
    Primary Survey: Assessment and Stabilization 10
    Secondary Survey 21
    The Pediatric Trauma Team: A Modular Concept 22
    Pediatric Trauma: The Continuum of Care 34

Chapter 3—Traumatic Head Injury 36
    Susan B. DeJong

    Epidemiology 36
    Pathophysiologic Principles 36

Types of Head Injuries	38
Neurological Assessment	51
Management of Increased Intracranial Pressure	56
Recovery from Head Injury	65

Chapter 4—Facial Trauma 68
Susan M. Gerhart

Facial Differences between Children and Adults	68
Etiology of Pediatric Facial Trauma	69
General Principles of Treatment	69
Soft Tissue Injuries	70
Facial Fractures	71
Ocular Trauma	74
Dental Injuries	75
Complications of Facial Trauma	76

Chapter 5—Spinal Cord Injury 79
Therese S. Richmond

Causes of Spinal Cord Injury	79
Prevention	79
Types of Spinal Cord Injury	80
Assessment and Management of the Spinal Cord-Injured Patient	81
Physiologic Nursing Diagnoses	82
Psychosocial Nursing Diagnoses	87

Chapter 6—Chest Trauma 91
Leslie Mancuso

Assessment of Thoracic Injuries	91
Chest Wall Injuries	92
Injuries to the Diaphragm	95
Pneumothorax	96
Injury to the Tracheobronchial Tree	98
Injuries to the Esophagus	99
Injuries to the Heart and Great Vessels	99

Chapter 7—Abdominal and Genitourinary Trauma 102
Lisa Marie Peckham and Lou Ann Kitchen

Mechanisms of Injury	102
Initial Assessment and Management	105

| | Abdominal Injury: Solid and Hollow Organ Trauma | 105 |
| | Genitourinary Trauma | 110 |

Chapter 8—Musculoskeletal Trauma ... 119
Connie Joy

	Mechanisms of Injury	119
	Special Considerations of Musculoskeletal Injuries in Children	120
	Initial Management of the Child with Multisystem Injury	123
	Management of Specific Musculoskeletal Injuries	127

Chapter 9—Transporting the Critically Injured Child ... 143
Teri S. Worthington

	Modes of Transport	143
	Equipment for Transport	144
	The Decision to Transport	146
	Initiating the Transport Call	147
	Preparing the Child for Transport	147
	Management and Stabilization En Route	148
	Safety and Risk Factors of Transporting Children	149
	Parental Concerns	152
	Documentation	152

Chapter 10—Burns ... 154
Joann Gallagher D'Italia

	Incidence and Etiology	154
	Initial Evaluation and Triage	154
	Determining the Burn Extent and Depth	158
	Care of Burn Wound	165
	Hypermetabolism	166
	Other Physiologic Alterations	167
	Inhalation Injury	167
	Electrical Burns	170
	Chemical Burns	171

Chapter 11—Pediatric Poisoning ... 173
Frances T. Gill

| | Nontoxic Ingestions | 174 |
| | History of Poisoning | 175 |

Emergency Management	176
Specific Toxins	180
Poisoning Prevention	189

Chapter 12—Submersion Injuries 193
Deborah P. Henderson

Terminology and Causes of Submersion Injuries	194
Fresh Water, Salt Water, and Cold Water Injury	194
The Submersion Incident	195
Prehospital Care of Submersion Injuries	196
Emergency Department Care	198
Management of Submersion Injuries	202
Severe Hypothermia	206
Admission to the Hospital	206
Prevention	208

Chapter 13—Child Abuse 211
Margaret Farmer Keil

Historical Background	211
Definition of Child Abuse and Neglect	212
Types of Abuse	212
Incidence of Abuse	213
Etiology and Precipitating Factors	215
Clinical Presentation of the Abused Child	217
Characteristic Physical Findings in Child Abuse	220
Diagnostic Tests and Procedures	224
Case Management	226
Nursing Interventions with Abusive Families	227

Chapter 14—Emotional Support of the Injured Child and Family 232
Tracy Kelly

Developmental Considerations	232
Nursing Roles in the Care of the Injured Child	235
The Family System	236
Planning Care	239

Chapter 15—Injury Prevention in Children 244
Karin Bannerot Braithwaite

Infants	244
Toddlers	247

Preschoolers	249
School-Aged Children	250
Adolescents	251
Conclusion	254
Index	**257**

Contributors

KARIN BANNEROT BRAITHWAITE,
R.N., M.S.N.
Faculty
Temple University
Philadelphia, Pennsylvania

SUSAN B. DEJONG, R.N., B.S.N.
Professional Consultant, Pediatric
Critical Care
Wynnewood, Pennsylvania

JOANN GALLAGHER D'ITALIA, R.N.,
M.S.N.
Clinical Nurse Specialist for Burns and
Reconstructive Plastic Surgery
St. Christopher's Hospital for Children
Burn Center
Philadelphia, Pennsylvania

SUSAN M. GERHART, R.N., M.N.
Education and Program Development
Specialist
St. Christopher's Hospital for Children
Philadelphia, Pennsylvania

FRANCES T. GILL, R.N., B.S.N., C.E.N.
Head Nurse, Emergency Department
The Children's Hospital of Philadelphia
Philadelphia, Pennsylvania

DEBORAH P. HENDERSON, R.N., M.A.,
C.E.N., C.C.R.N.
Administrator, California Emergency
Medical Services for Children Project
Harbor UCLA Medical Center
Torrance, California

CONNIE JOY, R.N., M.S.N., C.E.N.
Director of Emergency, Trauma, and
Maternal/Child Health
Director, Sky FlightCare
Aeromedical Helicopter Program
Brandywine Hospital and Trauma Center
Caln, Pennsylvania

MARGARET FARMER KEIL, R.N., M.S.N.
Head Nurse, Medical Unit
The Children's Hospital of Philadelphia
Philadelphia, Pennsylvania

TRACY KELLY, R.N., M.S.N., C.C.R.N.
Pediatric Clinical Nurse Specialist
Morristown Memorial Hospital
Morristown, New Jersey

LOU ANN KITCHEN, R.N., M.S.
Trauma Nurse Coordinator
Children's Hospital and Health Center
San Diego, California

LESLIE MANCUSO, R.N., M.S.N.
Instructor, Pediatric Critical Care
  Graduate Nursing Program
University of Pennsylvania
Philadelphia, Pennsylvania

LISA MARIE PECKHAM, R.N., M.S.
Children's Hospital and Health Center
San Diego, California

THERESE S. RICHMOND, R.N., M.S.N.,
  C.C.R.N.
Trauma Coordinator/Clinical Nurse
  Specialist
Thomas Jefferson University Hospital
Philadelphia, Pennsylvania

TERI S. WORTHINGTON, R.N.
Formerly, Nursing Coordinator,
  Emergency Transport Team
The Children's Hospital of Philadelphia
Philadelphia, Pennsylvania

HEIDI ZWICK, R.N., B.S.N.
Trauma Coordinator
Children's Hospital National Medical
  Center
Washington, D.C.

Preface

Trauma is responsible for more than half of all children who die between one and fifteen years of age and for one-third of those who die before their first birthday. The major causes of pediatric injury include motor vehicle accidents involving children as passengers, pedestrians, or bicycle riders; falls; fires; drownings; poisonings; and injuries received from adults through abuse. Because these injuries occur most frequently within the child's own environment or community, it is not surprising that most of the initial evaluation and care are provided within the emergency departments of local hospitals. Often, these early assessment and resuscitation efforts influence the child's ultimate outcome.

As with most types of health care delivery, expertise is greatly enhanced through opportunities for repetitive experience, such as when patients are cared for in regionalized systems with specialized care facilities. Nevertheless, severe pediatric injury occurs only about 25 percent as often as it does within the adult age group and across so large a geographic area that frequent, consistent contact with severe pediatric trauma in one hospital setting is uncommon. Hospitals generally evaluate and treat a far greater number of adults than children. Therefore, to decrease death and disability related to pediatric trauma, it is necessary to make a specific, conscious commitment to gaining information about the care of injured children.

Direct contribution to successful management of life-threatening injury in a child brings with it the responsibility for a wide range of skills and knowledge. Trauma nursing is rapidly becoming a recognized specialty with a unique body of knowledge requiring that technical and intellectual skills be translated into clinical action. Application of these skills to the pediatric patient must incorporate a consistent awareness related to the anatomical, physiological, and emotional differences of the child compared to the adult. It is these differences that prompted the writing of this book.

The impact of regionally organized trauma care cannot be underestimated in relation to the number of children who can be saved after severe injury. Chapter 1 assists in setting the tone of the book by emphasizing the importance of trauma system development. Chapter 2 discusses the resuscitation of a critically injured child, with attention not only to the care provided but to an optimal method of organizing a pediatric trauma team. Chapters 3 through 8 address the care of the child who has sustained specific body-system injuries. These include head, facial, spinal, chest, abdominal, genitourinary, and musculoskeletal trauma. Occasionally, an injured child requires transfer to a regional referral facility as a result of the level of care required; Chapter 9 was written to assist nurses in preparing to transport such a child. Chapters 10 through 13 deal with highly specialized and complex types of injuries. Burns, poisonings, drownings, and nonaccidental injuries remain significantly common within the pediatric age group, and each requires enormous resources and a high level of expertise to manage. Chapter 14 focuses on an area of pediatric trauma nursing that can greatly influence the care of any child: the response of the family. Nurses who work with children readily understand that the injured child is a member of a family unit which has also sustained injury. Emotional support to both the child and the family are essential to a positive outcome for all. The final chapter deals with the prevention of pediatric trauma throughout the normal stages of human growth and development. Successful prevention of severe injury is the best weapon against this childhood killer.

Each chapter is written by a clinically expert nurse who has made a career of pediatric or trauma nursing. They bring to their chapters the latest in pediatric trauma management as well as the belief that participating in the care of a critically injured child is one of the most important professional contributions that a nurse can make. Can there be any greater challenge?

Connie Joy, R.N., M.S.N., C.E.N.

Acknowledgments

The preparation of any book dictates a commitment not only to the topic but to the project itself. I am exceedingly grateful to each of the contributing authors for their ability and willingness to share their own expertise through writing. It has truly been an honor to work with nurses who, within their own professional careers, make a significant contribution to the care of children. I would especially like to thank Fran Gill for her assistance with this book and for her friendship and support. She is most certainly a role model for pediatric emergency and trauma nursing.

I would also like to express my sincere gratitude to Janet Joy for her assistance in preparing this manuscript and her meticulous attention to detail.

Last, I must thank my parents and sister for their love and encouragement and my husband, Rick, for his patience, understanding, and belief that this book was possible.

Chapter 1
Regionalization of Pediatric Trauma Care

Connie Joy

THE PROBLEM OF PEDIATRIC TRAUMA

The death of any child is a tragedy. In the case of childhood death due to trauma, most children before sustaining severe injury are physiologically and developmentally normal. They had thus far successfully avoided other childhood killers, such as congenital defects, infection, and cancer. Whenever a child dies, the potentials that existed for that life are lost not only to the child and the family but to society as well. Without the benefits of what that child may have offered, society as a whole is less of a strength overall.

Children between the ages of one and fourteen years are more likely to die from injuries than from any other cause.[1] This is not a recent problem but one that is demonstrating a significant upward trend. The National Safety Council in 1984 stated that trauma was identified as the cause of death approximately 10 percent of the time in persons over the age of 14 years.[2] Between the ages of one and fourteen years, however, more than 50 percent of deaths were related to traumatic injuries.[3]

These startling statistics alone should provide enough incentive to initiate the development of improved trauma care and trauma prevention programs for children. It is encouraging that regional trauma systems are actively being developed and implemented at a rapid rate throughout the United States. Currently, thirty-one states have some type of identified trauma system either established or within developmental stages.[4] Nevertheless, emphasis on the need for addressing the special requirements of injured children, and the promotion of trauma care systems that specifically deal with the pediatric age group, has been slow to evolve.

In the adult population, the development of a regionalized, systematic approach to trauma care has undeniably demonstrated the ability to reduce trauma death and the long-term effects related to severe injury.[5-8] Similar findings have been documented for the pediatric patient.[9,10] Research has shown that separate individuals such as paramedics, nurses, physicians, and other health care professionals can be highly trained and skilled in providing care to critically injured children. Yet, individual effort has little effect on significantly decreasing the numbers of children who die from trauma. In reality, the difference occurs when the activities of each of these professionals are coordinated within a regionally organized system of pediatric trauma care.

RATIONALE FOR A REGIONALIZED APPROACH TO PEDIATRIC TRAUMA CARE

Accidental injury is always unexpected. Therefore, the most vital aspect of any trauma system is that the system itself never be caught unprepared. Accidental trauma carries with it the unknown variables of when, who, where, and how severe. It is these variables that become the propelling force behind the establishment of a system of trauma care that is prepared to handle the unexpected. Anticipation and preparation are the best first-line defenses against traumatic injury. The hallmark of the beginning of a trauma system is the ability to convert these unknowns into obtainable information and then to react with an appropriate, lifesaving response.

The rationale for developing any type of health care system revolves around the need to supply the general population with a specific resource when it is required. In relation to pediatric trauma care, the immediate availability of specialized resources must be ensured on a 24-hour basis. There must also be provision for a continuum of care from the initial time of injury through the entire recovery period. The simple availability of these resources alone is not enough, however. State-of-the-art pediatric trauma care requires the highest level of expertise possible in treating injured children. These two concepts, availability of resources and level of expertise, lead to the impetus behind the designation of specific facilities within a given geographical region as pediatric trauma centers.

Availability of Resources

Specialized pediatric trauma care requires enormous resources that are not available within all hospitals at all times. These include surgeons with extensive training and experience in pediatric surgery and nurses who are specialized in the care of critically injured and recovering children. Other necessary professionals, such as social workers, respiratory therapists, and radiologists, must also have a high level of understanding of pediatric care. Required resources also include equipment that is essential to the care of the injured child. Availability of all types and sizes of equipment appropriate for every age group must be guaranteed, along with the expertise in their use.

The cost of these resources in time, energy, and money can be high, making their constant availability prohibitive in many hospitals. In addition, the actual number of professionals with extensive pediatric trauma experience is limited. The problem is often simply that there are not enough resources to go around.

Level of Expertise

Experience is one of the best teachers. Evidence of this point has been displayed on learning curves that demonstrate increases in knowledge and improved performance with increased practice and repetition. With pediatric trauma care, judgment, skills, and teamwork are improved by consistent contact with a significant volume of trauma patients who supply the opportunity for learning. Hospitals with frequent experience in treating critically injured children undeniably offer better care to such patients than hospitals receiving only an occasional traumatically injured child. Therefore, within a geographically regionalized system of trauma care, the specialized needs of the child should be recognized through the designation of specific facilities as pediatric trauma centers. Only then can centralization of resources and channeling of patients to those resources occur. This in turn will positively affect the outcome of pediatric injury and the incidences of death.

ESSENTIAL ELEMENTS OF A REGIONAL PEDIATRIC TRAUMA CARE SYSTEM

Commitment

Commitment is the first essential ingredient for optimal care of the critically injured child. It begins on a regional basis, extending far beyond the community boundaries that exist for any individual hospital. The question of whether or not there has been enough investment of time, personnel, money, and political emphasis in combating this childhood health problem must be answered by those agencies responsible for the quality of health care within a given geographical area. The development of an accreditation, designation, or categorization process then occurs; this requires the commitment and cooperation of many health care agencies and facilities. This is most readily apparent in the collaboration of multiple services throughout a region and the willingness of each to contribute required resources.

Commitment is also institutional. This is most visibly demonstrated by the trauma patient being viewed as having high priority within the institutional setting. Efforts to further convey this commitment should center around establishing defined methods of providing the care necessary for the injured child and family and contributing to improved pediatric trauma care in a global sense. Examples of how this commitment can be demonstrated include the following.

1. The establishment of trauma care protocols, which set the standard for care as well as provide educational resources for pediatric trauma care.
2. The immediate mobilization at all times of appropriate personnel to the receiving area of the institution to begin resuscitation, thus interrupting the dynamic dying process of a critically injured child.
3. The immediate and continued availability of necessary resources until the patient is fully recovered (for example, social services and school tutorial programs).
4. Consistent surveillance and intervention for all complications that can potentially claim the life of an injured child or limit his or her future ability to live independently and with quality.
5. Provision of a means to regain physical losses through rehabilitation.

6. Recognition of the child as an integral part of a family structure, and incorporation of the family into the system of trauma care.
7. Adoption of a leadership role in supplying advanced trauma education and training for health care professionals both within the institution and in the prehospital setting and other facilities.
8. Active involvement in injury-prevention programs both within the hospital and in the community it serves.
9. Aggressive quality assurance efforts that evaluate all aspects of the trauma care system and the medical/nursing care delivered to trauma patients.
10. Consistent contribution to the existing body of knowledge through active trauma data collection and research programs, with dissemination of information.
11. Maintenance of the institutional policy that the pediatric trauma system will be kept highly visible as a means of ensuring appropriate use of the system.

The hospital that has made a commitment to provide pediatric trauma care will be called on as a regional resource for needed information and assistance by both the public and other health care facilities. Any hospital with a trauma center holds itself out as providing a higher standard of care than what is ordinarily offered by most hospitals. It therefore must be prepared to respond through the provision of services, some of which will extend far beyond its own front doors.

Last, commitment is personal on the part of individuals who lend their time, energy, and expertise to the cause of improving pediatric trauma care. Personal commitment can be demonstrated through the deliverance of high-quality direct patient care, active individual search for increased knowledge related to trauma care, efforts related to sharing information through lectures or publishing, and the creative accomplishments of those who develop standards and protocols that directly influence the quality of trauma care provided.

Although the element of commitment is intangible, it must have great strength to endure many of the struggles that are inherent in any trauma system development process.

Cooperation

The second essential element of a regionalized approach to pediatric trauma care is cooperation. Trauma system development is undeniably a political process. Organizations and groups involved include governmental agencies who represent public health concerns; prehospital and hospital associations; physician, nursing, and other professional organizations; and public and community service groups. They must be prepared to work in concert with each other as a team, all with the same goal of improved trauma care.

It is usually difficult to bring all these groups together, however, and to sort through issues that would lead to optimal trauma care while at the same time protecting the interests of each specific group. One method used to resolve many of the political problems related to trauma system development is the placement of ultimate authority for the system with a specific organization. This organization is then accountable for the justification, planning, implementation, continued operational surveillance, and evaluation of the trauma care system on a regional basis. One example of this concept in action was the legislative establishment of the Pennsylvania Trauma Systems Foundation in 1984. This agency was granted the legal authority to accredit hospitals as trauma centers in the state of Pennsylvania. The Trauma Systems Foundation sets the standards for both adult and pediatric trauma centers, which are based on the work done by the American College of Surgeons' Committee on Trauma.[11] The Trauma Systems Foundation accepts and reviews applications from hospitals desiring trauma center accreditation and then organizes and oversees a site survey team visit to the applying hospital. These survey teams are composed of administrative, nursing, and medical experts in trauma care from throughout the country. On the basis of recommendations made by the site survey team, decisions regarding trauma center accreditation are made by the Trauma Systems Foundation. In addition, the Foundation is responsible for ensuring that the care received by injured persons treated in Pennsylvania trauma centers meets the required standard of care. This is done through centralization of trauma patient data, which are collected by a trauma registry system within each trauma center.

The success of any regionalized trauma care system is highly dependent on the cooperation of the emergency medical services (EMS) system. The concept of "getting the right patient to the right hospital at the right time" refers to the coordination of efforts immediately after the accident.[12] Vital to this concept is the use of a triage method that can guide the decision-making process of prehospital personnel whenever they deal with an injured person. The concept of triage is of particular importance when working with injured children. The number of hospitals having pediatric trauma capabilities within any geographical region is limited. Therefore, a rapid, accurate method of triage and transport, with provision of appropriate care, is essential to the salvage of a critically injured child.

Cooperation is also essential between hospitals that have trauma capability and those that do not. It must be recognized that the geographical distribution of facilities with pediatric trauma capability cannot ensure that the trauma center will be the hospital nearest the location of the injury, or even within a 20- to 30-minute transport time. Therefore, patterns of transfer for injured children requiring advanced trauma care must be established between designated pediatric trauma centers and nondesignated hospitals to guarantee the highest level of trauma care possible.

Last, within each hospital desiring trauma center designation there should be esprit de corps. The critically injured child requires multiple services throughout the acute and recovery phases. The development of a sense of unity and common goal facilitates the cooperative contribution of needed resources and brings with it a movement toward a team effort. This is perhaps one of the most exciting and satisfying processes for all those actively involved in hospital-wide trauma system development.

Competence

The final essential element of pediatric trauma care is competence. It has already been discussed that frequent exposure to critically injured children directly relates to increased opportunities for improved performance. Nevertheless, because of the lower incidence of severe pediatric trauma cases compared to adult cases, competence cannot be ensured solely through experience. The achievement of a high level of skill in the care of pediatric trauma patients begins with a well-managed organizational structure that promotes learning through various means.

Pediatric trauma care teams can include a wide range of nursing and medical specialists. Opportunities in trauma care education must be provided for each area of specialty, including nurses responsible for prehospital or interhospital transport, emergency resuscitation, intraoperative care, postanesthesia recovery, acute intensive care, post–acute surgical care, and rehabilitation. Physicians who fulfill numerous trauma system roles also must be provided with training, leading to proficiency in trauma care. Courses such as Advanced Cardiac Life Support and Advanced Trauma Life Support are available for physicians, nurses, and prehospital care providers, providing both didactic and hands-on experience. One problem with these programs is that, although a small portion of each deals with the ill or injured child, the vast majority of information pertains to the adult. Currently a few groups are making efforts to prepare educational programs that address the specific care requirements of the child.

Continuing education specifically designed for pediatric trauma centers is important in ensuring the preparedness of trauma team members. Assessment of the current knowledge and skills of all personnel involved in the care of the injured child is an important first step in the development of training programs. Trauma continuing education programs must be founded on this knowledge base and then designed to allow the professional to build on it, incorporating the most current information available in trauma care. Accessible resource individuals who have a high level of experience and expertise are also important, so that information is readily available when new experiences are encountered. A successful method of training new trauma team members is the frequent rehearsal of roles through mock trauma drills. The regular case review and critique of selected patients is also a valuable learning tool.

Hospitals with a recognized regional trauma program are called on to contribute heavily to educational offerings for both their own hospital personnel and other professionals outside the facility. In addition, whenever a hospital assumes responsibility as a pediatric trauma center, it also assumes a leadership role in the education of the public, especially in the area of trauma prevention and the accessibility of trauma care.

Perhaps one of the most important aspects in ensuring competence and quality care is the consistent evaluation of all aspects of trauma system performance. Much has been written regarding the value and validity of medical evaluation and its relationship to improved trauma care. Nevertheless, ensuring competence within a hospital-wide, regionally established trauma system is a difficult and elusive process. It requires examining care from the moment of injury through discharge or death, with consideration given to all the interactions that occur within any regionalized trauma system. This includes the evaluation of the availability, responsiveness, and performance of each of the following:

- EMS system
- referral hospitals
- intrahospital transfer systems
- trauma hospital
- rehabilitation facility.

System performance is evaluated by determining compliance with system criteria and standards and by assessing the quality of care delivered throughout each phase. The ultimate objective of system evaluation is to determine the effect of the system on the outcome of injured children and to modify, update, and improve the system whenever possible. This leads to increased individual and system competence.

IMPROVING PEDIATRIC TRAUMA CARE

The development and proliferation of trauma systems across the country has significantly changed the standard of trauma care. Data collection systems such as hospital-based, regional, and national trauma registries provide an extremely important mechanism for identifying causes of pediatric morbidity and mortality. The information gained from these registries can assist professionals in determining methods of minimizing etiological risks and improving nursing and medical management, and it can provide a basis for system comparison and evaluation. The recent heightened awareness about how the injured child differs from the adult has highlighted the need for trauma system development addressing the special needs of the child. Pediatric trauma care is beginning to attract the attention of nurses and physicians and is becoming a recognized specialty by a small but growing group of dedicated professionals. Future pediatric trauma care and trauma system development is a product of today's research. There continues to be a critical need for pediatric trauma investigation and funding. Improved trauma care for children depends on it.

NOTES

1. J. Alex Haller, Jr., "Problems in Children's Trauma," *Journal of Trauma* 10(1970):269–71.
2. "Accident Facts," *National Safety Council* (Chicago, 1984).
3. National Center for Health Statistics, "Monthly Vital Statistics Report," 33(22 June 1984).
4. R.H. Cales and R.W. Heilig, *Trauma Care Systems* (Rockville, Md.: Aspen Publishers, Inc., 1986), 315.
5. R.H. Cales, "Trauma Mortality in Orange County: The Effect of Implementation of a Regional Trauma System," *Annals of Emergency Medicine* 13(1984):1–10.
6. David R. Boyd and R. Adams Cowley, "Comprehensive Regional Trauma/Emergency Medical Services (EMS) Delivery Systems: The United States Experience," *World Journal of Surgery* 7(1983):149–57.

7. D.K. Lowe et al., "Patterns of Death, Complication and Error in the Management of Motor Vehicle Victims: Implications for a Regional System of Trauma Care," *Journal of Trauma* 23(1983):503–509.

8. J.G. West and R.H. Cales, "Impact of Regionalization: The Orange County Experience," *Archives of Surgery* 118(1983):740–44.

9. C. McKoy and M.J. Bell, "Preventable Traumatic Deaths in Children," *Journal of Pediatric Surgery* 18 (1983):505.

10. Max L. Ramenofsky et al., "Maximum Survival in Pediatric Trauma: The Ideal System," *Journal of Trauma* 24(1984):818.

11. Committee on Trauma, "Hospital and Pre-Hospital Resources for Optimal Care of the Injured Patient," *Bulletin of the American College of Surgeons* 68(1983).

12. Donald D. Trunkey, "Overview of Trauma," *Surgical Clinics of North America* 62(1982):3–7.

Chapter 2
Initial Assessment and Stabilization of the Critically Injured Child

Heidi Zwick

The arrival of a critically injured child at an emergency facility can result in confusion and anxiety if personnel feel unprepared because of lack of training or resources. The key to an efficient, coordinated response to the pediatric patient is an understanding of assessment, management, and treatment principles. Predetermined protocols must translate these principles into an organized team effort.

The approach to the injured child is discussed here in a format that has become an accepted national standard through the Advanced Trauma Life Support course sponsored by the American College of Surgeons.[1] This format prioritizes the approach to the injured patient into a primary and secondary survey. The primary survey involves direct intervention into clinical indicators of life-threatening conditions in the priority order of airway, breathing, circulation, disability, and exposure. The secondary survey is a thorough head-to-toe examination that seeks to identify other, previously undetected injuries.

The major anatomic and physiologic differences between the pediatric and the adult patient are identified and form the basis for understanding the assessment and stabilization measures that follow. The team concept and treatment protocols are then described as a method of applying these principles to practice.

UNIQUE ASPECTS OF THE CHILD

There are several ways in which children differ from adults, regardless of type or extent of injury. These general differences provide a basis for understanding the pediatric patient.

Children, generally, are free of pre-existing disease. A child can be treated for injuries without concern for chronic heart or lung disease complicating the presentation. As a result, children often have better outcomes than many, less healthy, injured adults.

Children have a small anatomy, which results in different patterns of injury from the same mechanism of injury. For example, a car bumper striking a child may cause extremity, abdominal, thoracic, and head injuries, whereas an adult may sustain only leg injuries. This small size also means that organs are in closer proximity to each other, so that multiple injuries are more likely. The various sizes of children require that supplies, equipment, and medication dosages be adjusted to their size and weight; a single standard cannot be applied to all.

The different developmental stages of children present a special challenge. Their response to injury, as well as to medical personnel, is based on their developmental stage and can complicate assessment, especially in cases of neurological impairment. For example, infants cannot localize pain and respond with a generalized movement of all their extremities. This is an appropriate response but may be perceived as a decreased level of consciousness if the developmental stage is not taken into account. The approach to the child and the care given must also be based on the developmental stage to be effective. For example, all children need reassurance and explanation. For infants, this may be provided by a calm, consistent voice throughout the resuscitation. For adolescents, this involves providing detailed descriptions of interventions being performed, allowing them to assist or to chose among alternatives if possible, and being sensitive to their need for privacy by using drapes or blankets as much as possible.

When a child is injured, the family is also injured. The family members must be made to feel a part of the treatment team by being included, as much as possible, in the care regimen from the moment of injury. Parents who understand the injuries, interventions, plans, and prognosis can assist in eliciting their child's trust, cooperation, and adjustment to injury.

PRIMARY SURVEY: ASSESSMENT AND STABILIZATION

Airway

A child's airway is structured differently from an adult's (Figure 2-1). The oral cavity is small in proportion to the tongue, allowing the tongue more easily to obstruct the airway. The submandibular tissue is thin, potentially permitting any pressure in this area to push the tongue back into the airway. The airway is at risk of obstruction because the passages are narrow and short and because the mucous membranes lining them are delicate and easily traumatized. The often hypertrophied tonsils and adenoids present a fragile and difficult obstruction to nasal intubation. The vocal cords are distensible, cartilaginous, and easily damaged. The narrowest diameter of the airway is the cricoid ring, whereas in the adult it is at the glottis. This places the child at risk for edema and subglottic stenosis if endotracheal tubes are too large and cause trauma to the airway. Intubation angles are different because the larynx lies at the level of the third vertebra, more anterior and cephalad than in the adult. The larynx and trachea are soft and collapsible, especially when the head is hyperextended or hyperflexed.

Assessment

The first priority for assessment of any trauma patient is the airway. The child is observed for signs of respiratory distress. This may include circumoral cyanosis or nasal flaring. The child may use accessory muscles to breathe and exhibit supraclavicular, sternal, intercostal, or subcostal retractions. Distress may also be exhibited by agitation,

Initial Assessment and Stabilization 11

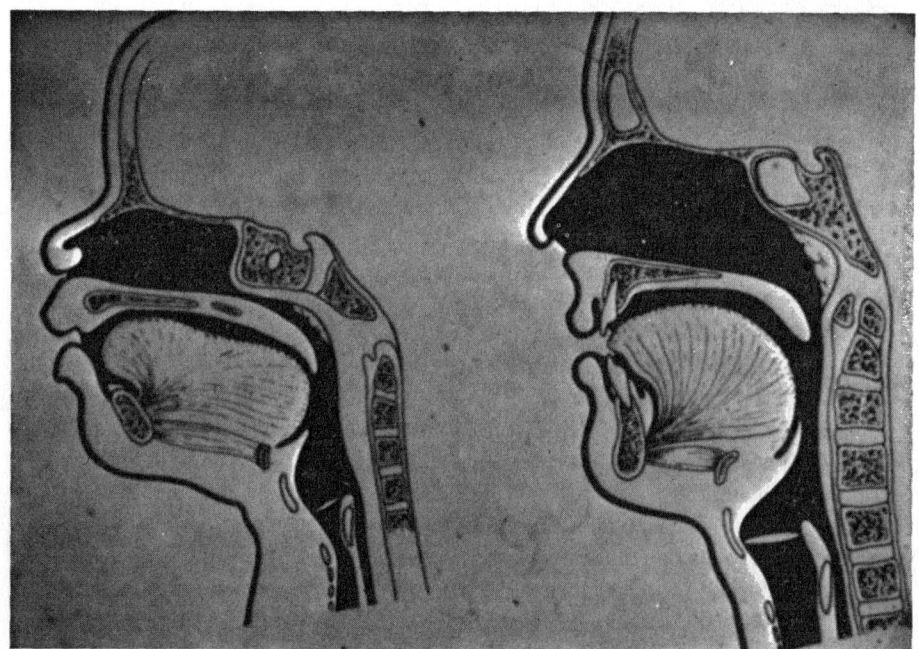

Figure 2-1 Comparison of the Pediatric and Adult Airway. *Source:* Reprinted from *Pediatric Trauma Care* by M.R. Eichelberger and G.L. Pratsch (Eds.), p. 52, Aspen Publishers, Inc., © 1988.

anxiety, or decreased level of consciousness due to hypoxia. Stridor or hoarseness may be an indication of a crushed or obstructed airway. Any external trauma to the face or neck such as bruising, apparent fractures, bleeding, or subcutaneous emphysema should be assessed. The mouth should be examined for blood, loose teeth, or visible foreign objects.

Stabilization

Stabilization of the airway is based on the observed symptoms and is conducted in an orderly fashion from simple to complex maneuvers.

All pediatric trauma patients have a potential cervical spine injury. The first priority of any airway maneuver is manual in-line cervical immobilization and, if available, the application of an appropriately sized rigid collar. The collar should be measured in width from the top of the shoulder to the chin when the head is in the neutral position. This will allow the bottom edge of the collar to rest on the shoulder while the chin is held in alignment. If the collar is too short, support will be inadequate. If the collar is too tall, it will hyperextend the neck and may compromise the airway. The child must also be immobilized manually on the backboard because no collar by itself provides sufficient immobilization if the child attempts to move. This is maintained until a lateral cervical roentgenogram of C1–7 is obtained to screen for any injury.

All injured children are initially given oxygen at a rate of 5 to 10 L/min. Measurement of arterial blood gases should be included in the routine laboratory tests to determine the need for continued oxygen.

Cervical spine immobilization and oxygen administration apply to all pediatric trauma patients. All other airway maneuvers are based on observed distress and proceed in a stepwise fashion. Intervention for a child with labored or absent respirations begins with a jaw thrust or chin lift, with fingers placed on the bony prominences of the jaw, to pull the tongue forward from a potentially obstructing position. If the child is still in respiratory distress, blood, vomitus, or a foreign object may be obstructing the narrow airway passages, so that suctioning the mouth and oropharynx may be lifesaving.

If positioning and suction do not relieve the patient's respiratory distress, mask-assisted ventilation is the next maneuver. The mask must be sized so that a tight seal is formed over the nose and mouth. The bag must also be sized so that the positive pressure delivered is not too great for the child's lung capacity. Fingers used to anchor the mask to the face must rest on bony prominences, not the thin submandibular tissue, so that the tongue is not displaced backward.

An oral airway should be used with caution in a patient who is not completely obtunded because it may cause vomiting and aspiration. The intervention of choice with an obtunded patient is intubation, so that oral airways should only be considered a temporary measure until intubation can be accomplished. If an oral airway is to be used, it must be sized to the patient by measuring from the earlobe to the corner of the mouth. An airway that is too short can push the tongue back into the oropharynx, and one that is too long can obstruct the trachea. The airway is inserted by means of a direct, rather than a rotating, technique with the assistance of a tongue blade. An esophageal obturator airway is contraindicated in children.

If ventilation is still inadequate or if the child remains obtunded with a Glasgow Coma Scale score of 8 or less (see Table 2-9), intubation is required while maintaining the head in the neutral or "sniffing" position. The nasotracheal route is used only if oral trauma precludes the oral route because the nasal passages are narrow with easily traumatized mucous membranes, tonsils, and adenoids. The endotracheal tube size is estimated by matching the diameter of the tube to that of the child's external nares or distal phalanx of the little finger; Table 2-1 lists tube sizes by patient age. Uncuffed tubes are used for children younger than 8 years of age to minimize subglottic ulceration and, later, stenosis.

The trachea is shorter in children than in adults, and the tube is passed only 2 to 3 cm below the vocal cords to avoid endobronchial intubation or perforation. Ventilation is provided with a hand resuscitator with an oxygen flow rate of 5 to 10 L/min. The anterior and cephalad position of the epiglottis makes placement of the endotracheal tube into the esophagus a common error. Tube placement must be checked carefully by auscultating for bilateral breath sounds at both the apices and bases of the lungs, checking for bilateral and equal chest excursions, and observing for the absence of cyanosis, gastric distention, or subcutaneous emphysema. An anteroposterior chest roentgenogram is obtained to confirm tube position above the carina of the trachea.

Accidental displacement of the orotracheal tube is common because of its shallow placement in the short trachea. The tube must be securely taped in place, but until that occurs, the fingers holding the tube should be anchored on the bony prominences of the face to avoid displacement due to hand movement.

Table 2-1 Recommended Tracheal Tube Sizes in Relation to Age

Age	Internal Diameter (mm)
Premature (2.5 kg)	2.5
Term newborn	3.0
6 months	3.5
12 months	4.5
18–24 months	4.5
4 years	5.0–5.5
6 years	5.5–6.0
8 years	6.0–6.5
10 years	6.5
12 years	7.0
14 years	7.5
Adults	8.0–9.5

Note: Children of the same age vary in size; occasionally a tube 0.5 mm smaller or larger in internal diameter (ID) may be required. A general formula giving the tube ID (in millimeters) for children older than 2 years of age is Age (years)/4 + 4.5.

Source: Reprinted from *Pediatric Trauma Care* by M.R. Eichelberger and G.L. Pratsch (Eds.), p. 54, Aspen Publishers, Inc., © 1988.

Intubation of children should always be accomplished with sedation to avoid further elevating potentially increased intracranial pressure. The only children who do not require sedation before intubation are those with a Glasgow Coma Scale score of 3 and flaccid paralysis. All others are sedated according to recommended doses (Table 2-2).

In very rare cases it may be impossible to intubate a child, and an emergency cricothyrotomy may be required. This is accomplished, as in adults, by insertion of a 14- to 16-gauge needle through the cricothyroid membrane. If this is not possible or unsuccessful, a surgical cricothyrotomy or tracheostomy is performed by an incision through the cricoid membrane.

Table 2-2 Recommended Sedation for Pediatric Intubation[2]

Patient Condition	Sedation and Procedure
Reactive patient with stable cardiovascular status and no need for rapid airway control	Thiopental or thiamylal, 2 to 4 mg/kg Ventilate with bag-mask for 3 minutes Use cricoid pressure unless patient is retching Intubate
Reactive patient with stable cardiovascular status and mandatory rapid airway control	Atropine, 0.02 mg/kg Thiopental or thiamylal, 2 to 4 mg/kg Succinylcholine, 2 mg/kg Ventilate with bag-mask for 60 seconds Use cricoid pressure unless patient is retching Intubate
Reactive patient with unstable cardiovascular status and no concern for increased intracranial pressure	Same as stable cardiovascular status, mandatory rapid airway control; thiopental or thiamylal may be omitted

Breathing

Children differ from adults in several ways that affect their ability to oxygenate and ventilate adequately, especially when they sustain thoracic injury. The skeletal structure of a child is more pliant than that of an adult, which reduces the incidence of fractures when the same amount of force of injury is sustained. Pulmonary contusions without rib fractures are more common in children because the kinetic energy of a blunt force is absorbed by the lung tissue rather than by the rib as it fractures. This also means that rib fractures are more ominous in children because more force is required to sustain the fracture.

The mediastinum is flexible in children, so that it can shift widely due to a pneumothorax or hemothorax. This can impinge dramatically on the contralateral lung, the heart, the great vessels, and the trachea and cause greater ventilatory distress than in the adult.

Children are prone to aerophagia because they swallow air when crying. Gastric dilation can impinge upward on the diaphragm, inhibiting diaphragmatic excursions and severely compromising ventilatory effectiveness. Small children have poorly developed chest muscles and use their abdominal muscles to move their diaphragms. This can cause compromised ventilatory capacity if there is abdominal distention or with inflation of the abdominal compartment of pneumatic antishock trousers.

Children have thin chest walls, so that breath sounds can be difficult to assess. The sounds are easily referred from one area to another and may be incorrectly perceived as being present even when an endotracheal tube is incorrectly placed in the esophagus. The lungs are therefore auscultated for equal and bilateral breath sounds at both the apices and the bases.

Children also have relatively small blood volumes, so that bleeding into the thoracic cavity can easily result in hypovolemic shock.

Assessment

Assessment of the child for ventilatory compromise involves maintaining observation for respiratory distress, especially if it continues after patency of the airway has been established. The child is observed for retractions, nasal flaring, anxiety, decreased level of consciousness, or deviation of the trachea. Young children, who use their abdominal muscles for ventilation, may exhibit a "see-saw" movement between the chest and abdomen with respiratory distress. The chest wall is inspected for contusions, lacerations, deformity of the rib structure, and unequal chest movement. The thoracic cavity is auscultated for equal and bilateral breath sounds at both the apices and bases. Because of the pliant skeletal structure, significant thoracic injury may be present without rib fractures as a clue.

Stabilization

Stabilization of the breathing component involves immediate intervention if clinical assessment indicates a life-threatening condition. Therefore, if the child exhibits signs of respiratory distress, unequal breath sounds, and unstable vital signs, a pneumothorax or hemothorax must be suspected and needle decompression accomplished without benefit of a chest roentgenogram. A needle thoracentesis is performed in the midaxillary line at the level of the nipples in the fourth or fifth intercostal space with a 14- to 20-gauge needle. Insertion at the apex presents a small target area in children and therefore a greater potential for error than in adults. After initial decompression is signified by a rush of air the needle is removed, and at the same landmarks a thoracostomy tube is inserted (Table 2-3). This is inserted without a trocar, directed toward the apex of the lung, and attached to a suction drainage device (Table 2-4).

If a hemothorax is suspected, a large bore needle should be used and directed posteriorly and inferiorly. Because of the relatively small blood volume of a child, fluid resuscitation must be accomplished before evacuation of a significant hemothorax to prevent exsanguination. If this is not done before evacuation, the thoracostomy tube should be clamped if excessive blood is detected. If an ongoing bleeding rate equal to or greater than 1 to 2 mL/kg/hour is detected through the chest tube, the child should be prepared for thoracotomy.[3]

Insertion of a nasogastric tube is also mandatory in children because of the diaphragmatic compromise resulting from aerophagia. Simple gastric decompression may alleviate severe ventilatory compromise in a child (Table 2-5). If there are potential maxillofacial injuries or signs of a basilar skull fracture (such as Battle's sign, raccoon eyes, otorrhea, or rhinorrhea), the orogastric route should be used instead.

Circulation

Because of their small size, children have a relatively small blood volume: 80 to 85 mL per kilogram of body weight. Although bleeding from a laceration in adults may represent an insignificant blood loss compared to their overall volume, an equal amount of bleeding in a child may result in hypovolemic shock.

Children compensate physiologically for hypovolemia and do not show a change in blood pressure until they have lost at least 20 percent of their blood volume. The most reliable indicator of shock in the pediatric patient is delayed capillary refill of greater than 2 seconds (or the time it takes to say "capillary refill"). Other indicators include tachycardia of greater than 130 beats/min, pallor, cool and mottled extremities, narrowed pulse pressure, and decreased level of consciousness. A systolic blood pressure of less than 80 mmHg indicates at least a 20 percent blood volume loss in 95 percent of the pediatric population.[4]

Venous access is difficult in children because of their small size. Percutaneous access is attempted first but is limited to two attempts before proceeding to a cutdown.

Table 2-3 Average Thoracostomy Tube Sizes

Patient Age	Tube Size
Infant	12F
Young child (<30 kg)	20F to 24F
Older child (>30 kg)	28F

Source: Adapted from Trauma Service Manual, p. 11, Washington, D.C. Children's Hospital National Medical Center, 1986.

Table 2-4 Fill Level in Water-Seal Chamber of Chest Drainage Device

Patient Age	Fill Level
Infant	10 cm
Older child	20 cm

Source: Adapted from *Trauma Service Manual,* p. 11, Washington, D.C. Children's Hospital National Medical Center, 1986.

Intraosseous infusion may provide an acceptable alternative for quick intervention. Fluid boluses are delivered by intravenous push because flow is inhibited by the relatively small-bore catheters. Also, boluses are given as small, specific volumes, 10 to 20 mL/kg, which precludes the effective use of a pressure bag applied to the intravenous solution container.

If shock continues unabated despite fluid replacement, the use of pneumatic antishock trousers may be considered, which are available in pediatric and toddler sizes, in addition to the adult size. Their greatest use is for major pelvic fractures with massive retroperitoneal bleeding. They must be used with caution in children, however, because (1) the saphenous vein and intraosseous infusion sites for venous access may be precluded; (2) pulmonary edema may result when they are used in conjunction with volume replacement; and (3) if the abdominal compartment is inflated the child's normal abdominal breathing pattern is impaired, and the pliant diaphragm is forced upward, compromising ventilatory status.[5] Therefore, if pneumatic antishock trousers are used, personnel must be prepared to provide previously unrequired ventilatory assistance.

Assessment

Assessment of the pediatric trauma patient for circulatory derangements begins with a quick survey of the child for any actively bleeding wounds. Assessment for hypovolemic shock includes observing for a capillary refill time of greater than 2 seconds after pressing on the nail beds or soles of the hands or feet and releasing. The child is observed for pallor or mottling, cool extremities, and decreased level of consciousness. Also, a heart rate of greater than 130 beats/min or a pulse pressure of less than 20 mmHg signals hypovolemia. Fluid resuscitation is initiated on the basis of any combination of these factors without waiting for a corresponding drop in systolic blood pressure. Systolic blood pressure is observed to determine whether volume losses are greater than 20 percent of total blood volume, as indicated by a systolic pressure of less than 80 mmHg.

Table 2-5 Average Nasogastric and Bladder Catheter Sizes

Patient Age	Catheter Size
Infant	8F
Child	10F
Adolescent	14F

Source: Adapted from *Trauma Service Manual,* p. 10, Washington, D.C. Children's Hospital National Medical Center, 1986.

Stabilization

Stabilization for the circulatory component of resuscitation begins with direct pressure to any bleeding wounds to prevent further blood loss. Manual pressure is maintained until hemostasis is obtained, and a pressure dressing is then applied.

All critically injured children should have two intravenous catheters inserted, one above and one below the diaphragm, if possible. Percutaneous insertion is attempted two times depending on the patient's condition. If profound shock is present, the surgeon proceeds more quickly to a cutdown. The preferred site is the greater saphenous vein at the ankle; other sites for cutdown include the antecubital fossa or femoral veins (Table 2-6). Use of a subclavian venous catheter has a high incidence of pneumothorax and vessel laceration in children; it is indicated only as a last resort and is inserted by the most senior physician.

Intraosseous infusion provides an acceptable alternative if venous access cannot be obtained. Sites include the tibia, one fingerbreath below the tubercle, and the femur, 2 to 3 cm above the external condyles in the midline. An 18-gauge spinal needle or a large-bore, short bone marrow needle with stylet is inserted through the periosteum, and marrow is aspirated into a saline syringe to check the needle placement. The line can then be utilized for volume replacement or emergency medications with absorption times that are equivalent to venous routes.[6]

If the child shows no evidence of hypovolemic shock, the intravenous lines are run at the child's maintenance rate for 12 to 24 hours (Table 2-7). If any of the previously described signs and symptoms of shock are assessed, fluid resuscitation is instituted as described in Table 2-8.

If the child exhibits continued instability despite adequate volume replacement, there may be a newly formed or previously undetected tension pneumothorax. If one is suspected, pleural decompression may alleviate the instability. Muffled heart sounds and a paradoxical pulse of greater than 10 mmHg may indicate a hemopericardium or pneumopericardium; if suspected, a pericardiocentesis should be performed. If neither of these conditions is found and if the systolic blood pressure is less than 80 mmHg, pneumatic antishock trousers may be applied. If the systolic pressure drops to 60 mmHg, the legs of the garment may be inflated. If severe pelvic fracture is suspected, the abdominal compartment may be inflated with intervention for probable ventilatory compromise anticipated by the airway team.

If the child continues to exhibit unstable vital signs after the above treatment regimen or requires blood volume replacement greater than 50 percent of the total volume, immediate surgical intervention in the operating suite should be considered. Emergency

---

Table 2-6 Average Intravenous Catheter Sizes

Patient Age	Catheter Size
Infant	20- to 22-gauge
Young child	18- to 20-gauge
Older child	16- to 18-gauge

Table 2-7 Maintenance Fluid Volume Requirements per 24 Hours

Patient Weight (kg)	Volume
0 to 10	100 mL/kg
11 to 20	1000 mL + 50 mL/kg for each additional kilogram over 10 kg
21 to 70	1500 mL + 20 mL/kg for each additional kilogram over 20 kg
>70	2500 mL (adult requirement)

thoracotomy should be considered as a last resort for a child who (1) is refractory to any of the described interventions, (2) has a penetrating wound to the heart, (3) has massive or continuous intrapleural hemorrhage, (4) has an open pneumothorax with a major defect of the chest, or (5) has massive intra-abdominal hemorrhage requiring aortic cross-clamping.[7]

Disability

Children differ from adults in several ways that affect their response to head injury. A child's head is proportionately larger and heavier in relation to the size of the body and has less musculoskeletal support. As a result, children tend to lead with their head when falling or when involved in acceleration-deceleration forces, making head trauma the most common injury of childhood.

Children have a lower incidence of mass brain lesions requiring operative intervention. They also have a greater incidence of elevated intracranial pressure, which may be related to a tendency toward cerebral hyperemia in the early stages of head injury. Young children have cranial sutures that are unfused, which allows for easier decompression of elevated intracranial pressure. Open fontanelles, however, may allow direct injury to brain tissue and gross bleeding, leading to hypovolemic shock. This should be considered when infants show evidence of shock with no visible signs of external bleeding or thoracic or abdominal trauma. There is also a higher incidence of hypovolemic shock related to scalp lacerations because of the increased vascularity and large surface area that is susceptible to traumatic forces.

Assessment

A rapid neurologic assessment is performed on a child to identify any potential head injury. The child's level of consciousness is assessed by means of the Glasgow Coma

Table 2-8 Protocol for Fluid Resuscitation for Hypovolemic Shock

Patient Condition	Procedure
Any presenting signs or symptoms of hypovolemic shock (see text)	Crystalloid (Ringer's lactate), 20 mL/kg intravenous push (IVP)
Signs or symptoms still present or reappear	Crystalloid, 20 mL/kg
Signs or symptoms still present or reappear	O− or type-specific packed red blood cells, 10 mL/kg; or whole blood, 20 mL/kg IVP
Signs or symptoms still present or reappear	O− or type-specific packed red blood cells, 10 mL/kg; or whole blood, 20 mL/kg IVP

Scale (Table 2-9), which scores motor and verbal responses and eye opening; the scoring must be based on the child's age and developmental level to be accurate. The pupils are also assessed for symmetry and reactivity to light.

Stabilization

Posttraumatic seizures within the first 24 hours of injury are relatively common in children and usually do not require medication because they often are self-limiting. The occasional child who progresses to status epilepticus can generally be successfully treated with diazepam, 0.3 mg/kg given slowly by intravenous push. Such children do not generally require any long-term anticonvulsant therapy.[5]

Children with a severe head injury (Glasgow Coma Scale score of 8 or less) require intubation with the use of sedative agents to prevent further increase in intracranial pressure. When intubated, they must be hyperventilated to a Po_2 of at least 80 to 100 torr and a Pco_2 of 25 to 30 torr. If a focal neurological deficit exists, mannitol, 0.5 mg/kg may be given intravenously to provide a margin of safety during computerized tomography (CT) scan.[8] If there is any evidence of hypovolemic shock, the child is treated according to the protocol shown in Exhibit 2-1. If the child has stable vital signs and no evidence of hypovolemic shock, intravenous fluids are restricted to two-thirds maintenance volume. The solution may be changed to 5 percent dextrose in one-half normal saline. When the cervical spine has been cleared by roentgenography, the head of the stretcher is elevated 30°.

Table 2-9 Glasgow Coma Scale

Adapted for Children*		Traditional Coma Score†	
Eye Opening		Eye Opening	
Spontaneous	4	Spontaneous	4
To sounds	3	To speech	3
To painful stimulation	2	To pain	2
None	1	Nil	1
Motor Responses		Motor Responses	
Spontaneous movement	6	Obeys commands	6
Localizes to pain	5	Localizes pain	5
Withdraws	4	Withdrawal	4
Reflex flexion	3	Abnormal flexion	3
Reflex extension (decerebrate)	2	Extensor rigidity	2
None (flaccid)	1	Nil	1
Verbal Responses		Verbal Responses	
Appropriate words or social smile; fixes and follows	5	Oriented	5
Cries, but consolable	4	Confused	4
Persistently irritable	3	Inappropriate	3
Restless, agitated	2	Incomprehensible	2
None	1	Nil	1

Sources: *Reprinted with permission of Thomas G. Luerssen, Assistant Professor, Division of Neurosurgery, University of California Medical Center, San Diego, California; and †reprinted from *Lancet*, Vol. 2, p. 81, with permission of The Lancet, Ltd., © 1974.

Exhibit 2-1 Protocol for Monitoring Vital Signs in Pediatric Head Trauma

> Monitor vital signs every 5 minutes for 20 minutes; continue monitoring every 5 minutes, if necessary, until the following criteria are met:
> - pulse is stable within 5 beats of each reading with a rate of less than 130 beats/min
> - respiration is stable within 5 respirations of each reading with a rate of 20 to 30 per minute
> - blood pressure is stable within 5 mmHg of each reading, with systolic pressure greater than or equal to 80 mmHg
> - neurologic signs are not deteriorating.
>
> Temperature is taken once but is repeated every 5 to 10 minutes if the reading is above or below 36° to 38°C.
> Repeat if the child becomes unstable.
>
> *Source:* Reprinted from *Trauma Service Manual*, p. 14, Washington, D.C. Children's Hospital National Medical Center, 1986.

Children who have any evidence of head injury should be evaluated by a neurosurgeon. Any child with unresponsive or asymmetric pupils, focal deficits, lateralizing signs, or seizures or who is obtunded is further evaluated by CT scan. Operative intervention is required if a mass lesion or depressed skull fracture is identified.

Exposure

Exposure, for children, refers to their risk of devastating hypothermia. Children have thin skin and little subcutaneous fat. They also have a high ratio of body surface area to underlying mass, which allows large insensible water losses by evaporation or conductive and convective heat losses. Infants less than 6 months of age and comatose children lack a shivering mechanism. The hypothermia that results from these factors can cause increasing metabolic acidosis, hypoxia, cardiac dysrhythmias, and pulmonary hypertension.

Assessment

Assessment for hypothermia must include observing the child for all signs and symptoms associated with shock: delayed capillary refill, pallor, cool and mottled extremities, tachycardia, and decreased level of consciousness. The presence of these symptoms despite adequate fluid resuscitation may indicate a hypothermic child. A core temperature must be obtained and should remain in the range of 36° to 38°C.

Stabilization

Radiant warmers and warmed intravenous fluids should always be used with pediatric trauma patients to prevent hypothermia in an often cool resuscitation area where all the child's clothing has been removed. If the patient is hypothermic on arrival, warmed blankets and warmed, humidified oxygen may also be used. In cases of severe hypothermia, warm saline may be used in nasogastric and peritoneal lavages.

SECONDARY SURVEY

The primary survey addresses life-threatening injuries in a priority order that is based on physiologic derangements and clinical assessments. The secondary survey is a head-to-toe examination that seeks to identify previously undetected injuries and allows continual reassessment of primary survey findings at the same time.

Assessment

Secondary survey assessment is done in a thorough, systematic manner from head to toe with the use of inspection, palpation, and auscultation techniques. The most potentially painful examinations of the abdomen and perineum are reserved for last so that the child's reaction to them does not obscure other portions of the survey.

The head is inspected and palpated for swelling, depressions, and lacerations. The anterior fontanelle of an infant is inspected for either depression or bulging. The face is inspected for any depressions, swelling, asymmetry, or lacerations and the individual structures of the eyes, ears, nose, and mouth for any evidence of obvious injury. Examination of the eyes allows for reassessment of neurological status through pupillary symmetry and reaction to light. The ears and nose are assessed carefully for any drainage of clear or bloody fluid, which indicates a potential leak of cerebrospinal fluid. The child's airway and breathing status is reassessed by observing for nasal flaring and circumoral cyanosis.

Cervical spine immobilization is maintained during assessment of the neck unless roentgenographic results are available. The collar should be loosened while manual immobilization is maintained so that the neck may be examined for deformity, swelling, tenderness, or venous distention.

The chest is inspected for contusions, abrasions, deformity, and asymmetry of chest wall movement. Primary survey findings are reassessed by examining for retractions, observing respiratory rate and depth, and auscultating for clear and equal breath sounds bilaterally.

The extremities are inspected for lacerations, contusions, deformities, or swelling. Warmth, pulses, sensation, and tenderness to palpation or range of motion are also checked.

The abdomen is examined for distention, contusions, abrasions, rigidity, and tenderness. Bowel sounds are confirmed by auscultation.

Last, the perineal area is examined for contusions, swelling, and bleeding. The pelvis is assessed for stability with gentle pressure or a gentle rocking motion. A rectal examination is performed to check for any hematomas, lacerations, or a high-riding prostate, and a stool smear is checked for blood.

Several diagnostic tests that allow further assessment of the child should be routinely performed. Blood studies include complete blood cell count, electrolytes, coagulation studies, blood urea nitrogen, amylase, glucose, creatinine, and bilirubin; a sample is obtained for type and cross-match. Samples should be drawn during the primary survey when venous access is obtained for insertion of intravenous lines. Arterial blood gases are also measured at this time. All children receive a standard radiologic examination, which must consist of a lateral roentgenogram of the cervical spine that includes C-1 through C-7 and an anteroposterior view of both the chest and abdomen. Testing for the presence of blood must be done in the resuscitation area on samples of stool, nasogastric aspirate, and urine.

Stabilization

Stabilization during the secondary survey includes insertion of a nasogastric tube to decompress the stomach and to decrease the risk of aspiration. This may have been accomplished during the breathing component of the primary survey if stomach distention was severely inhibiting ventilation. If maxillofacial trauma or a suspected basilar skull fracture exists, decompression may be accomplished through the orogastric route.

A bladder catheter is inserted if examination of the perineum and pelvis show no obvious injuries and if the rectal examination is also negative (see Table 2-5). If there is any potential for a urethral injury, catheter insertion should be delayed until further radiographic examination can be accomplished. If the patient is awake, alert, and without precluding injuries, he or she may be allowed to attempt to void spontaneously. The child should not leave the resuscitation area, however, without a urine hematest; catheterization is still necessary if the child is unable to void.

Any open wounds are cleaned and bandaged. If time and patient condition permits, suturing should be done at this time. Further diagnostic studies such as CT scan should not be delayed, however, if they are indicated. Any potential fractures are splinted to provide stabilization, and further radiologic examination is performed to determine the extent of bony injury.

The need for specialty consultations, further radiologic examination, and operative intervention is determined by the findings in both the primary and secondary surveys. The trauma surgeon should remain the coordinator of care because he or she has the broadest perspective on all the priorities for care. Specialists should be consulted for their expertise in each area of injury and become a valuable addition to the team in determining further diagnostic procedures and treatment.

If abdominal injuries are suspected, the child is usually evaluated by CT scan. Peritoneal lavage is rarely used for children because of its invasive nature and because of the efficacy of CT scanning in identifying injuries.[9] Lavage is used only in an unstable patient who is unresponsive to fluid resuscitation to determine whether operative intervention is required or in a patient with suspected bowel disruption from either blunt or penetrating trauma who is at risk for peritonitis.

Operative intervention for blunt trauma in children is generally more conservative than in adults, especially for abdominal trauma.[9] Many major defects of the liver and spleen often heal completely in children over a period of 6 to 12 months with no complications. Indications for laparotomy are given in Exhibit 2-2.

THE PEDIATRIC TRAUMA TEAM: A MODULAR CONCEPT

The members of a pediatric trauma team must be thoroughly familiar with the concepts and priorities of pediatric trauma care as presented in the previous sections. The

Exhibit 2-2 Indications for Laparotomy

1. Child remains in unabated shock despite adequate fluid resuscitation.
2. Child requires replacement of more than 50 percent of the total blood volume by transfusion.
3. Child shows clinical or radiographic evidence of peritonitis, bladder rupture, urethral transection, or rectal lacerations or injury to the pancreatic, bowel, or renal vasculature.

Source: Reprinted from *Pediatric Trauma Care* by M.R. Eichelberger and G.L. Pratsch (Eds.), p. 54, Aspen Publishers, Inc., © 1988.

team approach translates these concepts into predetermined roles and responsibilities that permit an efficient, organized, and systematic response to the needs of the injured child. The team model presented here was developed by an interdisciplinary group at Children's Hospital National Medical Center in Washington, D.C., to provide a consistent standard of quality care for any injured child.

The team is formed by seventeen people from throughout the hospital who together provide all the necessary expertise and resources to meet the needs of the pediatric trauma patient. All the members are available in the hospital 24 hours per day and, after notification by a "Trauma Stat" on a group-call paging system, respond to the resuscitation area within 1 to 2 minutes. The response of personnel from different areas of the hospital prevents depletion of staff from any particular area and causes minimal interruption of care for other children.

The response team design is based on a modular structure with a predetermined protocol of personnel, roles, and responsibilities. Each role has specific delineated tasks and is assigned to a separate clinical or support area (such as radiology, intensive care nursing, and anesthesia). The responsibility for the education and training of participating team members is assigned to each respective area so that education is ongoing and reproducible. Once the individuals are trained in the separate tasks necessary for an efficient resuscitation, they are incorporated easily into the team structure. Performance and protocol compliance is evaluated during training by each separate area and, on an ongoing basis for the entire team, by the trauma coordinator.

Team Interactions

The team is divided into an inner core team and an outer core team (Figure 2-2). The inner core team provides clinical care to the child. The outer core team comprises representatives of all the necessary resources of the hospital that allow the care to continue without distraction or interruption.

The inner core team consists of nine members. It is led by the surgical coordinator, a surgical attending or senior pediatric surgical fellow, who is responsible for determining the care priorities of the child and for directing the team according to the established protocol. The inner core team is further divided into several smaller care teams. On the patient's right is the surgical team, consisting of a senior surgical resident and an intensive care nursery nurse, who perform any necessary surgical procedures (such as

24 Pediatric Trauma Nursing

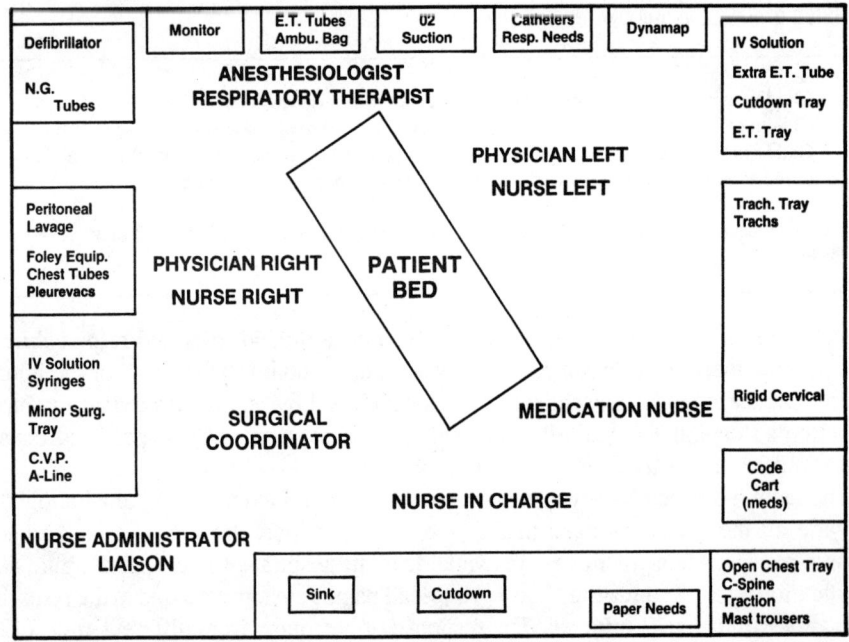

Figure 2-2 Trauma Resuscitation Bay. *Source:* Reprinted from *Pediatric Trauma Care* by M.R. Eichelberger and G.L. Pratsch (Eds.), p. 12, Aspen Publishers, Inc., © 1988.

---

cutdown or thoracostomy). On the patient's left is the medical team, consisting of a pediatric intensivist and an emergency room nurse, who provide necessary medical support (such as intravenous access and medication administration). At the child's head is the airway team, consisting of a pediatric anesthesiologist and a respiratory therapist, who provide a patent airway and cervical spine protection. Also within the inner core is a nursing support team, which includes a nurse-in-charge from the emergency room, who is responsible for documenting all team actions and patient responses, and a medication nurse from the pediatric intensive care unit. The resuscitation area is designed around the team structure so that the necessary supplies and equipment are available and easily accessible.

The responsibilities of the inner core team are divided by priority into the primary and secondary surveys. Team actions during the primary survey seek to identify and treat life-threatening derangements in the areas of airway, breathing, circulation, disability, and exposure. These can often be stabilized simultaneously as a result of structure and expertise of the team. After these areas are stabilized the team proceeds to a transition phase, which marks the beginning of the secondary survey. During the transition phase, a standard radiologic assessment is accomplished. Final clinical recognition of injury then proceeds with stomach and bladder decompression and a head-to-toe examination.

The outer core team, which consists of eight individuals, is located outside the door to the resuscitation bay so that crowding and confusion around the child are eliminated.

This team is led by the nursing administrator liaison, a senior nursing administrator who acts as a liaison between the needs of the inner core team and the resources of the hospital. An operating room nurse provides assistance to the inner core team with any major surgical procedures (such as tracheostomy or open thoracotomy) and prepares the operating room for any anticipated procedures. An emergency room attending physician provides any needed medical support to the inner core team (for example, during cardiac arrest) and provides a medical liaison with the family. A social worker provides immediate and continuous support to the family through the initial hours of care. Personnel from radiology, clinical laboratory, central supply, and security also respond to provide their expertise and resources.

This overall organization provides all the resources to the critically injured child that are needed most acutely within the first moments after arrival. The modular structure allows personnel to learn and understand their roles and to interact easily with the rest of the team. Confusion and chaos are replaced by calm efficiency, and priorities are not forgotten. With this basic understanding of team structure, the roles and responsibilities can be completely outlined.

Inner Core Team

Surgical Coordinator (Surgical Attending or Senior Pediatric Surgical Fellow)

The surgical coordinator must be familiar with all the principles of pediatric trauma and the priorities and methods of assessment and stabilization. The surgical coordinator must also be familiar with the roles and responsibilities of all team members so as to direct them properly in their interventions.

Direction to team members is provided by incorporating the assessments made by all the individuals into an overall plan. To do this, the coordinator must be able to "step back" from the action of the team and assess the "big picture" without becoming overly involved in the details of hands-on care. The coordinator must be expert, however, in all the techniques of resuscitation and able to intervene if any of the individual team members should require assistance. The coordinator also must quickly verify assessments being made so as to ensure their accuracy and the resulting priorities of treatment. This individual should therefore be an active participant in both the primary and secondary surveys and less actively involved in the actual procedures.

After the child has been stabilized and the primary and secondary surveys completed, the surgical coordinator determines the need for any specialty consultations (for example, with neurosurgery, orthopedics, urology, ENT [ears, nose, and throat], plastic surgery, ophthalmology, dental surgery, or cardiovascular surgery). The coordinator then determines the triage sequence before the child leaves the resuscitation bay (radiology, operating room, intensive care, or general care unit). These decisions are coordinated with the nursing administrator liaison and the operating room trauma nurse.

The coordinator keeps the family informed of the child's condition through the emergency room attending physician and the social worker during the resuscitation. After the child is stabilized and triage decisions have been made, the coordinator meets with the family personally to summarize the care to that point and anticipated findings or problems. The coordinator obtains any necessary permits for care from the parents and continues to meet with them through the first hours of care as needed.

If for any reason the surgical attending or fellow is delayed or unable to respond to the trauma resuscitation, the emergency room attending in the outer core team fills this role.

Airway Team: Pediatric Anesthesiologist and Respiratory Therapist

Pediatric Anesthesiologist (Attending or Fellow). The pediatric anesthesiologist is responsible for protection of the patient's cervical spine and for airway management. This individual is assisted by the respiratory therapist and works cooperatively with the rest of the response team.

The anesthesiologist performs all airway maneuvers in orderly fashion from simple to complex. He or she ensures that oxygen and cervical spine protection are provided to all patients and, if necessary, attempts to establish a patent airway with a jaw thrust, suctioning, and pneumatic antishock trouser–assisted ventilations. If further assistance is required, the anesthesiologist determines the sedation needed and requests that the correct dose be drawn up and administered. This individual then intubates the child, checks that the tube is correctly placed and secured, and provides ventilatory assistance with a hand resuscitator. The anesthesiologist must also monitor the child's central nervous system status by evaluating the level of consciousness, pupil size and symmetry, and pupillary reaction to light.

When oxygenation and ventilation have been successfully established, the respiratory therapist may assume responsibility for airway management.

Respiratory Therapist. The respiratory therapist assists the anesthesiologist in protecting the cervical spine and stabilizing the child's airway. The therapist may assume responsibility for airway management when the patient is stable.

The therapist ensures that the patient receives oxygen at a rate of 5 to 10 L/min. He or she assists the anesthesiologist in preparing the equipment required for airway management and checks that suction and oxygen apparatus is in good working order. The therapist assists with airway maneuvers such as suctioning and monitoring endotracheal tube placement. The therapist also guarantees in-line immobilization of the cervical spine until it has been cleared of injury by roentgenographic examination.

If a child requires ongoing ventilatory support, the therapist accompanies the patient as a member of the transport team to ensure that ventilation and oxygenation are provided throughout the transport event. The therapist remains with the patient until relieved by respiratory services on the patient care unit.

Surgical Team: Physician Right and Nurse Right

Physician Right (Senior Surgical Resident). Physician right is responsible for performing all right-sided procedures for the patient and all surgical procedures in priority order. This individual works in cooperation with physician left in accomplishing these tasks and is assisted by nurse right.

In the primary survey, the airway component is accomplished primarily by the airway team. Physician right must not compromise the airway or cervical spine protection during any procedures. If a cricothyroidotomy should be necessary, physician right assists the surgical coordinator in performing the procedure.

Breathing or ventilatory compromise must be assessed after a patent airway has been established. Physician right must auscultate for equal and bilateral breath sounds. In a severely compromised patient with a suspected hemothorax or pneumothorax, a needle thoracentesis and tube thoracostomy are performed without benefit of chest roentgenogram.

The circulatory component of resuscitation is then addressed by assessing the child for hypovolemic shock: delayed capillary refill, pallor, cool or mottled extremities, and decreased level of consciousness. Nurse left provides continual monitoring of vital signs to identify a heart rate of greater than 130 beats/min or a systolic blood pressure of less than 80 mmHg.

Circulatory compromise is treated first by direct pressure to any actively bleeding wounds and is maintained either manually or with a pressure dressing. Physician right then proceeds to insertion of an intravenous line on the child's right side through a percutaneous stick, if possible, or by performing a cutdown procedure.

After intravenous access has been established, physician right proceeds to fluid resuscitation if signs of shock are present. This is done cooperatively with physician left so that the child receives the fluid resuscitation described in Table 2-8. Throughout this sequence, physician right repeatedly assesses the child for a newly developed pneumothorax or muffled heart sounds signifying pericardial tamponade. If tamponade is suspected, physician right assists the surgical coordinator in performing pericardiocentesis.

If shock remains unabated, the surgical team may apply pneumatic antishock trousers. They are also responsible for the decompression sequence if the trousers are no longer required. This is done slowly, one compartment at a time, while nurse left carefully monitors the child's blood pressure.

Unabated shock in spite of the described interventions may require that the child be prepared for surgical intervention in the operating room. Physician right assists the surgical coordinator in the operating room or if an immediate open thoracotomy is needed in the resuscitation bay. During cardiac arrest of a pediatric trauma patient, physician right works closely with the surgical coordinator to reverse any mechanical reasons for the arrest (for example, insertion of bilateral chest tubes, pericardiocentesis, or open thoracotomy if indicated).

After the life-threatening injuries have been stabilized in the primary survey, physician right assists the radiology technician in the radiologic evaluation that is done during the transition phase. Physician right assists with any patient movement required for placement of roentgenographic plates while cervical spine immobilization is maintained by the respiratory therapist. During the lateral exposure, physician right maintains gentle, downward pressure on both arms of the patient to permit visualization to C-7 on the film.

After the transition phase, the surgical team performs several diagnostic tests and therapeutic interventions. Physician right performs a rectal examination and ensures that the stool is tested for blood immediately. The surgical team then inserts a bladder catheter and a nasogastric tube. This is done cooperatively and may be accomplished by either the physician or the nurse. Physician right must ensure that both nasogastric aspirant and urine are tested for blood immediately by the nursing support team.

The head-to-toe examination for the secondary survey is then performed by physician right, with findings verified as necessary by the surgical coordinator. Specialty consultations are requested, depending on the findings of the clinical examination and the diagnostic tests performed.

Before the child is transported to the radiology suite, operating room, or care unit, physician right must ensure that all physician documentation is complete. This includes a trauma score, physical examination, standard admission orders, an admitting progress note, and permits for treatment that are signed by the parents. Physician right then accompanies the patient to radiology, the operating room, or the appropriate care unit. The physician remains with the patient until he or she is transferred to the bedside caretakers or the operating room staff and continually monitors the child for developing compromise to airway, ventilation, circulation, or neurological status.

Nurse Right (Intensive Care Nursery Nurse). Nurse right works cooperatively with nurse left to accomplish bedside care for the child and assists physician right with right-sided surgical procedures. If the child has burn injuries, this position is filled instead by a burn unit nurse. Notification for the change is accomplished by the group-call of "Trauma Stat: Burn."

When the child arrives in the resuscitation area, nurse right exposes the patient by cutting off all clothing. The nurse turns on the cardiorespiratory monitor and places the electrocardiogram leads on the patient.

Nurse right assists physician right in all the interventions for the child in priority order. If a thoracostomy tube is to be inserted, nurse right prepares the thoracostomy tray and the suction drainage device to be used. He or she then assists with insertion procedures and attaches the tube to the suction device.

To assist with circulatory stability, nurse right applies direct pressure to all open, bleeding wounds, secures them with a pressure dressing when hemostasis is achieved, and applies dressings to any other wounds that are noted. The nurse prepares for and assists with all right-sided intravenous lines and monitors all right-sided infusions, blood products, and lavages and all right-sided outputs (such as blood, urine, drainage, and vomitus), announcing ongoing totals to the nurse-in-charge. Nurse right also assists physician right to apply and inflate the pneumatic antishock trousers.

Nurse right operates the trauma table as needed to accomplish Trendelenburg's position, head elevation, or ease of patient access. He or she must monitor exposure of the child and prevent or reverse hypothermia and thus is responsible for operating the warming lamps to maintain the child's core temperature. This is done cooperatively with nurse left, who monitors the child's vital signs.

Nurse right prepares all the equipment for bladder catheter and nasogastric tube placement, then inserts or assists physician right to insert them. Before patient transport, nurse right ensures that all right-sided lines are secured, that the patient identification bracelet is in place, and that the patient is properly placed on a transport monitor. The nurse may be designated a member of the transport team by the nursing administrator liaison. He or she then accompanies the patient to radiology, the operating room, or the appropriate unit while monitoring for any instability and assisting physician right with appropriate interventions.

Medical Team: Physician Left and Nurse Left

Physician Left (Pediatric Intensive Care Fellow). Physician left works in cooperation with physician right and is assisted by nurse left. This individual is responsible for left-sided procedures and medication administration.

During the primary survey, physician left begins with circulatory stabilization. The physician immediately seeks to gain venous access through a percutaneous stick. When venous access is obtained, the physician draws enough blood for the required specimens and gives them to the medication nurse (12 mL for complete blood cell count, electrolytes, coagulation studies, creatinine, glucose, amylase, blood urea nitrogen, and bilirubin). Physician left then establishes an intravenous line. When the line is secured, physician left then draws an arterial blood sample for blood gas analysis. If venous access cannot be obtained, the physician establishes access by the intraosseous route.

If the patient exhibits any signs of shock, physician left begins with the protocol for fluid resuscitation with Ringer's lactate and packed red blood cells as described in Table 2-8. This is done in cooperation with physician right so that the child receives the correct amount of fluid as rapidly as possible.

Physician left monitors the electrocardiogram and distal pulses of the child throughout the resuscitation. If any medications are required, physician left is responsible for assigning the correct dosage and for administration.

If the patient is in cardiac arrest, physician left forms a medical resuscitation team with the emergency room attending, determining medication doses and administering them along with fluids. This is done at the same time that the surgical team is seeking to reverse any mechanical reason for the arrest.

During the secondary survey, physician left assists in the continuous evaluation of the child's respiratory and circulatory status. Physician left may insert an arterial line at this point if indicated by the patient's condition and if required for adequate monitoring. If the child remains unstable, the physician may become a part of the transport team to provide medical assistance in case of arrest during transport or in radiology.

Nurse Left (Emergency Room Nurse). Nurse left works cooperatively with nurse right in providing all bedside care required for the child and assists physician left in accomplishing all left-sided procedures.

When the child arrives in the resuscitation bay, nurse left exposes the patient with nurse right by cutting off all clothing. Beginning with the first contact, nurse left communicates with the child, providing reassurance and explanations appropriate to the child's developmental level throughout the resuscitation event.

Nurse left closely monitors the child's status throughout the primary and secondary surveys. He or she obtains vital signs (temperature, pulse, blood pressure, and neurologic signs) every 5 minutes for a minimum of 20 minutes and announces them to the nurse-in-charge for appropriate documentation. Nurse left continues to monitor vital signs according to the protocol in Exhibit 2-1.

Nurse left assists with stabilization of the circulatory component by preparing all equipment needed for insertion of intravenous lines on the left side of the child. The nurse assists with blood drawing and line insertion and secures all left-sided lines. Nurse left monitors and controls all left-sided infusions, blood products, and lavages and all left-sided outputs (blood, urine, drainage, and vomitus) and announces ongoing totals to the nurse-in-charge for appropriate documentation. Nurse left also coordinates deflation or inflation of pneumatic antishock trousers with the surgical team by closely monitoring the child's blood pressure. In the event of a cardiac arrest, nurse left performs chest compressions until relieved by other personnel to return to normal protocol responsibilities.

Nurse left may be designated a member of the transport team by the nursing administrator liaison. He or she then accompanies the patient to radiology, the operating room, or the appropriate unit while continuing to monitor for any instability and assisting physician right in appropriate interventions.

Nursing Support Team: Medication Nurse and Nurse-in-Charge

Medication Nurse (Pediatric Intensive Care Unit Nurse). The medication nurse works cooperatively with the entire resuscitation team and assists the medical team with blood drawing procedures and medications. Before the patient's arrival, the nurse obtains succinylcholine and pancuronium from the medication refrigerator and draws up and labels four 6-mL syringes of normal saline and one 5-mL syringe of normal saline for Foley catheter balloon inflation (3 mL for a number 8 catheter). The medication nurse also prepares all the necessary blood-drawing equipment, including syringes, needles, and specimen tubes.

The medication nurse is responsible for knowing all drug actions, incompatibilities, and dilutions. This individual is responsible for preparing all medications and infusions requested by physician left and for communicating to the team the exact dose in milligrams that is being provided. The nurse assembles all pressure lines and transducers that may be required and prepares any medications that may be needed during transport. He or she places the correct amounts of blood in the proper tubes to be sent to the laboratory. The medication nurse also assumes other duties and responsibilities to assist the team as directed by the nurse-in-charge (for example, assisting in patient restraint).

If the patient is in cardiac arrest, the medication nurse draws up and labels the drugs listed in Table 2-10. These medications are arranged on the medication cart in alphabetical order with the flushes and are replenished immediately after use so that at least one dose is always available. Doses for these medications are calculated by patient age and weight as shown in Table 2-11. All other drugs are provided according to the dose requested by physician left. The medication nurse also prepares infusions, such as dopamine or epinephrine, that may be required.

The medication nurse may be designated a member of the transport team by the nursing administrator liaison. He or she then accompanies the patient to radiology, the

Table 2-10 Cardiovascular Resuscitation Drugs

Drug	Dose (per kilogram of body weight)
Sodium bicarbonate, 8.4 percent solution (1 mEq/mL)	1 mEq (1 mL)
Epinephrine, 1:10,000	10 μg (0.1 mL)
Atropine, 0.1 mg/mL	0.02 mg (0.2 mL)
Dextrose, 25 percent	2 to 4 mL

Source: Reprinted from *Cardiovascular Resuscitation Drugs for Children,* Washington, D.C. Children's Hospital National Medical Center, 1988.

operating room, or the appropriate unit while monitoring for any instability and assisting physician right with appropriate interventions.

Nurse-in-Charge (Emergency Room Nurse). The nurse-in-charge records the entire resuscitation event, acquiring data from all team members (including vital signs, input, output, and sizes of inserted tubes and catheters) to communicate to the surgical coordinator and other team members the status of vital signs, summaries of fluid infusions, pending medication times, and trends in the child's condition on a frequent basis. The nurse-in-charge assists the medication nurse in labeling all blood specimens and noting the time at which they are sent to the laboratory.

The nurse-in-charge monitors all the nursing activities and patient interventions while anticipating any needs and communicating them to the nursing administrator liaison. Before patient transport, the nurse-in-charge telephones a report to the receiving unit and ensures that all the appropriate paper work is completed and that any necessary equipment, supplies, medications, and personnel are ready to transport. The nurse-in-charge coordinates the release of team members from the resuscitation event with the surgical coordinator and nursing administrator liaison and may be designated a member of the transport team.

Outer Core Team

Nursing Administrator Liaison

The nursing administrator liaison (Monday through Friday, Director of Emergency Room Nursing Services; at all other times, Assistant Director of Nursing or Hospital Nursing Supervisor) is a senior nursing administrator who directs the outer core team and

Table 2-11 Average Patient Weight by Age

Patient Age	Average Weight
Newborn	3–5 kg
1 year	10 kg
3 years	15 kg
5 years	20 kg
8 years	25 kg
10 years	35 kg

serves as a communications link between the resuscitation bay and any needed hospital resources. This individual has the seniority and authority to coordinate hospital systems and resources to meet the needs of the patient. He or she provides a contact person for both the inner and the outer core to reduce confusion and to provide organization.

The nursing administrator liaison initiates and expedites the triage process to facilitate patient disposition. This may involve communicating with the admissions office, operating room, radiology, nurse staffing office, and receiving unit regarding the status of the child and anticipating the time of transfer and required equipment, supplies, and personnel. The nursing administrator liaison also adjusts nursing staff to ensure nursing care of the trauma patient during and after the resuscitation. This individual coordinates the release of team members from the resuscitation bay with the surgical coordinator and the nurse-in-charge and designates nurses to accompany the child during transport.

The nursing administrator liaison maintains the members designated by protocol in the inner and outer core teams to reduce confusion in the area. He or she receives and reports laboratory results to the resuscitation team, contacts requested consultants, and communicates with administration, public relations, and the police as needed. Before patient transport, the nursing administrator liaison ensures that consultants have examined the child, that the chart is complete, that the transport team is prepared, and that the receiving unit is ready for the child.

Emergency Room Attending Physician

The emergency room attending physician acts as the trauma team coordinator if the surgical coordinator is not able to be present. This physician also provides medical back-up for the team and works cooperatively with physician left during cardiac arrest to provide medical resuscitation. The attending physician remains aware of the progress of the resuscitation throughout the event, even if he or she is not initially required to participate, and is available to the team if senior medical consultation is required.

If not required for the coordinator function, the attending physician debriefs prehospital personnel, family, and police to determine the mechanism of injury, treatments provided before arrival, essential medical history, and allergies. The physician reports these components to the team and then serves as a medical liaison to the family while the rest of the team is involved in the resuscitation.

Social Worker

The social worker greets the family as soon as they arrive and escorts them to a separate, quiet waiting area. This individual relays information to the family, provides emotional support, and acts as a liaison between the family and the resuscitation team.

On the family's arrival, the social worker first seeks to learn the events surrounding the injury and the family's perceptions and feelings. He or she then explains to the family how trauma cases are handled and what they can expect, in general, to happen. If the emergency room attending physician is unable to see the family, the social worker documents any significant medical history or allergies and reports this information to the nursing administrator liaison. The social worker then acts as a liaison between the family and the resuscitation team throughout the resuscitation event and for the first several hours if needed. The social worker provides the family with continuous support and updated information about the child's general condition and plan for treatment and remains with them through discussions with medical staff to assist them in understanding the information presented. The social worker also provides the team with information about the family's level of understanding and needs. The social worker assesses the family's strengths and weaknesses in coping with the trauma and assists them in locating their personal support resources outside the hospital.

When the child leaves the resuscitation bay, the social worker assists the family with the admission process and escorts them to the appropriate waiting room or to the child's bedside. He or she informs the staff of the parents' presence and, if possible, introduces them. This individual makes appropriate referrals to in-patient social workers for continued support and documents all information on the patient's chart.

If the child dies in the resuscitation bay or within the first few hours, the social worker remains with the family and encourages them to express their grief and shock and any feelings of guilt that they may have. The social worker helps them to contact family and friends and to begin arrangements for the funeral if they wish. He or she assists them in their decision to view the child's body, prepares them for the interview with the medical examiner, provides them with names of significant personnel involved in the resuscitation attempts for follow-up contact, and communicates with them the next day and more often if appropriate.

Operating Room Trauma Nurse

The operating room trauma nurse remains outside the resuscitation bay unless required to assist the surgical coordinator and physician right with a major operative procedure (such as open thoracotomy or tracheostomy). If this is required, the trauma nurse enters the bay to act as scrub nurse and is responsible for the surgical trays and equipment in the room.

If no emergency surgical procedure is to be performed, the trauma nurse returns to the operating suite and prepares for any anticipated surgical procedures. The trauma nurse calls in additional operating room personnel if needed and maintains communication with the surgical coordinator, anesthesiologist, and operating room staff as to patient condition, disposition, and anticipated needs. When the patient arrives in the operating room, the trauma nurse assists with the surgical procedure and the transfer of the child to the receiving unit.

Laboratory Technician

The laboratory technician waits outside the resuscitation bay for blood specimens to be drawn. When these are available, they are handed to the nursing administrator liaison who, together with the technician, reviews the samples and laboratory slips for accuracy and completeness. If no errors are found, the technician transports the blood samples to the appropriate laboratories and expedites their processing on a priority basis. The technician then ensures that the laboratory results are reported promptly by telephone to the nursing administrator liaison.

Radiology Technician

The radiology technician remains outside the resuscitation bay until the transition phase. At the direction of the surgical coordinator, the technician enters the bay and obtains lateral cervical spine, anteroposterior chest, and anteroposterior pelvis films. Other portable films may be obtained on an emergent basis at the discretion of the surgical coordinator (for example, views of an open fracture).

After obtaining the films, the technician is responsible for processing, developing, and expediting the return of the films to the resuscitation bay for review by the team.

Central Supply Technician

On first responding to the "Trauma: Stat" call, the central supply technician brings several cups of ice for blood specimens to the resuscitation bay. This individual then remains stationed outside the bay to obtain any necessary supplies or equipment when supplies in the bay are exhausted or if certain supplies are not normally stocked in the room. These may include medications from the pharmacy or supplies from other areas of the hospital. The central supply technician also delivers additional laboratory specimens after the laboratory technician returns to the laboratory.

Security

The security guard responds on all trauma resuscitation calls to secure the arrival area (either the helicopter pad or the ambulance entrance) and to ensure the safety of the patient and the transport team. During the resuscitation event, the security guard monitors the trauma bay area for unauthorized personnel or visitors and clears the hallway and elevator for transport of the patient.

PEDIATRIC TRAUMA: THE CONTINUUM OF CARE

The personnel assigned to the pediatric trauma team can be adapted to the resources of any facility as long as the following principles of the model are recognized:

- a pediatric resuscitation protocol must be designed that outlines the responsibilities necessary for an effective resuscitation and that assigns those responsibilities to predetermined roles
- personnel on the team must be trained in the concepts of pediatric trauma
- consistent personnel who have been trained to fill those roles must be available 24 hours a day
- appropriate supplies and equipment must be available in the resuscitation bay.

These components will assist in providing an effective and efficient stabilization but represent only one step in providing quality trauma care for the child.

Pediatric trauma care represents a commitment on the part of hospital administration and staff to provide consistent, quality care along a continuum from the moment of injury through integration back into the community. The resuscitation bay does not constitute a pediatric trauma center. The critically injured child requires trained and knowledgeable pediatric specialists in the prehospital arena, during hospitalization, and in the postdischarge, rehabilitation environment. This network of interdisciplinary care providers must be supported by an institutional commitment to management structure, quality assurance programs, education, advocacy, and research.

Not all communities can provide the resources necessary for a pediatric trauma center. Regional centers must be established that provide a system of care that recognizes the uniqueness of childhood injury. This care may be provided in a general hospital environment but must ensure that the child's care does not suffer from the simultaneous commitments made to adult patients. The regional center must maintain an open-door policy and stand ready 24 hours a day to accept any child in need of these specialized resources.

Prehospital providers and emergency facility personnel must be prepared to provide specialized, quality emergency care for any injured child. Recognition of a child's unique needs must not end with stabilization, however. Emergency care providers must ensure that the child and family are transported to the most effective institution to provide the full continuum of pediatric care. Only in this way can the medical community provide a true commitment to pediatric trauma care.

NOTES

1. American College of Surgeons Committee on Trauma, "Advanced Life Support," in *ATLS Instructor Manual* (Chicago: 1986).
2. *Trauma Service Manual* (Washington, D.C.: Children's Hospital National Medical Center, 1986), 15.
3. M.R. Eichelberger and K.D. Anderson, "Sequelae of Thoracic Injury in Children," in W.R. Hix and B.L. Aaron, eds., *Residual of Thoracic Trauma* (Mt. Kirsco, New York: Futura Publishing Co., Inc., 1987), 252.
4. E.A. Mangubat and M.R. Eichelberger, "Hypovolemic Shock in the Pediatric Patient: A Physiologic Approach to Diagnosis and Treatment," *Trauma: Clinical Update for Surgeons* 2(1984):13.
5. D.J. Johnson, *Head Trauma Protocol* (Washington, D.C.: Children's Hospital National Medical Center, 1987).
6. W.A. Rosetti et al., "Intraosseous Infusion: An Alternative Route of Pediatric Intravascular Access," *Annals of Emergency Medicine* 14(1985):9.
7. *Trauma Service Manual*, 8.
8. D.J. Johnson, "Head Injury," in M.R. Eichelberger and G.L. Pratsch, eds., *Pediatric Trauma Care* (Rockville, Md.: Aspen Publishers, Inc., 1988), 91.
9. K.D. Newman, M.R. Eichelberger, and J.G. Randolph, "Abdominal Injury," in M.R. Eichelberger and G.L. Pratsch, eds., *Pediatric Trauma Care* (Rockville, Md.: Aspen Publishers, Inc., 1988), 102.

Chapter 3

Traumatic Head Injury

Susan B. DeJong

There are many circumstances that can significantly alter a child's neurological system. This chapter focuses on how trauma changes the intracranial equilibrium of the child. Discussion includes the physiology of intracranial pressure (ICP) and types of head injury frequently seen and highlights age-specific problems and the resultant critical care management of increased ICP. The goals in managing the child with a traumatic head injury are to preserve cerebral and physical function, to prevent secondary brain injury, to provide appropriate rehabilitation, and to reintegrate the child and family back into society.

EPIDEMIOLOGY

Head trauma is a major health problem in the United States; nearly five million children sustain some form of head injury every year, ranging from minor accidents at home or on the playground to the serious accidents seen with motor vehicle accidents or falls from a great height. Fortunately, most injuries seen can be classified as minor. Annually, however, more than 500,000 children are hospitalized after head injury, and nearly 4,000 die. Approximately 400 to 500 children die each year in the United States from bicycle-related injuries.[1] Children who die within the first 2 hours of sustaining a head injury probably die from primary brainstem damage. Additionally, 15,000 children who survive traumatic head injury require prolonged hospitalization and rehabilitation. Of this 15,000, 50 percent suffer major sequelae if coma exceeds 24 hours. Approximately 2 percent to 5 percent remain handicapped for life.[2]

PATHOPHYSIOLOGIC PRINCIPLES
The Monro-Kellie Doctrine

The forces that exist inside the injured brain can be understood by reference to the Monro-Kellie doctrine, which is essentially as follows. The volume of the cranium is constant and comprises three components: blood, brain, and cerebrospinal fluid (CSF).

Insults to the cranium, such as hyperemia, contusions, lacerations, and hematomas, are considered space-occupying lesions. Because the cranium is a fixed, rigid container, changes in the volume of one or more of these components or the addition of a lesion must be offset by a change in the volume of another component. If not, there will be a rise in the intracranial pressure.

Normally, the brain seeks to maintain cerebral equilibrium by compensating for changes by means of cranial structures. This is done by partial collapse of the cisterns, the ventricles, or the vascular system. During this compensatory period, the ICP remains in a safe range. When these compensatory systems have been exhausted, however, the ICP rises rapidly. Herniation occurs, and cerebral blood flow to the medulla is severed.

The Volume-Pressure Curve

The relation of pressure to volume in the cranium is illustrated in Figure 3-1. The volume of the intracranial contents can increase without changing the ICP while

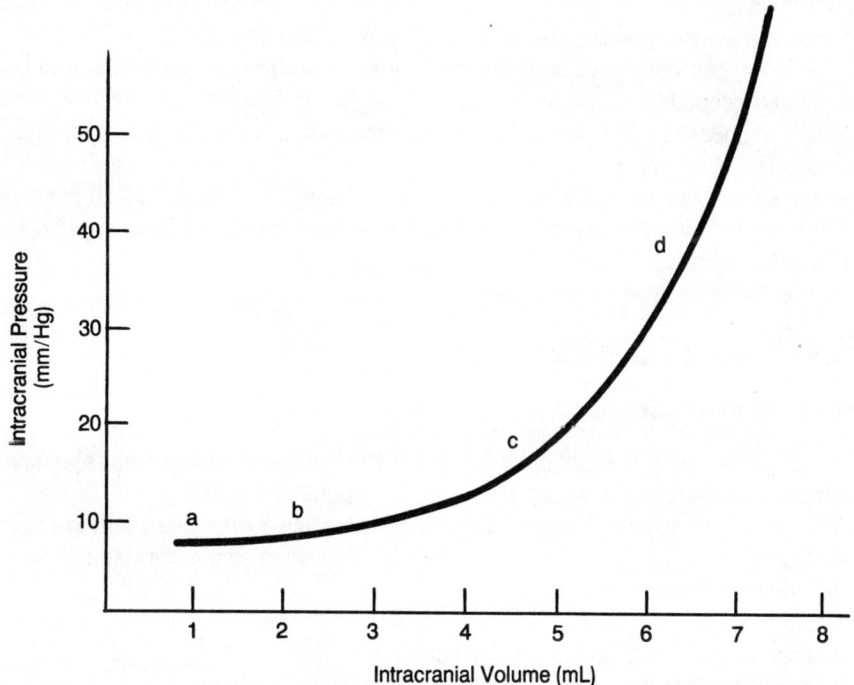

Figure 3-1 Volume-Pressure Curve. This curve demonstrates the relation between the volume of the intracranial contents and the ICP. Between points a and b there exists an element of compliance: as intracranial volume is added, the ICP remains the same. From point b to c the compliance decreases, and for every small amount of volume added there is a large increase in the ICP. Between points c and d, there is little or no compliance. At this point a small amount of volume creates a tremendous amount of pressure. Additional volume due to fluid overload, increasing $Paco_2$ and decreasing Pao_2, and acidosis can also contribute to vasodilation and therefore a rising ICP.

compensatory mechanisms remain intact. As soon as the brain loses its ability to compensate, however, there is a sharp rise in the ICP. Thus when a child loses the ability to compensate and becomes clinically symptomatic, the child is on the steep portion of the curve, indicating that sudden, severe elevations in ICP can occur.

Cerebral Perfusion Pressure

The response of the ICP to increasing volume is related to the location and type of lesion. How changes in ICP relate to changes in volume is called compliance. Poor compliance is when a small increase in volume creates a large increase in ICP. Clinically, compliance of the traumatized brain is measured by calculating the cerebral perfusion pressure (CPP). This is done by subtracting the ICP from the mean arterial pressure (MAP):

$$CPP = MAP - ICP$$

Increases in CPP indicate increased cerebral blood flow. A decrease in the CPP, which frequently is a poor diagnostic indicator, can mean reduced cerebral blood flow and an alteration in oxygen and glucose supplies to the brain. In the head-injured child, a CPP of 50 mmHg is acceptable. An acute increase in ICP can lead to cardiorespiratory arrest. When this happens the ICP becomes equal to the systemic arterial pressure, which prevents cerebral perfusion.

It is imperative that each ICP spike be treated as though indicating that all compensatory mechanisms have been exhausted, because there is no assurance that an additional insult will be tolerated.

TYPES OF HEAD INJURIES

Primary and Secondary Brain Injury

A current concept in the pathophysiology of head injury is primary and secondary head injury. Primary head injury occurs at the moment of impact and is directly proportional to the degree and type of trauma delivered to the brain and cranium. Physiologic dysfunction can occur in the absence of gross anatomic disruption, and the dysfunction often far exceeds anatomic injury.[3]

Secondary brain injury results from those events that, when left untreated, exacerbate the primary injury. Cerebral ischemia, edema, and increased ICP are the result of systemic hypotension, hypercapnia, and hypoxia. When untreated, these events can make potentially reversible lesions permanent, and new lesions can appear from the anoxic damage. This leads to increased mortality and morbidity. The prevention of secondary head injury is the primary purpose of critical care management.

It is because of this concept that the child who arrives in the emergency room comatose and with fixed, dilated pupils and loss of brain stem reflexes is now aggressively managed. These injuries are thought to be diffuse white matter injuries, not primary, irreversible lesions. If the injury is to the brainstem, the child may die within 2 hours of sustaining the injury.

Posttraumatic Hyperemia

Another concept unique to the head-injured child is posttraumatic cerebrovascular hyperemia. Because the child has an immature brain, there is probably an immediate rise in the cerebral blood volume that results directly from the trauma. Cellular injury occurs along with increased lactic acid production. This metabolic acidosis is compensated by dilation of the cerebral vasculature in an attempt to excrete excess hydrogen ions and to normalize the pH. The increase in the cerebral blood flow further increases the ICP. Increases in carbon dioxide and decreases in oxygen have the same effect on the cerebral blood flow and the resultant ICP. A diffuse, swollen brain with an increased ICP can be detected on computerized tomography (CT); the information gained from such scans helps in determining the appropriate drugs to administer for the traumatized brain.

Herniation

As demonstrated in Figure 3-1, an increase in ICP is tolerated for a brief period of time. Infants and children have an additional margin of expansion because their cranial sutures are not completely fused until approximately 6 months of age and their fontanelles close at approximately 20 months of age. Complete ossification is thought to occur at approximately 12 years of age.

As the ICP continues to rise, CSF is shunted into the subarachnoid spaces in the spinal column or the cerebral blood flow reduces to compensate. Should the ICP increase acutely and normal measures of compensation or displacement be inadequate to relieve it, the brain is forced to move within the intracranial vault. Because the brain is viscoelastic, it can normally tolerate some displacement and compression. The brain can be displaced from one compartment to another, depending on the pressures within the compartments. An example of this is the rapidly expanding epidural hematoma.

When the brain cannot tolerate further compression or displacement, a condition called herniation develops. The site at which herniation occurs indicates the intensity of the ICP and the sequelae that may be seen (Figure 3-2).

Uncal Herniation

The temporal lobe or uncus is the most frequently identified area where herniation occurs. With uncal herniation, there is displacement of the temporal lobe and the uncus of the parahippocampal gyrus. As the uncus shifts medially to accommodate the intracranial lesion, the adjacent midbrain, the oculomotor nerve (cranial nerve III), and the posterior cerebral artery are compressed.[4]

Clinically the child complains of headache, which is caused by distortion of the dura and the basal cerebral blood vessels; this is followed by deterioration of the child's level of consciousness. Other signs and symptoms include early dilation of the ipsilateral pupil (from damage to cranial nerve III) and, when left untreated, contralateral hemi-

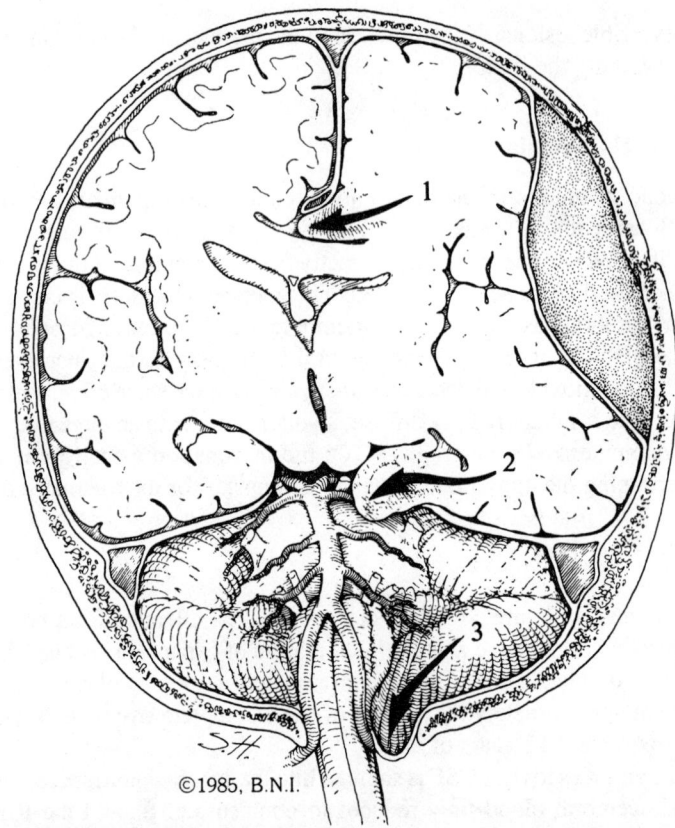

Figure 3-2 Herniation: Transtentorial, Uncal, and Tonsilar. The brain shifts to accommodate the expanding hematoma. Arrow 1 indicates the cingulate gyrus displaced below the falx to the contralateral side. Arrow 2 indicates the uncus of the parahippocampal gyrus displaced medially against the midbrain and cranial nerve III. Arrow 3 indicates displacement of the brainstem downward through the tentorial hiatus. *Source:* Courtesy of Steve Harrison.

---

paresis or decerebrate posturing.[5] The next sign of continued herniation is dilation of the opposite pupil, which is followed by motor involvement, altered respiratory function, and, terminally, bradycardia, systemic hypertension, and respiratory arrest.[6] This series of events is common to all lesions if they are left untreated, producing transtentorial herniation.

In children younger than 4 years of age, bradycardia may be the first sign of impending herniation and rising ICP. If herniation is not diagnosed promptly, what could have been an optimum recovery with reversal of herniation will instead lead to a fatal outcome; this irreversible stage may be reached within minutes. Recovery appears to be related to the degree of neurological function present at the time at which ICP was relieved. An attempt to relieve the herniation should always be made in the child, regardless of the clinical signs, because children tolerate brainstem compression better than adults.

Transtentorial Herniation

A second kind of herniation occurs under the falx cerebri from one side of the supratentorial space to the other. The clinical sign is loss of leg function (unless the patient is comatose), which results from anterior cerebral artery compression.

Tonsilar Herniation

A third type of herniation occurs when the cerebellar tonsils are compressed into the foramen magnum. This happens with diffuse brain swelling and is clinically difficult to diagnose because clinical signs referable to the foramen magnum are often absent. Some children develop headache, stiff neck, or vomiting. This kind of herniation can result in sudden respiratory and cardiac arrest.[7]

Cerebral Edema

Cerebral edema occurs when the brain swells as a result of injury. Although cerebral edema is thought of as pathologic, unless it interrupts neurologic function or causes increased ICP it can be present yet undetected.

Hyperemic Cerebral Edema

When brain swelling is directly related to massive increases in cerebral blood flow, it is called hyperemic cerebral edema. This response is often triggered by hypercapnia, hypoxia, or lactic acidosis. The brain responds to these symptoms by vasodilating to rid itself of toxic substances and to maintain its supply of oxygen and glucose.

Cytotoxic Cerebral Edema

The cerebral edema seen with swelling of the cellular components is called cytotoxic cerebral edema, in which interstitial volume decreases and allows fluid to accumulate within brain cells. Even though the edema is within the cells, there is also a change in the permeability of the capillary endothelial cells and in the ionic transport control. This leads to an overall increase in water content in the brain.

The exact mechanism of cytotoxic edema is unclear. It is thought that cytotoxic and vasogenic edema have similar characteristics. Cytotoxic edema may be the result of injuries producing hypoxia, hypoglycemia, ischemia, and hypo-osmolality. It is the type of edema most frequently seen in critically ill pediatric patients.

Vasogenic Cerebral Edema

Vasogenic cerebral edema is caused by an alteration in the blood-brain barrier, which allows water and proteins freely to enter the interstitial space. How the blood-brain barrier is altered is unclear. Once the defect is present, however, vasogenic edema spreads freely. Fluids migrate freely from the intravascular space into the interstitium because of hydrostatic pressure, so that molecules of all molecular sizes and diffusing capacities continue to cross the blood-brain barrier.

Vasogenic cerebral edema occurs much faster in the white matter than in the gray matter because the former is more compliant, or less resistant to flow.[8] Resolution of vasogenic edema is by reabsorption of excess fluid by glial cells. A small amount of fluid is transported into the ventricles through the CSF.

Scalp Lacerations

Lacerations of the scalp are frequently seen in both minor and severe head injuries. The scalp's rich vascular supply allows for quick and often uneventful healing. Without proper management, however, serious infection or disfigurement can occur.

In managing scalp injuries, it is helpful to understand the composition of the scalp. The scalp is composed of five planes of tissue (these can be remembered by using the mnemonic SCALP): (1) skin; (2) dense connective tissue containing the blood supply to the scalp; (3) the epicranial aponeurosis, which is a condensation of fascia of the frontalis and occipitalis muscles; (4) loose connective tissue; and (5) the pericranium, which is the periosteum of the calvarium (Figure 3-3).[9]

Simple scalp lacerations can be treated in the emergency room by thorough cleaning and suturing if necessary. Lacerations without tissue loss can be closed as follows.[10]

1. Cleanse the area with an antimicrobial solution. Remove as little hair as possible by cleaning and positioning it away from the edge of the laceration.
2. Control bleeding of scalp arteries by ligation and electrocoagulation. Lidocaine (1 percent) can also help to control blood loss.
3. Conservatively débride dead tissue. Because of the scalp's rich blood supply, even sites of severe contusions often heal successfully.
4. Remove any foreign bodies.
5. Delicately handle tissue.
6. Approximate skin edges with 3-0 to 5-0 monofilament nylon suture. Remove sutures in 5 to 7 days.

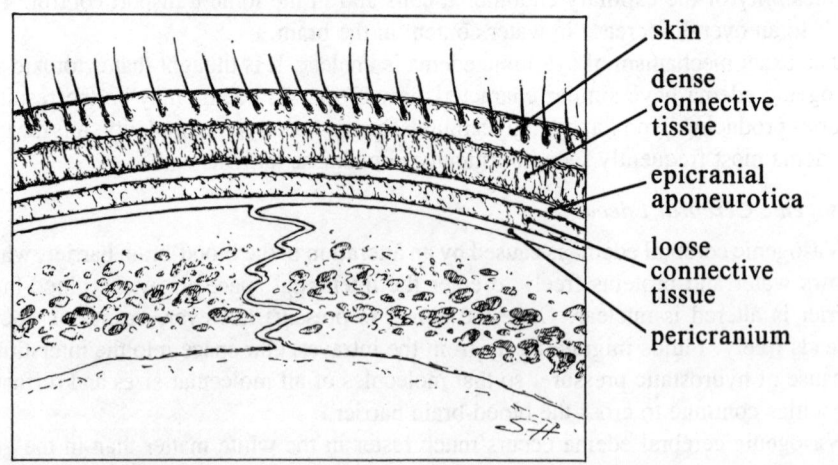

Figure 3-3 Layers of the Scalp. *Source:* Courtesy of Steve Harrison.

Tetanus prophylaxis should be administered if needed. If avulsions or other scalp defects larger than 2 cm are present, a plastic surgeon or neurosurgeon should be consulted. Antibiotics are not indicated because with proper management the incidence of infection is less than 1 percent.

Scalp Hematomas

Evaluation of whether scalp swelling is diffuse or focal can help to determine the type of hematoma that may be present. Transillumination can also be helpful in determining the location and type of hematoma (Figure 3-4).

Subgaleal Hematoma

The loose connective plane is composed of small cavities and spaces below the aponeurosis. When this tissue is injured, infection and blood can accumulate. The most common hematoma in this area is the subgaleal hematoma (Figure 3-5), which is frequently a complication of the linear skull fracture. This type of hematoma is seen most often in the older child. Clinically, swelling is diffuse and transillumination decreased. Management is conservative because the fluid is generally reabsorbed within a few weeks. Aspiration is contraindicated because there is a risk of infection.

Cephalohematoma

Cephalohematomas occur when there is an accumulation of fluid in the subperiosteal plane. Cephalohematomas are rarely large because the pericranium is tightly joined at the site of the cranial sutures, which inhibits fluid from crossing the suture line. Clinically, cephalohematomas are usually associated with focal scalp swelling in the

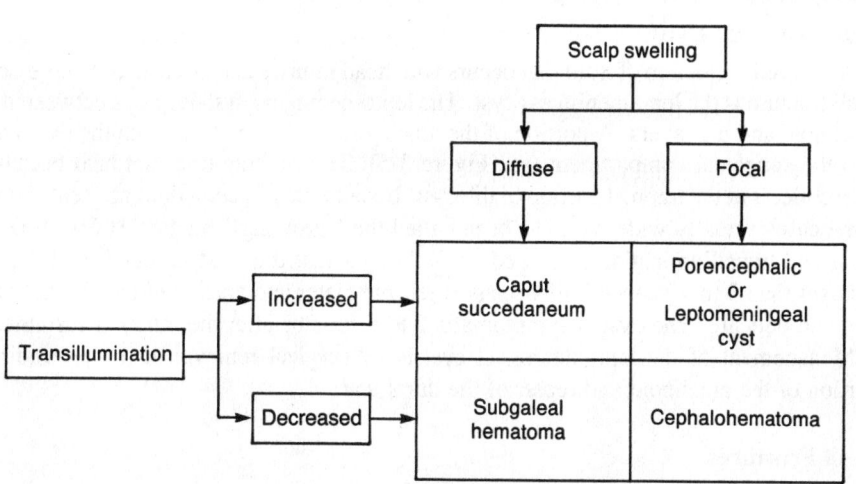

Figure 3-4 Evaluation of Scalp Swelling: Tracing the Cause. *Source:* Reprinted from *Contemporary Pediatrics*, Vol. 3, p. 34, with permission of *Contemporary Pediatrics*, © 1986.

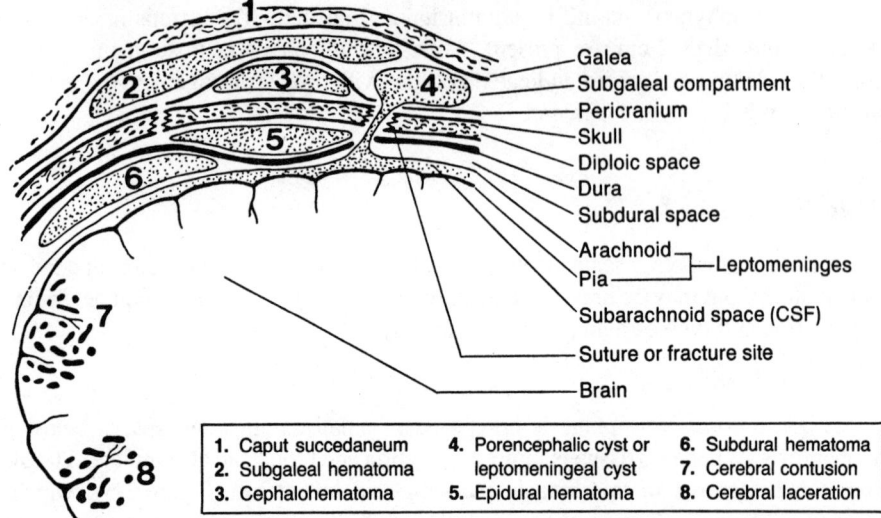

Figure 3-5 Anatomy of Head Trauma: Evaluating Sites of Traumatic Brain Injury. *Source:* Reprinted from *Contemporary Pediatrics*, Vol. 3, p. 26, with permission of *Contemporary Pediatrics*, © 1986.

parietal region. Cephalohematomas are often associated with mid- or high-forceps delivery during childbirth.

Caput Succedaneum

Caput succedaneum is a diffuse collection of fluid within the layers of the scalp. Swelling can extend across suture lines, and transillumination is increased. This swelling is seen most frequently in the newborn. As with the cephalohematoma, treatment is usually not necessary.

Leptomeningeal Cyst

A delayed collection of fluid that occurs with head injuries and often after a depressed skull fracture is the leptomeningeal cyst. The leptomeningeal cyst develops between the arachnoid and pia layers. A portion of the arachnoid then extends through the dura and into the subgaleal compartment (see Figure 3-5). The fracture does not heal because CSF collects in the trapped portion of the cyst. Because this fracture does not heal and in some cases actually widens, it has been called the "growing" fracture.[11] Swelling is focal and transillumination increased. It is thought that this cyst is found in children younger than 3 to 4 years of age because their pia mater and arachnoid membranes are thin and delicate. The cyst is symptomatic 2 to 6 months after the injury is sustained.

Management of the leptomeningeal cyst is by surgical removal of the protruding portion of the arachnoid and repair of the dural tear.

Skull Fractures

The clinical status of the patient is not assessed exclusively by the presence or absence of a skull fracture. Often major brain injury is not evident, while at other times significant injury accompanies skull fractures.[12] The skull accepts a large proportion of the impact force of trauma, which spares the underlying brain.

Linear Fractures

A simple or linear skull fracture is one in which the bone remains approximated and the underlying dura is not pierced. This type accounts for approximately 75 percent of all skull fractures in children.

Clinically, the scalp can be swollen, ecchymotic, and tender. Evaluation of the skull should include determining the fracture location and the neurological status of the patient. When this fracture occurs in the temporal lobe area, there is a risk of injury to the middle meningeal artery. If this location is identified, observation and hospitalization are necessary because of the delayed risk of an epidural hematoma. Healing occurs within 6 months in the infant and within 1 year in the older child.

A subgaleal hematoma is a common occurrence with a linear skull fracture, developing within a few days or weeks. This hematoma can be large and fluctuating. The fluid is frequently thought to be CSF on skull films, but should not be aspirated.

Depressed Skull Fractures

If a depressed skull fracture is closed, it is rarely a neurosurgical emergency. Only if focal seizures or a focal neurological deficit are manifested is surgery indicated. Depressed fractures are considered significant when the skull is depressed more than 5 mm or when the outer table lies below the inner table of the skull. Depressed fractures are cause for concern because they can bruise or lacerate the underlying brain. The dura is often torn, increasing the risk of infection. Good skull films can determine the extent of the injury. If needed, a CT scan can be done to evaluate further the degree of brain involvement.

Diastatic Fractures. Diastatic fractures are seen with depressed and sometimes with linear fractures. Diastatic fractures are traumatic separations of cranial bones at the cranial suture site. They most frequently affect the lambdoid suture and occur in the first 4 years of life.[13] Leptomeningeal cysts ("growing" fractures) can develop at the site of a diastatic fracture. Therefore, these fractures require close monitoring, especially in children younger than 3 years of age.

Compound Depressed Fractures. Compound depressed skull fractures are managed in the same manner as other compound injuries. They are meticulously cleaned, débrided, and examined for foreign bodies. The CT scan is helpful in that it can show bony fragments and also underlying cerebral injury.

Clinically, the patient may present with contusion and edema of the scalp. Depending on the brain involvement there can be alterations in the level of consciousness. If surgical intervention is needed the fracture is elevated, and any existing tears in the dura are repaired. With a compound skull fracture the first priority is to maintain homeostasis. This can be done by using Rainey clips at the wound edges. The open wound is cleansed gently with saline and povidone-iodine. Antibiotic coverage with a broad-spectrum agent, such as oxacillin (150 mg/kg/day), is indicated. Tetanus status again needs to be evaluated.

Basilar Skull Fractures

The basilar skull fracture occurs at the base of the skull, often extending to the ears and nasal passages. This fracture usually creates tears in the dura, although the underlying brain is usually not injured. These dural tears allow free communication of CSF from the subarachnoid space to the upper respiratory system. About 5 percent to 15 percent of all head injuries are basilar skull fractures.

The diagnosis of basilar skull fracture is a clinical one, made on the basis of presenting signs and symptoms. The classic presentation of basilar skull fractures includes (1) periorbital cyanosis (raccoon eyes), (2) an ecchymotic area over the mastoid bone (Battle's sign), (3) presence of blood behind the tympanic membrane or in the external canal due to tearing of the tympanic membrane, (4) presence of bleeding in the nose or nasopharynx, and (5) CSF otorrhea (leakage of CSF from the external ear canal) or rhinorrhea (leakage from the nasopharynx).

Cranial nerves should be assessed because cranial nerve palsies sometimes occur. Commonly involved cranial nerves are the olfactory (I), the acoustic (VIII), and the facial (VII).

Skull films are rarely obtained when a basilar skull fracture is suspected because the complexity of bony structures in the base of the skull makes the fracture difficult to identify on roentgenography. CSF rhinorrhea and otorrhea are of special concern because they can create open pathways for infection. Rhinorrhea can often be overlooked in children because they swallow the fluid, making its presence difficult to detect. A dipstrip can be used to evaluate nasal drainage for glucose. False positives can occur, however, because normal nasal secretions can contain glucose. Another test for CSF leakage is to place a sterile gauze pad at the ear or nose to collect a sample of drainage. If a yellow halo appears around the serosanguinous area, CSF is probably draining. This test is also inconclusive, however, because plasma can make a similar appearance. If it is necessary to determine conclusively whether CSF is in the drainage, radioactive albumin is injected into the subarachnoid space through a lumbar puncture. This can be traced as it drains from the nose or ears. Persistent leakage of CSF may require CT evaluation and surgical repair of the meninges.

Management is essentially twofold: first, preventing further tears in the dura, and second, preventing infection. To prevent further dural tearing, the child's head should be elevated at all times to minimize or stop the rhinorrhea. Vigorous coughing and nose blowing should be minimized. Sneezing should not be inhibited. The Valsalva maneuver should be avoided because it can increase pressure on the tympanic membrane and lead to further dural tearing. Suction catheters and nasogastric tubes should only be inserted with the guidance or order of a physician.

Prevention of infection is key. Patients are admitted for observation for 48 to 72 hours and are monitored closely to prevent them from putting objects or fingers into their nasopharynx or ears. Suction catheters and nasogastric tubes are often contraindicated because they present a risk of introducing infection.

Most basilar skull fractures heal spontaneously within 7 to 10 days. Children with basilar skull fractures were once treated prophylactically with broad-spectrum antibiotics, but it has been shown that the incidence of meningitis is not significantly reduced. Current practice is to monitor these patients for infection, only treating them with antibiotics if signs and symptoms of meningitis develop.

Closed Head Injuries

Cerebral Concussion

Cerebral concussion is defined as a transient phase of unresponsiveness or loss of awareness after head injury. Symptoms occur on impact and can persist for several seconds, minutes, or, infrequently, hours. Concussions are usually caused by blunt trauma to the head. The force of impact is less than that causing skull fractures. A concussion is most likely to occur if the head moves freely after the impact, so that an acceleration-deceleration injury (often with rotation) is produced. Shearing stresses are placed on the brainstem, resulting in trauma to the reticular activating system. When this system is injured, the brain's center for wakefulness and attentiveness is inactivated. The diagnosis of a concussion is made when the child regains consciousness and demonstrates no other signs of neurological deterioration.

Amnesia

Concussions are frequently associated with amnesia. In the unwitnessed period of unconsciousness, a memory loss is often the clue that a concussion has occurred. Amnesia associated with concussions can be of three types: temporary retrograde, permanent retrograde, and temporary posttraumatic (anterograde).

Temporary retrograde amnesia is a memory loss of events that occurred several years before the injury. With this type of amnesia, memory usually returns within several hours or days. Permanent retrograde amnesia is a memory loss involving those events occurring a few seconds to minutes immediately before the injury. With this type of amnesia, direct recall never returns. Anterograde amnesia is a memory loss of new information, in which the child is unable to retain new information since the injury. With this type of amnesia, the child typically asks questions repeatedly. This type of memory disturbance usually resolves within 24 hours.

Clinically, the child who sustains a concussion and loses consciousness may also present with vital sign changes. Often there is a decrease in respirations, decreased heart rate, and decreased blood pressure. Corneal and gag reflexes are present but depressed.

Postconcussion syndrome is common and includes the symptoms of headache, malaise, vertigo, anxiety, or fatigue. These may last for several days or weeks.

Pediatric Concussion Syndrome

The pediatric concussion syndrome, which is unique to children, occurs after what appears to be a minor head injury. Clinically, the child may lose consciousness for a brief period of time. The child reawakens readily and demonstrates good neurological improvement. The child remains lucid for several minutes to hours before neurological status deteriorates and vomiting begins. Ultimately, the child presents with loss of consciousness, unilateral or bilateral pupil dilation, Babinski's sign, and decerebrate posturing. This syndrome has three possible outcomes: (1) spontaneous resolution, (2) persistence for several days with gradual resolution, and (3) progression to coma and, without critical care intervention, brain death.[14]

Because of the occurrence of this syndrome in children, any child who sustains a concussion should be hospitalized for 24 hours for neurological evaluation. Any changes in the child's neurological status should be reported immediately to the physician.

Cerebral Contusions

Cerebral contusions occur when the brain is injured with resulting hemorrhage, edema, and bruising. They are often related to blunt trauma, acceleration-deceleration forces, or rotational forces that traumatize the brain. If the injury is directly under the site of impact, it is called a coup injury. If the injury occurs on the opposite side from the impact, it is called a contrecoup injury.

The signs and symptoms of contusions are related to the degree of brain tissue injury, cerebral edema, and intracranial bleeding. Severe intracranial bleeding can develop into subdural or epidural hematomas. The cerebral edema present can lead to increased ICP. Focal brain injury can be manifested by seizures.

The type of seizure associated with contusions and, often, lacerations is called posttraumatic epilepsy. The risk of developing posttraumatic epilepsy increases with depressed skull fractures and when the child has sustained a concussion with loss of consciousness for more than 1 hour. The risk also increases with the severity of the head injury. Approximately half the children who develop posttraumatic epilepsy eventually undergo resolution of the seizures. Some children continue to experience several seizures a year.

Treatment of posttraumatic epilepsy is the same as that for nontraumatic seizures. Phenytoin (Dilantin®) is the first drug used because it enters the brain rapidly. If seizures persist, other drugs such as paraldehyde and diazepam (Valium®) are administered. Prophylactic administration of anticonvulsants has not been shown effective.

A clinical diagnosis of cerebral contusions can be made when specific focal neurological signs or focal seizures are present. Confirmation of contusions is made after CT scan evaluation. Management of contusions is dependent on the presenting signs and symptoms. Generally it is supportive unless there are signs of increased ICP.

Intracranial Hematomas

Intracranial hematomas are vascular injuries that occur as the result of head injury. Often significant trauma can occur regardless of whether there is a skull fracture. When neurological deterioration is noted in the presence of skull fractures, an intracranial hematoma is a likely diagnosis.

Epidural Hematomas

An epidural hematoma is a collection of blood above the dura and below the skull. It most often occurs in the temporoparietal area. Of all epidural hematomas, 75 percent are associated with skull fractures, frequently a linear skull fracture of the squamous bone occurring across the groove of the middle meningeal artery. Frequently the source of bleeding is a lacerated middle meningeal artery.

Interestingly, there are few epidural hematomas in children younger than 2 years of age. The reason for this may be that fixation of the middle meningeal artery does not occur until approximately 2 years of age. Before 2 years, this artery is not embedded into the temporal bone, allowing it to rotate and perhaps to avoid injury. It has also been noted that the dura has close adhesion to the skull in early childhood, which may decrease the likelihood of epidural bleeds.

The child with an epidural hematoma has usually sustained a relatively minor blow to the head with or without loss of consciousness. Often the clinical presentation can be misleading because some children with epidural hematomas lose consciousness and awaken, whereas others lose consciousness and never awaken. Only about 30 percent to 50 percent of all children with epidural hematomas experience the classic lucid period with subsequent increasing headache, dilated pupil ipsilateral to the hematoma, and neurological deterioration. Therefore, when the signs and symptoms of neurological deterioration present, the child is in danger of a rapidly rising ICP.

A CT scan should be done immediately to diagnose the epidural bleed. If unavailable or if the child is critically ill, a skull film is often adequate to identify the location of the hematoma. Critical care management usually includes a craniotomy with surgical evacuation of the hematoma. The child should be placed in the intensive care unit and should have an ICP monitor inserted for at least 72 hours, because this is the time of greatest risk to the brain. If the bleeding is venous in nature, the child may present with signs of decreasing level of consciousness (headache, nausea, vomiting, and papilledema) within 1 to 2 weeks.

Less than 25 percent of children with acute epidural hematomas have seizures after the injury. Approximately 25 percent of children who sustain an epidural hematoma die. Those who survive have minimal sequelae (Table 3-1).

Table 3-1 Epidural and Subdural Hematomas: A Comparison

Clinical Features	Acute Epidural Hematoma	Acute Subdural Hematoma
Frequency	Less	Greater
Skull fracture	75%	30%
Source of bleeding	Usually arterial	Venous
Age of Patient	Usually older than 2 yrs	Usually younger than 1 yr
Laterality	Usually unilateral	Usually bilateral
Seizures	Less than 25%	75%
Preretinal and retinal hemorrhages	Less than 25%	75%
Increased ICP	Present	Present
CT configuration	Usually lenticular	Usually curvilinear or crescent-shaped
Mortality	25%	Less than 25%
Morbidity	Low	High

Source: Reprinted from *Contemporary Pediatrics*, Vol. 3, pp. 24–46, with permission of *Contemporary Pediatrics*, © 1986.

Subdural Hematomas

A subdural hematoma is a collection of blood below the dura mater and above the pia-arachnoid. Subdural hematomas are commonly venous bleeds resulting from tearing of the bridging meningeal veins. Of all subdural hematomas, 75 percent are bilateral. They are seen most often in infants with a peak frequency at 6 months of age. An acute subdural hematoma can occur as the result of child abuse, accidental injury, motor vehicle accident, or birth trauma. With subdural hematomas associated with difficult labor and delivery (frequently breech presentation and low Apgar scores), the infant presents with neurological deterioration within 12 hours of birth. The infant usually has bulging fontanelles, retinal hemorrhages, and respiratory distress.

In infants younger than 1 year of age, subdural hematomas are frequently the result of child abuse. Whenever the extent or severity of the injury does not agree with the history given by the significant caregiver or does not fit the normal developmental process of the child, child abuse must be considered. Subdural hematomas caused by shaking the infant have been referred to as the "Shaken Infant Syndrome." A recent study has shown that shaking alone in an otherwise healthy infant is unlikely to cause subdural hematomas and that some form of impact is necessary to produce severe head injury.[15]

On admission, these children are frequently comatose with bulging fontanelles; fixed, dilated pupils; retinal hemorrhages; and seizures. If the child is apneic on admission, the clinical course is ominous. If child abuse is suspected, the patient should be admitted and appropriate documentation completed and addressed to a child protection agency.

Chronic subdural hematomas occur in children younger than 2 years of age. Again, these are often the result of child abuse. Pathophysiology includes a tearing of the meningeal veins with a slow accumulation of blood in the subdural space. The onset of neurological symptoms is seen over several weeks, resulting from a slowly rising ICP. Most chronic subdural hematomas are bilateral and should be treated as if they were acute.

In the older child, the most common causes of subdural hematomas are motor vehicle accidents and falls. In urban settings, direct blows to the head by an assailant have become an increasingly common cause within the adolescent population.[16]

Management is as follows. After the patient is intubated and hyperventilated, bilateral fontanelle taps are performed. A fontanelle tap must be lateral from the midline by at least 2 cm to avoid the large draining veins. After 5 to 20 mL of subarachnoid fluid is removed, there is frequently a softening of the fontanelle, a decrease in pupil size, and a decrease in motor tone.[17] Sometimes a catheter is left in the subdural space and connected to a closed drainage system and removed after 24 hours.

After the initial stabilization, a CT scan is obtained. The CT scans are rarely impressive, usually showing increased density due to bleeding or a small posterior interhemispheric subdural hematoma.[18] If skull films are obtained old hematomas are frequently identified; these are often associated with child abuse. These hematomas have resolved over time, and the blood in the subdural space was reabsorbed.

Most children with a subdural hematoma require good critical care management because they are at risk for developing acute cerebral edema and seizures. Surgery is rarely indicated. In the older child, there is frequently an associated cerebral contusion, laceration, or massive edema. In this population, there is a greater likelihood that the lesion will require surgery. Aggressive postoperative management of increased ICP is necessary.

When the hematoma is uncomplicated, mortality is 10 percent; when there is cerebral involvement the mortality increases to 60 percent to 80 percent. Mortality and morbidity from subdural hematoma seem to be closely related to the child's level of consciousness at the moment of critical care intervention and the duration of increased ICP.[19]

NEUROLOGICAL ASSESSMENT

When a child sustains a head injury it is frequently in association with other injuries. Therefore, it is essential that the child admitted to the emergency room or critical care unit be rapidly assessed for the degree and extent of all life-threatening injuries. The treatment of any unconscious child admitted should follow the ABCs of resuscitation (airway, breathing, and circulation). Once the airway is secured and the circulation restored, the child should be assessed neurologically with the Glasgow Coma Scale.

The Glasgow Coma Scale provides a consistent and uniform method of neurological evaluation. It can also help to predict the outcome of a head-injured child.

The Glasgow Coma Scale is divided into three parts: eye opening, best verbal response, and best motor response. Points are assigned according to the child's responsiveness in each section. These points are then totaled. A score of 3 or less is indicative of deep coma, and a score of 15 indicates normal neurological function. There has been much debate over the reliability of this scale in children, but with some adaptation it can be easily applied (see Chapter 2).

Assessment of Key Cranial Nerves

It is imperative that several cranial nerves be assessed when the head-injured child is evaluated. A close evaluation of these reflexes can aid in determining whether neurological deterioration is occurring.

Pupil Responses

The pupils are innervated by the optic (II) and the oculomotor (III) cranial nerves. Normally the pupils are round with a smooth border, approximately 2 to 5 mm in diameter (Figure 3-6), and respond to light by constricting briskly. To test the light response of the pupils, the room must be dark. A bright light (such as that of a penlight) is held approximately 8 inches from the eyes. This light is slowly moved from the periphery to in front of the eye. If the patient is awake, he or she is asked to focus on a distant point, not on the light, to exclude accommodation (see below). The optic and oculomotor cranial nerves are considered intact if the pupils constrict briskly to the light. Reactivity is important to assess along with size, shape, and symmetry of response.

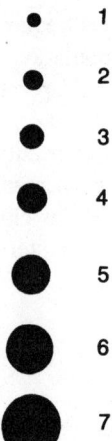

Figure 3-6 Guide to Pupil Size (in Millimeters).

Changes in pupil reactivity from brisk to sluggish, or changes in symmetry between the right and left pupil, are important indicators of changes in cerebral equilibrium.

Hippus is rapid and rhythmic contraction and dilation of the pupils in response to light; it indicates the balance between sympathetic and the parasympathetic function. When hippus is noted it often is an indicator of injury or insult to the sympathetic or parasympathetic fibers. Injury to the sympathetic fibers (located in the pons) causes small, nonreactive pupils bilaterally. Injury to the parasympathetic fibers (located in the midbrain) causes dilation of the pupils. When these fibers are impinged upon because of increased ICP, hippus is much more pronounced.[20]

Other factors can affect pupil size. Pupil constriction, or miosis, can occur from morphine administration; hemorrhages in the pons, which affect the sympathetic fiber responses; and poisoning.[21] Factors that cause pupil dilation include atropine administration; hypothermia; large doses of sympathomimetic agents, such as dopamine or epinephrine; and pain.[22] Prolonged oxygen deficit, possible midbrain dysfunction, or extensive brain damage can all be potential causes of fixed and dilated pupils.

When there is increased ICP, the oculomotor nerve is depressed. This causes pupil dilation ipsilateral to the site of the pressure and an absent direct light response. The pupils should be tested frequently, depending on the clinical status of the patient. Any pupil change should be reported immediately to the physician.

Accommodation is the process by which a clear visual image is formed as the eyes focus on a near and then a distant object. To do this the eyes must converge and the pupils must constrict, and there is a thickening of the lens through the contraction of the ciliary muscles. In the test for this response, the child focuses on a light as it is shone into the eye; pupil constriction should be observed.

When cerebral edema exerts pressure on the optic disk, papilledema results. The diagnosis is made when the retinal veins appear to be engorged and the optic disk is distant when viewed with an ophthalmoscope. Papilledema indicates that the ICP has been increased for at least 24 hours. Clinically, the child may complain of blurred or double vision and headaches.

Corneal Reflex

The corneal reflex is controlled by the trigeminal nerve (V). This cranial nerve is large, innervating the face in three branches. The corneal reflex is tested by gently stroking the cornea with a wisp of cotton; the normal response is blinking or tearing. If the response is absent, it may indicate coma or brainstem insult.

Startle Reflex

The startle reflex is controlled by the acoustic nerve (VIII). This reflex is tested by clapping or initiating other loud noises near the child's ear. The normal response is movement as if surprised, grimacing, or blinking. This reflex can also be tested by auditory stimulation in the brainstem auditory-evoked response test. This test has potential value in predicting patient outcome.

Caloric Reflex

The caloric reflex, also known as the oculovestibular reflex, is controlled by the trochlear (IV) and abducens (VI) nerves. This reflex can be tested when there is an intact tympanic membrane. The head of the bed is elevated at least 45°. The physician places a small catheter or syringe into the external canal of the ear and slowly instills about 15 mL of iced saline. The normal response in a comatose patient is nystagmus with deviation of both eyes toward the irrigated ear. If deviation does not occur, brainstem injury is present (Figure 3-7).

Doll's-Eye Reflex

The doll's-eye reflex, also known as the oculocephalic reflex, is controlled by three cranial nerves: the oculomotor (III), the trochlear (IV), and the abducens (VI). If a cervical spinal fracture is suspected, this reflex should not be tested. To evaluate this reflex, the child's head is rapidly turned from side to side while the eyelids are held open. The normal response is movement of the eyes in the opposite direction from that in which the head is turned (Figure 3-8). When this reflex is lost, the eyes appear to stay in a midline position as the head is moved from side to side, just as if they were the eyes of a doll. Loss of the oculocephalic reflex is indicative of brainstem dysfunction.

Gag Reflex

The gag reflex tests the glossopharyngeal nerve (IX). In the test for this reflex, a tongue blade or suction catheter is used to stimulate the posterior pharynx. The normal response is to gag or cough. Absence of this reflex indicates pressure on or damage to cranial nerve IX in the medulla. Clinically, the child may drool and is unable to swallow, which increases the risk of aspiration.

Diagnostic Tests

Computerized Tomography

The CT scan is crucial in the evaluation of head injury in children. The CT scan is a series of skull images that are combined by a computer and analyzed to form a total

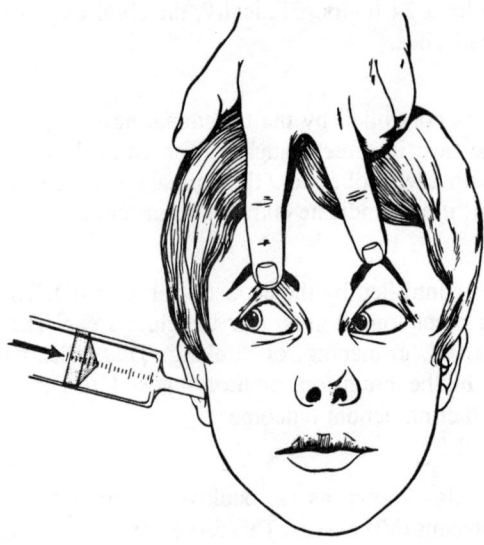

Figure 3-7 Caloric (Oculovestibular) Reflex. This drawing depicts a normal response to iced saline injected into the external ear. *Source:* Reprinted from *Critical Care Quarterly*, Vol. 2, No. 1, pp. 23–44, Aspen Publishers, Inc., © 1979.

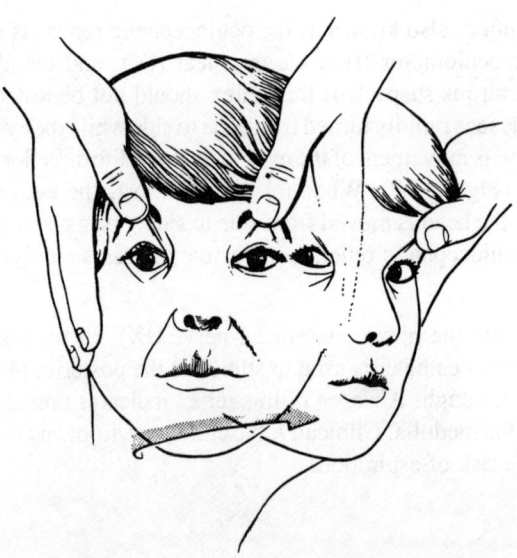

Figure 3-8 Doll's-Eye (Oculocephalic) Reflex. This drawing illustrates the normal response in a comatose patient: deviation of the eyes in the opposite direction from that in which the head is turned. *Source:* Reprinted from *Critical Care Quarterly*, Vol. 2, No. 1, pp. 23–44, Aspen Publishers, Inc., © 1979.

image of the intracranial contents. The advantage of the CT scan is its ability to image simultaneously several different planes within the head. White and gray matter and space can be differentiated intracranially. The CT scan provides the maximum amount of diagnostic information to the physician concerning what is happening in the intracranium of the injured child. Whenever possible, the CT scan is the preferred diagnostic test compared to skull roentgenograms, angiograms, or ventriculograms.

The use of the CT scan has been shown to have a definite effect in reducing morbidity and mortality in children with severe symptomatic head trauma. In a recent study, the CT scan was found to be valuable in assessing head injuries that appeared to be less severe clinically as determined from deteriorating Glasgow Coma Scale score, changes in pupillary light responses, neurological findings, vital signs, and level of consciousness. The study concluded that the use of the CT scan in initial evaluation and follow-up may prevent missed or delayed diagnosis of significant intracranial injury.[23] In managing increased ICP, the CT scan can be helpful diagnostically in understanding sudden clinical changes.

In managing the child with a head injury, the benefits of the CT scan are certainly greater than the risks. The amount of radiation is minimal, about 2 rad or the equivalent of a four-view series of skull films. Often the CT scan does not require sedation, so that neurological evaluation is not jeopardized. Compared to the total cost of hospitalization of a head-injured patient, the cost of CT imaging is small; when compared to the cost of a preventable death or permanent handicap, it is small indeed.

Magnetic Resonance Imaging

Recently, magnetic resonance imaging (MRI), a diagnostic imaging modality that does not use ionizing radiation, has become available. MRI uses the alignment of hydrogen nuclei under the influence of an externally applied magnetic field to produce images. When an energy pulse is delivered to the area under study, a maximal response appears as a white area and a minimal response appears as a black area.

It is thought that the greatest value of MRI is in evaluating diseases of the central nervous system. For head injuries it can be a good diagnostic indicator. For example, MRI is extremely sensitive in detecting blood and can therefore provide the diagnosis of a subarachnoid hemorrhage quickly and accurately.

The greatest handicap in using MRI with head-injured children is the time that it takes to obtain an image. Although MRI is more accurate than the CT scan, it takes several minutes for each image to be obtained. During this time the child must remain still. For the acute brain injury this may not be possible because sedation may be contraindicated and time may not allow for this extensive examination. MRI is presently about 10 percent to 25 percent more costly than CT.

History

An important part of the initial neurological assessment is the precipitating history of the injury. Historical data obtained from even the most lucid head-injured patients are often of limited value.[24] Often it is difficult for children to verbalize information in an uncomfortable environment and with unrecognized caregivers, so that it is important to question available witnesses concerning the traumatic event. Valuable witnesses are the emergency transport personnel and the family if the accident was witnessed by them. On arrival in the emergency room, emergency transport personnel should provide a detailed description of the potential cause of the accident, the mechanism of injury, a flow sheet of vital signs, and an assessment of neurological function. This information is extremely important in children and can influence and direct the nature of their care. For example, if the fact that the child lost consciousness is not communicated, the child could be prematurely discharged from the emergency room. Because of the risk of pediatric concussion syndrome, any child who sustains a concussion must be hospitalized for observation for 24 hours.

It is also necessary to obtain a complete history database for the child. Information should include an assessment of growth and development and health, social, spiritual, and family histories.

MANAGEMENT OF INCREASED INTRACRANIAL PRESSURE

Initial Assessment and Management

The immediate focus of attention on the neurologically injured child is prevention of secondary injury. Hypoxia, hypotension, and hypovolemia (often due to massive hemorrhage) insult the tissues and compromise the brain. Life support measures of resuscitation take precedence over specific neurological functions; when there is evidence that a head injury is present, however, additional measures can be taken simultaneously.

Airway and Ventilation

Children with head injuries often exhibit distinct breathing patterns that demonstrate the degree of brain involvement. Often there is an initial pattern of slow, deep, irregular breaths. This serves to increase the child's total oxygen volume through passive hyperventilation. This pattern can change to hyperventilation accompanied by a metabolic acidosis. Periodic breathing is observed when there is brainstem dysfunction. Finally, ataxic breathing due to a lack of muscle coordination and from insult to the medulla may be seen.

If the child is comatose with severe head injury, manual ventilatory control should be maintained with 100 percent oxygen. An artificial airway is immediately inserted by means of the rapid-sequence intubation method, which does not hyperextend the neck. This technique provides optimal results with minimal elevations in the child's ICP. It is performed only when there is a stable systemic arterial blood pressure because the administration of thiopental could precipitate a decrease in systemic blood pressure. The child is anesthetized with thiopental, 3 to 5 mg/kg, administered intravenously. Pancuronium, 0.2 mg/kg, is then immediately administered intravenously to provide neuromuscular relaxation. Together, these two drugs provide optimal conditions for nasally intubating the head-injured child. Pressure at the cricoid ring occludes the esophagus, preventing potential aspiration of gastric contents.

Nasal intubation is generally preferred with head injury (unless contraindicated because of a basilar skull fracture or facial trauma) because the child may suck or bite on an oral endotracheal tube. This can interfere with appropriate ventilation. As soon as the correct size endotracheal tube is inserted and secured, a nasogastric tube is inserted to aspirate the stomach and to prevent aspiration. Once the stomach contents are evacuated, the child is passively hyperventilated with large tidal volumes and 100 percent oxygen. The goal is to reduce significantly the arterial carbon dioxide pressure. The rapid-sequence induction and intubation technique with thiobarbiturate and pancuronium protects the brain, provides complete relaxation allowing atraumatic exposure of the glottis and insertion of the tracheal tube, and minimizes reflux of gastric contents.[25]

Once the child is intubated, the bed should be placed in an upright position with the head of the bed elevated 30° to enhance venous return from the brain. If there has been prolonged bag and mask ventilation, this position can enhance diaphragmatic exertion. After arterial blood gas analysis, the child is ventilated with the appropriate oxygen concentration and correct ventilator settings.

Circulatory Support

Vital signs and systemic perfusion should be carefully and continuously assessed. The child rarely demonstrates hypotension as a result of head injury but more frequently as a result of hemorrhage. The vital sign change seen with rising ICP is increased heart rate. Pain and hemorrhage can also cause tachycardia. The classic Cushing's triad (increased systemic arterial pressure with widened pulse pressures, bradycardia, and apnea) is rarely demonstrated in children. As ICP rises, the child is often tachycardic and hypertensive. Increased pulse pressures and apnea are often late signs of increased ICP.

Tissue Perfusion

The child should be assessed for adequate systemic perfusion. This is done by assessing pulses, skin temperature, capillary refill, nail beds, and mucous membranes. Children often exhibit cyanosis as a late sign of respiratory failure. Diagnostically, an admitting serum hematocrit value should be obtained to identify any existing hemorrhage. The child's circulating blood volume should be calculated, and if there is a loss of more than 5 percent to 7 percent of the total volume the loss should be replaced.

Fluid replacement in the head-injured child should be done carefully. Expanding the circulating blood volume supports systemic perfusion but at the same time increases the cerebral blood volume, thereby increasing ICP. Closely monitoring the mean arterial blood pressure is helpful in ensuring adequate systemic and cerebral perfusion pressures. Ideally, an arterial cannula should be inserted into a systemic artery; this provides a continuous digital reading of mean arterial pressure and allows painless sampling of arterial blood for blood gases and other laboratory studies.

Adequate systemic circulation and cerebral perfusion pressures can be maintained by keeping the mean arterial pressure at 65 torr or higher. Therapy directed at decreasing ICP can have an adverse effect on systemic perfusion. Fluid restriction and osmotic diuretics can cause hypovolemia, whereas barbiturates and hypothermia can cause systemic hypotension.

Fluid Balance

In the absence of major hemorrhage, the child's fluid intake may be restricted to one-half to two-thirds maintenance volume; in addition, the child receives nothing by mouth and has an intravenous line inserted. The desired clinical situation is the lowest cardiac filling pressure that is consistent with adequate systemic pressure and cardiac output, a serum osmolality of 300 to 320 mOsm/L, and a urine output of 0.5 to 1.0 mL/kg/hr.

Maintenance intravenous fluids are usually 5 percent or 10 percent dextrose in 0.45 percent saline. If the child becomes hypovolemic, 5 percent albumin or fresh frozen plasma is given. Initial fluid restriction is prophylactic: by decreasing the overall circulating blood volume, cerebral blood volume will be decreased along with the ICP.

Urine Output

Because fluids are restricted, the urine output should be monitored closely. If injuries are severe, a urinary catheter should be inserted immediately. If blood is noted on insertion, the physician should be notified immediately. If the child's urine output falls below 0.5 mL/kg/hr, the physician should be consulted to evaluate whether the child is volume depleted, in renal failure, or has poor systemic perfusion to the kidneys.

The urine should be dipsticked to determine pH and to test for the presence of glucose, protein, ketones, and blood. It is recommended that catheter care be done regularly because the catheter provides entry for bacteria.

Drugs

Furosemide. Diuretics can rapidly change ICP within 15 minutes of administration. Administration of furosemide (Lasix®, 0.5 to 1.0 mg/kg) is recommended in the first 24 hours after injury. Mannitol is not recommended because it can cause transient vasodilation, thereby increasing cerebral blood flow and further injuring the traumatized, hyperemic brain.[26]

Dexamethasone. The use of steroids is always an issue of question and controversy. Steroids are not used for the rapid treatment of ICP because the peak time of effectiveness is about 12 to 15 hours. If steroids are to be used, dexamethasone (Decadron®) is the drug of choice because of its minimal salt-retaining properties. Dexamethasone at 1 mg/kg/day (the normal dosage) has shown no significant effect. Only higher than normal dosages (1.5 mg/kg/day) have been shown to reduce posttraumatic brain edema.[27] Dexamethasone can be administrated intravenously or intramuscularly in four divided doses per day for 5 days. After this schedule it is discontinued by gradually tapering the dose over several days.

In the critically injured child, the dangers associated with steroid administration are increased susceptibility to infection due to inhibition of the immune system and gastric bleeding due to hyperacidity of the gastric mucosa. Nursing management should include routine monitoring of the pH of the gastric contents from a nasogastric tube. When the pH is less than 5, administration of an antacid is recommended. The physician can also order cimetidine hydrochloride. Cimetidine inhibits acid secretion and can decrease the amount of antacid needed. If total fluid volume must be maintained at a low value, cimetidine can help decrease the volume. The standard dosage is 20 to 40 mg/kg/day in four divided doses.

In addition to antacids and cimetidine, good handwashing and aseptic technique must be followed at all times.

Secondary Assessment and Management

Secondary assessment and management is primarily directed toward the prevention of secondary brain injury and is immediately activated when there is neurological deterioration.

Hyperventilation

Often when the severely head-injured child arrives in the emergency room, there are spontaneous respirations. To ensure that the ICP is not elevated unnecessarily, the child is intubated and passively hyperventilated. The goal of hyperventilation is to reduce the child's arterial carbon dioxide pressure, thereby reducing ICP. Because carbon dioxide is a vasoconstrictor, a reduction in the arterial pressure will decrease cerebral blood flow. A decrease in pressure from 40 to 20 torr reduces cerebral blood flow to nearly 60 percent of normal.[28] This is why ICP elevations are so rapidly corrected when manual hyperventilation is instituted. Therefore, the first therapy for acute ICP spikes in the head-injured child is immediate removal of the child from mechanical ventilation and administration of manual hyperventilation.

The child's ventilator settings are adjusted to maintain arterial carbon dioxide pressure between 20 and 25 torr and the arterial oxygen pressure above 90 torr. If the ICP is uncontrollable, the carbon dioxide pressure can be further reduced to 15 torr.[28] The child's jugular venous oxygen tension should be monitored to observe how much oxygen is returning from the child's brain. This enables determination of whether the brain is being adequately perfused. Monitoring is accomplished by threading a catheter into the jugular venous bulb of the jugular vein. Cerebral blood flow and cerebral metabolic rate can also be measured through this catheter. Normal jugular venous oxygen tension is 35 torr.

Neuromuscular Blockade

For adequate hyperventilation, use of a paralyzing agent is necessary. This prevents overriding of the set respiratory rate, alterations in tidal volume (due to the child bucking the ventilator), and a potential rise in ICP from the child biting or gagging on the endotracheal tube.

The paralyzing agent of choice is pancuronium bromide (Pavulon®). Continuous neuromuscular blockade is established by an initial intravenous bolus of 0.2 mg/kg and then a continuous intravenous infusion at 0.1 mg/kg/hr. If a continuous infusion is not desired, then the child can receive intermittent boluses of 0.2 mg/kg. Often the first indicator that pancuronium has worn off is when the child triggers the ventilator-assist control and begins to breathe at the established respiratory rate.

Even though the child is unable to move, he or she can still perceive surrounding activity. Perceptions are often altered, however. It is crucial to explain everything to the child to decrease anxiety and fears, which may be evidenced by a rising ICP. Most physicians order sedation for the child with drug-induced paralysis. If not, the nurse should actively seek this order. The recommended sedation is morphine sulfate (0.1 to 0.2 mg/kg intravenously) and diazepam (Valium®, 0.04 to 0.20 mg/kg intravenously). Frequently sedation is ordered every 3 to 4 hours as needed for procedures; thus a sedative is given when ICP increases before or during procedures.

Continuous pancuronium infusions alter the normal physiologic processes of the child. Eye care is imperative because the child is unable to blink. Instillation of natural or artificial tears prevents corneal abrasions.

Respiratory Care

Because so many clinical indicators are removed when the nurse is caring for a head-injured child, frequent and consistent clinical assessment is important. Any child with an artificial airway should be evaluated frequently by auscultating and assessing the quality of breath sounds and by evaluating the endotracheal tube for patency, placement, and stability. If the child is paralyzed and unable to cough or gag, nursing measures should be directed toward preventing aspiration.

For pulmonary physiotherapy and suctioning, the child should first be manually hyperventilated with 100 percent oxygen to reduce ICP. The child is then suctioned rapidly, and manual hyperventilation is begun. Ideally, two nurses should perform this task to ensure that an appropriate ICP is maintained at all times.

Most children admitted to a pediatric intensive care unit have an ICP line inserted. Care should be exercised when turning the child so that intravenous lines and the ICP bolt are not kinked or disconnected. At all times the head should remain in a 30° upright, neutral position. If the head is turned to one side with obstruction of the internal jugular vein, there may be a sudden increase in ICP; the ICP should return immediately to normal when the head is returned to the neutral position.

Arterial Line

An arterial line must be inserted concurrently with intubation and hyperventilation of the child. This line allows blood samples to be obtained painlessly. The arterial line allows for continuous assessment of the child's mean arterial pressure, from which the cerebral perfusion pressure can be calculated. Arterial blood gases should be obtained routinely and whenever the child's condition changes.

Skin Care

Good skin care is important to prevent skin breakdown. The use of a foam ring under the child's head can prevent hair loss and skin breakdown. High-top sneakers are worn to prevent foot drop. Parents are encouraged to participate in general care when appropriate.

Intracranial Pressure Monitoring

For children who sustain head injury, the simplest and safest ICP monitoring device is the subarachnoid screw or bolt. Insertion of the bolt into the subarachnoid space ensures that healthy brain tissue is not destroyed and that infection is not introduced. Insertion is usually done by a neurosurgeon under local anesthesia. It can be done at the bedside in the emergency room or pediatric intensive care unit.

The intracranial bolt is connected to a nonflush system that is connected to a sensor, a transducer, and a recording or monitoring instrument. This system enables continuous monitoring of the mean ICP and calculation of the cerebral perfusion pressure. The ICP line should never be routinely flushed. If there is a question of patency, the ICP line is flushed by the physician by injection 0.1 mL or less of normal saline solution. In the noncompliant brain, this small increase in volume can significantly elevate the ICP. Newly designed fiberoptic ICP monitors are replacing bolts in many situations.

The ICP line should be recalibrated and rebalanced (rezeroed) every time the child is repositioned or every 2 to 4 hours. Frequently, the neurosurgeon requests that the level of the third ventricle or the tragus of the external ear be the point of reference for rebalancing the transducer.

Normal ICP wave forms are a series of rhythmic oscillations. Normal ICP ranges from 0 to 10 torr with an upper limit of 15 torr. Any elevation of 16 to 20 torr that persists for longer than 30 minutes should be treated.

A waves or plateau waves usually are the ICP spikes that occur with hyperemia. Appearance of these waves should be treated as a neurologic emergency. The A waves are 50 to 100 torr in amplitude and usually occur when there is already increased ICP (Figure 3-9).

B waves have low amplitude and are frequently seen oscillating with respirations. They often lose clarity because they are rhythmic in nature.

C waves also have low amplitude. The significance of C waves is not known, but it is thought that they may indicate an altered equilibrium in the cranium that reflects a new volume-pressure relation. Some experts hold that these waves reflect and oscillate with the mean systemic arterial pressure.

Osmotic Therapy

In the first 24 to 48 hours of management, administration of mannitol can cause a transient vasodilation in the recently traumatized, hyperemic brain; after this time, however, it is often the diuretic of choice. Mannitol is a hypertonic agent that is effective in decreasing cerebral edema. It is frequently administrated to control spontaneous elevations in ICP (ICP spikes).

The recommended dose of mannitol is 0.25 to 1.00 g/kg. When given in response to an ICP spike, it is usually effective within 20 minutes. Manual hyperventilation may be necessary initially to bring the ICP to a normal range as the mannitol is being administrated. Whenever there is a rapid increase in ICP, the nurse should always use manual hyperventilation as the initial therapy. Use of a Foley catheter is necessary to measure accurately the diuresis from mannitol administration.

When mannitol is administered to the head-injured child, the child is already in a low-volume state because fluids have been limited. It is imperative that parameters to monitor the extent of dehydration be utilized. Generally, dehydration is gauged according to the serum osmolality and the urine specific gravity. The optimal dehydration state is when

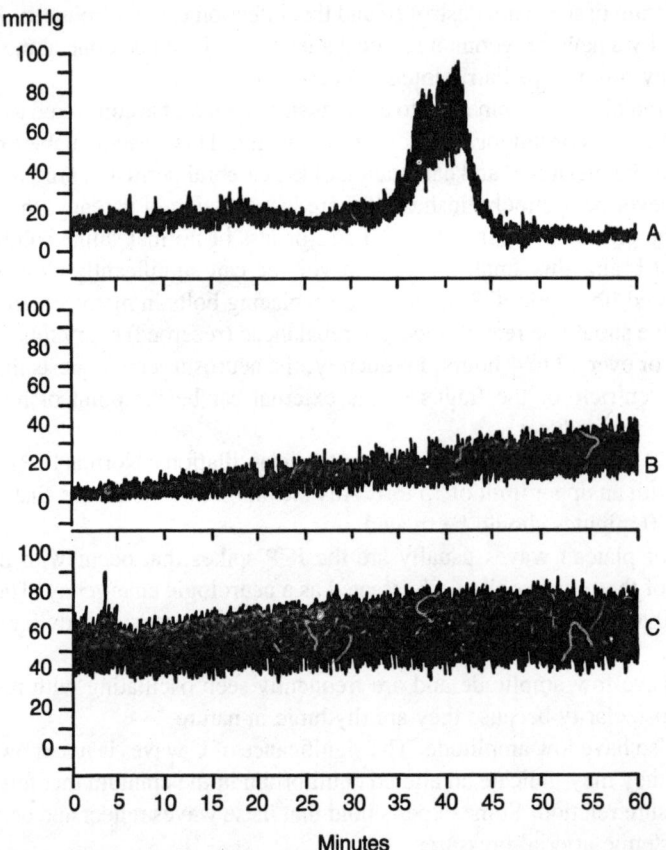

Figure 3-9 ICP Waves. **(A)** A waves: amplitude, 50 to 100 mmHg; duration, 5 to 20 minutes. **(B)** B waves: amplitude, 0 to 50 mmHg; frequency, 0.5 to 2.0 per minute. **(C)** C waves: amplitude, 0 to 20 mmHg; frequency, 4 to 8 per minute. *Source:* Reprinted from *Journal of Neurosurgical Nursing*, Vol. 9, p. 145, with permission of American Association of Neuroscience Nurses, © December, 1977.

---

the serum osmolality is between 290 to 310 mOsm/L. If mannitol is given frequently, the serum and urine osmolality and electrolytes must be checked often. Monitoring these parameters closely can prevent the adverse effects of osmotic agents. If the serum osmolality approaches or exceeds 320 mOsm/L, caution in administering mannitol is indicated because osmotic or mannitol rebound can occur.

Osmotic diuresis occurs when water is removed from healthy brain tissue and transported to the blood across an osmolar gradient. Normally the osmotic agent is prevented from entering the brain tissue by the blood-brain barrier. In the injured brain after maximal diuresis, however, the blood-brain barrier is ineffective, and the osmotic agent begins to leak into the tissue. This causes a higher concentration of the osmotic drug in the brain than in the blood. To equalize this, water flows freely into the brain.

This gradient reversal is what causes the rebound swelling. When this occurs, mannitol is no longer clinically effective until the serum osmolality falls to a lower level.

Other problems associated with osmotic diuretics, specifically mannitol, are renal dysfunction, electrolyte imbalance, and severe hypovolemia resulting in low cerebral perfusion pressure.[29]

Unresponsive Intracranial Hypertension

When the therapy described above does not effectively lower the child's ICP, then additional measures to reduce the ICP must be introduced. These measures are considered both controversial and routine. If the child continues to have uncontrolled increased ICP, a barbiturate coma may be induced to place the child in a state of hypothermia. The use of a barbiturate coma and hypothermia reduces the cerebral metabolic rate and cerebral blood flow, causing the ICP to decrease.

The two short-acting barbiturates most often administered are thiopental and pentobarbital (Nembutal®). Coma induction is achieved with pentobarbital, whereas thiopental is more often used to control random bursts of ICP.

Barbiturate coma reduces the cerebral metabolic rate and allows the brain to survive brief periods of ischemia. Optimal reduction of the cerebral metabolic rate is achieved when the electroencephalogram (EEG) shows an isoelectric state. To monitor this rate the child is connected to a bedside EEG. Barbiturates (specifically thiopental) have also been shown to protect the brain by producing free radical scavengers.[30] Free radicals are formed during ischemic insults on brain tissue.

A bedside biopolar EEG monitor consisting of two leads is used for all children in barbiturate coma. The leads are needle electrodes placed subcutaneously in the child's head. The type of electrical tracing seen in barbiturate coma is a burst suppression pattern.

The EEG monitor indicates when isoelectric activity occurs, so that minimal drug administration is needed. Throughout the course of barbiturate coma, the EEG should be monitored for any bursts of activity. This activity is treated with thiopental if the ICP increases. The electrodes should be replaced every 24 hours and the skin cleansed with povidone-iodine solution.

Induction of Coma

The child is given an initial bolus of sodium pentobarbital, 3 to 5 mg/kg, over 30 minutes. When the bolus dose is completed, the child is placed on a continuous intravenous infusion at 2 mg/kg/hr.[31] Therapeutic blood levels are helpful in determining the level of coma. At a level of 2 mg/dL, the child should still demonstrate burst suppression on the bedside EEG. If this level is unable to control ICP, then the infusion is increased to achieve a level of 3 mg/dL. At this level, the child is likely to have severe hypotension and can become dependent on vasopressors to maintain adequate perfusion.[32] At 4 mg/dL or more the child will require circulatory support.

Hypotension is initially treated by expending the circulating blood volume with colloid infusions. If the child's mean arterial pressure does not stabilize, then a dopamine infusion is begun at 4 to 12 µg/kg/min. The goal of both colloid and dopamine administration is to maintain the mean arterial pressure above 65 torr. If the ICP continues to rise, additional therapy to induce hypothermia may be introduced before barbiturate doses are increased.

Barbiturate Infusion

Barbiturate infusion is continued for at least 72 hours because maximal cerebral swelling occurs 48 to 72 hours after the injury. Once the barbiturate coma is established, drugs for neuromuscular blockade can be discontinued. All neurological parameters are diminished during barbiturate coma. It is imperative that all monitoring systems be working precisely because clinical neurologic evaluation of the child is impossible. Strict attention to all body systems is necessary to prevent the hazards of immobility.

When the child has had a stable ICP for 24 hours, then the barbiturates can be tapered. During the weaning process, if the child demonstrates any dangerous elevations in ICP the dose is returned to the last effective level. During this recovery period, baseline ICP of 20 torr is accepted with spikes to 25 torr left untreated. Therapy remains at this level until there is another 24-hour period free from ICP increases. During this time it is crucial to assess for neurologic reawakening. It may be difficult to evaluate whether the child is having an ICP spike or is waking in response to treatment.

Barbiturate Withdrawal

It is not uncommon for the child who has been in barbiturate coma to go through a period of withdrawal after coming out of coma. Symptoms frequently seen are tremors, agitation, delirium, visual hallucinations, and difficulty in controlling speech and fine motor activity.[33] These symptoms can last from a few days to a week. If possible, the child should be moved to a quiet area of the pediatric intensive care unit. Lights should be turned on only when necessary, and the child should be disturbed as infrequently as possible. If the child is uncomfortable during withdrawal, diazepam may be administered. It is not uncommon for the child to have difficulty sleeping for several days and then to fall into a deep sleep. The child's behavior is usually more appropriate after waking from this deep sleep.

Parents require a great deal of support during this time because it is often frightening and exhausting for them as their child experiences withdrawal symptoms. Most children do not remember the events that happened while they were in the pediatric intensive care unit, and there is comfort in that fact. Children must often be reoriented to where they are and what they are doing.

Hypothermia

If the barbiturate coma does not reduce the ICP, then surface hypothermia is instituted. The child is cooled with hypothermia blankets. A monitored esophageal or a rectal thermometer should be used to assess continually the temperature. The goal is to stabilize the core temperature at around 31°C; reduction of body temperature from 37° to

31°C decreases cerebral metabolism and blood flow by approximately 40 percent, with a concomitant reduction in cerebral blood volume and ICP.[34] Care should be taken in lowering the temperature because, if the temperature is too low, rewarming may be difficult and the child could spontaneously fibrillate. When the child's temperature falls to 34°C, the blankets should be turned off to allow the child's temperature to rise slowly.

Initially the body responds to the lowered temperature sympathetically with shivering, vasoconstriction, increased oxygen consumption, bronchodilation, and an increase in body function.[35] While in barbiturate coma the child does not experience these adverse effects.

Complications associated with hypothermia are as follows. Fluids and electrolytes shift easily into the interstitial tissues, causing hypovolemia and electrolyte imbalance (hyperkalemia and hypernatremia); intravenous access is difficult because fluid is third spaced; skin may break down due to the pressure of the dependent edema; and immune and inflammatory responses may be altered, making the child more susceptible to infection. At all times meticulous care with good attention to handwashing should be administered to the child in this vulnerable condition. Drug requirements should be reassessed and possibly reduced because of slowed hepatic and renal excretion. Because standards for electrolytes at low body temperature are not available, monitoring altered potassium and sodium is difficult. Therefore the child is rewarmed as the ICP will permit.

Rewarming

The process of rewarming must be done slowly, at a controlled rate of 0.5° per hour, until the temperature reaches 35°C. When the temperature is restored to this level, the child will gradually equilibrate to become normothermic. By slow rewarming, severe fluid shifts and cardiovascular instability can be prevented. If the child is not in a barbiturate coma, neuromuscular blockade may need to be restarted to reduce shivering and subsequent rises in ICP. Any significant and prolonged rises in ICP warrant a return to the immediately disconnected therapy. Therapy continues until there is a 24-hour period free of ICP elevations. After the child is weaned from hypothermia and barbiturate coma, the neuromuscular blockade can be discontinued and the child weaned from ventilatory support.

RECOVERY FROM HEAD INJURY

Children who sustain head injury and recover to consciousness and generally good function usually do so in about 3 weeks after the injury. Behavioral problems, shortened attention span, and irritability last much longer.[36] The best prognosis for a full recovery is in patients with a Glasgow Coma Scale score on admission of 5 or more. The highest mortality and morbidity are in those children who arrive in the emergency room with decerebrate posturing or flaccidity. Whether the child arrives flaccid with spontaneous respirations or apneic may affect the outcome. Children with spontaneous respirations appear to have a better chance for neurologic recovery.

Problems in school should be followed up with a neuropsychologist's evaluation to identify the problem and to correct it. Psychological testing of this group of children demonstrates significant slowing of response, reduction in performance IQ compared to the preinjury state, and difficulty with auditory and visual perception, all of which markedly limit school performance.[37] The child may have difficulty in adjusting to a different body image if there is a focal injury present that could change artistic or athletic abilities.[38] Attention should be directed toward reintegrating the child into his or her peer group at school and at home. It is recommended that the child have neuropsychological testing before returning to school and a neurologic examination every 3 years.

Behavioral problems are often triggered by parental response. Therefore every effort must be made to ensure that the family is comfortable with the child's condition before discharge. Throughout hospitalization it is important to encourage the parents to talk to and touch their child. If they can begin to help provide care while the child is in the hospital, they will be much better prepared to deal with their feelings at discharge. They should not be made to feel as though their child is unavailable to them; this only serves to set up feelings of powerlessness and anger.

As the child approaches the rehabilitative stage, the parents are in the best position to direct care because they know the behavior patterns of their child. In this way care can be planned that will maximize the child's potential.

The challenge for nurses caring for the child who sustains a head injury is to prevent secondary brain injury. The nurse must observe and respond to those subtle neurologic changes that may herald a neurologic crisis. It is the nurse who bridges the gap between the patient and the complex intensive care technology and brings sensitivity and caring to the family and child. Nurses with good assessment skills and knowledge of appropriate intervention and management techniques are needed so that secondary brain injury is prevented. In this way the nurse plays a crucial role in ensuring that the child has a good chance for neurologic survival.

NOTES

1. Barry Weiss, "Bicycle Helmet Use by Children," *Pediatrics* 77(1986):677–79.
2. Russell C. Raphaely et al., "Management of Severe Pediatric Head Trauma," *Pediatric Clinics of North America* 27(1980):715–27.
3. J.H. Wisoff and F.J. Epstein, "Management of Pediatric Head Trauma," in W.B. Zimmerman, ed., *Critical Care Pediatrics* (Philadelphia: W.B. Saunders Co., 1985), 368–77.
4. Kim H. Manwaring and Robert F. Sapetzler, "Head and Central Nervous System Injury in the Child," in Randall E. Marcus, ed., *Trauma in Children* (Rockville, Md.: Aspen Publishers, Inc., 1986), 39–56.
5. D.A. Bruce, L. Schut, and Leslie M. Sutton, "Neurosurgical Emergencies," in Stephen Ludwig and Gary Fleisher, eds., *Textbook of Pediatric Emergency Medicine* (Baltimore, Md.: Williams & Wilkins, 1983), 1012–26.
6. Bruce, Schut, and Sutton, "Neurosurgical Emergencies," 1012–26.
7. Ibid.
8. Robert C. Jorden, "Pathophysiology of Brain Injury," *Critical Care Quarterly* 5 (1983):1–11.
9. Manwaring and Sapetzler, "Head and Central Nervous System Injury," 39–56.
10. Ibid.

11. N. Paul Rosman, "Pediatric Emergencies: Managing Acute Head Trauma," *Contemporary Pediatrics* (November 1986):24–46.
12. Manwaring and Sapetzler, "Head and Central Nervous System Injury," 39–56.
13. Rosman, "Pediatric Emergencies," 24–46.
14. Raphaely et al., "Management of Severe Pediatric Head Trauma," 715–27.
15. A.C. Duhaime et al., "The Shaken Baby Syndrome: A Clinical, Pathological, and Biomechanical Study," *Journal of Neurosurgery* 66(1987):409–15.
16. Wisoff and Epstein, "Management of Pediatric Head Trauma," 368–77.
17. Bruce, Schut, and Sutton, "Neurosurgical Emergencies," 1012–26.
18. Ibid.
19. Ibid.
20. Donna H. Groh, Sherry W. Benica, and Susan B. DeJong, "Neurological Disorders," in Janis B. Smith, ed., *Pediatric Critical Care* (New York: John Wiley & Sons, 1983), 198–264.
21. Judy Harr and M.F. Hazinski, "Neurological Disorders," in M.F. Hazinski, ed., *Nursing Care of the Critically Ill Child* (St. Louis: C.V. Mosby Co., 1984), 360–454.
22. Ibid.
23. Fred Rivara et al., "Poor Prediction of Positive Computed Tomographic Scans by Clinical Criteria in Symptomatic Pediatric Head Trauma," *Pediatrics* 80(1987):579–84.
24. George W. Tyson et al., "Acute Care of the Head Injured Patient," *Critical Care Quarterly* 2(1979): 23–44.
25. Raphaely et al., "Management of Severe Pediatric Head Trauma," 715–27.
26. Bruce, Schut, and Sutton, "Neurosurgical Emergencies," 1012–26.
27. Groh, Benica, and DeJong, "Neurological Disorders," 198–264.
28. Raphaely et al., "Management of Severe Pediatric Head Trauma," 715–27.
29. Mark A. Eiler, "Pharmacologic Therapeutic Modalities: Osmotic and Diuretic Agents," *Critical Care Quarterly* 5(1983):44–51.
30. Raphaely et al., "Management of Severe Pediatric Head Trauma," 715–27.
31. Ibid.
32. Ibid.
33. Ibid.
34. Ibid.
35. Groh, Benica, and DeJong, "Neurological Disorders," 198–264.
36. Raphaely et al., "Management of Severe Pediatric Head Trauma," 715–27.
37. Ibid.
38. Ibid.

Chapter 4

Facial Trauma

Susan M. Gerhart

Children and adults are exposed to the same situations in which facial trauma occurs, yet major facial trauma is less common in children. The child's age, size, and physiology alter the type and mechanism of injury. These differences also contribute to wide variances in the severity of facial injuries experienced by children and significantly influence modalities of care. This chapter outlines the type of facial injuries commonly experienced in the pediatric multiple trauma patient and explores the medical and nursing care that is required.

FACIAL DIFFERENCES BETWEEN CHILDREN AND ADULTS

Because the face of a child is proportionally smaller in relation to the total surface area of the body than that of an adult, the child is less prone to facial injury. The extent of projection of the facial skeleton is relatively small, and major trauma, when it occurs, is more likely to be transmitted to the frontal bone.

Children are smaller and lighter than adults, and their height and body mass produce less momentum. Together with the greater thickness of soft tissue, this results in the dissipation of less energy on impact. The facial bones of a child are softer and more resilient; therefore facial bone fractures tend to be less severe, with undisplaced and comminuted fractures being most common.

During the first few years of life, the crowns of the developing permanent teeth are incompletely formed, the ratio of bone to tooth substance is relatively high, and unerupted tooth buds alter the face's structural integrity. In addition, the frontal, maxillary, and sphenoidal sinuses are rudimentary, and cartilaginous growth centers are extensive.

Despite these physiologic features, facial trauma remains a significant problem in the pediatric population. Of multiply injured pediatric patients, 57 percent have facial injuries.[1] One study reported that in an 8-year period more than two-thirds of all children with facial trauma had associated trauma-related medical and dental injuries.[2]

ETIOLOGY OF PEDIATRIC FACIAL TRAUMA

The etiology of facial injuries in children is determined to a greater or lesser extent by the child's age and developmental level. Before the age of 5 years, most children are relatively closely supervised. Dog attacks and the so-called "coffee table" laceration of the forehead are common injuries. Throughout childhood and adolescence, children are exposed to the sudden deceleration injuries of automobile accidents, either as passengers or as adolescent drivers. After 5 years of age, the child's increasing independence from parents, participation in peer activities, and attendance at school result in falls from a great height; blunt trauma caused by swings, baseball bats, and the like; and bicycle accidents. Athletics becomes a significant cause of injury in the teenage years. It is during adolescence that the pattern and severity of facial trauma begins to simulate that of adults.

Although the annual incidence of facial fractures has remained fairly stable, over the past few years the mechanisms of injury have changed considerably. The etiology of facial fractures in children has been influenced by several factors, including increased emphasis on the use of seat belts and child restraint devices and an overall increase in high-speed travel. The result of these changes is a slight decrease in the frequency of traffic accidents as an etiology of facial injury but an increase in the severity of facial fractures. For example, traffic accidents formerly resulted in isolated facial fractures, but now multiple facial fractures are often accompanied by extensive lacerations and other soft tissue injuries. Vehicular trauma, however, continues to be responsible for more than 30 percent of all facial trauma in children.[3]

Sports-related facial fractures occur most commonly in contact sports, such as football and ice hockey, in addition to sports such as horseback riding. The frequency of bicycle accidents has also demonstrated a rapidly rising trend.[4] In an attempt to reduce the number and severity of facial injuries associated with sports, there has been an ever-increasing emphasis on prevention and protective devices. Mouthguards are perhaps the most common form of protective device now worn in contact sports, but 25 years ago little consideration was given to the protection of the mouth, jaws, and teeth.[5] Sports-related injuries to the head and facial regions are often caused by direct frontal impact or impact to the mandible from below, but, more important, an impact to the lower jaw may be transmitted to the skull and brain primarily through the mandibular condyles.

Studies have also reported violence as an increasing cause of facial fractures in children and adults.[6,7]

GENERAL PRINCIPLES OF TREATMENT

The primary goals in healing injuries to the face include restoring the function of the facial structures and restoring the child's appearance. The abundant blood supply predisposes facial wounds to good healing and enables these two goals to be accomplished simultaneously.

Although treatment of a facial injury is rarely an emergency in itself, fatalities can occur should the child's airway become compromised or should exsanguinating hemorrhage occur. Immediate management must be directed toward airway maintenance and preservation of hemodynamic status (see Chapter 2). In addition, careful assessment of neurologic function is imperative because any significant injury to the face results in dissipation of energy through the cranium and cervical spine.

Unlike the situation for adults, in whom definitive treatment of facial fractures may be delayed for up to 10 days, the child's thick vascular periosteum, osteogenic ability, and increased metabolic rate contribute to rapid healing of facial fractures. Early reduction is required to prevent malunion. This increased healing potential also results in a greater tendency for hypertrophic scar healing.

Laryngeal Trauma

Laryngeal injuries occur when the head and neck are in hyperextension. In this position the upper airway becomes fixed against the vertebral column, and when a blow is delivered to the laryngeal cartilage significant damage can result. This type of injury is less likely to occur in children than in adults because the child's larynx is more cartilaginous, more mobile, and less prominent. Nevertheless, direct laryngeal trauma may occur if the child is thrown forward onto a sharp object.

The child's airway must be protected and an airway established particularly if there is any indication of laryngeal obstruction. Signs and symptoms of laryngeal obstruction may include contusions of the neck, cervical emphysema, marked swelling of the cervical region, and lowering of the voice pitch. If the larynx is fractured, endotracheal intubation is usually contraindicated. Direct surgical repair and tracheotomy should be performed as soon as the child's condition permits.

Anesthesia in Pediatric Facial Trauma

Children with facial injuries present a particular challenge. Repair of simple lacerations that require only local anesthesia in an adult may necessitate heavy sedation, restraint, or general anesthesia in the child.

Fear of pain, of separation, and most of all of the unknown are the overwhelming reactions of the injured child. The anxiety produced by the injury itself, the environment of the emergency department, and the reaction of the parents all combine to affect the child's ability to cope with an unfamiliar situation. The choice of anesthetic should be determined not only by the child's age, developmental level, and reaction to injury but also by the child's ability to cooperate, the size and location of the laceration, and the precision required for repair. Every effort should be made to optimize the initial repair.[8]

SOFT TISSUE INJURIES

Facial soft tissue injuries may range from contusions and abrasions to massive avulsions. As with any facial injury, return to normal function and appearance are the primary goals of management. In general, treatment depends on the type, extent, and location of the injury and follows the general principles defined for the adult.

Facial Lacerations

Most facial lacerations result from falls, and laceration of the supraorbital ridge—the so-called "coffee table" laceration—is the most commonly occurring childhood facial injury. When necessary facial lacerations can be sutured, although adequate anesthesia is required to permit a satisfactory cosmetic result.

Lacerations involving the facial nerve are surgically repaired only when they occur in the distal third of the nerve. Medial to this area, the facial nerve branches and enters the facial musculature; surgical repair is therefore not required.[9]

Intraoral lacerations result when the child falls with a stick or other pointed object in the mouth. These injuries only require repair when injury to the main salivary duct or carotid artery is suspected.

Bite Injuries

It has been reported that in North America one person of two hundred seventy-five will sustain a dog bite injury every year and that children represent the largest proportion of this population. Of all dog bite injuries, 75 percent involve the head, face, and neck.[10] The injury usually occurs in a domestic setting and involves a friendly dog that is known to the victim. The mechanisms of injury involve biting, clawing, and crushing forces, which result in wounds with a characteristic pattern of punctures, lacerations, and avulsions.

Most dog bites can be repaired after thorough débridement. Risk related to rabies is geographically determined, and the local branch of the Department of Health is the most accurate source of information and guidance regarding treatment.[11]

Human bites are invariably heavily contaminated and should not be closed. Although they may result from an intentional act in young children, they most commonly occur in teenagers during a fistfight when a clenched fist strikes an opponent's teeth. Vigorous débridement and irrigation, local wound care, and antibiotic therapy are indicated for these injuries.

FACIAL FRACTURES

Facial fractures in children younger than 12 years of age represent an extremely small percentage of the total number of facial fractures that occur annually. The anatomic and physiologic differences between children and adults are responsible for the relative rarity of these injuries.

When facial fractures occur, management presents particular challenges that are not present when caring for adults.

1. Early reduction is required to avoid malunion; any deformity tends to worsen after a poor or incomplete reduction.
2. Immobilization after reduction is difficult because developing teeth occupy space within the maxilla or mandible, and injuries to either structure may alter the teeth's growth potential.

3. Deciduous and incompletely developed teeth cannot be used for internal fixation. This presents particular difficulty in the child with mixed dentition.[12]
4. General anesthesia is required for treatment of pediatric facial fractures. Even procedures such as placement of arch bars or interdental wiring, which can be completed under local anesthesia in the adult, require general anesthesia in the child.

Nasal Fractures

Nasal fractures are the most common facial fracture in children. In childhood, the nasal bones contain a midline suture that is a weak point when the mechanism of injury is a direct blow. Trauma to the lower two-thirds of the nose may result in nasal septal injury and possibly septal hematoma formation. Nasal fractures are a significant injury in children because of the exceedingly high incidence of growth disturbances that occur from the nasal fracture or from septal hematoma. Signs and symptoms of a nasal fracture include edema, ecchymosis, pain, crepitus, and distortion.

Nasal injury in children is treated conservatively. After 3 to 4 days, edema is usually sufficiently resolved to allow careful examination and identification of any displacement. Closed reduction can then be performed. In most patients, closed reduction is the preferred approach to nasal fractures.[13] After reduction, the nose is packed and splinted. The packing is usually removed at 48 hours and the splint at 1 to 2 weeks.[14]

Mandibular Fractures

The mandible is the second most commonly fractured facial bone. Because of its U shape, it is particularly susceptible to multiple fractures; in more than 50 percent of patients mandibular fractures are multiple. Signs and symptoms include improper tooth alignment and pain with motion.

The mandibular condyle is the major growth center of the mandible. Particularly during the first 3 years of life, a fracture of the condyle can compress the growth center and predispose the child to long-term problems. Although more difficult to diagnose, fractures of the condylar neck are more easily treated than other mandibular fractures.

Minor crack fractures of the mandible usually do not require immobilization. Unilateral fractures or fractures of the condylar neck should be treated by encouraging movement while actively training muscles to prevent deviation and malocclusion. When the fracture is multiple or unstable or occurs in the body of the mandible, interdental fixation may be required; 3 weeks of immobilization is usually sufficient to ensure union.

Mid-Face Fractures

Fractures of the middle third of the facial skeleton may involve the maxilla, the nasoorbital complex, or the zygomatic bones. Displaced fractures of the LeFort classification type are rarely seen in children younger than 8 years of age.

The mechanism of injury of a mid-face fracture involves considerable force, so that an injury that would cause a LeFort III fracture in adults often results in death of the child because of concomitant head injuries. In addition, the lack of pneumatization of the frontal, ethmoidal, and sphenoidal sinuses in young children prevents the displaced fracture usually seen in the LeFort group.

When a mid-face fracture is present, however, surgical repair is complex. The mandible is established as a solid base on which all other repairs are built. The fractured portion of the mid-face is fixed between a stabilized mandible and the next highest stable point on the facial skeleton. Because of the problems associated with internal fixation in children, this may be best accomplished by external traction from a plastic head cap or halo apparatus.

Zygomatic Complex Fractures

The site and prominence of the zygoma or cheekbone makes this bone prone to injury in the adult. Such injuries are less common in children. In the child younger than 8 years the maxillary sinus, which underlies the zygoma, is not fully developed and pneumatized, making these injuries extremely rare.

Zygomatic complex fractures are most often caused by violence, traffic accidents, falls, and sports-related injuries.[15] Flattening of the cheek is a primary sign, provided that edema is not so severe as to obscure it. Other symptoms include sensory disturbances, anesthesia of the infraorbital region, diplopia, or unilateral nosebleed.

Undisplaced fractures can be treated conservatively, but displaced, unstable, or comminuted fractures may require open reduction. The treatment modality involving use of a contrast material–filled balloon catheter to stabilize zygomatic fractures in adults is contraindicated in children because of the location of permanent tooth buds.

Orbital Fractures

Depressed fractures of the orbital floor are termed "blow-out" fractures. The mechanism of injury suggests that, after blunt trauma, increased pressure of the orbital contents causes downward fracture of the thin floor of the orbit. Edema and gravity combine, and the orbital contents sag into the maxillary sinus.

"Blow-in" fractures occur in patients with severe skull or facial fractures. Downward fracturing of the floor of the anterior cranial fossa or upward bulging of the orbital floor after a severe blow to the maxillary sinus characterize the mechanism of injury. In addition, buckling forces on the walls of the orbit contribute significantly to the mechanism of injury.[16]

Treatment of these fractures consists of open exploration, repositioning, and insertion of a bond or silastic graft.

Postoperative Management of the Child with a Facial Fracture

Postoperative management of the child who has had a surgical reduction of a facial fracture is challenging and complex. Important points to be considered when planning for care include the following.

1. Airway obstruction is the major hazard in the immediate postoperative period.
2. The head should be raised 45° as tolerated, and ice should be applied postoperatively to minimize edema.
3. If a nasotracheal tube has been used for anesthesia, it may be left in place for 24 hours or until the child can tolerate extubation.
4. Tracheotomy is performed in patients with severe edema of the neck or lower facial region, in patients with maxillary or mid-face fractures that prevent use of a nasotracheal tube, or to accomplish intermaxillary fixation in unconscious patients.
5. A nasogastric tube is used for gastric decompression; vomiting and the accumulation of secretions are hazardous because it may be difficult if not impossible to suction the child's mouth.
6. All patients with intermaxillary fixation must have a wire cutter attached to the bed at all times. Should the child vomit or demonstrate signs of airway obstruction, the wires must be cut and the jaws opened.

OCULAR TRAUMA

The child at play is a ready target for ocular trauma. The National Society for the Prevention of Blindness has estimated that more than 100,000 eye injuries resulting from play or sports occur annually in school-aged children and that 90 percent of these injuries are preventable.[17] Community education programs must address the risks associated with playing sports and the benefits of protective equipment to reduce the incidence of ocular trauma in children.

Corneal Injuries

Trauma to the cornea may damage the corneal epithelium directly; it usually results from a foreign body. The exposure of nerve endings and the irritation by the upper lid cause acute pain, photophobia, blepharospasm, and profuse tearing. More severe symptoms occur when the abrasion is caused by fingernails, animal claws, or evergreen needles. With these types of injury, the cornea will heal but will frequently break down several weeks or months later, causing a recurrence of symptoms.[18]

Treatment of corneal injuries consists of removal of the foreign body (if present), use of antibiotic ointment or drops, and patching the eye until the cornea heals. A corneal abrasion heals in approximately 24 to 48 hours.

Blunt Ocular Trauma

The most common result of severe blunt trauma to the eye is traumatic hyphema, or presence of free blood in the anterior chamber. About 80 percent of traumatic hyphemas occur in males between 1 and 15 years of age.[19]

Small hyphemas are usually uncomplicated; large hyphemas have a poor prognosis primarily related to the risk of recurrent hemorrhage, which is associated with glaucoma, corneal staining, and reduced vision. Most rebleeds occur within 4 to 5 days. Therefore, during this period, management includes bed rest, daily measurement of intraocular pressure, cycloplegia, and occasionally topical corticosteroids. Rebleeding complicates 10 percent to 35 percent of traumatic hyphemas, and 32 percent of these patients require surgical intervention to reduce intraocular pressure.[20] The risk of recurrent hyphema is reduced by avoidance of aspirin and treatment with antifibrinolytic agents.[21]

Penetrating Ocular Trauma

Penetrating eye injuries may involve the orbit, may include retention of an intraocular foreign body, and may result in retinal damage, vitreous hemorrhage, traumatic cataract, decreased vision, or enucleation. The degree of damage depends on the depth of the wound and the structures involved. Intracranial damage has been reported after eye injuries that were initially believed to be localized to the lid and orbit. Eyelid lacerations in penetrating injuries may be small, but the bone of the orbital roof is thin and easily fractured.[22] Assessment must include the mechanism of injury and neurologic status to plan and implement appropriate care.

Sympathetic Ophthalmia

The most serious complication of penetrating ocular injuries is sympathetic ophthalmia. This is an acute inflammation that occurs in the uninjured eye and is thought to be an allergic response of the uveal pigment initiated in the injured eye. The inflammation may begin at any time after 10 days following the traumatic injury. Frequent assessment of both eyes is required because this complication can be controlled or treated with corticosteroids or immunosuppressive agents. Because sympathetic ophthalmia may result in severe impairment of vision, enucleation of the injured eye may be required to prevent or minimize risks.[19,23,24]

DENTAL INJURIES

Dental injuries that occur in childhood can have long-term implications. Considering the value that society places on appearance, loss of or damage to permanent dentition is a significant problem for the child. Every effort to preserve natural dentition after injury must be made. Although most dental injuries must be managed by a dentist or oral surgeon, prompt, appropriate treatment can often avoid the unnecessary loss of teeth.

Deciduous Teeth

Traumatic injury to primary dentition usually coincides with the onset of walking. The toddler's imperfect balance contributes to many bumps and falls, and dental trauma during this period is almost always limited to maxillary incisors.

If the injury is limited only to the crown of the tooth, sharp edges are ground smooth and parents are instructed to ensure that follow-up roentgenograms are obtained every 6 months until the permanent tooth is fully erupted. Pulpal necrosis can sometimes follow apparently minor trauma, so that dental assessment is required should the tooth begin to darken. Root fracture and displacement or avulsion of deciduous teeth usually require extraction. Proper treatment of injuries to deciduous teeth rarely results in problems with permanent dentition.

Permanent Teeth

Although some dental injuries are unavoidable, contact sports are implicated in many dental injuries. A reduction in dental injuries of up to 90 percent has been reported with the use of a properly fitted mouthguard.[25]

Tooth preservation is the goal of treatment for traumatic injuries to permanent teeth. Treatment may include restoration, endodontics, or splinting depending on the tooth involved and the severity of the injury.

The total displacement of a permanent anterior tooth is a true dental emergency. Reimplantation is the goal of treatment, but there is strong evidence that the chance of success of reimplantation is inversely proportional to the tooth's extraoral period. When reimplantation occurs within 2 hours of injury, short-term root reabsorption almost always occurs. Once reinserted, the tooth must be immobilized for 6 weeks. Children whose injured permanent teeth have fully matured roots should have endodontic treatment within 2 to 3 weeks of reimplantation. Root fracture, gross caries, extensive alveolar bone fractures, or an extraoral period of greater than 2 hours all preclude reimplantation.[26]

COMPLICATIONS OF FACIAL TRAUMA

Although facial injuries may result in significant initial deformity in both children and adults, such deformity is more significant in children because it is frequently exacerbated by growth. Young children have greater growth potential and therefore greater potential for deformity. For example, injury to the condylar head usually produces severe growth disturbance of the mandible if the injury occurred before age 3. This same injury may produce moderate deformity in children younger than 12 years of age and only minor deformity in older children.

Injury to bony growth centers that arrests growth may result in a deformity that worsens as the rest of the face grows normally. Growth disturbances occur mainly after mandibular or nasal fractures; mid-face fractures usually result in residual deformities as well.

Treatment of established arrested condylar growth is complex and includes surgical intervention to minimize deformity with subsequent serial bone grafts that are timed immediately before anticipated periods of active growth.

Nasal growth changes are unpredictable. A long-term study reported a 63 percent incidence of external deformity and a 38 percent incidence of nasal septum deformities after nasal fractures treated by closed reduction.[27] It is difficult to predict the outcome on the basis of the child's age, mechanism of injury, or other associated traumatic injuries.

Nursing care of the child with facial trauma is directed toward careful assessment and creative and empathetic intervention and support for the child and family. A disfiguring injury is itself alarming, but the treatment required (suturing, mandibular immobilization, repair of orbital fractures, enucleation, and so forth) may terrify the parents as well as the child. A calm approach is essential to enhance their coping abilities.

NOTES

1. Ian R. Munro, "Facial Bone Injuries," in *Care for the Injured Child* (Baltimore, Md.: Williams & Wilkins Co., 1975), 114.
2. Mark A. Fortunato, Allen Fred Fielding, and Louis H. Guernsey, "Facial Bone Fractures in Children," *Oral Surgery* 53(1982):230.
3. Munro, "Facial Bone Injuries," 114.
4. Christian Lindqvist et al., "Maxillofacial Fractures Sustained in Bicycle Accidents," *International Journal of Oral and Maxillofacial Surgery* 15(1986):15.
5. P.J. Chapman, "Orofacial Injuries and the Use of Mouthguards by the 1984 Great Britain Rugby League Touring Team," *British Journal of Sports Medicine* 19(1985):34–35.
6. Hans Starkhammar and Jan Olofsson, "Facial Fractures: A Review of 922 Cases with Special Reference to Incidence and Aetiology," *Clinical Otolaryngology* 7(1982):405.
7. C. Michael Hill et al., "Facial Fractures—The Results of a Prospective Four-Year Study," *Journal of Maxillofacial Surgery* 12(1984):267.
8. David A. Billmire, Henry W. Neale, and Richard O. Gregory, "Use of IV Fentanyl in the Outpatient Treatment of Pediatric Facial Trauma," *Journal of Trauma* 25(1985):1079.
9. Robert L. Walton, Juris Bunkis, and Gregory L. Borah, "Maxillofacial Trauma," in Donald D. Trunkey and Frank R. Lewis, eds., *Current Therapy of Trauma—2* (Philadelphia: B.C. Decker, 1986), 183.
10. Nathan E. Wiseman, Harvey Chochinov, and Virginia Fraser, "Major Dog Attack Injuries in Children," *Journal of Pediatric Surgery* 18(1983):533–35.
11. Hugh G. Thompson, "Skin and Subcutaneous Tissue Injuries," in Judson G. Randolph, Mark M. Ravitch, Kenneth J. Welch, and Eoin Aberdeen, eds., *The Injured Child; Surgical Management* (Chicago: Year Book Medical Publishers, 1979), 139.
12. Norman L. Rowe, "Fractures of the Facial Skeleton in Children," *Journal of Oral Surgery* 26(1968):506.
13. Hans Dommerby and Mirko Tos, "Nasal Fractures in Children—Long-Term Results," *Otorhinolaryngology* 47(1989):272.
14. Munro, "Facial Bone Injuries," 121.
15. James P. Ganley et al., "Aspirin and Recurrent Hyphema after Blunt Ocular Trauma," *American Journal of Ophthalmology* 96(1983):797.
16. Gary T. Raflo, "Blow-In and Blow-Out Fractures of the Orbit: Clinical Correlations and Proposed Mechanisms," *Ophthalmic Surgery* 15(1984):114.
17. Paul F. Vinger, "Sports-Related Eye Injury: A Preventable Problem," *Survey of Ophthalmology* 25(1980):47–48.
18. John S. Crawford, "Eye Injuries," in *Care for the Injured Child* (Baltimore, Md.: Williams & Wilkins Co., 1975), 94.
19. Valdo P. Oleari, "Nursing Care of the Child Who Requires Eye Surgery," in Dianne Fochtman and John G. Raffensperger, eds., *Principles of Nursing Care for the Pediatric Surgery Patient* (Boston: Little, Brown & Co., 1976), 119.

20. Matthew A. Thomas, Richard K. Parrish II, and William J. Feuer, "Rebleeding after Traumatic Hyphema," *Archives of Ophthalmology* 104(1986):206–10.
21. Ganley et al., "Aspirin and Recurrent Hyphema," 800.
22. Jeff Mono, R.D. Hollenberg, and J.T. Harvey, "Occult Transorbital Intracranial Penetrating Injuries," *Annals of Emergency Medicine* 15(1986):589–91.
23. Janet Lowe, "Nursing Management of Eye Injuries," *Nursing (London)* 2(1983):495.
24. Crawford, "Eye Injuries," 98.
25. Chapman, "Orofacial Injuries," 34.
26. F. Dungy Arlington, "Dental Injuries," in *Care for the Injured Child* (Baltimore, Md.: Williams & Wilkins Co., 1975), 123–29.
27. Dommerby and Tos, "Nasal Fractures in Children," 272–77.

Chapter 5
Spinal Cord Injury

Therese S. Richmond

Spinal cord injury in children complicates developmental issues by adding an unparalleled situational crisis. This type of injury affects each body system and reverberates throughout the psychosocial spheres to family and significant others. It affects more people between the ages of sixteen and thirty than all other age groups combined. Only 4.9 percent of all spinal cord injuries affect children between infancy and fifteen years. Males account for 82 percent of all injuries.[1] Because of the age distribution of spinal cord injuries in the United States, the focus of this chapter is primarily the older child and adolescent who sustain such an injury.

CAUSES OF SPINAL CORD INJURY

Within the age group between infancy and fifteen years, motor vehicle accidents are the major cause of spinal cord injury; this mechanism is followed by sports injuries, personal violence, and falls.[2,3] The incidence of spinal cord injury increases as the year progresses to longer days and warmer temperatures, steadily rising through July and then declining at a constant rate until February.[4]

PREVENTION

Prevention is a key element of spinal cord injury management. Because of the devastating nonreversible nature of these injuries, a primary focus must be prevention. Prevention of spinal cord injury is not unlike that of trauma in general (see Chapter 15), but there are aspects of spinal cord injury prevention that are unique to the population at risk for it. Emphasis should be placed on preventions that are related to the mechanisms described above.

In motor vehicle accidents, secondary impact is usually the causative factor of spinal cord injury. Fracture-dislocation injuries rarely result from direct impact on the vertebral column. They occur in unrestrained people during the secondary impact with the windshield, dashboard, or other care structures.[5] Restraints appropriate to the child's age group significantly decrease the incidence of spinal cord injury.

Diving and football are the major sports implicated as causes of spinal cord injury. Diving is the only totally preventable cause of such injuries. Children must be taught and receive continual reinforcement that playing in water is fun but that they should not take unnecessary risks. Key factors in preventing spinal injuries resulting from diving are presented in Exhibit 5-1. The National Football Association has implemented rules to protect the head and spinal cord from injury. These rules have significantly improved the safety of school and official games. Nevertheless, children must be taught that all rules that apply to officiated football games must be carried to their evening and weekend "pick-up" games.

Alcohol is implicated as a factor that places the person at greater risk for spinal cord injury due to impaired judgment. Alcohol can also contribute to an increased degree of spinal injury because of dulled pain and diminished awareness, leading to continued movement and further injury.[6]

TYPES OF SPINAL CORD INJURY

The core foci of clinical assessment and management of spinal injuries are the determination of the level of neurologic deficit and the completeness of the lesion. Spinal cord injuries are divided into two major categories: complete and incomplete. A complete injury is defined as a total loss of voluntary movement and sensation below the level of the lesion. On the basis of current medical knowledge and capabilities, the person sustaining a complete spinal cord injury has no hope of recovering significant neurologic function.[7]

Incomplete spinal cord injury is characterized by a variable loss of voluntary movement or sensation below the level of the lesion. Preservation of sacral sensation during the acute phase provides solid evidence that the injury is incomplete.[8] The degree and pattern of loss is dependent on the types of spinal tracts injured and the severity of the injury. Unlike the situation with complete spinal cord injury, the person sustaining an incomplete injury is likely to show some degree of neurologic improvement.[9] The type and amount of function regained is difficult to ascertain during the acute phase of the injury. Two types of incomplete spinal cord injury commonly result from traumatic injury: central cord syndrome and Brown-Séquard syndrome (Exhibit 5-2).[10]

Exhibit 5-1 Key Factors in Preventing Spinal Cord Injury

- Do not dive into shallow or unknown depths of water.
- Jump feet first, the first time.
- Dive correctly: when entering the water, the body should already be curving upward to the surface.
- Do not play at the edge of the pool or on the diving boards.
- Avoid diving into waves in the ocean because currents can make seemingly deep water shallow.

Exhibit 5-2 Incomplete Spinal Cord Injury Syndromes

Central cord syndrome	Brown-Séquard syndrome
Cause: Most commonly caused by severe hyperextension injury or tumor growing within the spinal cord.	**Cause:** Most commonly caused by an invasive implement such as bullet, knife, or icepick.
Pathophysiology: The tracts of the spinal cord are organized such that the cervical fibers are carried most central to the cord while the sacral fibers are on the outermost portion of each respective tract. Any injury in which the major pathologic process is in the center of the spinal cord will more severely affect cervical and thoracic fibers.	**Pathophysiology:** This syndrome results from hemisection of the spinal cord. The clinical findings are directly related to where each major tract decussates. Corticospinal tract (motor) decussates in the brain and then descends. The dorsal column tracts (touch and vibration) ascend on entry to the spinal cord and decussate in the brain. The spinothalamic tract (pain and temperature) decussates within a few segments of entry into the spinal cord and ascends on the side opposite of entry.
Clinical presentation: Upper extremities are more severely affected than lower extremities. Sensory loss is variable.	**Clinical presentation:** Motor function, the ability to perceive touch and vibration, is lost on the same side of the injury below the level of the lesion. The ability to sense pain and temperature is lost on the opposite side of the injury below the level of the lesion.

Source: Reprinted from *Focus on Critical Care*, Vol. 12, No. 3, pp. 23–33, with permission of The C.V. Mosby Company, © 1985.

The neurologic level of the lesion is determined by clinical examination of movement, sensation, and reflex activity. The level of the lesion has major implications in the acute phase of injury because of the intimate relation between neurologic level and ventilatory capability. In the rehabilitative phase, the level of the lesion is the primary determinant of functional outcome.

Quadriplegia or quadriparesis are terms used to describe an injury to the cervical spinal cord resulting in neurologic deficit to all four extremities. Paraplegia or paraparesis describes an injury to the thoracic, lumbar, or sacral spinal cord, resulting in neurologic deficit to the lower extremities.

ASSESSMENT AND MANAGEMENT OF THE SPINAL CORD–INJURED PATIENT

The child who sustains a spinal cord injury represents a challenge that requires creative and sensitive nursing care. During adolescence especially, the individual is enmeshed in developmental crises. A spinal cord injury compounds this period by introducing a situational crisis beyond compare. The future orientation of adolescence coupled with resistance to any notion of adult domination creates tension during the acute and rehabilitative phases of spinal cord injury.[11] Many people view spine-injured patients as having no future. Additionally, the multisystem physiologic derangements that result from spinal cord injury require that the health care providers (adults) manage many of the functions that the child had previously mastered (such as bowel and bladder function, breathing, and feeding).

The assessment and management of the spine-injured child centers on the nursing diagnoses and medical implications common to this injury. Nursing diagnosis provides a framework that highlights major aspects of care. For effective, efficient, and holistic care of the spine-injured patient, however, a well-developed multidisciplinary approach such as that used in the thirteen federally funded model spinal cord injury centers is essential.[12] All specialty areas of treatment are equally important and must work together with good communication among patient, family, and all health care providers.

Although the focus of this chapter is management of the spinal cord–injured patient during the emergent and acute phases, anticipation and inclusion of rehabilitation is crucial. Failure to anticipate the rehabilitation needs of a paralyzed patient is one of the great pitfalls during the early treatment.[13]

PHYSIOLOGIC NURSING DIAGNOSES

Potential for Injury Related to Vertebral Instability

Protection of the spinal cord from actual or potential vertebral instability is of primary concern during prehospital, emergency, and acute management of the patient sustaining multiple trauma. Up to 25 percent of cervical spinal cord injuries result in permanent neurologic deficit as a result of improper handling.[14] Any mechanism of injury that could result in flexion, hyperextension, rotation, or compression of the vertebral column places the patient at high risk for sustaining injury to the spinal cord.

Immobilization at the scene of injury involves placing the patient on a backboard and securely fastening the head and body to the board with sandbags and tape across the forehead and chin to keep the cervical spine in a neutral or "sniffing" position.[15] Chin straps in obese children or large teenagers can cause hyperextension and should be used cautiously. Soft or hard cervical collars do not effectively immobilize the cervical spine; they serve only to remind both patient and health care provider not to flex or hyperextend the neck. Cervical collars can present a hazard by constricting a neck that is swelling from expanding hematoma or subcutaneous emphysema.[16] Additionally, forcing a child into a collar that is too large can result in hyperextension, worsening the injury and compromising the airway.[17]

Upon arrival at the emergency department, the patient remains on the backboard until the cervical spine (and, if dictated by clinical findings or history, other areas of the spine) is definitively cleared. Clearance of the cervical spine requires lateral cervical spine roentgenograms, which visualize the top of the first thoracic vertebra.[18] Encouraging the patient to relax or pulling the shoulders downward enhances the visualization of all seven cervical vertebrae.[19]

because the pathophysiology is neuromuscular failure. The three-pronged approach includes clinical assessment, measurement of arterial blood gases, and assessment of ventilatory parameters.

The aspects of clinical assessment, which assume priority, are inspection and auscultation. Inspection of muscles used, diaphragmatic mobility, respiratory rate, breathing pattern, and ability to cough and clear secretions is crucial in monitoring the potential for neuromuscular failure.[30] Auscultation of breath sounds initially focuses on aeration of the lung base and on secretion retention secondary to the inability to cough effectively.

Arterial blood gas values are of limited use as indicators of ventilatory failure. The goal of acute care is to identify the patient in distress (for example, by an acute increase in arterial carbon dioxide pressure) before failure becomes a major clinical issue. Monitoring of end-tidal carbon dioxide is effective and more cost-efficient than repeated analysis of blood gases.

The mainstay of assessment is ventilatory parameters. The cause of the ineffective breathing pattern is neuromuscular failure, so that the trends of ventilatory parameters identify the patient who is beginning to fail before the onset of clinical signs and symptoms or definitive changes in blood gases.

Although all ventilatory parameters are important, a key parameter is vital capacity. A measurement of baseline vital capacity is obtained and repeated every 4 hours. A downward trend in vital capacity is indicative of diaphragmatic fatigue, which is a prelude to acute ventilatory failure.

Management

Mechanical ventilation can be instituted when vital capacity is critically reviewed and acted on, before the onset of an emergency situation. There is no particular value of vital capacity at which mechanical ventilation is mandatory, but the trend of vital capacity provides a firm basis from which to make an informed decision.

Ventilatory support may be short term or lifelong, depending on the level of the lesion. When the injury is above the level of C3-4, lifelong ventilation is expected unless diaphragmatic pacing is instituted.[31] At C-4 and below the patient should be able to maintain adequate ventilation independently, and the goal is a ventilator-free life.

Decreased Cardiac Output

Spinal (neurogenic) shock occurs at the time of the injury and resolves over several days.[32] Spinal shock is defined as a loss of all neurologic innervation below the level of the lesion.[33] The loss of sympathetic innervation results in peripheral vasodilation, decreased venous return of the heart, and decreased cardiac output.

Assessment

During the emergent phase of spinal cord injury, the differentiation between spinal shock and hypovolemic shock is crucial. Because the underlying pathophysiologic mechanisms are different, the clinical differentiation is relatively simple. Hypovolemic shock results from volume deficit, with sympathetic outflow resulting in vasoconstriction and increased heart rate to maintain blood pressure; the clinical presentation consists of hypotension, tachycardia, and cool, clammy extremities. The pathophysiology of spinal shock is lack of sympathetic innervation, with vasodilation and decreased venous return resulting in hypotension, bradycardia, and warm, dry extremities. This triad of symptoms occurs within 30 to 60 minutes of injury.[34]

Management

The hemodynamic repercussions of spinal shock may or may not require medical intervention. The determination of need for intervention is based on the adequacy of end organ perfusion. If urinary output and mental status indicate that perfusion is adequate, no intervention is required. If peripheral perfusion is compromised, however, therapy must be initiated. Hypoxemia and hypothermia contribute to bradycardia, which can worsen spinal shock. Atropine or a temporary transvenous pacemaker may be used if the bradycardia leads to a hypoperfusion state. Sufficient volume expansion is usually adequate to manage hypotension, although a direct-acting α-adrenergic drug may also be used.

Impaired Gas Exchange

Impaired gas exchange can be due to a number of etiologies. These include, but are not limited to, secretion retention secondary to impaired cough and pulmonary embolism secondary to deep vein thrombosis.

Secretion Retention Secondary to Impaired Cough

The inability to cough effectively assumes priority status in planning nursing intervention. Secretion retention can result in profound hypoxemia, particularly when mucus plugs occlude a major bronchus. Prevention strategies are instituted immediately on the patient's admission to the critical care unit and are required to sustain life.

Three nursing interventions are beneficial in this situation: chest physiotherapy, incentive spirometry, and quad-assist coughing. Chest physiotherapy is effective in mobilizing secretions for coughing and suctioning. This can be accomplished on any type of bed and in any immobilization device. Incentive spirometry performed ten times each hour while the patient is awake maximizes deep breathing and the opening of alveoli. Incentive spirometry can be adapted to a patient with a tracheostomy through the use of elbow connectors. Quad-assist coughing is an effective method of replacing the patient's absent abdominal musculature. After a series of deep breaths, the patient initiates a cough while the nurse provides a strong, upward abdominal thrust between the umbilicus and the xyphoid process. Effective quad-assist coughing can obviate the need for intubation for secretion clearance and repetitive suctioning.

Pulmonary Embolism Secondary to Deep Vein Thrombosis

Pulmonary embolism is a complication for which the spinal cord–injured patient is at high risk. The forerunner, deep vein thrombosis, can occur within 48 hours of injury;

routine monitoring and institution of preventive interventions for this condition are mandatory. Assessment of deep vein thrombosis includes measuring the calf and thigh to document objectively the presence of swelling and monitoring for a low-grade temperature. Other signs such as Homan's sign are of no use in the insensate patient. Routine diagnostic screening studies such as intermittent plethysmography and ^{125}I fibrinogen scans can help with early identification of deep vein thrombosis. Venography is the definitive diagnostic test. Prevention of deep vein thrombosis may include low-dose heparin, intermittent inflation boots, electrical muscle stimulators to enhance venous return, and early mobilization.

The prevention of pulmonary embolism is accomplished by treatment of documented deep vein thrombosis. Therapeutic heparinization is the treatment of choice. If the patient has contraindications for heparinization, the use of a vena cava filter is considered.

Pulmonary embolism should be suspected with the onset of acute hypoxemia unrelated to secretion retention. The classic signs and symptoms of pulmonary emboli such as tachycardia, tachypnea, shortness of breath, air hunger, and hypotension may be significantly muted in the spine-injured patient. Hypoxemia without these additional signs and symptoms should still raise the suspicion that a pulmonary embolism is the cause. Treatment is usually heparinization, although more aggressive therapies such as fibrinolytic therapy and interventional arteriography may be considered.

Impaired Temperature Regulation Related to Poikilothermia

During the early phases of spinal cord injury, the patient is at risk for severe alterations in body temperature. The normal homeothermic capacity is lost, and the patient becomes poikilothermic.[35] Poikilothermia causes the individual to assume the temperature of the immediate environment.

Impaired temperature regulation can result in hypothermia or hyperthermia, depending on environmental temperature. Hypothermia worsens the bradycardia of spinal shock, whereas hyperthermia can easily be misinterpreted as an indication of infection, which is a common occurrence in spinal cord injury.[36] Close monitoring of temperature coupled with control of environmental temperature and appropriate dressing of the patient can prevent this complication.

PSYCHOSOCIAL NURSING DIAGNOSES

Impaired Verbal Communication

Impaired verbal communication has a physiologic basis in intubation and tracheostomy; nevertheless, the nursing diagnosis of impaired verbal communication is of psychosocial concern. The plan of care must extend beyond the provision of a method for the patient to communicate physiologic needs to include a system for higher level communication that encourages discussion of the child's response to the injury.

In the early phases of injury, two methods are highly successful. The best of the two is lip reading. In a spinal cord injury center, which deals with hundreds of patients each year, the nursing staff by necessity are excellent lip readers and are able to carry on high-level conversations with patients with relative ease. This is enhanced by consistency of care, whereby a selected group of staff soon come to know a patient's idiosyncrasies in communication.

The second method may be necessitated if lip reading is unsuccessful or if the family cannot learn to lip read. The use of a letter board permits the freedom of full communication but in a more time-consuming manner. Quadriplegic patients cannot point to the letters with their hands and must use a mouth-held pointer (which is not realistic in the acute setting) or indicate the letter by eye contact (which is difficult at best with a twenty-six letter alphabet board). Dividing the board into quadrants is beneficial in that only seven or eight letters are in a quadrant, creating a narrower selection and an easier validation process.

Whatever the method, communication with both the health care providers and the family is a high priority in the early phase of injury. Nursing time must be devoted to the family to support and improve their communication skills.

Alteration in Family Process

Spinal cord injury catapults the family into acute disarray with the promise of long-term alterations in family process. The assessment and management of the family and their incorporation into the plan of care must start in the emergent phase and continue throughout hospitalization. The family is the most important contextual influence in the child's growth and development and will continue to be so after a spinal cord injury.[37] Because the child's life will never be the same, the family's life is also changed forever. The spine-injured patient is cognitively intact, so that the patient and family have the opportunity to deal with the physiologic and psychologic issues simultaneously.

Baseline assessment of the family's level of functioning before the injury is essential. The family system is more than the sum of its parts, so that assessing individual members does not produce complete information regarding the family unit as a whole.[38] The family's coping ability is affected by societal and health care alterations and also by the effects of illness within the family system.[39] The goal of management during the crisis phase is the return of the family to the preinjury level of functioning or to an improved level of functioning.[40] Strategies to achieve this goal include maintaining open lines of communication, incorporating the family into the plan of care and the delivery of care, allowing private time for the patient and family, and including the family in a family-support group (if available). One study demonstrated that, in the first 72 hours after the patient's admission to intensive care, the family's primary need was to receive as much information about the patient as possible.[41]

The focus on the family must be intense because they will probably become the primary caregivers. Therefore, the injury has occurred to them as well as to the patient. From the outset a focus must be to help the patient and family believe that there is a future, because the belief that there is no future creates a loss of hope and abandonment of life.[42] Psychological support including psychologists, psychiatric liaison nurses, and social workers is considered optimal.

Powerlessness

Powerlessness is the "perceived lack of control over a current situation or immediate happening."[43] During the acute phase of injury, the lack of control is not only perceived but actual. If the injury occurred in adolescence, a time for attaining and maintaining independence is now a time of total dependence. The adolescent is thrust back to early childhood, once again developing trust, learning to control bladder and bowels, and learning once again to feed himself or herself.[44]

The physical basis of powerlessness in the emergent and intensive care phases is real; the psychological basis is initially real and is the focus of nursing management. Because of the imbalance of authority and power that occurs in the relationship between patient and caregiver, the dependent patient is vulnerable to the emotional message of the caregiver.[45] This is highlighted in the adolescent's relationship with the adult nurse. Nurses must be sensitive to patients' feelings and consistently reconfirm their individuality and personhood. Unless this forms the basis of the relationship, no strategies will be effective in helping the adolescent resume control after a spinal cord injury.

NOTES

1. S.L. Stover and P.R. Fine, *Spinal Cord Injury: The Facts and Figures* (Birmingham: University of Alabama, 1986).
2. A. McGuire, "Issues in the Prevention of Neurotrauma," *Nursing Clinics of North America* 21(1986): 549–54.
3. Stover and Fine, *Spinal Cord Injury*.
4. Ibid.
5. W. Adelstein and P. Watson, "Cervical Spine Injuries," *Journal of Neurosurgical Nursing* 15(1983): 65–71.
6. T.A. Hall, "The Injured Patient's Injured Neck," *Emergency Medicine* (April 15, 1984):24–48.
7. L.J. Cerullo and M.R. Quigley, "Management of Cervical Spinal Cord Injury," *Journal of Emergency Nursing* 11(1985):182–87.
8. T. McSweeney, "Injuries of the Cervical Spine," *Annals of the Royal College of Surgeons of England* 66 (1984):1–6.
9. B.S. Green et. al., "Acute Spinal Cord Injury: Current Concepts," *Clinical Orthopaedics and Related Research* 154(1981):125–35.
10. T.S. Richmond, "The Patient with a Cervical Spinal Cord Injury: A Critical Care Challenge," *Focus on Critical Care* 12(1985):23–33.
11. K.A. Long, "Pitfalls to Avoid and Positive Approaches in the Nurse-Adolescent Relationship," *Perspectives in Psychiatric Care* 23(1985):22–26.
12. Stover and Fine, *Spinal Cord Injury*.
13. Hall, "The Injured Patient's Injured Neck," 24–48.
14. Ibid.
15. D.F. Dean, "The Child with Possible Spinal Cord Injury," *Emergency Medicine* (May 15, 1982): 123–151.
16. Green et al., "Acute Spinal Cord Injury," 125–35.
17. Dean, "The Child with Possible Spinal Cord Injury," 123–51.
18. Cerullo and Quigley, "Management of Cervical Spinal Cord Injury," 182–87.

19. D. Nikas, "Resuscitation of Patients with CNS Trauma," *Nursing Clinics of North America* 21(1986): 693–704.
20. Cerullo and Quigley, "Management of Cervical Spinal Cord Injury," 182–87.
21. D. Brunette and G.L. Rockswold, "Neurologic Recovery Following Rapid Spinal Realignment for Complete Cervical Spinal Cord Injury," *Journal of Trauma* 27(1987):445–47.
22. Cerullo and Quigley, "Management of the Cervical Spinal Cord Injury," 182–87.
23. Green et al., "Acute Spinal Cord Injury," 125–35.
24. Adelstein and Watson, "Cervical Spine Injuries," 65–71.
25. Green et al., "Acute Spinal Cord Injury," 125–35.
26. Cerullo and Quigley, "Management of Cervical Spinal Cord Injury," 182–87.
27. J.P. Kostuik, "Indications for the Use of Halo Immobilization," *Clinical Orthopaedics and Related Research* 54(1981):46–50.
28. McSweeney, "Injuries of the Cervical Spine," 1–6.
29. D.L. Jeffrey, "The Hazards of Reduced Mobility for the Person with a SCI," *Journal of Rehabilitation* 52 (1986):59–62.
30. M.E. Rinehart and D.A. Nawoczenski, "Respiratory Care," in L.E. Buchanan and D.A. Nawoczenski, eds., *Spinal Cord Injury: Concepts and Management Approaches* (Baltimore, Md.: Williams & Wilkins Co., 1987).
31. H. Garrido et al., "Permanent Artificial Respiration by Diaphragm Pacemaker in Tetraplegic Children," *Paraplegia* 24(1986):276–81.
32. McSweeney, "Injuries of the Cervical Spine," 1–6.
33. D. Feustal, "Alterations in Neuron Innervation Associated with Spinal Cord Lesions," *Journal of Neurosurgical Nursing* 13(1981):48–52.
34. Adelstein and Watson, "Cervical Spine Injuries," 65–71.
35. Ibid.
36. K. Walters and J.R. Silver, "Gastrointestinal Bleeding in Patients with Acute Spinal Injuries." *International Rehabilitation Medicine* 8(1986):44–47.
37. S. Murphy, "Family Study and Nursing Research," *Image: Journal of Nursing Scholarship* 18(1986): 170–74.
38. A.L. Whall, "Nursing Theory and the Assessment of Families," *Journal of Psychiatric Nursing and Mental Health Services* 19(1981):30–36.
39. L.L. Northouse, "Who Supports the Support System?" *Journal of Psychiatric Nursing and Mental Health Services* 18(1980):11–15.
40. T.S. Richmond and M. Craig, "Family-Centered Care for the Neurotrauma Patient," *Nursing Clinics of North America* 21(1986):641–51.
41. L. Daley, "The Perceived Immediate Needs of Families with Relatives in the Intensive Care Setting," *Heart and Lung* 13(1984):231–37.
42. S.S. Hickey, "Enabling Hope," *Cancer Nursing* 9(1986):133–37.
43. M.J. Kim, G.K. McFarland, and A.M. McLane, eds., *Pocket Guide to Nursing Diagnoses* (St. Louis: C.V. Mosby Co., 1984).
44. S.E. Bourdon, "Psychological Impact of Neurotrauma in the Acute Care Setting," *Nursing Clinics of North America* 21(1986):629–40.
45. N. Drew, "Exclusion and Confirmation: A Phenomenology of Patients' Experiences with Caregivers," *Image: Journal of Nursing Scholarship* 18(1986):39–43.

Chapter 6
Chest Trauma

Leslie Mancuso

Pediatric trauma continues to be one of the leading health problems today. The major cause of injury and death to children older than 1 year of age is accidents. Statistics indicate that approximately 50 percent of deaths of children in the United States are due to major traumatic injuries.

Thoracic injuries in children are a serious threat to their survival. Studies have documented that the incidence of mortality associated with pediatric thoracic trauma ranges from 7 percent to 14 percent.[1] Thoracic trauma is rarely seen as an isolated injury but is usually discovered concomitantly with head or abdominal injuries (or both).

As with other traumatic injuries, the most common mechanism of injury in thoracic trauma is impact of a blunt force. Children involved in automobile or sports-related accidents may sustain blunt injuries associated with rapid deceleration. Although penetrating thoracic trauma in children is uncommon, specific injuries incurred by weapons have been identified. One mechanism of injury that is unique to children involves the mechanical equipment used in the management of pediatric patients, such as mechanical ventilators and suction catheters.[2]

Specific growth and developmental factors influence the type of thoracic injuries observed in children. A child has a compliant thorax. The structures are cartilaginous and therefore extremely flexible. A child's mediastinum moves freely compared to an adult's. Therefore the heart can be easily displaced, the great vessels moved, the lungs compressed, and the trachea shifted. The cardiac output is impeded as these structures move.

Aerophagia is seen in children after a traumatic injury. As the stomach distends the diaphragmatic excursion is compromised. Therefore the child's respiratory efforts must increase dramatically.

ASSESSMENT OF THORACIC INJURIES

Thoracic injuries can pose a serious threat to resuscitation efforts. Therefore an initial assessment of the chest must be instituted. It is not unusual for a child to have no external marks indicating a chest injury but to have sustained a major internal injury. Thus it is imperative that the child's respiratory rate and depth and symmetry of ventilatory movements be assessed. An unequal chest expansion may be indicative of a hemothorax, pneumothorax, or tension pneumothorax. Clinical signs of respiratory distress such as retractions, nasal flaring, and dyspnea may be the result of chest injuries. The breath sounds should be auscultated and the point of maximal impulse determined.

Although penetrating trauma is not often observed in children, initial assessments must include examining the patient for any overt evidence of chest trauma. The anterior and posterior sides of the chest should be assessed for wounds caused by penetrating devices such as knives. Small-caliber bullets can cause small penetrating wounds in the child. Injuries that may accompany this type of wound are open pneumothorax, ruptured trachea or bronchus, and ruptured esophagus and diaphragm. Specific injuries such as penetrating injury to the heart, ruptured esophagus, ruptured bronchus, and traumatic diaphragmatic hernia require an immediate thoracostomy.

CHEST WALL INJURIES

Because thoracic injuries are seen infrequently in children in comparison to adults, their recognition and management may be slightly different. Indicators of chest wall injury include hypotension, tachycardia, tachypnea, paradoxical chest wall motion, and chest wall tenderness or crepitus. These manifestations suggest chest wall injury and possible pulmonary dysfunction. Because of the child's cartilaginous bones and elastic thorax, specific injuries are less likely to occur.

Rib Fractures

Because the child's thorax is compliant, a major chest injury may be sustained without fracturing the bony thorax. Rib fractures, although rare, may be seen in the childhood age group. Injuries associated with rib fractures vary depending on the location of the injury. The upper ribs are somewhat protected by the clavicles; therefore if there is any fracture to ribs one through four there may also be extensive traumatic injuries. If the upper ribs are damaged, bronchial, tracheal, or aortic rupture is often suspected.

Middle thoracic fractures may result from anteroposterior compression or from a direct blow.[3] This area of the ribs is most frequently fractured. If the force is strong, there is an increased tendency for the ends of the ribs to penetrate the lung tissue and to cause serious pulmonary damage. A pneumothorax or hemothorax may accompany middle rib fractures.

The cause of lower rib fractures is often direct blows. Ribs ten through twelve are mobile and therefore rarely fractured. Often a rupture of the liver, spleen, or kidney is associated with these fractures. A flail chest and a tension pneumothorax can be seen with lower rib fractures as well.

There is a strong association between the number of ribs fractured and the severity of the thoracic trauma. Abdominal injury, extremity fractures, and complications resulting from the injury tend to follow a linear progression in terms of the number of fractured ribs.[4] The survival rate may be directly influenced by the number of rib fractures.

Rib fractures can be easily determined when the child experiences localized pain on taking deep breaths, coughing, or changing position. Local muscle spasms occur initially, and then the pain increases in severity. The area is tender during palpation. A grating sound may be auscultated over the fracture.

Rib fractures usually heal within 3 to 6 weeks with rest and pain-relief medications. The child is encouraged to do deep-breathing exercises to prevent atelectasis. Intercostal nerve blockers have been used infrequently to control severe pain.

Sternal Fractures

The sternum, like the ribs, is flexible and cartilaginous. Therefore, injury to the sternum in children is relatively rare. Fracture may be caused by a critical blow to the chest, by an object such as a steering wheel, or by a crushing chest injury. Sternal fractures, if present, are usually seen with esophageal rupture, tracheobronchial rupture, and diaphragmatic injuries.

The diagnosis of a sternal fracture is made by a lateral chest roentgenogram. Clinically, the child exhibits local tenderness, swelling, and crepitus.

The treatment modalities for sternal fractures depend on the extent of the injury. Accompanying injuries must be addressed before surgery. If there is pain with motion, dislocation of the heart, or severe depression of the chest wall an open reduction is performed.

Flail Chest

A flail chest is the consequence of a blunt or crushing chest trauma. Flail injuries may be either anterior, involving the sternum, or lateral, involving the ribs. There is a higher incidence of flail chest with fractures of the sternum.[5] Flail chest involves multiple lateral or anterior fractures of adjacent ribs, which leave the other ribs in effect free floating. As the child inspires, the floating portion of the rib cage does not move outward but collapses inward with the negative intrathoracic pressure. The opposite occurs during expiration. The child also demonstrates paradoxical chest wall motion with respiration, in which each side of the chest appears to move independently. Therefore, as one side rises the other moves down. The child also exhibits signs of respiratory distress, including dyspnea and cyanosis.

As the situation progresses, severe asphyxia occurs. The size of the flail determines the extent of the asphyxia. The severity is dependent on the amplitude of the paradoxical motion and the vigor of the patient's expiratory efforts.[6] As the asphyxia worsens, the flail motion increases. The child's condition deteriorates as air is rebreathed from one lung to the other and as bronchial secretions increase. Auscultation reveals decreased or diminished breath sounds on the affected side along with respiratory stridor. Subcutaneous emphysema may be present on palpation.

Isolated flail chest has a good prognosis, but usually this condition is accompanied by other cardiac and pulmonary injuries. These injuries pose serious threats to the child's life.

Initially, while resuscitation efforts begin, the injury should be splinted with firm gentle pressure by hand or with a sandbag or pillow. The child may be positioned with the injured side down so that the flail segment is somewhat stabilized.

Intubation and mechanical ventilation are instituted when there is evidence of increasing anxiety and restlessness, tachycardia, decreased tidal volume, and low arterial oxygen pressure and high carbon dioxide pressure. If the child is comatose, endotracheal intubation is begun immediately. If mechanical ventilation is necessary, the child is placed on a positive-pressure respirator. A Swan-Ganz catheter may be placed. Sedation is often used to alleviate the pain with respirations and thus to encourage the child to breathe deeply. Other methods that have been suggested for the management of flail chest include fluid restriction, diuretics, steroids, and intercostal nerve blockade.

Traumatic Asphyxia

Traumatic asphyxia is seen in children as a result not only of their flexible thorax but of the absence of valves in the venous system of the inferior and superior venae cavae.[7] Asphyxiation occurs as a result of direct compression of the chest wall, as is seen when the child is trampled in a crowd or run over by a vehicle. The compression is usually anterior and posterior between the compressant force and a hard surface, but it may result from an indirect force with the patient in a jackknife position.[8] With this type of trauma other injuries should be suspected, such as a ruptured aorta, bronchus, or diaphragm; pulmonary contusion; and flail chest with sternal fractures.

The child with traumatic asphyxia classically presents with severe cyanosis of the face and neck and with petechiae on the head, neck, and chest. The patient may also exhibit subconjunctival and retinal hemorrhages, so that visual disturbances occur in some instances. The nasal buccal mucosa may have petechiae or ecchymoses. Other clinical manifestations seen with these children are tachypnea, disorientation, hemoptysis, epistaxis, and signs of respiratory insufficiency. The child may lapse into a comatose state as a result of increased intracranial pressure.

If the child has an accompanying pneumothorax or pulmonary contusion, the treatment modalities described below must be instituted. Because of the severe respiratory compromise, intubation and mechanical ventilation are usually necessary. Chest tubes are often inserted to drain fluid and air from the chest. Intracranial pressure must be monitored if there is evidence of an increase. Other treatment modalities are instituted on the basis of the other injuries sustained.

Pulmonary Contusion

The most common cause of potentially lethal chest injury in children is pulmonary contusion. A pulmonary contusion should be anticipated whenever a child has a chest injury and, in particular, if bruising is noted on the chest. A direct blunt traumatic injury such as an automobile-pedestrian accident is the most common cause.

This trauma damages the parenchymal tissues of the lung causing edema and hemorrhage, which leads to severe respiratory distress and sometimes tracheal obstruction. The edema is the result of the capillary endothelium becoming permeable, allowing plasma to move freely into the alveoli. Therefore the alveolar-capillary interface is no longer effective.

A child with a pulmonary contusion often presents initially with mild, if any, symptoms. Within a few hours, however, the child develops hemoptysis, wheezes, rales, decreased breath sounds, and an elevated temperature. After 2 to 6 hours, there is a decrease in arterial oxygen pressure and an increase in carbon dioxide pressure. The child exhibits restlessness, tachypnea, tachycardia, and further symptoms of respiratory insufficiency.

The chest roentgenogram will reveal a clear lung field during the first few hours, with subsequent consolidation that does not conform to segmental or lobar distribution. This increased density should clear within several days, but small areas have been seen as long as 1 year after the accident.

The goal of the initial treatment is to prevent large increases in interstitial pulmonary edema. Therefore, fluid resuscitation is performed carefully. A Swan-Ganz catheter is often placed to monitor the pulmonary capillary wedge pressure to prevent fluid overload. Albumin has been used in some medical centers for osmotic purposes; the serum osmolarity is maintained at 300 mOsmL. Diuretics are also used to further restrict the amount of pulmonary interstitial fluid.

The pulmonary status is closely monitored. Serial measurements of arterial blood gases are obtained. The child's airway is maintained, and endotracheal intubation and respiratory support may be required. Positive end-expiratory pressure is applied, which places the child at risk for a spontaneous or tension pneumothorax; the arterial oxygen saturation should be kept at 90 percent. A neuromuscular blocker may promote effective ventilatory assistance. If continued mechanical ventilation is necessary after 2 weeks, a tracheostomy is performed.

The child is at risk for infection with a pulmonary contusion. Therefore, prophylactic antibiotics may be administered until the consolidation on the chest roentgenogram disappears.

INJURIES TO THE DIAPHRAGM

The diaphragm is at risk for rupture with forceful blunt trauma to the lower chest and upper abdomen.[9] This injury may result from a fall from a height or from an automobile accident. A penetration of the diaphragm can occur from a gunshot wound.

A rupture of the diaphragm occurs most frequently on the left side. There are two reasons for this. First, the liver may provide a protective barrier for the right side of the diaphragm, whereas the left side has no internal protection. Second, children injured as pedestrians in motor vehicle accidents in the United States are more likely to be presenting their left side to traffic.

Most lacerations occur with ragged edges in the central part of the diaphragm. This allows the abdominal organs to pass freely into the thoracic cavity. The most common organs to herniate are the stomach, the spleen, and the splenic flexure of the colon. The amount of displaced organ varies depending on the size of the defect. With a large defect, the herniation continues because of the large pressure difference between the negative intrathoracic pressure and the positive intra-abdominal pressure. As the abdominal viscera are displaced into the thorax, the mediastinum shifts and impedes the cardiac output. The lung tissue is compressed, leading to atelectasis.

Diagnosis of a diaphragmatic hernia may be delayed unless the child presents with acute symptoms. The child will be dyspneic and have left chest pain and continuing respiratory distress. On percussion, there are mixed areas of dullness. The child will have decreased breath sounds and possible audible bowel sounds in the chest. A scaphoid abdomen may be readily detected on physical examination.

The chest roentgenogram may show a collapsed lung with air and fluid present, a mediastinal and tracheal shift, and extrapleural fluid. The diaphragm is indistinct and high, with varying amounts of abdominal contents visible in the thoracic cavity. Placement of a nasogastric tube may provide a clear indication on a roentgenogram that there is a diaphragmatic hernia with displaced abdominal viscera.

If acute diaphragmatic hernia is detected, immediate surgery is performed. If possible, an intra-abdominal approach is used because of the potential for concomitant injury to the abdominal viscera.

PNEUMOTHORAX

Pneumothorax is the most commonly occurring entity in pediatric thoracic injuries. It can be caused by either blunt or penetrating trauma. The most common cause is blunt injury. The pneumothorax exists because of air leakage. It is seen most often as the result of a tear in the tracheobronchial tree, an esophageal perforation, or a penetration of the chest wall. Because of the flexibility of the thorax, a pneumothorax may be present without rib fractures. If a rib fracture is detected, the child should be examined for the possibility of pneumothorax.

The symptoms of a child with pneumothorax may vary greatly. The child may be asymptomatic or have signs of severe respiratory distress. The child may exhibit dyspnea, tachypnea, pain, and agitation. The physical examination may reveal decreased breath sounds on the ipsilateral side and tracheal deviation. There is often hyperresonance to percussion and subcutaneous emphysema. A chest roentgenogram is obtained to confirm the diagnosis.

If the child is in severe respiratory distress, a needle aspiration is performed immediately to withdraw the air from the pleural space. A chest tube is then inserted. This tube, when attached to a water seal and suction device, provides information about the existence of persistent leaks. A persistent air leak may be indicative of a bronchopleural fistula, intrapulmonary placement of the tube, esophageal rupture, or a leak around the tube at the entrance site on the chest or at one of the connectors.[10]

Open Pneumothorax

A penetrating trauma often results in an open pneumothorax. Other causes for an open pneumothorax are ejection of the child from a car or a fall on a sharp object. A child with an open pneumothorax exhibits restlessness, cyanosis, subcutaneous emphysema, and mediastinal shift. The child's condition continues to deteriorate, leading to shock. With a large wound mediastinal flutter occurs, whereby the mediastinum moves to one side or the other depending on the phase of respiration. During inspiration, air moves through the largest opening or the wound. As the lung collapses air passes from it to the intact lung, and the mediastinum shifts to the functioning lung. During expiration, air again exists through the largest opening route or the wound. The lung expands partially, and air from the functional lung is rebreathed into the partially collapsed lung.[11]

An open pneumothorax may be categorized according to the extent of the wound. With a moderately sized wound there may be no pulmonary laceration, whereas with a large wound there may be significant pulmonary collapse.

The open wound should be covered immediately with an airtight seal. In the field, sterile towels or a gloved hand can be used until a dressing is applied. On arrival in the emergency room the dressing should be examined. Optimally a petroleum jelly–gauze dressing should be applied when the patient has stabilized.

Tension Pneumothorax

With a tension pneumothorax, air enters freely into the pleural space but is unable to exit during expiration. This injury is the result of a tear in the lung or pleura that acts as a one-way valve.[12] The intrapleural pressure then increases, causing the collapse of the injured lung.

As a result of the collapsed lung, there is progressive impairment of venous return, a decrease in cardiac output, and cardiovascular collapse. The mediastinum shifts widely. Clinical examination reveals diminished or absent breath sounds, tracheal deviation, poorly moving hemithorax, hyperresonance on percussion, and subcutaneous emphysema.

A needle aspiration must be performed immediately to equilibrate the intrapleural pressure with atmospheric pressure. A chest tube may then be inserted.

Subcutaneous Emphysema

Subcutaneous emphysema occurs as a result of the leakage of interstitial air into the pleurae. It may be caused by a major disruption in the pleurae or intercostal muscles, as with rib fractures with a pneumothorax. The outward movement of air from the mediastinum may be caused by a ruptured bronchus or esophagus.

Once the source of the subcutaneous emphysema is detected and treated, the process is self-limiting. The extent of the subcutaneous crepitus should be noted. Treatment for the emphysema is directed toward managing the underlying primary injury. Subcutaneous air has no physiologic effect and is absorbed easily.

INJURY TO THE TRACHEOBRONCHIAL TREE

Tracheal Injuries

Tracheal injuries are the result of blunt or penetrating trauma. This disruptive injury to the airway may be the consequence of various types of mechanisms. An infant younger than 18 months of age usually sustains tracheal damage from vigorous attempts at pharyngeal suctioning or during an emergency bronchoscopy. Child abuse may be a cause of tracheal injury in older children.

The most frequent injuries occur in the cervical trachea. This is often seen as a result of a hyperextension mechanism. The child may be struck by an object while biking or sledding. If the child holds the breath on impact, the trachea becomes rigid and is prone to rupture.

The trachea can rupture either longitudinally or transversely; the most common type of rupture is transverse. The rupture is usually within 2 cm of the carina. The child may have an incomplete transverse rupture or a complete and total rupture. With a complete and total rupture, the lower portion of the trachea usually dislocates.

The symptoms of cervical tracheal injury include cyanosis, severe inspiratory stridor, hemoptysis, and subcutaneous emphysema. The child coughs and exhibits increasing respiratory distress with dyspnea and retractions.

A high tracheal injury requires surgical intervention and a tracheotomy. A low tracheal injury necessitates a thoracotomy. If the child has severe respiratory distress, a tracheotomy may be required immediately as a resuscitation measure. If intubation is performed, bronchoscopy is preferred to blind intubation to establish the airway because the false lumen may be cannulated and submucosal insertion can convert a partial to a complete respiratory obstruction.[13] The airway is allowed to stabilize and heal for 5 to 6 days, after which corrective repair is performed.

Bronchial Injuries

The bronchial area most commonly injured in children is that within 2.5 cm of the carina. Sudden compression of the anterior and posterior chest and compression of the semirigid bronchus against the spine can lead to a major tracheobronchial rupture.

Less than 50 percent of children with bronchial injuries present initially without symptoms. Those who do exhibit symptoms have dyspnea, hemoptysis, subcutaneous and mediastinal emphysema, and evidence of airway obstruction with mediastinal shifting. If a tension pneumothorax is detected with mediastinal emphysema, a tracheobronchial disruption should be seriously considered.[14] If hemoptysis is present with a blunt thoracic trauma, a bronchoscopy should be performed.

Chest roentgenograms of a bronchial tear may reveal a displacement of the collapsed lung, a deformity of the bronchial air pattern, and small air collections alongside the bronchus. Bronchography is useful in defining the extent and site of the injury. Bronchoscopy also reveals the state of the distal portion of the tracheobronchial tree below the level of the transection.

Once the injury is identified, an endotracheal tube is placed to the opposite mainstem bronchus as an immediate resuscitation effort. Positive-pressure ventilation is used. Most injuries require an early surgical intervention to prevent bronchial stenosis. If the bronchial injury is chronic, surgical removal of the stricture is recommended.

INJURIES TO THE ESOPHAGUS

Rarely in children is there a direct injury to the esophagus, except perhaps from a gunshot wound. This is due, in part, to the extensive protection provided by the mediastinum. The most common cause of esophageal rupture is a result of instrumentation.[15] In infants, perforation of the upper esophagus can be caused by the rough insertion of a nasogastric tube. Ingestion of a sharp object such as an open safety pin may rupture the esophagus. Blunt esophageal rupture may result from the child striking the dashboard or steering wheel in an automobile accident.

Perforation of the esophagus may be exhibited by mediastinal or subcutaneous emphysema and severe cardiovascular collapse. Other signs that may alert a nurse to an esophageal injury are restlessness, severe substernal chest pain, cyanosis, pneumothorax, hydrothorax, and pneumomediastinum.[16] The pain may be so critical that swallowing is impossible. A cough when swallowing is usually a late sign of a fistula between the esophagus and the respiratory tract. During auscultation a mediastinal crunch (Hamman's sign) is audible. Fluoroscopy is used to diagnose the injury.

In esophageal injuries in neonates, symptoms include obstruction to the passage of the nasogastric tube and excessive oropharyngeal secretions.[17] Diagnosis is by administration of contrast material into the esophagus and subsequent radiology.

Injuries can occur from ingestion of a corrosive substance; this is often seen in toddlers. This type of injury burns the lining of the esophagus. The child should be treated immediately with antibiotics and steroids and be allowed no food by mouth. Many surgical alternatives are available for treating such an injury.

In injuries of the intrathoracic esophagus, the child is managed with liberal fluid resuscitation and antibiotic therapy. A thoracotomy is performed immediately.

When a child presents with a possible esophageal injury, a chest tube is inserted to drain fluid and air from the thorax. The drainage should be assessed for evidence of bilious or gastric drainage. High amylase content in the drainage is indicative of esophageal perforation. Esophagography or esophagoscopy is performed to confirm the diagnosis. Surgical intervention is then initiated.

INJURIES TO THE HEART AND GREAT VESSELS

It is rare for a child to have a penetrating wound of the great vessels. Such an injury is usually diagnosed by signs of massive hemothorax.

Aortic Rupture

Aortic rupture may occur as the result of a blunt force to the chest, a vertical or horizontal deceleration injury, or a crushing injury. Automobile accidents most often are the cause of this type of injury. Rupture usually occurs in the descending aorta below the level of the subclavian. The injury may be a tear in the intima, a partial rupture, or a complete transection.

The child exhibits specific symptoms depending on the nature and extent of the injury. If the child is alert on admission, the most common complaint is a severe chest pain that radiates from the midscapular region to the back. The clinical manifestations may include symptoms of shock with diminution of the femoral pulses. There may be a discrepancy in blood pressure between the right and left arms. A left hemothorax may be detected. Some children have a hoarseness or cough due to tightening in the area of the left laryngeal nerve or left mainstem bronchus. The child is restless as a result of cardiovascular collapse, which affects the cerebral circulation. Heart murmurs are unusual, although a harsh systolic murmur over the precordium may be detected.

The most significant indication of aortic rupture is a widened mediastinum on chest roentgenography. Other indications are loss of sharpness of the aortic knob and movement inferiorly of the left mainstem bronchus. These characteristics do not absolutely confirm the diagnosis but are indicative of a type of mediastinal vessel hemorrhage.

For any child with a suspected aortic rupture, a chest roentgenogram should be obtained immediately after the cervical spine roentgenogram is taken. If a widened mediastinum is identified, an aortogram is indicated. An aortogram provides information about the extent and location of the tear. As soon as the diagnosis of a tear is made, emergency surgery is performed.

Cardiac Tamponade

A complication of injuries to the heart and major intrathoracic vessels is cardiac tamponade. A small volume of blood around the heart can severely compromise cardiac function. Cardiac output may diminish dramatically.

Clinical manifestations of cardiac tamponade include hypotension despite vigorous fluid resuscitation. The child has an elevated central venous pressure, paradoxical pulse, tachycardia, and peripheral vasoconstriction. Muffled heart sounds are a late sign of cardiac tamponade.

If cardiac tamponade is suspected, a needle aspiration is performed immediately. As the aspiration continues, the nurse should observe for improvement of the cardiovascular status. The circulating blood volume in a child is approximately 80 mL/kg; any loss of 5 percent to 7 percent of the circulating blood volume indicates a large blood loss necessitating a blood transfusion.

Hemothorax

A hemothorax can be caused by either blunt or penetrating trauma. Blood collects in the pleural space, eventually leading to a collapse of the affected lung. Any injury to the internal mammary vessels, intercostal artery, pulmonary vessels, cardiac chambers, or aorta may lead to hemothorax. Children can lose approximately 40 percent of their circulating blood volume with one hemothorax.

The signs and symptoms of hemothorax vary depending on the severity of the injury. Because the circulating blood volume in a child is small in comparison to that of an adult, bleeding in the chest can readily initiate a hypotensive state. The clinical picture includes cyanosis, ventilatory embarrassment, decreased or absent breath sounds on the affected side, poorly moving hemithorax, mediastinal shifting, and signs of shock. Dullness may be audible over the affected side during percussion. A pneumothorax may accompany a hemothorax.

The initial goal for treating a hemothorax is the immediate evacuation of blood from the pleural space with a chest tube. A thoracostomy tube near the seventh or eighth intercostal space allows the hemothorax to drain, reexpands the lung, and provides a means of monitoring ongoing bleeding.[18] The blood volume should be rapidly replaced. If bleeding persists, the presence of other injuries must be considered.

NOTES

1. T. Mayer et. al., "The Modified Injury Severity Scale in Pediatric Multiple Trauma Patients," *Journal of Pediatric Surgery* 15(1980):719–26.

2. M. Eichelberger and J. Randolph, "Thoracic Trauma in Children," *Surgical Clinics of North America* 61(1981):1181.

3. E. Golladay, *Injuries to the Heart and Chest in Children* (Mount Kisco, N.Y.: Futura, 1983), 111.

4. Ibid., 112.

5. R.F. Wilson, C. Murray, and D.R. Antonenko, "Nonpenetrating Thoracic Injuries," *Surgical Clinics of North America* 57(1977):17.

6. F. Blarsdell and L.D. Trunkey, *Cervicothoracic Trauma* (New York: Threme Inc., 1986), 344.

7. J.A. Haller and J.S. Donahoo, "Traumatic Asphyxia in Children," *Journal of Trauma* 11(1971):453.

8. Golladay, *Injuries to the Heart and Chest*, 145.

9. K.J. Welch, "Thoracic injuries," in J.G. Randolph, ed., *The Injured Child* (Chicago: Yearbook Medical Publishers, 1980), 217.

10. Golladay, *Injuries to the Heart and Chest*, 111.

11. B. Brooks, *The Injured Child* (Austin: Univ. of Texas Press, 1985), 258.

12. P. Perdue, "Life-Threatening Respiratory Injuries," *RN* 4(1981):31.

13. Golladay, *Injuries to the Heart and Chest*, 111.

14. M.M. Kirsh, M.B. Orringer, D.M. Behrendt, and H. Sloan, "Management of Tracheobronchial Trauma," *Annals of Thoracic Surgery* 22(1976):93.

15. Eichelberger and Randolph, "Thoracic Trauma in Children," 1188.

16. P. Perdue, "Life-Threatening Respiratory Injuries," 32.

17. S.B. Lee, "Esophageal Perforation in the Neonate: A Review of the Literature," *American Journal of Diseases in Children* 130(1975):329.

18. Eichelberger and Randolph, "Thoracic Trauma in Children," 1188.

Chapter 7

Abdominal and Genitourinary Trauma

Lisa Marie Peckham and Lou Ann Kitchen

Traditional beliefs and practices regarding diagnosis and management of abdominal injuries in children have been questioned during the past 15 years. Innovations have been refined that have improved the outcome for children who would otherwise have died or suffered severe morbidity at an earlier time. Although intra-abdominal injuries account for a small percentage of total pediatric trauma deaths, failure to diagnose and manage these injuries promptly and successfully accounts for most preventable deaths after multiple trauma.[1]

MECHANISMS OF INJURY

Blunt Abdominal Injury

Blunt trauma to the abdomen can cause lethal injury without visible signs of damage. The liver and spleen are the solid and relatively friable organs that frequently hemorrhage after blunt abdominal wall injury in children. Children's Hospital and Health Center (CHHC) in San Diego has seen more than 1700 patients since being designated a regional pediatric trauma center in August 1984. As of October 1987, CHHC has treated 44 liver injuries and 38 spleen injuries (Tables 7-1 and 7-2). The most severely injured children in this series were those injured by automobiles: struck as a pedestrian, struck as a cyclist, or injured as a passenger. These mechanisms of injury should produce a high index of suspicion for blunt abdominal trauma.

Penetrating Abdominal Injury

Penetrating abdominal injury is less common than blunt abdominal injury in children, accounting for less than 10 percent of pediatric injuries. Penetrating wounds occur primarily from gunshots and stabbings. These injuries often cause confusion and are anxiety-producing for the nurse who is more familiar with blunt trauma. The nurse may tend to focus on the obvious penetrating injury, overlooking airway control and circulatory management. In the patient with penetrating injury, vena cava injury may be

Table 7-1 Hepatic Injury, August 1984 through October 1987, Seen at Children's Hospital and Health Center (CHHC)

Series		Child Struck as Pedestrian	Passenger	Miscellaneous*	Gunshot Wound	Child on Bicycle	Stabbed
Number of patients	44	20	10	9	2	2	1
Age (years)	5.96	5.5	5.6	6.4	8	7	2
Male	26	11	4	7	1	2	1
Female	18	9	6	2	1	–0–	–0–
Trauma score	10.3	8.2	11	12.1	15	16	16
Injury severity score	37	45	35	26	22	17	4
Probability of survival	0.64	0.48	0.69	0.77	0.96	0.99	0.99
Survivors	36	14	9	8	2	2	1
Nonsurvivors	8	6	1	1	–0–	–0–	–0–
Observed survival	0.81	0.70	0.9	0.88	1.0	1.0	1.0

*Includes falls, crushes, all terrain vehicle, and the like.
Source: The Pediatric Trauma Center at Children's Hospital and Health Center, San Diego, California, with permission of Frank P. Lynch, M.D.

Table 7-2 Splenic Trauma, August 1984 through October 1987, Seen at CHHC

Series	Child Struck by Cyclist	Pedestrian	Gunshot Wound	Passenger	Child on Bicycle	Miscellaneous*
Number of patients	38	3	19	1	5	3	7
Age (years)	7.3	8.3	6.0	6	4.9	6	10.3
Male	23	3	11	–0–	2	2	5
Female	15	–0–	8	1	3	1	2
Trauma score	10.7	9.0	8.6	14	10.6	15.7	15.5
Injury severity score	36	47	47	38	33	18	11
Probability of survival	0.62	0.41	0.40	0.91	0.55	0.99	0.99
Survivors	27	1	11	1	4	3	7
Nonsurvivors	11	2	8	–0–	1	–0–	–0–
Observed survival	0.71	0.33	0.57	1.0	0.80	1.0	1.0

*Includes falls, crushes, all terrain vehicle, and the like.
Source: The Pediatric Trauma Center at Children's Hospital and Health Center, San Diego, California, with permission of Frank P. Lynch, M.D.

present. If possible, one intravenous access line should be started above the diaphragm. O⁻ blood should be ready to administer promptly on the patient's admission. In determining whether the patient requires an immediate exploratory laparotomy, it is not necessary to diagnose which abdominal organ is injured; it is only necessary to know that there is a life-threatening injury requiring surgical repair.[2]

All gunshot wounds that penetrate the abdomen should be explored operatively. Peritonitis, blood from an orifice, pneumoperitoneum, or evisceration is indicative of abdominal penetration. These findings are easily assessed on physical examination and abdominal roentgenograms.[3] The nurse should assess and document entrance and exit wounds. The exit wound will not always be found posterior to the entrance site because bullets can ricochet inside the abdomen. The exit wound, if present, may therefore be far removed from the entrance point.[4]

INITIAL ASSESSMENT AND MANAGEMENT

Successful management of the pediatric trauma patient requires a systematic approach to assessment and resuscitation (see Chapter 2). Prompt, efficient assessment with simultaneous treatment of potentially life-threatening conditions is necessary because failure rapidly to institute needed therapy may increase morbidity and mortality.

Assessment of the abdomen is generally considered part of the secondary survey. Unless the abdominal injury is obviously the major site of trauma (for example, if there is a penetrating wound or rapid increase in size due to massive bleeding), it is cared for after any respiratory difficulties, circulatory compromise, or depressed level of consciousness are addressed. Depending on the circumstances and experience of the team, however, much of the assessment and treatment can be done simultaneously.

ABDOMINAL INJURY: SOLID AND HOLLOW ORGAN TRAUMA

Trauma resulting in injury to the abdomen is caused most frequently by mechanisms of injury that produce blunt, high-force trauma, as when the child is struck as a pedestrian or a passenger in a motor vehicle accident or when the child falls or is crushed. All these mechanisms tend to produce multisystems injuries, which can be devastating and can complicate early diagnosis and treatment.[5] The associated injuries are sometimes more apparent,[6] and significant intra-abdominal bleeding can obscure and lead to delay in diagnosis of the abdominal injury.

Blunt abdominal trauma in children often results in solid organ injury, commonly involving the liver or spleen and leading to bleeding and possible hemorrhage. Although there are usually associated injuries, intraperitoneal hemorrhage resulting from injury to the liver or spleen is the most urgent concern. The liver is the most commonly injured solid organ after abdominal trauma and the most formidable cause of exsanguinating abdominal hemorrhage.[7] Of children with major liver injuries, 40 percent die before reaching the hospital. Of these injuries, 80 percent involve the right lobe and 20 percent involve the vena cava or a major hepatic vein.[8] The spleen is involved in approximately 25 percent of injuries to the abdomen. Delay in diagnosis of these injuries is associated with high morbidity and mortality. Early, accurate radiologic evaluation by means of computerized tomography (CT) decreases unnecessary delay in diagnosis and management of liver and spleen injuries.

Pancreatic injury occurs in only 5 percent of pediatric patients with abdominal injury.[9] Because the pancreas lies anterior to the vertebral column, blunt forces can cause compression of the gland against bone and lead to contusions. Motor vehicle accidents, child abuse, and impact from bicycle handlebars are common causes of injury. Injuries to the pancreas include contusions, hematomas, disruption of the structural framework, and capsule injury to the ductal system.[10] The pancreas is usually injured along with other organs, such as the spleen and bowel, and pancreatic trauma is rarely the cause of death.

The stomach, small intestine, and large intestine are hollow, air-containing structures. Hollow viscus injuries are uncommon in childhood. Blunt injury does not usually cause lethal hemorrhage in these organs.

Initial physical assessment should be directed toward recognition of patients who are hemodynamically unstable as a result of abdominal trauma. Uncontrollable hemorrhage, evidenced by a falling hematocrit or unstable blood pressure, requires a coagulation profile and then blood transfusions to maintain a hematocrit of 35 percent. Persistent hemorrhage requiring blood transfusions exceeding 50 percent of the patient's calculated blood volume in a 24-hour period or inability to maintain a stable blood pressure necessitate immediate surgical intervention. Operative intervention is recommended only if hemodynamic stability cannot be maintained. Hemodynamically stable patients require a thorough clinical physical assessment including radiologic evaluation. Although minor controversy concerning its use still exists, it is well established that contrast-enhanced CT is the imaging modality of choice for the evaluation of the hemodynamically stable child with abdominal injury.

Physical Examination

The mechanism of injury guides the nurse in physical assessment. Examination of a child's abdomen is difficult, and findings can be misleading in the unconscious child or the conscious child with lower rib fractures, contusions of the abdominal wall, pelvic fractures, or gastric dilation.[11] Repeated examinations by the same nurse are most useful in detecting physiologic abnormalities or changes that require further diagnostic evaluation or medical attention.

The skin should be assessed for contusions, lacerations, and protruding tissue. Abdominal distention, patterns of ecchymosis, pulsations, and peristaltic waves may be visible. Upper quadrant distention suggests gastric dilation, and diffuse lower quadrant distention suggests bleeding. The following signs of intra-abdominal injury should be assessed, communicated to other team members, and well documented.[12]

1. *Kehr's sign.* Free blood in the abdomen irritates the diaphragm and the phrenic nerve. Pain is referred along the nerve, causing pain in the left shoulder, which indicates splenic liver injury.

2. *Selt belt sign.* Ecchymosis over the lower abdomen results from compression of a lap-type seat belt against the iliac crest and lower abdomen. This sign indicates that severe force was applied against the abdominal viscera.
3. *Cullen's sign.* A rare manifestation from a ruptured spleen is periumbilical ecchymosis, which is caused by intra-abdominal bleeding.

The patient who has sustained blunt abdominal trauma should be closely observed if he or she complains of abdominal pain. Pain can be referred or associated with other body cavities. Location, duration, and character of the pain should be communicated to other team members and well documented.

Abdominal trauma that decreases bowel sounds is usually caused by an irritant outside the bowel. Irritants decrease or cause cessation of peristalsis, resulting in absent sounds. Increased bowel sounds may be a result of irritants inside the intestine. Absent bowel sounds are more indicative of intra-abdominal pathology than increased bowel sounds.

Percussion to determine position, size, and density of underlying structures is particularly useful in confirming gastric dilation. Identifying abnormal sounds by means of percussion requires experience and clinical skill. It is most useful in nonacute situations.

The abdomen is palpated to elicit tenderness or to detect rigidity. All four quadrants should be palpated. When the fingers are pressed firmly over an area and quickly released, the pain felt on release is rebound tenderness, which is a sign of peritoneal irritation.

Diagnosis and Treatment of Solid Organ Injuries

Traditional concepts regarding diagnosis and treatment of pediatric abdominal injuries have been challenged during recent years. The increased use of sophisticated imaging techniques such as radionuclide scintigraphy, ultrasonography, and CT in the last decade has contributed to improved characterization of the extent of the injury. Much of the current literature states that CT is the most appropriate, accurate, and rapid imaging technique for diagnosis of solid organ injury. CT is noninvasive, clinically reliable, injury-specific, and immediately available in all trauma centers. It enables the classification of solid organ injuries, as shown in Exhibits 7-1 and 7-2. With CT, the nature and extent of the injury can be classified with a high degree of accuracy. This classification is useful in guiding nonoperative management.

Most patients with abdominal injuries have sustained multisystems injuries, including head injury. It is simple to include the abdomen in a CT study after the head is scanned. For the unconscious child who requires emergency neurosurgical intervention (a situation in which there is no time to obtain an abdominal CT scan) in whom diagnosis of a hemoperitoneum would necessitate concomitant laparotomy, diagnostic peritoneal lavage is done. This can be accomplished in the emergency department or in the operating room. Appearance of frank blood requires immediate operative intervention. Absence of bloody return leads to the infusion of 0.9 percent sodium chloride solution at 10 mL/kg.[13] Lavage is considered positive if one of the following is present[14]:

Exhibit 7-1 Classification of Splenic Injury

Class I	Localized capsular disruption or subcapsular hematoma without significant parenchymal injury.
Class II	Single or multiple capsular and parenchymal disruptions, transverse or longitudinal, that do not extend into the hilum or involve major vessels. Intraparenchymal hematoma may or may not coexist.
Class III	Deep fractures, single or multiple, transverse or longitudinal, extending into the hilum and involving major segmental blood vessels.
Class IV	Completely shattered or fragmented spleen or one separated from its normal blood supply at the pedicle.
Subclass	
A	Without other associated abdominal injury.
B	With other associated abdominal injury.
B_1	Solid viscus injury.
B_2	Hollow viscus injury.
E	With associated extra-abdominal injury.

Source: Reprinted from *Journal of Pediatric Surgery*, Vol. 12, pp. 3–10, with permission of Grune & Stratton, Inc., © 1977.

Exhibit 7-2 Classification of Hepatic Injury

Class I	Capsular avulsion or parenchymal fracture less than 1 cm deep.
Class II	Parenchymal fracture 1 to 3 cm deep; subcapsular hematoma less than 10 cm in diameter; peripheral penetrating wound.
Class III	Parenchymal fracture less than 3 cm deep; subcapsular hematoma less than 10 cm in diameter; central penetrating wound.
Class IV	Labor tissue destruction; massive central hematoma.
Class V	Hepatic venous or retrohepatic caval injury; extensive bilobar disruption.

- 100,000 red blood cells per milliliter of lavage fluid
- 500 white blood cells per milliliter of lavage fluid
- bile
- bacteria on Gram's stain

If hemodynamic stability can be achieved, nonoperative management is preferred for both liver and spleen injury. Children are hospitalized for at least 1 week. Serial examinations and complete blood cell counts must be performed routinely. Criteria for discharge are normal laboratory values and resolution of abnormal findings on CT. At discharge the parents should be counseled to keep the child confined to the home with limited activity for 1 month. At 1 month, a CT scan should be performed to monitor the healing process.

The most important impetus for splenic preservation has been the observation of postsplenectomy sepsis. The incidence of infection in asplenic children is eighty-five times greater than normal; also, infection occurs in 1.5 percent of all splenectomized children and has a mortality rate of approximately 50 percent. The advantage of operative salvage compared to nonoperative observation is still controversial; some investigators recommend operative intervention only if hemodynamic stability cannot be achieved.[15] Indications for surgical intervention include multisystem injuries requiring exploration, hemodynamic instability, multiple splenic fragments on CT, or persistent bleeding requiring blood transfusions exceeding 50 percent of the patient's calculated blood volume in a 24-hour period.[16]

If total splenectomy is required, the child should be immunized with pneumococcal vaccine and receive prophylactic antibiotics. Parents must be educated about the risk of postsplenectomy sepsis. If there are any indications of febrile episode, the child must be assessed by a physician.

Diagnosis and Treatment of Hollow Organ Injuries

Hollow viscus injuries are difficult to diagnose. Signs of injury are subtle, and diagnosis is sometimes delayed. Serial clinical examination is the most useful diagnostic tool. Several hours after injury, peritoneal lavage may be positive for an increase in white blood cells, bile, or bacteria. No diagnostic study can completely exclude visceral injury. Surgical exploration is often required.

An abrasion or contusion in the upper abdomen should raise the suspicion of a stomach injury. Bloody nasogastric drainage, tympanic sounds elicited when percussion is performed over the liver, or detection of free air or a nasogastric tube in an abnormal position on roentgenography are all indicative of stomach injury.[17] A perforated stomach produces a board-like abdomen with intense pain in the conscious patient. Flat plate, upright, and lateral decubitus films are the diagnostic images of choice for evaluation of stomach injuries. With perforation, acute peritonitis develops within hours. Surgery is always required.

The small bowel is fixed to the retroperitoneum at two points: the ligament of Treitz, and the cecum. Rapid deceleration injury may lead to partial or complete transection of the small bowel at or near one of these two fixed points. A child with a ruptured bowel may have minimal symptoms, although frank peritonitis is inevitable. Occasionally, the small bowel is crushed against the vertebral column. The resulting perforation and leakage may take 3 to 4 days to become obvious. If suspected, surgical exploration is required.

Trauma to the anorectum occurs rarely, but when it does it is usually due to child abuse. Rectal injury is best assessed by direct inspection because the rectum is an extraperitoneal structure. Examination under general anesthesia is the best method for a thorough examination of the rectum. A rectal tear is best treated by rectal irrigation, direct repair, a diverting colostomy, a mucus fistula, and presacral drainage anterior to the coccyx.[18]

GENITOURINARY TRAUMA

Genitourinary injuries occur frequently in children. They typically occur in association with other injuries that are immediately life threatening, however. Consequently, they may be neglected in the initial assessment of the multiply injured child. Although genitourinary injuries are rarely life threatening, they may be a significant cause of morbidity, especially if they are not recognized early.[19,20] The diagnosis of genitourinary trauma necessitates a high index of suspicion guided by knowledge of the mechanism of injury and clinical and diagnostic findings.

The ultimate goal in the management of genitourinary trauma in children is the preservation of tissue and function. In addition, efforts are made to minimize posttraumatic strictures, urinary fistulas, incontinence, hypertension, impotence, and testicular dysfunction.[21] These complications are especially important to avoid in the child, who potentially has many years to live with them.

Initial Evaluation

Although genitourinary injuries occur frequently in children, they are often subtle and require careful assessment for accurate diagnosis. Any child with abdominal or flank tenderness, pelvic fracture, lower rib fracture, or perineal swelling should be considered to have genitourinary trauma until proved otherwise.[22]

During the initial physical examination, the abdomen and flanks are examined for tenderness, masses, overlying abrasions and contusions, or flank ecchymosis (Grey-Turner's sign), all of which indicate retroperitoneal hemorrhage. The external genitalia are examined for swelling, ecchymosis, or blood at the urethral meatus, which suggest the possibility of a urethral injury. Signs of shock may be present and indicate massive bleeding; patients who present with profound shock usually have associated injuries, however.[23] Exhibit 7-3 lists physical signs associated with genitourinary injury.

In children with a suspected genitourinary injury, the bladder should be catheterized and urinalysis performed. Catheterizing the child serves to decompress the bladder, provides a means of following urine output, decreases urinary extravasation in cases of bladder interruption, prevents urinary obstruction due to clots, and provides a route for contrast material for studies.[24] The contraindication to urethral catheterization is the possibility of urethral injury, which is manifested by perineal swelling, blood at the meatus, or inability to void. Forcing a catheter in these conditions may convert a partial urethral tear into a complete one. In such cases, a suprapubic bladder tap is indicated to decompress the bladder and collect a urine sample for analysis.

Any degree of hematuria demands further clinical investigation, even if clinical suspicions of genitourinary trauma are low. Gross or microscopic hematuria is present in most genitourinary injuries. The degree of hematuria does not correlate with the severity of the injury, however.[25,26] Significant genitourinary injuries may produce only microscopic hematuria or no hematuria at all, and minor injuries can result in gross hematuria.

Additional laboratory tests for suspected genitourinary injuries include serial measurements of hematocrit and electrolytes. Rising blood urea nitrogen and creatinine levels indicate renal dysfunction, and a declining hematocrit indicates further bleeding.

Exhibit 7-3 Physical Signs of Genitourinary Injury

Renal
  Hematuria
  Flank or abdominal pain
  Flank abrasion, contusion, or ecchymosis
  Previous renal abnormality
Bladder
  Hematuria
  Abdominal pain
  Inability to void
  Pelvic fracture
  Renal injury
Ureteral
  Deceleration injury with hyperextension
  Flank pain
  Flank mass
  Penetrating injuries
  Hematuria
Urethral
  Blood at urethra
  Inability to void
  Lower abdominal or pelvic pain
  Scrotal hematoma or perineal swelling
  High-riding prostate
  Hematuria

Source: Reprinted from *Emergency Management of Pediatric Trauma* by T. Mayer (Ed.), p. 343, with permission of W.B. Saunders Company, © 1985.

Radiologic evaluation consists of an abdominal radiograph in the resuscitation room, which may show bony fractures or fragments of penetrating foreign bodies. Infusion pyelography or CT is performed as part of the initial diagnostic evaluation of all patients with significant abdominal trauma, regardless of the presence or absence of hematuria.[27] Many hospitals prefer contrast-enhanced CT because it allows excellent visualization of the genitourinary anatomy as well as simultaneous assessment of other intra-abdominal organs. In addition, studies have shown CT to be a more sensitive indicator of renal injuries than infusion pyelography.[28,29]

Renal Injuries

In children, the kidney is one of the most commonly injured organs as a result of blunt abdominal trauma. Renal injuries account for approximately 5 percent of all childhood trauma.[30] Children are more vulnerable to renal injuries than adults because of their smaller amount of perinephric fat, their underdeveloped posterior abdominal muscles and thoracic cage, and the larger size of the kidney relative to their total body size.

Pre-existing renal abnormalities are present in approximately 10 percent of trauma cases.[31] Hydronephrosis is the most common abnormality; others include ectopic kidneys, horseshoe kidneys, and tumors. Frequently these abnormalities are not known before the trauma. A pre-existing anomaly should be suspected when hematuria that seems to be disproportionate to the mechanism of injury is present. With hydronephrosis, relatively minor trauma may result in major renal damage.[32]

Mechanism of Injury

Renal injuries are most commonly caused by blunt trauma. Motor vehicle accidents (involving the child as either passenger or pedestrian), falls, sports injuries, and child abuse are the most common mechanisms of injury.[33] Rapid deceleration forces may crush the kidney against the ribs or vertebrae, resulting in parenchymal lacerations or contusions. Fractured ribs may also directly lacerate the kidney. The vascular pedicle, which is fixed, may also be stretched during sudden deceleration, resulting in tears of the renal vein or artery.[34]

Approximately 40 percent of patients with renal injuries have associated injuries.[35] The head, spleen, liver, and long bones are the most frequently injured body areas. Of left kidney injuries, 25 percent are accompanied by splenic injuries. Liver injuries are associated with right renal injuries but are relatively uncommon.

Diagnosis

Renal injury should be suspected in any child with a history or physical evidence of trauma to the abdomen, flank, lower chest, or back. In addition, any patient with a head injury and depressed level of consciousness should be evaluated for possible abdominal and renal injury. The signs and symptoms of renal trauma vary depending on the general condition of the child and presence of other associated injuries as well as on the type and severity of renal injury.

Hematuria is the hallmark of renal trauma and is present in most patients, but again the degree of hematuria does not correlate with the severity of the injury.[36,37] The absence of hematuria does not rule out renal injury if other signs suggest its possibility. Abdominal rigidity or a palpable flank mass may be present as well as superficial abrasions, contusions, or ecchymosis. Flank and abdominal pain are usually present. Paralytic ileus may also occur if intraperitoneal damage is present.

Classification of Renal Injuries

Many classification systems for renal injuries have been used such as the one shown in Figure 7-1. In addition, the three categories proposed by Hodges, Gilbert, and Scott are widely used and are based on the patient's clinical condition and radiographic findings[38]:

1. Grade I (minor injuries) includes simple contusions and confined small lacerations with intact capsule. Clinical signs are stable, and intravenous pyelography or CT findings are normal or show minimal injury. This type of injury is the most common.
2. Grade II (major injuries) includes lacerations with extension through the renal capsule with or without involvement of the pyelocaliceal system or

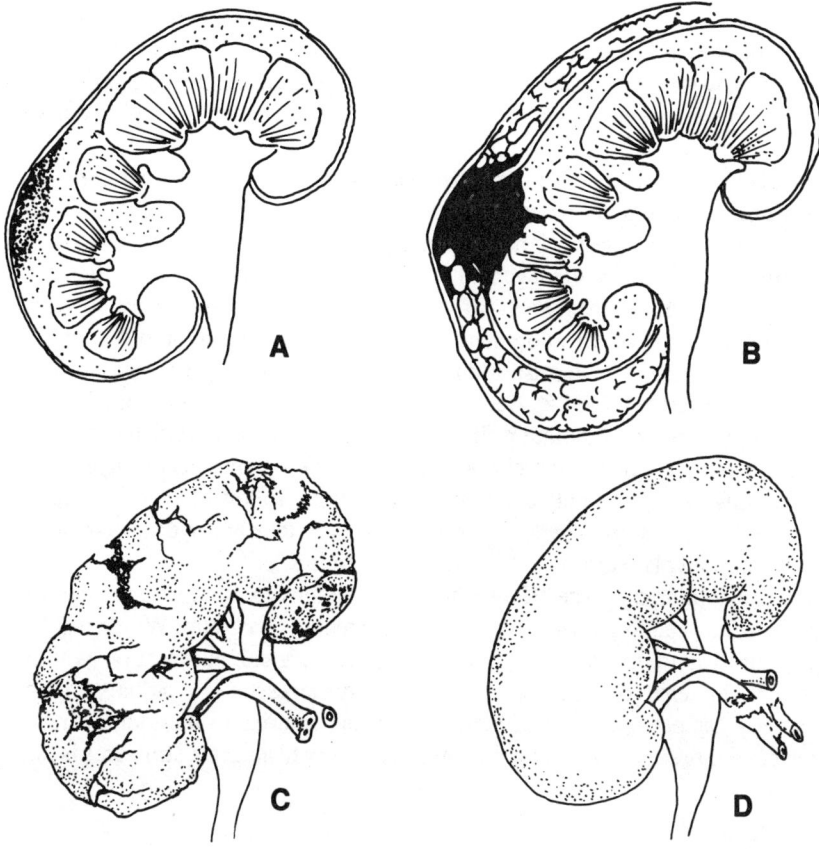

Figure 7-1 Classification of Renal Injuries. (**A**) Subcapsular hematoma, usually associated with renal contusions. (**B**) Renal cortical laceration with hematoma extending into the perirenal space. (**C**) Multiply fractured kidney; nephrectomy is frequently indicated for this type of injury. (**D**) Renal pedicle injury with avulsion of artery and vein. *Source*: Reprinted from *Traumatic Injuries of the Genitourinary System* by W.S. McDaugal and L. Persky, p. 115, with permission of Williams & Wilkins Company, © 1981.

---

extrarenal extravasation. These injuries are also associated with stable clinical signs.
3. Grade III (critical injuries) includes major vascular injuries, shattered kidneys, or injuries associated with uncontrollable hemorrhage or unstable clinical signs (or both).

Management

Approximately 85 percent of kidney injuries are minor and can be managed nonoperatively. Management consists of bed rest, symptomatic care, and observation including frequent monitoring of vital signs; serial determinations of hematocrit, blood urea nitrogen, and creatinine levels; and urinalysis. Hematuria (gross or microscopic) may persist for up to 1 month, but prolonged restricted activity is not needed.[39] Healing proceeds rapidly with minimal scarring because the general architecture of the kidney is preserved and because bleeding is contained by Gerota's fascia. Delayed sequelae are rare.

The remaining 15 percent of injuries are major or critical injuries, one-third of which require immediate exploration because of associated abdominal injuries.[40] The management of patients with grade II injuries remains controversial. The trend is toward conservative, nonoperative management because careful management results in kidney salvage in 80 percent to 90 percent of cases.[41–43] The child is closely observed and managed in an intensive care unit setting. Relatively high urine output is maintained initially by intravenous administration of fluids and then by oral fluids once any associated ileus has resolved.[44] Bed rest is mandatory until hematuria clears and is followed by progressive ambulation. If clinical deterioration with evidence of increasing blood loss occurs, surgical intervention may be necessary. Intravenous pyelography is used for follow-up assessment. In addition, patients are followed over the long term to evaluate for hypertension. The long-term risk of hypertension, hydronephrosis, infection, and parenchymal atrophy is difficult to determine.[45,46]

Critical renal injuries (grade III) are the least common type of injury, and there is little dispute as to the need for early operative management in this group. With renal vascular injuries, survival of the affected kidney requires surgical intervention within 4 to 6 hours. A shattered or fragmented kidney may necessitate a partial or complete nephrectomy for persistent blood loss. Penetrating injuries to the kidney are rare in children but require surgical exploration because injury to adjacent structures is likely.[47]

Ureteral Injuries

Traumatic disruption of the ureter from the renal pelvis is a rare injury because the ureteropelvic junction is deep in the retroperitoneum and is protected by the paraspinal muscle and the spine. Because penetrating injuries are rare in children, the mechanism of injury is usually extreme hyperextension of the trunk caused by sudden acceleration or deceleration. The great elasticity and mobility of the child's spine makes such an injury possible, whereas in the adult the degree of hyperextension necessary to tear the ureter is usually lethal.[48] Blunt ureteral injuries are often associated with vertebral fractures and central nervous system, renal, bladder, and other visceral injuries.[49]

Signs of ureteral injury are flank pain and an enlarging flank mass. Hematuria is an unreliable sign because it is not present in all patients and may be transient or only microscopic.

Ureteral injuries are frequently overlooked in the initial assessment of the trauma patient. The intravenous pyelogram may not always demonstrate extravasation, especially if there is poor visualization of the collecting system or if delayed films are not taken. Retrograde pyelography may be necessary for diagnosis.[50,51]

Management is always operative. Surgical repair usually involves reanastomosis of the ureter. Urinary diversion, either temporary or permanent, is sometimes necessary. If recognized early and treated appropriately, ureteral injuries usually heal well without significant sequelae. If recognition is delayed, however, repair is complicated by scarring, fibrosis, and ureteral strictures and fistulas.[52]

Bladder Injuries

A child's bladder is vulnerable to rupture because it is more of an abdominal than a pelvic organ, especially when full. Most bladder injuries are secondary to severe blunt trauma. Occasionally, penetrating injuries to the suprapubic area may lacerate the bladder. Bladder injuries frequently occur in association with other organ injuries, particularly pelvic fractures and renal injuries. The mortality rate in patients with a ruptured bladder is high (up to 60 percent), usually as a result of severe associated injuries.[53,54] Delay in diagnosis and treatment after 24 hours greatly increases the mortality rate.[55]

The bladder may rupture intraperitoneally or extraperitoneally. Intraperitoneal rupture usually occurs at the bladder dome when the bladder is full at the time of trauma. This results in signs of peritonitis with azotemia and acidosis. Extraperitoneal rupture occurs at the bladder neck and results in more subtle findings. Difficulty in voiding, incontinence, lower abdominal pain, suprapubic tenderness, and hematuria should raise the suspicion of extraperitoneal rupture. Bladder injuries frequently are overlooked because of associated injuries and the sometimes subtle findings.

Diagnosis is best made by cystography. In the male, retrograde urethrography should be done before any attempt is made to pass a catheter because of the high degree of association between bladder injury and urethral injury.[56,57] A plain film of the abdomen may show evidence of intraperitoneal fluid or a pelvic fracture.

Treatment varies with the degree and type of injury. Minor extraperitoneal extravasation may be treated with catheter drainage and antibiotic coverage only. Large extravasation injuries require closure of the defect and suprapubic cystostomy.[58] Once repaired, bladder injuries usually heal well without significant complications.

Urethral Injuries

Injury to the urethra most commonly results from pelvic fractures, straddle injuries, or urethral manipulation. Most injuries occur in males, whose urethra is longer and less well protected than that of females. Proximal urethral injuries are generally associated with pelvic fractures, and distal injuries are almost always secondary to a straddle injury.[59,60]

Blood at the meatus, urinary retention, lower abdominal or pelvic pain, and external evidence of lower abdominal or perineal trauma are all signs of urethral injury. Extravasation of blood and urine may be visible as fluid accumulates in the scrotum or penis in the male or labia in the female. Rectal examination revealing a superiorly positioned prostate in the male, or a soft mass in the female, helps confirm such a diagnosis.

When a urethral injury is suspected, it is important that a urethral catheter not be inserted. Catheterization may convert a partial tear into a complete one or may disrupt a pelvic hematoma. Retrograde urethrography should be performed to determine the location and extent of the damage.

A great deal of controversy remains in the management of these injuries. One form of therapy involves the creation of a suprapubic cystostomy with no attempt to repair the urethral disruption. After 3 to 6 months, the resultant stricture is repaired. Another option involves primary repair of the urethral injury, leaving a urethral catheter in place as a stint for 14 to 21 days. There are advantages and disadvantages to each form of therapy. Complications include impotence, incontinence, strictures, fistulas, chordee, diverticula, and salpingitis.[61,62]

Genital Injuries

The genitalia can be injured in various ways, including motor vehicle accidents, sporting activities, accidental mutilation, burns, and sexual abuse. Genital injuries are not uncommon in the child; however, most of these injuries are not serious.[63]

Blunt trauma can result from straddle injuries, falls, kicks, or other trauma. These injuries can be painful, and swelling, ecchymosis, and hematoma are common. Small scrotal and vaginal hematomas are usually treated conservatively, whereas large hematomas may need to be surgically explored. Treatment of crush injuries depends on their severity. Minor injuries are managed with ice packs and analgesics, and more severe injuries may require pressure dressings to control swelling and bleeding.[64] Catheterization may be required, but associated urethral trauma should be excluded by physical examination and urethrogram if necessary.

Fracture of the corpus cavernosum in young males is rare but requires surgical repair. Penile deviation, marked swelling, and hematoma are visible with this injury.[65] Testicular injuries are also rare in prepubertal males because of the small size and mobility of the child's testicles. Scrotal ultrasonography may be used to assess for a ruptured testicle. If ultrasound is positive, the testicle should be explored on an emergency basis.[66]

Various injuries in both sexes can result from sexual abuse. These include severe bruising and perineal tears, abrasions and hematomas on the penile shaft, anal fissures, and lacerations of the anal canal or vagina. Sexual abuse should be suspected in any child with injuries inconsistent with the history or type and degree of genital injury. A thorough physical examination should be performed, preferably under general anesthesia. Careful documentation of the injuries is essential, with photographs if possible. Specimens should be collected both for semen identification and bacterial cultures for sexually transmitted diseases.

NOTES

1. N.E. Peterson, "Apparent Exceptions to the Usual Patterns in Renal Trauma," *Journal of Urology* 121(1979):489.
2. John Barrett, "Penetrating Abdominal Trauma," *Trauma Quarterly* 1(August 1985):55–61.

3. Ibid., 57.

4. Julie Mull Strange, "Abdominal Trauma," in Virginia D. Cardona, ed., *Trauma Nursing* (Oradell, N.J.: Medical Economics Books, 1987).

5. Eduardo M. Suson, Donald Klotz, Jr., and Peter K. Kottmeier, "Liver Trauma in Children," *Journal of Pediatric Surgery* 10(1975):411.

6. Peterson, "Apparent Exceptions to the Usual Patterns in Renal Trauma," 490.

7. William L. Buntain, Frank P. Lynch, and Max L. Ramenofsky, "Management of the Acutely Injured Child," in Kimball I. Maull, ed., *Advances in Trauma*, vol. 2 (Chicago: Year Book Medical Publishers, Inc., 1987), 43–86.

8. S.S. Gallagher et al. "The Incidence of Injuries Among 87,000 Massachusetts Children and Adolescents: Results of the 1980–81 Statewide Childhood Injury Prevention Program Surveillance System," *American Journal of Public Health* 74(1984):1340–47.

9. Judy A. Estroff and Johan G. Blickman, "Imaging in Pediatric Abdominal Trauma," *Emergency Care Quarterly* 3(February 1988):48.

10. Barbara Bennett Jacobs and Lenworth M. Jacobs, Jr., "Anatomy of the Abdomen," *Emergency Care Quarterly* 3(February 1988):7.

11. Nabil N. Jacir and Martin R. Eichelberger, "Pediatric Abdominal Trauma," in Randall E. Marcus, ed., *Trauma in Children* (Rockville, Md.: Aspen Publishers, Inc., 1986), 69–74.

12. Barbara Bennett Jacobs and Lenworth J. Jacobs, Jr., "Assessment of the Abdomen," *Emergency Care Quarterly* 3(February 1988):15.

13. Buntain et al., "Management of the Acutely Injured Child," 43–86.

14. Joshua M. Careskey, "Abdominal Trauma in Children," *Indiana Medicine* (April 1985):283–86.

15. Buntain et al., "Management of the Acutely Injured Child," 43–86.

16. Ibid.

17. Jacir and Eichelberger, "Pediatric Abdominal Trauma," 69–74.

18. Ibid.

19. M.O. Koch and W.S. McDougal, "Genitourinary Trauma in Children," in Randall E. Marcus, ed., *Trauma in Children* (Rockville, Md.: Aspen Publishers, Inc., 1986), 77–97.

20. S.J.M. Monstrey et al., "Urological Trauma and Severe Associated Injuries," *British Journal of Urology* 60(1987):393–98.

21. Koch and McDougal, "Genitourinary Trauma in Children," 77–97.

22. Thom A. Mayer, "Initial Evaluation and Management of the Injured Child," in *Emergency Management of Pediatric Trauma*, ed. Thom A. Mayer (Philadelphia: W.B. Saunders Company, 1985), pp. 1–38.

23. T.S. Morse, "Renal Injuries," in R.J. Touloukian, ed., *Pediatric Trauma* (New York: John Wiley & Sons, 1978), 461–72.

24. Mayer, "Initial Evaluation and Management," 1–38.

25. Ibid.

26. Koch and McDougal, "Genitourinary Trauma in Children," 77–97.

27. Ibid.

28. M.P. Karp et al., "The Role of Computed Tomography in the Evaluation of Blunt Abdominal Trauma in Children," *Journal of Pediatric Surgery* 16(1981):316–23.

29. M.P. Federle et al., "Computed Tomography in Blunt Abdominal Trauma," *Archives of Surgery* 117(1982):645–50.

30. T.S. Morse and B.H. Harris, "Non-Penetrating Renal Vascular Injuries," *Journal of Trauma* 13(1973):497.

31. Morse, "Renal Injuries," 461–72.

32. R.G. Middleteon et al., "Genitourinary Injuries in Children," in T.A. Meyer, ed., *Emergency Management of Pediatric Trauma* (Philadelphia, Penn.: W.B. Saunders, 1985), 341–52.
33. N. Javalpour, P. Guinam, and I.M. Bush, "Renal Trauma in Children," *Surgery Gynecology and Obstetrics* 136(1973):237–45.
34. P.M. Livne and E.T. Gonzales, "Genitourinary Trauma in Children," *Urology Clinics of North America* 12(1985):53–64.
35. Middleteon et al., "Genitourinary Injuries in Children," 341–52.
36. Monstrey et al., "Urological Trauma," 393–98.
37. W.A. Mandour et al., "Blunt Renal Trauma in the Pediatric Patient," *Journal of Pediatric Surgery* 16(1981):669–76.
38. C. Hodges, D. Gilbert, and W. Scott, "Renal Trauma: A Study of 71 Cases," *Journal of Urology* 66(1951):627–31.
39. Middleteon et al., "Genitourinary Injuries in Children," 341–52.
40. Livne and Gonzales, "Genitourinary Trauma in Children," 53–64.
41. Buntain et al., "Management of the Acutely Injured Child," 43–86.
42. Mandour et al., "Blunt Renal Trauma," 669–76.
43. S.C. Evins, W.B. Thompson, and R. Rosenblum, "Non-Operative Management of Severe Renal Lacerations," *Journal of Urology* 123(1980):247–52.
44. Buntain et al., "Management of the Acutely Injured Child," 43–86.
45. Ibid.
46. Middleteon et al., "Genitourinary Injuries in Children," 341–52.
47. Ibid.
48. E.F. Reda and R.L. Lebowitz, "Traumatic Ureteropelvic Disruption in the Child," *Pediatric Radiology* 16(1986):164–66.
49. Koch and McDougal, "Genitourinary Trauma in Children," 77–97.
50. Ibid.
51. Livne and Gonzales, "Genitourinary Trauma in Children," 53–64.
52. Reda and Lebowitz, "Traumatic Ureteropelvic Disruption," 164–66.
53. J. McConnel, M. Wilkerson, and P. Peter, "Rupture of the Bladder," *Urologic Clinics of North America* 9(1982):293–96.
54. W.G. Guerrieru, "Trauma to the Kidneys, Ureters, Bladder, and Urethra," *Surgical Clinics of North America* 62(1982):1047–58.
55. A. Cass, "Bladder Trauma in the Multiply Injured Patient," *Journal of Urology* 115(1974):667–70.
56. Middleteon et al., "Genitourinary Injuries in Children," 341–52.
57. Livne and Gonzales, "Genitourinary Trauma in Children," 53–64.
58. Buntain et al., "Management of the Acutely Injured Child," 43–86.
59. Middleteon et al., "Genitourinary Injuries in Children," 341–52.
60. Livne and Gonzales, "Genitourinary Trauma in Children," 53–64.
61. Koch and McDougal, "Genitourinary Trauma in Children," 77–97.
62. Livne and Gonzales, "Genitourinary Trauma in Children," 53–64.
63. D. Muram, "Genital Tract Injuries in the Prepubertal Child," *Pediatric Annals* 15(1986):616–20.
64. G.T. Kauber, "Genitourinary Trauma in Children," *Emergency Care Quarterly* 3(1987):51–56.
65. Middleteon et al., "Genitourinary Injuries in Children," 341–52.
66. Kauber, "Genitourinary Trauma in Children," 51–56.

Chapter 8

Musculoskeletal Trauma

Connie Joy

Children are different from adults. This concept has been well established in all clinical fields of nursing and medicine and certainly holds true in the area of childhood musculoskeletal trauma. The reaction of an injured child differs from that of an adult both physiologically and psychologically. Musculoskeletal trauma is one of the areas in which these differences are most pronounced.

A child is a continually growing organism. Much of the most visibly apparent growth occurs within the musculoskeletal system and is most striking in the years from infancy through puberty. Orthopedic injury during childhood carries with it the risk of devastating, lifelong consequences. Injuries to upper extremities may have critical effects on both fine and coarse body movements, self-sufficient functioning, and important sensory requirements. Lower limb injury can result in a loss of functions that are performed automatically and yet are essential to mobility. Limb length inequality after pelvic or lower limb trauma may be much more disabling than length inequality in the upper limbs. The treatment of musculoskeletal injuries that occur during childhood must therefore be aimed toward allowing the growth process to continue with as little interruption as possible.

MECHANISMS OF INJURY

Orthopedic trauma is the most common childhood surgical emergency and is second only to soft tissue injury in overall trauma frequency.[1] The mechanism of orthopedic trauma involves either external forces acting on the body and bony structure itself, as with a direct impact, or internal forces caused by muscle contraction or ligament tension, as with a bending force. Bone breakage occurs because of the application of a loading force to the bone.[2] A fracture indicates that the ability of the bone to store and dissipate energy by temporary deformation has been exceeded. The major factors that determine the deformation potential and fracture resistance of a bone are

- the direction, magnitude, and rate of force application
- the size and shape of the bone

- the natural properties of the tissue that makes up the bone
- any previously existing defects that reduce the strength of the bone.

Loading forces are important to understand when discussing orthopedic injury. The types of applied forces that can result in bone fracture include bending, tension, compression, torsional, and combined loading. A loading force can be applied along the bone's long axis (axial loading) or transversely across the bone. In addition, the magnitude and rate of load application greatly determine the bone deformation.

Children are highly susceptible to musculoskeletal trauma largely because of their participation in typical activities of childhood. Falls are an extremely common cause of fractures, including falls from great heights, which are most frequently seen in urban settings.[3] Compared with adults, children spend more time running, climbing, and jumping, which leads to a greater number of musculoskeletal injuries, particularly when activities are combined with a comparatively limited appreciation for risk and danger. Additionally, with the advent of motorized tricycles and increased use of trail bikes, emergency departments are treating orthopedic injuries that are increasingly complex, extensive, and mutilating.[4]

Sports-related injuries are also of concern, although children have different injury patterns and severities from those of adults. This is due to the child's immature skeleton, different bone tissue properties, and smaller body mass.[5]

The most serious injuries tend to occur in motor vehicle accidents, when the child presents with either isolated bony and soft tissue injury or multisystem trauma. As an unrestrained motor vehicle occupant, a child can easily be tossed around the interior, ricochetting off its fixed structures multiple times. Often, because of their small size and body weight, children are catapulted from a motor vehicle with a long-distance trajectory that results in significant force on final impact.

The child pedestrian usually sustains injuries to the chest and femur when struck by the bumper and hood of a car. Head injuries as well as upper and lower extremity injuries result when the child collides with the ground after being struck. This mechanism is called Waddell's triad.[6]

Fractures are a common manifestation of child abuse and, are second in frequency only to injuries of the skin.[7] The probability that a fracture has been caused by intentional rather than accidental injury must be carefully considered on the basis of the correlation of the physical findings with the clinical history.

SPECIAL CONSIDERATIONS OF MUSCULOSKELETAL INJURIES IN CHILDREN

Comparison of Injury Types

Fractures are more common than dislocations, muscle sprains, and torn ligaments. Fractures are a common occurrence within the pediatric age group both as isolated injuries and in combination with other injured body systems. This is directly related to the strength and tolerance of living tissue when it undergoes impact. Throughout normal childhood development, the muscles, ligaments, and tendons are strong and resilient and are able to withstand the sudden extension that occurs with injury. The combination of slender bones and ligament attachments that are stronger than their associated bony structures results in more fractures than torn muscle tissues. In the adult, the stretching of less accommodating musculoskeletal tissue results in sprains, strains, and tears. For example, the type of injury that would produce torn ligaments and soft tissue damage in the knee of the adult can result in displaced epiphyseal fractures involving the distal femoral and proximal tibial epiphyses of the child.

Many types of fractures that occur frequently in childhood, such as greenstick, hairline, or buckle fractures, are not serious and with proper treatment heal well. Nevertheless, fractures involving intra-articular epiphyseal plate structures are considered serious and have the potential for permanent growth disruption.

Blood Loss

Children are less tolerant than adults of blood loss associated with musculoskeletal injuries. The blood volume of a child is based on the calculation of 80 to 85 mL per kilogram of body weight. Although the blood volume is proportionally less in children than in adults, blood volume represents a larger percentage of blood volume per kilogram.

One major concern related to blood loss, be it from musculoskeletal or other system injury, is that the most typical mechanism of trauma in children is by far blunt impact, so that severe external hemorrhage usually occurs much less frequently than in the adult trauma population. Therefore, recognition of internal blood loss requires critical judgment and a solid understanding of the subtle changes that can occur with incipient bleeding.

Internal bleeding resulting in significant blood loss occurs most commonly in five body areas as a result of a lack of nearby anatomical structures that would serve to apply pressure or tamponade bleeding within each area. These areas are (1) chest, (2) abdomen, (3) retroperitoneal spaces, (4) pelvis, and (5) thighs. Blood loss in the thigh related to a femur fracture can be particularly misleading because significant amounts of blood can be distributed up and down the long axis of the femur with little or no external evidence. Visible changes in thigh size may be attributed to fracture-related soft tissue swelling rather than blood volume loss. Circumferential measurements of both thighs should be made soon after the patient's admission to the emergency department and should be checked frequently against the baseline measurement. Even small changes in the circumference of the thigh may indicate a large percentage of total blood volume lost. One point to keep in mind is that concealed hemorrhage from multiple fractures may be the sole cause of shock in a child.

Diagnosis

One of the challenges in working with injured children is sorting through and identifying symptoms and piecing them together to formulate an accurate diagnosis. Frequently, children with minor injuries present without clearly defined complaints or with symptoms that change. Fearing increased pain at the hands of the medical or nursing staff, the child may deny or minimize the injury or may actually attempt to prevent any physical examination of the injured area. In addition, fractures or other injuries often occur during activities that parents have warned against, or the injury may have been inflicted by a parent or other adult caretaker. The child, fearing punishment, may change or deny the mechanism of injury, making accurate assessment even harder. Young children, especially toddlers, are notoriously difficult to examine and may say that their foot hurts when actually the site of the injury is the lower or even upper leg.

Radiological examination for fractures in children is by no means foolproof and should not be considered the only initial diagnostic measure. A history should be obtained and physical assessment with immediate immobilization of the injured area should be done before any radiological studies are performed. The site of injury should be determined as specifically as possible by observing for deformity, swelling, and abnormal neurosensory and circulatory findings distal to the suspected area of injury. This determination is important to avoid unnecessary or inappropriate radiological studies. Positioning and adequate immobilization of the child during the studies is often a challenge, and unsuccessful attempts can lead to misdiagnosis due to poor-quality films and a delay in definitive treatment.

Even with adequate radiographic examination, the normal bony changes that occur throughout childhood, such as the appearance of various epiphyseal plates and centers of secondary ossification, can easily be misinterpreted as fracture lines. If major difficulty is encountered in diagnosis, one of the easiest and best methods is to compare the uninjured limb to the injured one in both clinical and radiological examinations.

Whenever a child has been critically injured, priorities must be set that appropriately delay the treatment of non–life-threatening injuries. This may result in diagnostic delays or missed recognition of musculoskeletal injuries that may lead to significant morbidity.[8] Any suspicion of injury identified during the acute resuscitation process must be meticulously followed up to ensure adequate diagnosis and management.

Special Types of Fractures Limited to Children

Birth Fractures

The clavicle bone of a newborn is the most frequently fractured bone: fracture typically occurs during the difficult delivery of a large, broad-shouldered newborn. A lack of movement of one arm is the most apparent sign during the first hours after birth. Splinting the affected arm against the body with a sling and bandage wrap is the best management; callus formation typically occurs within 10 days.

The humerus is the next most commonly fractured bone in the newborn. Lack of arm movement combined with a history of a difficult breech delivery should lead to the suspicion of a humeral shaft fracture. Again, bandaging the arm to the chest for a period of 2 weeks allows the fracture clinically to unite satisfactorily.

Femur shaft fractures or traumatic separation of either the distal or the proximal femoral epiphysis are most likely to occur during the frank breech delivery of a newborn. Midshaft femur fractures are usually clinically apparent because of deformity and lack of normal leg-toward-torso movement. Bryant's skin traction is usually used for this injury for a period of approximately 3 weeks with good outcome. Separation of femoral epiphyseal plates is usually more difficult to detect, but with appropriate immobilization the child has a good prognosis for continued normal growth.

Spinal fractures occurring during the birthing process are rare but can be associated with complete and permanent paraplegia.

Epiphyseal Plate Fractures

As stated earlier, the child is a growing organism. Musculoskeletal injury in the child carries with it the risk of local growth disturbance and permanent growth arrest, potentially resulting in bony deformity and lifelong disability. The reasons for this are related to the unique anatomical aspects of the normal child's musculoskeletal system, specifically the epiphyseal growth plates at the proximal and distal ends of the long bones. These areas are responsible for much of the longitudinal growth of the child. Until full growth is obtained, when these areas of cartilage are transformed into dense bone, epiphyseal plate fractures should be suspected in any child who has received an injury and displays clinical symptoms suggestive of a fracture near the end of a long bone.[9] Diagnosis of these fractures is made by careful radiological examination (Table 8-1).

Healing

The simple statement "The younger the child, the faster the healing" is particularly true for musculoskeletal injuries. This is primarily related to the vigorous osteogenic activity that occurs within pediatric bone, which progressively decreases with age. For example, a femoral shaft fracture in an 8-year-old child typically unites within 8 weeks, whereas in an adult older than 20 years of age a comparable injury takes 20 weeks to heal.[10]

The union of epiphyseal plate fractures, specifically types I, II, and III, takes only half the time required for the healing of a fracture through the metaphysis of the same bone in the same child.

INITIAL MANAGEMENT OF THE CHILD WITH MULTISYSTEM INJURY

State-of-the-art trauma resuscitation requires an organized, planned approach that emphasizes the recognition and resolution of the most immediately life-threatening problems without delaying the management of less significant but important injuries. The key to the principles involved in pediatric trauma resuscitation, particularly relating to musculoskeletal injury, is that priority management need never compromise complete management.

A standard approach to trauma resuscitation is particularly important with children for several reasons.

Table 8-1 Salter and Harris's Classification of Epiphyseal Plate Fractures

Type	Description	Management	Prognosis
I	Complete epiphyseal separation without fracture. Most common in younger children with thick epiphyseal plates.	Closed reduction and cast immobilization.	Excellent unless the blood supply to the epiphysis is compromised.
II	Most common epiphyseal fracture. Separation of epiphyseal plate with a fracture through the metaphysis, producing a triangular fragment.	Closed reduction and cast immobilization.	Excellent unless the blood supply to the epiphysis is compromised.
III	Fracture through part of the epiphyseal plate and extending into the joint.	Open reduction and internal fixation usually required.	Good, with restoration of normal joint surface and vascularity.
IV	Fracture completely through the epiphyseal plate and extending through a portion of the metaphysis.	Open reduction and internal fixation.	At risk for interrupted longitudinal growth unless there is perfect anatomic alignment, which must be maintained until complete healing.
V	Crush injury to an area of the epiphyseal plate that is nondisplaced with no fracture line visible on roentgenography.	Immobilization and non-weight bearing for a minimum of 3 weeks to prevent further compression.	Poor. Injury is frequently identified only in retrospect after growth disturbance has occurred.

1. The distinction between localized and multisystem trauma may be difficult to determine initially. The type of mechanism of injury in an adult that would produce a single system injury may, in a small child, result in several body systems being injured simply because of their close proximity. One example of diagnostic difficulty in children is that severe pain from a leg fracture may mask symptoms of an injured abdomen.
2. The mechanism of injury in a child is most often blunt rather than penetrating, so that some serious injuries can be easily overlooked because they are less obvious at first.
3. Children can be difficult to examine because of their age, growth and development factors, and reaction to injury. In addition, practitioners' emotional reaction to a critically injured child, especially one in whom there has been significant anatomical rearrangement, can lead to major distraction, thus increasing the risk of not recognizing and treating a significant finding.

The key concept in trauma resuscitation is that the patient must be stabilized in a stepwise fashion, with each step secured before directing attention to other problems. The approach that is most useful is a primary and secondary assessment survey, which guides the practitioner through a comprehensive systematic evaluation. Without the primary and secondary survey guidelines, a hit-or-miss approach is used that could lead to the risk of delayed identification of injuries.

There are two goals common to all members of any pediatric trauma team as they work together to perform the initial stabilization of a critically injured child: (1) the immediate interruption of the dynamic dying process of a critically injured child, and (2) the prevention of disabilities. Although orthopedic trauma is rarely life threatening, it can be a major contributing factor to the prolonged instability of the patient. Most certainly, musculoskeletal injury can be limb threatening and can result in lifelong disability. For this reason, the second goal listed is important to keep in mind with orthopedic injuries. The ultimate function of an extremity or joint is much more important than the anatomically correct reduction of fracture fragments.

A comprehensive evaluation of the musculoskeletal system takes place during the secondary survey, and emphasis is placed on determining immediate and acceptably delayed interventions. A systematic head-to-toe assessment should be performed with simultaneous examination of the skin. Visual examination combined with physical manipulation of each bone and joint is necessary to provide adequate information. Findings that are important to identify and document include

- estimated blood loss attributable to each injury identified
- neural or vascular deficit distal to an injury
- open wound with fracture between joints or at a joint
- visible deformity, shortening, or angulation of a limb
- partial loss of a digit or limb
- complete loss of a digit or limb

- continued expansion of limb circumference
- positive pelvic crunch sign
- crush injury
- any injury suspected of resulting in compartment syndrome
- abnormal muscle or tendon function (or both)
- point tenderness or muscle spasms (or both)
- ecchymosis
- swelling
- crepitus
- abnormal movement between joints or at a joint.

Once an injury has been identified, the first priority is to estimate blood loss. Accurate assessment of the distal neurovascular status of all limbs, including color, capillary refill, temperature, pulses, sensation, movement, and level of pain, should follow soon after (Exhibits 8-1 and 8-2 and Table 8-2). Similar assessment should be performed after any treatment, including temporary splinting. Baseline assessments should be documented, with continued recording of injured extremity assessments to allow for trending. A neurovascular assessment flow sheet, which may be included on a general trauma flow sheet, can be helpful for this purpose (Exhibit 8-3).

Pulses should be identified and assessed both above and below the injured area. The use of an ultrasound doppler may be helpful if pulses are weak or nonpalpable or if the patient is an infant.

Significant findings should be communicated to the other members of the trauma team so that they will be alerted and cautious around that body area during resuscitation.

Exhibit 8-1 Peripheral Pulse Evaluation

> 0—Absent
> 1—Weakly palpable
> 2—Palpable
> 3—Strongly palpable
> 4—Bounding

Exhibit 8-2 Motor Strength Evaluation

> 5—100 percent strength; normal, complete range of motion against gravity and resistance
> 4—75 percent strength; good, complete range of motion against gravity and some resistance
> 3—50 percent strength; fair motion against gravity (without resistance)
> 2—25 percent strength; poor motion against gravity (without resistance)
> 1—10 percent strength; evidence of muscular contractility with no joint movement
> 0—None

Table 8-2 Nerve Function Evaluation

Nerve	Sensation	Motion
Peroneal	Prick web space between great toe and second toe.	Have child dorsiflex ankle and extend toes at metatarsal phalangeal joints.
Tibial	Prick medial lateral surface of sole of foot.	Have child plantar-flex ankle and flex toes.
Radial	Prick web space between thumb and index finger.	Have child hyperextend thumb, then wrist, then the four fingers at metacarpal phalangeal joints.
Ulnar	Prick distal end of small finger.	Have child abduct all fingers with fingers flexed.
Median	Prick distal surface of index finger.	Have child oppose thumb and little finger and flex wrist.

Appropriate management should be undertaken and planning begun as to the definitive treatment.

MANAGEMENT OF SPECIFIC MUSCULOSKELETAL INJURIES

Fractures

A clean break with two intact principle bone fragments, usually resulting from low-magnitude, slowly applied force loading, is considered a simple fracture. A comminuted fracture is a complete break with three or more fragments that typically results from rapidly applied, high-magnitude force loading.[11] Comminution of a fracture indicates an increased amount of surrounding soft tissue damage due to greater displacement of bone.

Fractures in which there is no break in skin integrity at the fracture site are considered closed. Treatment is anatomical alignment with adequate splinting applied for a length of time that is dependent on the type and location of the fracture. In open fractures, the skin over the fracture site is broken. A bone spike can penetrate the skin from within, or the skin can be punctured from without by the object causing the fracture. An open fracture is a contaminated wound and is considered an emergency and prompt surgery is indicated. It is helpful to grade the fracture to gain a clear understanding of the degree of injury.

Primary management of open fractures includes obtaining a wound culture, applying a sterile dressing, and administering tetanus toxoid if deemed necessary from the child's immunization record. Intravenous antibiotics, such as one of the cephalosporins and penicillin, are started in the emergency department. The child is then taken to the operating room for aggressive wound irrigation, meticulous débridement, and fracture alignment. Fracture stabilization may be accomplished by means of conventional closed-plaster cast techniques, internal fixation, or external fixation depending on the fracture pattern, location, degree of soft tissue injury, and the type and severity of other injuries that the child may have sustained.

Exhibit 8-3 Neurovascular Assessment Flow Sheet

NEUROVASCULAR ASSESSMENT

Time	Initial	Extremity	Color	Capillary Refill	Temperature	Pulse	Edema	Sensation	Movement	Other	Pain Level (0–4)

Key:

Extremity:
Right Arm —RA
Left Arm —LA
Right Leg —RL
Left Leg —LL
Bilateral Upper —BU
Bilateral Lower —BL
All Extremities —ALL

Neurovascular:
Color .... pink —Pk
Capillary Refill ..... rapid —Rpd
Temperature ...... warm —Wm
Pulse .... strong —Stg
Edema .... absent —Abs
Sensation .... good —Gd
Movement .... present —Pres
Pain Level 0–4   0: none   to   4: severe

pale —Pl   blue —Bl
sluggish —Sl   absent —Abs
cold —Cld   hot —Ht
weak —Wk   absent —Abs
mild —Mld   severe —Sev
tingling —Tng   numbness —Nb
absent —Abs

Fracture lines can extend in several different fashions and are either complete (when the fracture fragments are separated) or incomplete (when some portion of the fracture fragments remain attached).[12] An example of an incomplete fracture is a greenstick fracture, which occurs when the bone is angulated beyond the limits of its bending capability, resulting in a partial separation of the bone through the bone shaft. Other fracture lines are transverse (running crosswise, at a right angle to the long axis of the bone), oblique (running at a slant along the long axis), and spiral (running in a circular, slanting direction around the bone shaft).

Upper Extremity Fractures

Upper extremity bones are the most frequently fractured during childhood. Most of these fractures can be appropriately treated without interfering with the comprehensive management required for the multiply injured child. Nevertheless, upper extremity fractures can become a major source of functional disability when the special requirements of pediatric orthopedic injury management are not recognized.

The Shoulder (Clavicle, Scapula, and Proximal Humerus). The clavicle is the most frequently fractured bone during the developmental years of childhood.[13] Fractures typically involve the midportion of the bone, although they can occur anywhere. Mechanisms of injury related to clavicular fractures range from lateral compression during a difficult delivery to a simple fall on to an outstretched arm. Incomplete fractures are more common in the younger age group; older children most often sustain complete clavicular fractures. Clinical findings range from lack of arm movement in the infant to crepitation on palpation, deformity, pain, and tenderness.

Unless there is clinical evidence of vascular injury or neurovascular complication, such as damage to the subclavian vessels, most clavicular fractures can be treated easily.[14] A clavicle strap, currently available in several sizes appropriate for young age groups, or a figure-of-eight bandage can be used to hold the fracture fragments relatively still. Within 10 to 14 days fracture callus forms in abundance. Grossly displaced clavicle fractures may require alignment by pulling the shoulders up and back before applying the figure-of-eight harness. Addition of plaster to the harness may be necessary to maintain desired positioning and immobilization.

The scapula is a highly mobile bone that is resilient to most trauma except perhaps severe, direct impact. A major concern when scapula fractures are diagnosed should be the certainty that related thoracic injuries, such as pneumothorax, rib fractures, or vertebral fractures, have been ruled out.[15] Management of the fracture itself is usually accomplished with simple immobilization of the shoulder.

Fractures of the proximal humerus most often occur in late childhood and early adolescence and are associated with athletic activities or a fall on an outstretched arm with ...e shoulder in full extension. Adduction and external rotation create a shearing force across the weakest surface in the shoulder area, which is the proximal humeral growth plate. The typical fracture is a type I or type II epiphyseal plate fracture.[16] In the adult, the same mechanism of injury would produce a dislocation of the shoulder; in the child, the joint capsule is stronger than the epiphyseal plate, resulting in the fracture.

Management of these fractures depends on the amount of displacement. Typically, minimal reduction may be necessary, and the involved arm can be supported in a sling or bandaged to the trunk with an elastic wrap. Immobilization should be ensured for 4 to 6 weeks for older children, with sports and rough play restricted for an additional month. Open reduction of these fractures may be considered with severely displaced epiphyseal fractures that are unresponsive to closed reduction or for children who are head injured and whose movements are uncontrollable.

Upper Arm (Humerus and Elbow). Humeral shaft fractures are not common in childhood and are the result of a fairly severe impact when they do occur. Often these fractures are unstable, with mobile proximal and distal bone fragments that can be moved easily by unknowing care providers. This type of fracture should be immediately splinted on its discovery, before radiographic examination, so that movement at the fracture site does not occur. This decreases the risk of further injury to nearby structures and assists in controlling pain. Radial nerve damage is a particular risk in a distal to midshaft humeral fracture.[17] The radial nerve wraps closely around the humerus in this area. Injury to the radial nerve may result in wrist drop and paralysis of finger extensors.

Management of humeral shaft fractures rarely requires open reduction. Severely displaced fractures may require continuous skeletal traction with a pin in the olecranon for a few weeks to maintain alignment and to correct rotation. Most fractures can be managed by closed reduction and a shoulder spica cast for about 6 weeks. Minimally displaced humerus fractures require no reduction and heal in 3 to 4 weeks with immobilization by a sling and trunk wrap bandage, which splints the arm to the chest.

Elbow fractures and dislocations are common injuries in children, and management can range from simple to extremely complex. The high incidence of complications related to elbow injuries indicates that a careful evaluation of motor function, sensation, and vascular status of the forearm and hand should be made soon after injury. The radiological examination of the elbow can be difficult because of the ossification centers contributing to the formation of the elbow joint that are unique to childhood. Normal growth plates along with secondary ossification centers for each articulating and nonarticulating bone can both appear and close at ages ranging from 1 year up to 20 years. Often, normal growth plates may be mistaken for fracture lines, and minimally displaced fractures are overlooked.[18] For example, the secondary ossification center at the proximal end of the ulna appears between ages 10 and 12 years and closes between ages 14 and 16 years. During that time, if an injury to that area is suspected, this normal growth center may be mistaken for a fracture of the proximal ulna and treated as such.

One of the most common childhood musculoskeletal injuries is a transient subluxation of the radial head, resulting in a "pulled elbow" or "nursemaid's elbow."[19] Preschool-aged children (1 through 5 years old) are most vulnerable, with the peak incidence being between ages 2 and 3 years. The history is typically classic, although parents or caretakers may be reluctant to discuss the occurrence leading to the injury. It is usually the result of a combination of traction and pronation forces that commonly occurs when a parent, older sibling, or other caretaker exerts a strong pull on the extended elbow. This lifting force placed on the joint, combined with the opposing force produced by the weight of the child, produces a tear in the distal attachment of the ligament to the radial neck. The radial head can then protrude partially through this tear, resulting in a pinched ligament and significant pain. Presentation of the child is also often classic. The child suddenly begins to cry, refuses to use the arm, and cradles the forearm with the elbow slightly flexed as if to protect it. Any passive motion attempted during examination is vigorously resisted. Roentgenographic studies of the elbow are usually normal.

Treatment of this type of minor injury is simple. Firm and quick supination of the forearm while the elbow is flexed allows the trapped ligament to escape from the joint, and the child experiences immediate relief. The use of a sling for 2 weeks is recommended to allow the tear in the ligament attachment to heal. One of the most important treatment aspects is teaching the parents about the harmful effects of pulling or lifting their child by the hand. Health care professionals must also be aware of families who continually present to the emergency department with the same problem and must recognize that the child may also be experiencing repeated injury in other ways.

Lower Arm (Radius-Ulna, Wrist, and Hand). Fractures of the radial and ulnar shafts are extremely common in childhood and occur most frequently in the distal metaphyseal region. These fractures often follow falls from trees, gymnastic and sports activities, and bicycle or motor vehicle accidents.[20] Incomplete fractures, such as buckle or greenstick fractures, are most commonly seen in young children, whereas complete fractures occur most often in older children and adolescents because their cortical bone assumes more adult characteristics.

In most cases, management of radius-ulna fractures can be accomplished successfully with a molded above-elbow plaster cast in place for 3 to 6 weeks. An additional 2 to 4 weeks' protection in a short arm cast or splint may be necessary, with the avoidance of all contact sports for up to 2 to 3 additional months.

All radius and ulna fractures should be evaluated closely for the potential development of increasing compartment pressure due to swelling in the closed fascial space of the forearm.[21] The development of Volkmann's ischemia and permanent neurological deficit due to median nerve or, less commonly, radial and ulnar nerve compression is a threat that management must take into account. Complete information related to the assessment and management of compartment syndrome is discussed later in this chapter.

The growth centers, or epiphyses, of the wrist and hand appear at regular intervals throughout the developmental process and are useful in determining skeletal age and in estimating overall growth potential. Fractures of the wrist and hand are most common during the early teenage years, with sports being a major cause. Boys sustain these fractures 70 percent of the time, with the frequency of right and left hand injury being equal.[22]

Carpal fractures commonly occur as a result of forceful hyperextension of the hand. Pain and tenderness on the radial side of the wrist after a fall on an outstretched hand should raise the suspicion of a carpal fracture. Protective splinting should be placed immediately, with a short arm cast maintained for 4 to 8 weeks. Typically, uncomplicated wrist fractures heal well, and posttraumatic carpal instability is rare.

Metacarpal fractures are usually a result of direct impact. Again, contact sports, such as football and basketball, and fistfights account for most hand fractures within the older age groups. Young children sustain hand fractures from getting their hands and fingers trapped in a closing door, beneath a falling object, or beneath an adult foot when playing on the floor. Simple fractures that are not displaced may be successfully treated with splinting and soft dressing for 3 to 4 weeks. Occasionally, open reduction and anatomic realignment of fragments with fine wire fixation is required for displaced fractures.[23]

Phalangeal fractures or dislocations in children are caused by mechanisms of injury similar to those described above. Displaced phalangeal shaft fractures may be difficult to treat by closed methods and may require open reduction and pinning.

Other common childhood finger injuries include crush injuries of the nail bed and finger tip avulsion or amputation. These occur with surprising frequency and may or may not be associated with a bone fracture. Nail bed hematomas require the placement of an opening through the nail to allow drainage. A protective dressing should be placed over the finger and the parents warned that the fingernail may be lost. If the nail bed is intact a new nail will grow out in 3 to 4 months, usually without disfigurement. Injuries of the tip of the finger may involve the soft tissue, nail, and bone and are treated in several ways, depending on the extent of the injury. In most cases, attempts are made to reconstruct the finger tip through primary management soon after injury or through secondary reconstruction, which may involve the use of tissue from other parts of the hand (as with a pedicle flap).[24]

As in the adult, the poorly managed hand injury in a child can result in lifelong limitations that may affect both work and life style; furthermore, the child must live with these limitations for many years more than an adult. The advantages of specialized care of hand injuries cannot be overemphasized. Extensor or flexor tendon injuries can occur with almost any type of hand injury, as can either sensory or motor nerve damage. Vascular injury of the hand is one of the most difficult to repair. Operative repair by means of microtechniques is available in many pediatric regional referral centers. The management of the injured hand before referral of the patient to a specialist is critical, and often the best approach is a somewhat limited one. Once bleeding has been controlled by direct pressure and circulation has been assessed by comparing the color of the injured side to that of the uninjured side, specialized care should be sought within 1 to 3 hours. It is best to do nothing other than dress the hand in a sterile dressing with an immobilizing splint, place the arm in a high sling, and transfer the child to the individual who will be providing definitive care.

Spinal Fractures

Fracture of spinal bone is the result of extraordinary trauma. Motor vehicle accidents, falls, diving accidents, sports-related trauma, and trampoline mishaps account for most vertebral column injuries. The mobile cervical spine is most often involved in all age groups, the upper segments being most frequently injured in young children and the lower cervical levels in adolescents.[25]

Injury of the vertebral column may occur without associated spinal cord damage (for a discussion of spinal cord injury, see Chapter 5). Radiologic examination is essential, but findings may be difficult to interpret because of the normal ossification centers in the immature spine. These areas may be mistaken for fracture lines or fragments, and the normal hypermobility of the child's spine could be misinterpreted as subluxation. For these reasons, the existence of or the potential for spinal cord injury is never ruled out on the basis of simple radiologic studies. The cost of undiagnosed spinal injury is much too high.

Commonly obtained radiologic studies include a lateral cervical spine, flexion and extension views, and an open-mouth view of the base of the odontoid bone. Forward or backward displacement of individual vertebral bodies should normally not exceed 3 mm; greater displacement indicates cervical instability.

Both short- and long-term orthopedic management of bony spine injury depend on the degree of vertebral column instability. Adequate immobilization or surgical stabilization may be required regardless of the presence of spinal cord injury.

Lower Extremity Fractures

Isolated lower extremity fractures abound in the pediatric age group and frequently disrupt the entire family because of the injured child's changes in mobility. Lower extremity fractures in the multiply injured child present a real threat from blood loss, which contributes to a prolonged state of instability. The timing of the treatment of these fractures is extremely important in the critically injured child. Early definitive management may or may not have the greatest advantage over delayed management, depending on the child's overall condition.

Upper Leg (Pelvis and Femur). Like spine fractures, pelvic fractures occur as a result of significant impact. The pelvic bones of a child are much more cartilaginous than those of the adult, making the child's pelvis more flexible, yielding, and less susceptible to fracture. In addition, the pelvic girdle in childhood is narrow and does not afford the same amount of protection to internal organs as the adult pelvis. Therefore, one of the most important aspects of pelvic fractures in children is not the fracture itself but related injuries to nearby organs and structures. Extensive internal hemorrhage either in the peritoneal or retroperitoneal area may accompany a fractured pelvis. For example, a displaced pelvic fracture may tear a large arterial vessel, such as the superior gluteal artery, and the child may lose as much as 60 percent of the circulating blood volume into nearby tissue spaces.[26] Other nearby organs or structures are at risk for relational injuries. Hematuria, either gross or microscopic, is an important sign indicating the need for further evaluation. Catheterization should be performed cautiously with prior urologic consultation if there is any suspicion of genitourinary injury.

Initial diagnosis of a pelvis fracture is based on findings such as local swelling, tenderness, refusal to move the lower extremities, shortening of one leg, and a positive "pelvic crunch" sign, which occurs when the examiner compresses the wings of the ilium and pelvis together. Ecchymosis may also be apparent in the perineal area.

Immobilization is a critical first line of management of pelvic fractures. In the field, the patient's torso should be splinted with a long board, and pneumatic antishock trousers should be placed and inflated as indicated for splinting or shock control.

Pelvic fractures are usually classified as either stable or unstable, depending on whether the fractures interfere with the stability and integrity of the pelvic ring.[27] Types of unstable fractures include separation of the symphysis pubis, an opening in the pelvic ring, proximal upward movement of one half of the pelvis, or a "bucket handle" fracture, in which the fractured half of the pelvis rolls forward and inward. This type of fracture frequently occurs as a result of a crush injury, as when a child is run over by a vehicle. Unstable pelvic fractures may require open reduction with internal fixation to achieve alignment. An external fixation device somewhat like an arched Hoffman device may be used, especially if there are associated torso or abdominal injuries that cannot be enclosed in a spica cast. Skeletal traction may also be used to achieve alignment in displaced fractures.

Fractures of the femoral neck in the child are much more uncommon than in the adult because of the strength of that area in children. Nevertheless, these fractures are usually serious and carry with them a high incidence of complications.[28] Examination often reveals hip pain, limitation of active motion with resistance to passive movement, lateral rotation, and apparent shortening of the limb. As with pelvic fractures, associated injuries must be suspected and identified. The initial immobilization may use a Thomas half-ring splint, Hare traction, or other equipment in the appropriate size.

Management of displaced femoral neck fractures typically calls for internal skeletal fixation with spica cast immobilization usually for 3 months. When the blood supply of the femoral head is disrupted at the time of the fracture, posttraumatic avascular necrosis occurs in approximately 30 percent of patients.[29] This complication has also been reported in apparently nondisplaced femoral neck fractures.[30] There is little evidence of this until several months after the injury, when it is discovered that the ossific nucleus has stopped growing. The femoral head may then become deformed and require treatment similar to that used for children with Legg-Calvé-Perthes disease.

Fractures of the femoral shaft are a relatively common occurrence in childhood, partially owing to the slender diameter of the bone. As a child grows the femur increases in size and strength, and more force is required to produce a fracture. A transverse fracture is a result of a direct loading force applied perpendicular to the bone, such as when a child is struck by a car bumper. Spiral fractures occur after torsional loading, when a twisting force is applied. Examples of this mechanism include a fall with the leg caught under a bicycle or a football tackle. In the infant, femur fractures are surprisingly easy to inflict by adults through direct blows or by a combination of pulling and twisting forces.

Diagnosis of a displaced femoral shaft fracture is usually readily made through the classic presentation of a child with angulation, external rotation, and shortening of the affected leg. Early application of a splint is essential to prevent further injury to the femoral artery. Blood loss after a femoral fracture is significant; even patients who sustain a fracture with minimal displacement lose one to two units of blood at the fracture site during the first 48 hours.[31] This type of fracture may rapidly contribute to a picture of hypovolemic shock in a child with abdominal or chest injury or multiple other fractures. The use of a pneumatic antishock garment may be helpful in providing immobilization to the limb and in tamponading the fracture site.

The vast majority of uncomplicated femoral shaft fractures are treated with closed reduction and spica casting. Some fractures require continuous traction before casting. In a child who has sustained multiple injuries or severe head injury, however, the treatment plan may be more complex, and internal or external fixation may be required. An external fixation device is frequently used if the fracture is open with concomitant soft tissue damage.

Lower Leg (Knee, Tibia and Fibula, Ankle, and Foot). Injuries at the knee range from a relatively minor injury, such as traumatic dislocation of the patella, to a severe derangement or fracture, which can result in a poor prognosis for subsequent growth and function. It has been demonstrated that most of the missed musculoskeletal injuries in the multiple trauma patient are around major joints, such as the knee.[32] Therefore, careful examination is essential. In addition, it is helpful to remember that, in children especially, complaints of knee pain may be referred symptoms from a hip injury.

Fractures of the lower leg bones are common during childhood, again owing to their slender diameter. Fractures may occur singularly to either the tibia or the fibula, but frequently fractures occur in both bones. Open, comminuted tibial-fibular fractures are often seen in children who are involved in motorcycle and bicycle accidents as well as in those who fall from a height and land on their feet. These fractures are among the most difficult to treat successfully and usually require extensive surgical débridement, external fixation, and sometimes bone and skin grafting.

The lower leg comprises a tight skin and a muscle and bone compartment, much like the lower arm. Therefore, all fractures in this area indicate careful evaluation of vascular and neurologic function. Major vessels and nerves lie close to the tibia and fibula and may be damaged by fracture fragments. Internal compartment pressure may rise, causing ischemia. This is a surgical emergency that needs early recognition (see below).

With severe open crush injuries to the lower leg requiring almost complete vascular repair, the probability of functional survival of the distal third of the leg in an adult is extremely poor. Early amputation is frequently performed. In young patients, however, the prognosis is somewhat better, and limb salvage is aggressively attempted.

Fractures of the ankle bones are common in children and can produce significant morbidity if they are not treated properly. Ankle fractures during childhood almost always involve an epiphyseal plate, most commonly the distal tibial epiphysis. Fractures can be any of the types of epiphyseal plate injuries (I through V) discussed earlier and can occur from several different types of mechanisms. The most common mechanism is a combination of twisting and bending forces, such as when the foot is caught while the body rotates around it. If the foot is forced into an inverted position, injuries occur in the lateral malleolus or lateral ligaments. If the foot is forcibly everted, medial injuries occur. All injuries to the ankle area should be immobilized with a well-padded splint until all radiologic studies are completed.

Management of ankle fractures depends on the type of epiphyseal plate fracture that has occurred.[33] Open reduction and fixation may be necessary. Early growth plate closure after a fracture in this area is not uncommon and results in the possibility of a deformity.

Fractures of the metatarsal bones of the foot are uncommon in children. The most frequent mechanism of injury is crushing, such as when a child is run over by a vehicle. A child's foot can also be crushed or mangled if it is caught in a piece of machinery, such as a lawn mower. If the child has been multiply injured, the foot injury appropriately receives low priority during the initial resuscitation because it is not life threatening. Nevertheless, it can become a major cause of lifelong disability if it is not treated aggressively at the appropriate time.

Crush Injuries

Crush and avulsion injuries can range from minor to severe and are frequently unpredictable in terms of outcome. Crush injuries are typically poorly defined at the surface, leading to difficulty in determining the extent of damage within. The most important issue in working with crush injuries is their ultimate effect on distal structures.

Crush injuries are defined as injuries involving two or more tissue types (skin, bone, muscle, nerve, or blood vessels). The viability or functional ability of the tissue or distal structure must be questionable for the injury to qualify as a crush injury, although injuries range from minimally traumatic to irreversibly damaged.

The pathophysiology of a crush injury is relatively simple. Each tissue of the body has its own level of tolerance to the effects of the ischemia that occurs as a result of tissue disruption. Once oxygen delivery to the tissue is interrupted and the tolerance level is exceeded, the tissue dies.

The following classification system for crush injuries is based on expected functional impairment.[34]

1. Type I: damage of tissue is minor; functional impairment is not anticipated, even if tissues do not survive. Example: finger tip crush with loss of nail bed.
2. Type II: severe injury with tissue and functional loss. Example: injury resulting in nerve damage, impairment of muscle contraction, and bone loss.
3. Type III: catastrophic injury in which the survival of the limb is questionable or, in the case of multisystem injury, the life of the victim is further jeopardized.

Diagnosis

Diagnosis of crush injury is sometimes delayed because attention is being paid to the more visible injuries associated with a crush, such as skin loss and bone fracture. The mechanism of injury is an important component in history taking, and crush injuries should be suspected whenever high kinetic energy is absorbed and dissipated. Important elements that should raise the suspicion of a crush injury include tissue loss or contused tissue, loss of function, and diminished distal pulses and diminished sensation. Closed crush injuries may initiate a compartment syndrome, which leads to a cycle of tissue necrosis and edema, increasing pressure within fascial spaces, and venous and arterial obstruction with further tissue necrosis. Laboratory tests are useful in obtaining information to assist in determining the severity of tissue damage. Studies that can detect muscle damage during the early stages, and should therefore be obtained, include measurement of the circulating serum myoglobin, creatinine pyrophosphate kinase, potassium, creatinine, and blood urea nitrogen levels. Myoglobinuria is also a significant sign of a crush injury, and urine myoglobin levels should be measured for a minimum of 48 to 72 hours after injury to determine how long myoglobin remains in the urine. Acute tubular necrosis and renal failure are of great concern with large crush injuries, so that consistent and prolonged evaluation of kidney function is required.

Treatment

Initial management of a crush injury involves all the techniques for preventing further injury that are used with musculoskeletal injuries. Hemorrhage control, splinting, and application of protective dressing to open wounds should all be done. Frequent neurosensory and functional checks should be made to determine changes in the circulatory status distal to the injury. On the patient's arrival to the hospital, all open wounds should be cultured, irrigated, and covered with sterile dressings, and tetanus antitoxin and antibiotics should be administered. More definitive management includes consultation with a specialist, who may use studies such as angiography, electromyography, and thermography to assist in wound appraisal and determination of treatment. Typically, débridement, stabilization of fractures, and fasciotomy are required for type II and type III injuries, unless the type III injury is so severe that the injured area requires immediate amputation. The wound is left open, and serial débridement along with whirlpool therapy is often used. Hyperbaric oxygen therapy is also being used more frequently with crush injuries because it can facilitate a vast increase in oxygen delivery to the tissue.[35] The primary effects of hyperbaric oxygenation also include the reduction of edema due to vasoconstriction, which is a major contributing factor in the pathophysiology of a crush injury.

Amputation and Limb Salvage

The incidence of traumatic amputations during childhood increases steadily from birth and peaks in the midteen years. One of the most common mechanisms for complete amputation of a limb is railroad accidents, especially in the age group of 8 to 16 years.[36] Accidents with power tools and farm machinery also account for amputations, especially in rural areas. Finger tip amputations are surprisingly common in children and are due to heavy steel doors, bicycle chains, and lawn mowers. Curiosity, lack of coordination, and an inherent lack of understanding of danger are the major characteristics that predispose children to this type of injury.

Diagnosis

Amputations can be classified as either partial or complete and show various degrees of tissue and bone damage. A guillotine type of amputation creates a wound with clean, well-defined edges. This type offers the most successful opportunity for replantation. A crush or avulsion injury resulting in separation of a body part involves extensive damage to soft tissue, bone, nerve, and blood vessels and has a much poorer prognosis for limb salvage.

Treatment

In a complete amputation, it is easy to focus attention on the body part rather than on the child. As with all other traumatic injuries, the ABCs of resuscitation (airway, breathing, and circulation) are essential. When a complete amputation occurs, the severed blood vessels retract and clamp down, usually resulting in effective clotting and minimal bleeding. A sterile dressing soaked in normal saline should be applied to the stump, which is then splinted and elevated. An artery may be lacerated rather than severed, leading to profuse bleeding. Direct pressure with a soft dressing should be used along with elevation of the extremity. Tourniquets or clamping of blood vessels is contraindicated because this increases ischemia in the body part and damages vessels needed for revascularization. A child with amputation as an isolated injury, and with no evidence of shock process, should be medicated for pain and united with his or her parents as quickly as possible. The possibility of replantation of the severed part should be discussed with the family almost immediately, but there should be no false reassurance.

Care of the amputated part requires an effort aimed at decreasing warm ischemia time. The part should be gently rinsed with normal saline to remove gross dirt. The part should then be wrapped in dry sterile gauze, placed into a sealable plastic bag, and then placed on ice.[37] Caution should be taken not to place the part directly into saline or on ice because moisture will be absorbed by the tissue, causing it to swell and macerate and become necrotic.

Early cooling of the part is a critical aspect of care because the cooling process decreases metabolic and oxygen demands, thus extending the time within which successful anastomosis and circulatory reflow can occur. Caution should again be used to ensure that the part is not immersed in ice because cold injury can occur to the severed tissues.

Time limits for successful replantation depend on the body part involved and the length of time that the part remains uncooled. Digits, because of their lack of muscle tissue, can tolerate a longer period of time with ischemia. A digit that has remained uncooled for 8 to 10 hours may be replanted successfully; cooled digits may be replanted after 20 to 28 hours.[38] Other uncooled parts or limbs that have muscle tissue may be replanted within 6 hours, and appropriate cooling extends that time to 10 to 12 hours.

Not all amputation injuries are appropriate for replantation, although in children attempts are made more often because of their ability to regenerate nerves and to heal quickly. Additionally, children have a heightened ability to adapt to sensory and motor changes as well as to accept altered body images as normal for themselves.

Compartment Syndrome

The ultimate goal whenever working with a child who has sustained musculoskeletal injury is to ensure that after treatment optimal functioning will result. Complications can occur that may interfere with this outcome. Frequently these complications are related to loss of peripheral nerve function, which results in loss of extremity function. Development of compartment syndrome is one such complication.

Diagnosis

After traumatic injury to an area of the body that has tightly enclosed compartments, direct bleeding and the inflammatory process may contribute to increased pressure within that space. The two extremities most commonly affected are the forearm and the lower leg. Within the forearm are the superficial volar and the deep volar compartments. The lower leg contains the anterior, the lateral, the superficial posterior, and the deep posterior compartments.

Within each of these areas, muscles and nerves are surrounded by inelastic fascial tissue that allows for minimal expansion. Arterial flow is compromised and may be completely occluded when intracompartmental pressure compresses the capillary bed and venous vessels, causing diminished flow and backup at the arterial end. This rapidly results in muscle ischemia, edema caused by increased capillary leakage, and even higher intracompartmental pressure.[39] Capillary venous end pressure is normally low (18 mmHg) to facilitate the flow of blood from the higher-pressure arterial end. It is generally accepted that a tissue pressure of 30 mmHg or greater indicates blood flow compromise; a pressure of 50 mmHg or greater requires opening of the compartment, or fasciotomy, to relieve some of the pressure. Without aggressive management, irreversible functional loss may occur within 4 to 6 hours after tissue perfusion has been compromised.

Symptoms of compartment syndrome may be subtle initially. Evaluation includes "the five Ps."

1. Pain: the patient complains of pain out of proportion to the apparent injury, often describing it as a burning sensation. Pain on passive movement of the extremity due to stretching of the ischemic muscle is an important assessment.
2. Paresthesia: the patient complains of abnormal sensation, such as numbness, prickling, tingling (as if the extremity has "gone to sleep"), or heightened sensitivity. Diminished ability to discriminate between two points is also an important assessment.
3. Pallor: the limb may or may not become pale, depending on the amount of venous or arterial collapse. Capillary refill may be normal or may begin to demonstrate delay.
4. Paralysis: the patient experiences progressively worsening muscle weakness.
5. Pulselessness: pulse will usually be palpable on examination because the larger arteries remain open until the compartment pressures are extremely high. Therefore, the injured distal extremity that has strong pulses in no way eliminates the need to assess for compartment syndrome.

One of the most serious results of compartment syndrome is Volkmann's ischemia and contracture, which was first described more than 100 years ago. Compression of both forearm compartments may lead to diminished blood supply from the brachial artery. This in turn leads to a progressive neurologic deficit resulting in permanent contracture of the distal arm and hand.

Treatment

Initial management of a limb in which compartment syndrome is suspected includes resuscitation for shock if multiple injuries have occurred. Any state of shock further decreases arterial pressure, compromising tissue perfusion. Any tight dressings should be loosened and the limb placed in a neutral position. Elevation of the limb is contraindicated because this results in further impediment of arterial flow.

Actual compartmental pressure may be established through the use of a simple monitoring device that can be inserted into the muscle compartment at the patient's bedside.[40] This monitor can be used to evaluate the existence of increased compartment pressure as well as used for continuous monitoring.

Definitive management for compartment syndrome involves the decompression of all muscle compartments involved through a surgical fasciotomy. The incision is frequently left open for a period of time, with the limb splinted in a functional position. In severe compartment syndromes that require extensive fasciotomies and débridement, hyperbaric oxygen therapy may be used.

NOTES

1. Richard C. Davidson and Hugh G. Watts, "Musculoskeletal Trauma," in Kenneth J. Welch, Judson G. Randolph, Mark M. Ravitch, James A. O'Neill, Jr., and Marc I. Rowe, eds., *Pediatric Surgery* (Chicago: Year Book Medical Publishers, Inc., 1986), 189–96.

2. Dennis R. Carter, "Biomechanics of Bone," in Alan M. Nahum and John Melvin, eds., *The Biomechanics of Trauma* (Norwalk, Conn.: Appleton-Century-Crofts, 1985), 135–65.

3. Barbara Barlow et al., "Ten Years of Experience with Falls from a Height in Children," *Journal of Pediatric Surgery* 18(1983):509–11.

4. C.E. Thompson and S.D. Stroud, "The Motorized Tricycle: An Accident Waiting to Happen," *Journal of Pediatric Nursing* 12(1987):120–25.

5. Cyril B. Frank and Savio L.-Y. Woo, "Clinical Biomechanics of Sports Injuries," in Alan M. Nahum and John Melvin, eds., *The Biomechanics of Trauma* (Norwalk, Conn.: Appleton-Century-Crofts, 1985), 191–203.

6. M. Rang, *Children's Fractures* (Philadelphia: J.B. Lippincott Co., 1974), 132–42.

7. David Kerns, "Child Abuse," in Thom A. Mayer, ed., *Emergency Management of Pediatric Trauma* (Philadelphia: W.B. Saunders Co., 1985), 421–34.

8. R.E. Marcus, M. Mills, and G.H. Thompson, "Multiple Injury in Children," *Journal of Bone and Joint Surgery* 65A(1983):1290–94.

9. Robert B. Salter and William R. Harris, "Injuries Involving the Epiphyseal Plate," *Journal of Bone and Joint Surgery* 45A(1963):587.

10. James A. Ogden, *Skeletal Injury in the Child* (Philadelphia: J.B. Lippincott Co., 1983).

11. Y.C. Fung, "The Application of Biomechanics to the Understanding and Analysis of Trauma," in Alan M. Nahum and John Melvin, eds., *The Biomechanics of Trauma* (Norwalk, Conn.: Appleton-Century-Crofts, 1985), 1–16.

12. Peter Scoles, "Musculoskeletal Trauma," in Peter Scoles, ed., *Pediatric Orthopedics in Clinical Practice* (Chicago: Year Book Medical Publishers, Inc., 1982), 23–77.

13. Ibid.

14. T.B. Dameron and C.A. Rockwood, "Fractures and Dislocations of the Shoulder," in C.A. Rockwood, K.E. Wilkens, and R.E. King, eds., *Fractures in Children* (Philadelphia: J.B. Lippincott Co., 1984), 587.

15. Ogden, *Skeletal Injury in the Child,* 62.

16. T.B. Dameron, Jr., and D.B. Reibel, "Fractures Involving the Proximal Humerus Epiphyseal Plate," *Journal of Bone and Joint Surgery* 51A(1969):289–97.

17. Edward Jones and David Louis, "Median Nerve Injuries Associated with Supracondylar Fractures of the Humerus in Children," *Clinical Orthopedics* 150(1980):181–86.

18. George H. Thompson and John H. Wilber, "Fracture Management of the Multiply Injured Child," in Randall E. Marcus, ed., *Trauma in Children* (Rockville, Md.: Aspen Publishers, Inc., 1986), 99–146.

19. B.G. Weber, Charles Brunner, and Fredrick Freuler, *Treatment of Fractures in Children and Adolescents* (New York: Springer-Verlag, 1980), 44.

20. James V. Fowles, Nicolas Sliman, and M.T. Kassab, "The Monteggia Lesion in Children: Fracture of the Ulna and Dislocation of the Radial Head," *Journal of Bone and Joint Surgery* 65A(1983):1276–83.

21. F.A. Marson and R.G. Veith, "Compartmental Syndromes in Children," *Journal of Pediatric Orthopedics* 1(1981):33–41.

22. Thompson and Wilber, "Fracture Management of the Multiply Injured Child," 99–146.

23. Frances Stein, "Skeletal Injuries of the Hand in Children," *Clinical Plastic Surgery* 12(1980):65–81.

24. B. O'Brien et al., "Replantation and Revascularization Surgery in Children," *Hand* 12(1980):12–24.

25. Scoles, "Musculoskeletal Trauma," 23–77.

26. Robert B. Salter, "Musculoskeletal Injuries," in Thom A. Mayer, ed., *Emergency Management of Pediatric Trauma* (Philadelphia: W.B. Saunders Co., 1985), 353–89.

27. Martin L. Morden, "Pelvic Fractures in Children," in G.R. Houghton and George H. Thompson, eds., *Problematic Musculoskeletal Injuries in Children* (London: Butterworth, 1983), 159–77.

28. S.P. Kay and J.E. Hall, "Fracture of the Femoral Neck in Children and Its Complications," *Clinical Orthopedics* 80(1971):53.

29. Salter, "Musculoskeletal Injuries," 353–89.

30. F.C. Durbin, "Avascular Necrosis Complicating Undisplaced Fractures of the Neck of the Femur in Children," *Journal of Bone and Joint Surgery* 20(1980):684–87.

31. Scoles, "Musculoskeletal Trauma," 23–77.

32. R.N.W. Chan, D. Ainscow, and J.M. Sikorski, "Diagnostic Failures in the Multiply Injured," *Journal of Trauma* 20(1980):684–87.

33. T.F. Kling, Jr., R.W. Bright, and R. Hinsinger, "Distal Tibial Physeal Fractures in Children That May Require Open Reduction," *Journal of Bone and Joint Surgery* 66A(1984):647–57.

34. Michael B. Strauss and George B. Hart, "Crush Injury and the Role of Hyperbaric Oxygen," *Topics in Emergency Medicine* (April 1984):9–23.

35. O. Szekely, G. Szanto, and A. Takats, "Hyperbaric Oxygen Therapy in Injured Subjects," *Injury* 4(1973):294–300.

36. C.N. Lambert, *The Child with an Acquired Amputation: A Symposium* (Washington, D.C.: National Academy of Sciences, 1972), 1–5.

37. Robert Beasley, "General Considerations in Managing Upper Limb Amputations," *Orthopedic Clinics of North America* 12(1981):743–49.

38. Michelle M. O'Hara, "Emergency Care of the Patient with a Traumatic Amputation," *Journal of Emergency Nursing* 13(1987):272–77.

39. V.T. Tolo, "Complications of Musculoskeletal Injuries in the Multiply Injured Child," in Randall E. Marcus, ed., *Trauma in Children* (Rockville, Md.: Aspen Publishers, Inc., 1986), 199–225.

40. Mary Larson, Julie Leigh, and Lynn R. Wilson, "Detecting Compartmental Syndrome Using Continuous Pressure Monitoring," *Focus on Critical Care* (October 1986):51–56.

Chapter 9
Transporting the Critically Injured Child

Teri S. Worthington

The pediatric transport team serves as an essential component of the pediatric trauma system. With regionalization and the recent development of pediatric trauma centers throughout the United States, emphasis must be placed on providing the critically injured child with access to the pediatric referral tertiary care center directly from the scene of the accident or from the local hospital. An injured child is routinely transported initially by the local emergency medical service system to the nearest available hospital, which may not be accustomed to caring for critically injured children. It is the goal of the pediatric transport team to provide the injured child with a means of safe and effective transportation to more advanced care while providing quality care en route as close as possible to that available at the receiving pediatric center.[1]

This chapter focuses on the special needs and considerations of injured children during interhospital transport, or the movement from the primary receiving hospital to the pediatric referral center.[2] It also provides a detailed description and overview of the organizational structure of a pediatric transport system.

MODES OF TRANSPORT

Ground or ambulance transport is still by far the most common mode of transport. Ground transport is only best for short distances because response time is a major consideration in both prehospital and interhospital patient movement. The ambulance involved in interhospital transport should be fully equipped for the critically injured pediatric patient. The role of the ambulance driver should be determined by the contracting pediatric center, including expectations of availability and response time. Mobilization time (discussed below) should not exceed 30 minutes. Some centers may own an ambulance, and a designated driver may be stationed at the hospital to reduce response time.

The use of air transport systems, specifically helicopters, has flourished throughout the United States. The speed at which a patient can be transported is their major advantage. Most helicopters cover a 150-mile radius and travel at 120 to 150 miles per hour, whereas an ambulance travels at 55 to 65 miles per hour and covers a radius of only about 100 miles. The landing space that a helicopter requires is 60 by 60 square feet.[3] Therefore, the trauma team can land directly at the scene of an accident. In addition, helicopter transport may be beneficial in areas where traffic may be a problem.

For covering long distances, the most suitable mode of transport may be fixed-wing aircraft; these are most often augmented by either helicopter or ambulance transport. Patients may be flown to various locations throughout the country for specialized surgery or advanced medical care should the area of origin be rural or without advanced facilities nearby. Fixed-wing aircraft travel at speeds of more than 200 miles per hour and can cover much greater distances than helicopter or ambulance transports.

The effects of altitude on an injured child are important to consider before air transport, especially by way of fixed-wing aircraft. When ascending to high altitudes, the gases within the pleural spaces or gastrointestinal tract may expand. This may be particularly dangerous should the patient already have a potential for a pneumothorax or abdominal problems.[4] One way to counteract this effect is to place a nasogastric tube to eliminate abdominal distention; an existing pneumothorax can be relieved by placing a chest tube before transporting the patient by air. In addition, whether the child is wearing pneumatic antishock trousers (discussed below) or simply has an inflated endotracheal tube cuff, which may create excessive pressure, must be considered.[5]

Another problem related to air transport is that, although the percentage of oxygen in the atmosphere is constant (21 percent) at all altitudes, its partial pressure (Po_2) decreases as atmospheric pressure decreases with ascent to high altitudes, and the pressure of the other gases in the air mixture increases.[6] Therefore, it may be wise to consider supplying supplemental oxygen to the patient during air transport to prevent hypoxia and further compromise of the child's condition.

A pressurized cabin will aid somewhat in preventing these adverse effects of air transport. Near-atmospheric conditions can be achieved in a pressurized aircraft by increasing the barometric pressure within the cabin, thereby reducing the effective cabin altitude.[7]

EQUIPMENT FOR TRANSPORT

Included in the planning and preparation for transporting critically injured children is the organization of equipment specific for transport. Careful consideration should also be given to size and weight limitations. Medical equipment companies have begun to develop miniature equipment such as cardiac monitors, infusion pumps, and defibrillators specifically for transport vehicles (Exhibit 9-1). A reduced number of pieces of equipment is essential to the efficiency of transport care, and the transport team must be familiar with the location and use of all equipment, especially the items in the medication and airway equipment boxes.

Exhibit 9-2 gives a list of medications, intravenous line supplies and solutions, and airway and miscellaneous equipment that may be necessary when transporting critically injured children. After each transport, it is generally the responsibility of the transport nurse to restock and maintain the equipment for the next transport.

Transporting the Critically Injured Child 145

Exhibit 9-1 Transport Equipment

Medication, airway, and miscellaneous equipment boxes
Infusion pumps (pediatric)
Portable Dinamap or blood pressure cuffs
Portable defibrillator
Portable suction unit
Cardiac monitor
Ultrasonic doppler
Stretcher
Blankets
Spinal board and sandbags

Exhibit 9-2 Transport Medications and Supplies

MEDICATIONS

Sodium chloride
50 percent dextrose
Sterile saline
Potassium chloride
Oxacillin
Epinephrine
Heparin
Succinylcholine
Atropine
Isoproterenol
Calcium chloride
Chlorpromazine (Thorazine®)
Diphenhydramine (Benadryl®)
Procainamide
Promethazine (Phenergan®)
Digoxin
Propranolol
Phenytoin
Nipride
Hydralazine (Apresoline®)
Furosemide
Hydrocortisone
Gentamicin
Mannitol
Ketamine
Sodium bicarbonate
Sterile water

Calcium gluconate
Penicillin G
Potassium phosphate
Normal serum albumin (25 percent and 5 percent)
Pancuronium
Lidocaine
Dobutamine
Insulin
Physostigmine
Phenylephrine (Neo-Synephrine®)
Dexamethasone
Fentanyl
Dopamine
Neostigmine (Prostigmin®)
Diazepam (Valium®)
Phenobarbital
Morphine
Diazoxide (Hyperstat®)
Bretylium
Chloramphenicol
Ampicillin
Thiopental
Methylprednisolone
Phytonadione (AquaMEPHYTON®)
Naloxone (Narcan®)
Theophylline

INTRAVENOUS SOLUTIONS

Dextrose in water (5 percent and 10 percent)
5 percent dextrose in 25 percent normal saline (D5•2NSS)

5 percent dextrose in 50 percent normal saline (D5•5NSS)
Ringer's lactate

Exhibit 9-2 continued

INTRAVENOUS LINE SUPPLIES

Tape
Adaptors
Tourniquets
Povidone-iodine swabs
Heparin flush
Extension sets
Catheters (numbers 24, 22, 18, 16, and 14)
Central venous pressure catheters (numbers 10 and 11)
Benzoin swabs

T-connectors
Alcohol swabs
Tape remover
Bandages
Blood collection tubes
Needles
Syringes
Arm boards
Solusets

MISCELLANEOUS EQUIPMENT

Rubber bands
Measuring tape
Aquasonic doppler gel
Dextrosticks
Urine collection bags
Suture materials
Lumbar puncture needles
Disposable razors
Penlight
Foley catheters
Sterile gloves
Arterial blood gas syringes

Safety pins
Sterile sponges
Stopcocks
Electrodes and leads
Test tubes
Surgical blades
K-Y jelly
Thermometer
Feeding tubes and replogle tubes
Disposable sterile fields
Petroleum jelly gauze

PEDIATRIC AIRWAY SUPPLIES

Face masks
Laryngoscope handles and blades
Magill forceps
Tongue depressors
Chest tubes and connectors
Suction catheters
Oxygen and suction tubing
Endotracheal tubes (uncuffed, 2.5 to 7.0; cuffed, 5.0 to 9.0; extra long, 3.0 to 5.0)
Oxygen humidifier
Pediatric partial rebreather mask

Nebulization supplies (isoproterenol, racepinephrine [Vaponefrin®], metaproterenol [Alupent®], acetylcysteine [Mucomyst®], terbutaline)
Venturi system
Manometer
Plastic oral and nasal airways
Benzoin
Tracheostomy supplies
Pleurevac
Endotracheal tube stylets
Nasal cannulaes
Ambu bag

THE DECISION TO TRANSPORT

Multisystem trauma is defined as injury from external forces to two or more body systems.[8] Given evidence of significant injury and associated symptoms that may require surgery or specialized care beyond the capability of the primary hospital, the decision to transport should be carefully considered.

The significance of the "golden hour" is well known and appreciated in relation to critically injured adults.[9] The term "platinum half hour" could be used to describe the urgency related to a critically injured child and serves to reinforce the need for rapid and decisive response at the scene of the accident and then at the primary hospital. Caregivers have the responsibility to ensure that the child is given the highest level of care available. The community hospital should identify the nearest pediatric referral center in anticipation of the need for transport before the situation arises.

INITIATING THE TRANSPORT CALL

During the referral telephone call from the primary hospital to the pediatric trauma center, several pieces of information should be communicated to assist the pediatric trauma center in preparing for the child and to allow time for supportive medical instruction during initial resuscitation. This information should include the following.

1. Patient's age: the age of the child gives an indication of the specific sizes of equipment that will be required during transport and at the trauma center.
2. Patient's weight: the weight of the child is essential for proper medication. Most pediatric trauma centers today use kilograms as the weight measure (2.2 lb = 1 kg).
3. Mechanism or cause of injury.
4. Time of injury.
5. Complete description of each identified injury.
6. Description of treatment modalities currently in use, including airway and respiratory support (intubated or ventilated), cervical spine protection (hard collar or Gardner-Wells tongs), circulatory support (cardiopulmonary resuscitation, intravenous fluids), individual injury management (chest tubes, hemorrhage control, or splinting).

All this information, as well as the child's response to management and current condition and any additional diagnostic measures that have been completed, is helpful because it allows the pediatric center and transport team to anticipate a plan of care.

During the referral call, it is also essential for the transport team to provide the referring hospital with an estimated time of arrival.

PREPARING THE CHILD FOR TRANSPORT

To expedite the response and turnaround time once the transport team arrives at the referring hospital, it is helpful if the referring medical personnel have begun preparing the child for transport. While stabilization continues without interruption, a designated individual should gather all the necessary materials to deliver to the transport team. The medical chart, nursing and physician notes, and radiology and laboratory results should all be copied. Once the transport team arrives, a full and updated report of the child's condition should be given. The transport team joins in the child's care and begins their assessment and evaluation of the child. The referring personnel should feel comfortable either remaining involved in the continued support and management of the child or allowing the transport team to take over the child's care.

At this time, the transport team proceeds with their assessment of the child and performs any additional procedures or treatments that may be deemed necessary before transporting the child to the pediatric trauma center. Only the absolute essentials of stabilization should be performed before transporting.

MANAGEMENT AND STABILIZATION EN ROUTE

Once the child is considered stabilized for transport, a transport team member should call the accepting physician at the receiving hospital. A full report of the child's condition should be delivered along with an expected time of arrival at the pediatric center, allowing time for preparations to be confirmed and completed at the receiving unit.

All the transport equipment is gathered along with the necessary forms and medical charts, and the child is carefully moved to the transport stretcher. The vehicle is loaded, and the nurse and physician are positioned close by the child's side to continue assessing and monitoring the child's condition.

The findings from continuous monitoring and vital signs should be documented at least every 15 minutes en route. Although efforts to stabilize the child before transporting have been made, rapid deterioration in the transport vehicle en route must be anticipated and prepared for. In the event of such an occurrence, it may be best to pull to the side of the road if traveling by ground and to perform whatever procedures are necessary there. If airborne, efforts to stabilize the child must obviously be done as judiciously as possible.

Managing the child's airway and providing oxygen therapy and ventilatory support during transport can be challenging and require a great deal of knowledge and preparation. If a respiratory therapist does not happen to be a member of the transport team, delivering oxygen therapy and perhaps ventilatory support becomes a responsibility of the transport nurse or physician. Therefore, the transport nurse must be well educated in techniques of respiratory care.

There are various forms and methods of oxygen administration that may be used during transport, depending on the level of the child's respiratory compromise. Oxygen therapy during transport should be as simple as possible and should be monitored continuously throughout transport from both an equipment and patient standpoint.

The oxygen tank most suitable for transport is the compressed-gas E cylinder, which is a pressure- and flow-regulating device. The E cylinder has the capacity to hold 1.9 pounds (660 liters) of oxygen and weighs 13 pounds empty. The filling limit of the E cylinder is 2200 pounds per square inch.[10]

The duration of flow for an E cylinder may be obtained from the following calculation:

$$\text{Time (minutes)} = \frac{\text{Pressure (lb/in}^2)}{\text{Flow rate (L/min)}} \times 0.28$$

Example: $\frac{2200}{2} \times 0.28 = 308$ minutes

This calculation gives an indication of how long an E cylinder will last during transport with a given flow rate. For long transports or anticipated high flow rates, it may be wise to carry more than one cylinder. It may also be wise to use the transport vehicle's oxygen source, which is normally equipped with larger cylinders.

The oxygen tank should slide into position underneath the transport stretcher or be wheeled alongside the patient in a carrier. The tank must never be placed on the stretcher with the patient.

Oxygen administration is dependent on the child's needs during transport. Physiologic differences between a child's airway and an adult's should also be considered. Devices that may be suitable include a Venturi mask, which uses air entrainment to provide a high flow of a consistent oxgyen concentration; a nasal cannula, which is used only for patients requiring low flows of oxygen; a ventilation bag, which along with a mask or endotracheal tube provides 100 percent oxygen and spontaneous as well as manual ventilation; and a transport ventilator, which again provides pressure ventilation and various set concentrations of oxygen.

Oxygen therapy in whatever form should be continued and maintained as needed throughout transport. Continuous evaluation of the patient should include observing for clinical signs of respiratory distress or hypoxemia (such as tachypnea, cyanosis, retractions, nasal flaring, decreased activity, and apnea).

SAFETY AND RISK FACTORS OF TRANSPORTING CHILDREN

Safety requirements related to transporting critically injured children cannot be emphasized enough. There are several factors to consider for both the team personnel and the patient.[11]

The transport team members should be in generally good health and must be rested before transporting. Individuals must consider the physical requirements of transport, such as the routine need to lift relatively heavy objects (stretchers and isolettes), before joining a transport team. Needless to say, seat belts must be worn at all times while en route, but this does not preclude active provision of care during transport. The risk related to accidents should also be carefully considered by prospective transport personnel.

The child should be secured to the stretcher with seat belts, and the stretcher should be locked in place to the floor and sides of the transport vehicle. All intravenous lines and tubes should be labeled and secured to prevent them from becoming dislodged during turbulence and motion.

The cabin should be well ventilated, and an adequate temperature must be maintained. Blankets should be used to prevent hypothermia. Maintaining the child's temperature is

Exhibit 9-3 Emergency Transport Team Flow Sheet

THE CHILDREN'S HOSPITAL OF PHILADELPHIA EMERGENCY TRANSPORT RECORD

PATIENT NAME ____________

ADDRESS ____________

____

DOB/AGE ____________

TRANSPORT DATE ____________

WEIGHT ________ Kg

ADMIT TO ____________

DEPART CHOP @ ________

ARRIVE REFERRING @ ________

DEPART REFERRING @ ________

ARRIVE CHOP @ ________

TRANSPORT PERMIT SIGNED ________

ALLERGIES ________

LOCATION
H Referring Hospital
A Ambulance

REFERRING HOSPITAL ____________

CITY/STATE ____________

PHONE ____________

UNIT SC Nursery NB Nursery Pediatrics ER ICU OTHER ________

VENTILATION MODE
V = Ventilation NC = Nasal Camula
M = Mapleson FM = Face Mask
O = Oxyhood

IV SOLUTIONS
A ________
B ________
C ________

		VITAL SIGNS					VENTILATION					BLOOD GASES						INTAKE		
LOCATION	TIME	TEMP	HEART RATE	RESP RATE	BP	CHEMSTRIP	MODE / Airway	FiO_2	IMV	PIP / Peep	Color	pH	PCO_2	PO_2	BE	HCO_3	SOURCE	A	B	C

Source: The Children's Hospital of Philadelphia, Nursing Service Department, Philadelphia, Pennsylvania.

Transporting the Critically Injured Child

FORM #N-1323

HISTORY OF PRESENT ILLNESS, NURSING ASSESSMENT, OBSERVATIONS, PROCEDURES

MATERNAL AGE _____ Gravida _____ Para _____ Abortion _____ Apgars 1 _____ 5 _____

KEY: NEURO ASSESSMENT

Eye Opening:
- S-Spontaneous
- V-To Verbal Stim
- P-To Painful Stim
- N-None

Motor Response:
- O-Obeys Command
- L-Localizes Pain
- W-Withdraws To Pain
- F-Flexion To Pain
- E-Extension To Pain
- FL-Flacid

Verbal Response:
- O-Oriented
- C-Confused
- IA-Inappropriate
- IN-Incoherent
- N-None

Key Abbreviations
- DOB-Date of Birth
- SC-Special Care
- NB-Newborn
- VIT-Vitamin
- PIP-Peak Inspiratory Pressure

OUTPUT		MEDICATIONS	NEURO				
URINE	GI		EYE OPENING	VERBAL RESPONSE	MOTOR RESPONSE	PUPILS react	size
		VIT K _____					
		EYE GTTS _____					

SIGNATURES
TRANSPORT NURSE:
TRANSPORT PHYSICIAN:

crucial in that a decrease in body temperature will increase oxygen consumption, which may further compromise the child's condition.

The limited battery power of equipment in use should be considered, and power outlets in the transport vehicle should be used while en route to prevent equipment malfunction. Air and oxygen sources should also be considered and tanks checked before departure. Equipment should be positioned in the most accessible location because movement within the vehicle while en route is limited.

PARENTAL CONCERNS

When transporting a critically injured child, the parents or guardians must always be considered. The parents are likely to be upset and fearful for their child, especially with regard to the need for transport to a distant place. Often, caretakers become so involved in their efforts on the child's behalf that little time or consideration is given to the parents. Therefore, it is generally the responsibility of the transport physician or leader to spend time with the parents, explaining the need for transport and any procedures or surgery that may be necessary and offering support. This initial encounter with the transport team will instill feelings that may be reflected in the parents' subsequent attitude toward the overall care for their child at the pediatric trauma center.[12] Therefore, it is important to reserve a small amount of time to offer support and comfort. It is also important to be realistic without giving false hope.

Before departure, the transport team should allow the parents to visit with their child. This is essential in all cases but most certainly at times when the child's condition is grim. The transport team should provide the parents with directions to the pediatric trauma center and the patient unit and floor and obtain the parents' written consent to transport. It is generally not a good idea to permit the parents to ride along on transport because of space limitations and possible sudden deterioration in the child's condition en route. Therefore, it is best to suggest that a friend or family member bring the parents to the pediatric trauma center. They should be reminded to arrange child care for other siblings and to gather their own and their child's belongings for an overnight stay. Normally the parent will also be contacted by the social work department at the referral center on arrival. The social worker may aid in obtaining accommodations as well as offer support.

DOCUMENTATION

It is absolutely essential that good record keeping and documentation be a major factor of transporting critically injured children. The transport nurse and physician must include their forms as a permanent part of the child's record. Exhibit 9-3 is an example of an emergency transport team flow sheet that can be used for documentation; this form facilitates review for the overall quality assurance of the transport system.

NOTES

1. Dean F. Smith and Alvin Hackel, "Selection Criteria for Pediatric Critical Care Transport Teams," *Critical Care Medicine* (January 1983):10–12.
2. T. Mayer, "Transportation of the Injured Child," in *Emergency Management of Pediatric Trauma* (Philadelphia: W.B. Saunders Co., 1985), 508–23.
3. P. Campbell, "Transporting the Critically Ill and Injured Child," *Critical Care Quarterly* (June 1985):1–12.
4. L. Huber and N. Dunn, "Aeromedical Physiology: Implications for Neonatal Nurses," *Neonatal Network* (October 1982):10–18.
5. American Academy of Pediatrics, Committee on Hospital Care, "Guidelines for Air and Ground Transportation of Pediatric Patients," *Pediatrics* (1986):943–50.
6. Huber and Dunn, "Aeromedical Physiology," 10–18.
7. J.A. Dorsch and S.E. Dorsch, "Compressed Gas Containers," in *Understanding Anesthesia Equipment* (Baltimore: Williams & Wilkins, 1984), 1–15.
8. Barbara J. Lockwood, "Transport of Multisystem Trauma Patients from Rural to Urban Health Care Facilities," *Critical Care Quarterly* (December 1982):22–37.
9. Campbell, "Transporting the Critically Ill and Injured Child," 1–12.
10. Dorsch and Dorsch, "Compressed Gas Containers," 1–15.
11. American Academy of Pediatrics, "Guidelines for Air and Ground Transportation of Pediatric Patients," 943–50.
12. T. Morse, "Transportation of Critically Ill and Injured Children," *Pediatric Clinics of North America* 6(1969):565.

Chapter 10

Burns

Joann Gallagher D'Italia

INCIDENCE AND ETIOLOGY

One child is badly burned every 4 minutes.[1] Burn injuries rank second only to car accidents as a cause of death in children. The toll exacted by burn injuries in children is greater than that from any other pediatric trauma as a result of the disability and disfigurement that occurs at this early age.

Thermal injury resulting from spill scalds, immersion scalds, and contact with hot irons, pipes, and heaters is the predominant injury in the child less than 5 years of age. Flame burns from stoves, match play, and volatile liquids are common in the school-aged child. Chemical and electrical injuries represent a small percentage of burn injuries in children. Although flame burns cause the most devastating injuries to children of all ages, major scald injuries in infants and toddlers are just as life threatening.

INITIAL EVALUATION AND TRIAGE

Initial evaluation of the child with burns is similar to that of the child with multiple trauma because thermal injury affects all organ systems. Airway patency, ability to breathe, and adequacy of circulation are the first priorities in the assessment of any injured child. Carbon monoxide poisoning in the child caught in a house fire requires immediate treatment with 100 percent oxygen to reverse carboxyhemoglobinemia; airway obstruction due to rapid edema formation in the child with burns of the face or neck necessitates prophylactic intubation. Burns do not bleed; therefore, if bleeding is evident some associated trauma to the head, chest, abdomen, or long bones is the probable source. In children with major burns of more than 20 percent of the total body surface area, one large intravenous catheter will provide adequate access for fluids and should be inserted in unburned areas with strict aseptic technique. Monitoring of central venous pressure is usually unnecessary in the child with burns; if monitoring is required and peripheral lines are unavailable, the internal jugular vein or subclavian is used. An arterial line is used to monitor blood gases if a significant inhalation injury is present. Placement of an indwelling catheter to monitor urine output is necessary during the first 48 to 72 hours of fluid resuscitation. Acute gastric dilation and an adynamic ileus are common problems during the emergent phase; decompression with a nasogastric tube alleviates these problems. A nasogastric tube also provides a route for antacid therapy to prevent Curling's ulcer, which is a stress ulcer in burn patients. An accurate weight is obtained to calculate medication dosage and fluid administration.

As a result of the alteration in skin integrity, the child with a major burn is at great risk for developing hypothermia. The relatively larger surface area, smaller body mass, and thinner skin of the child compared to that of the adult contribute to greater heat loss. In response to cold stress, the child shivers to maintain body temperature because evaporative water loss exceeds the rate of heat production. Infants tolerate hypothermia poorly because of their immature temperature regulating center. Nonshivering thermogenesis, which is an active energy process that catabolizes brown fat in the presence of catecholamines, is activated to maintain heat. This process requires the expenditure of large amounts of oxygen, so that prolonged hypothermic episodes in young infants may result in excessive lactate production and acidosis.[2] Hypothermic infants with burn injuries of more than 15 percent of the total body surface area are more difficult to resuscitate with fluids than children who are normothermic.

The first-aid treatment of the burn wound is the application of cool, wet towels during the first 20 minutes to stop the burning process and to alleviate pain. Overzealous treatment by the application of ice is contraindicated and further complicates life-threatening conditions. After determining the child's temperature and extent of the injury, the child is wrapped in a warm, smooth, sterile sheet. Intravenous fluids stored in an air-conditioned emergency room may need warming before infusing. The eyes must be evaluated to determine the presence of abrasions or burns requiring topical therapy before they are swollen shut, making examination and treatment impossible. Hair serves as a nidus for infection in the scalp and must be shaved wherever burns are evident.

Combativeness after a burn injury, which is often interpreted as pain, may be due to hypoxia. During the emergent phase, pain medications (morphine sulfate, 0.1 mg/kg) are given intravenously. Until systemic circulation is restored, intramuscular and subcutaneous medications provide no pain relief because they pool in the tissue. When normal circulation returns, the accumulated doses are mobilized and cause cerebral and respiratory depression.

The child with a burn has lost the barrier against bacterial invasion. This child is a compromised host, so that precautions against infection must be taken during the many procedures initiated during the emergent period. Prophylactic penicillin directed toward endogenous streptococci is given as a short course in the early postburn period in children who are hospitalized. Gowns, gloves, and masks must be worn by all trauma team members (it should be kept in mind how frightening the trauma team, thus attired, must appear to the child).

The American Burn Association (ABA) has developed a severity index to classify burn injuries according to minor injury (requiring outpatient management), moderate injury (requiring hospitalization), and major injury (requiring admission to a burn care facility). The six triage criteria for determining severity are (1) age, (2) past medical history, (3) part of body burned, (4) concomitant injuries, (5) extent, and (6) depth. These criteria are an adaptation of the ABA severity index.

Exhibit 10-1 Emergency Department Wall Chart

ASSESSMENT AND INITIAL CARE OF SEVERE BURN PATIENTS

Guidelines for Hospital Emergency Departments*

1. STOP BURNING PROCESS
   Remove or cool hot clothing
   Extensive lavage of chemical burns

2. ADMINISTER CPR AS NEEDED

3. MAINTAIN VENTILATION
   Look for signs of inhalation injury (cough, singed nasal hair, soot, or edema in upper airway)
   OBSTRUCTED AIRWAY:
   Hyperextend neck, suction, endotracheal tube
   RESPIRATORY INSUFFICIENCY:
   Administer high concentration of oxygen until carbon monoxide is proven to be below toxic level
   Monitor ABG's
   Use endotracheal tube and respirator if necessary

4. ESTABLISH CIRCULATION
   Install I.V. line (#16 or #18 plastic cannula)
   Use Ringer's lactate, without glucose
   (2-4 cc/kg body weight/% BSA burned)
   Objective: At least 50 cc urine/hr in adults.
   1 mL urine/kg/hr in children
   BURNED EXTREMITY:
   Elevate, remove rings, bracelets, etc.

6. MAINTAIN BODY TEMPERATURE
   Avoid systemic hypothermia or chill, using dry blankets.

7. HISTORY AND PHYSICAL
   Type, area and depth of burn
   Other injuries (fractures, lacerations, etc.)
   Details of accident
   Pre-existing illness (e.g. diabetes)
   Use of alcohol, tobacco, drugs
   Allergies, medications

8. PREVENT ILEUS COMPLICATIONS
   Keep patient N.P.O.
   Nasogastric tube to drainage, for nausea, vomiting or distention, burns over 25% BSA

9. RELIEVE PAIN
   Give narcotics, 2-4 mg, morphine or equivalent, I.V. only, to achieve desired effect
   (Restlessness may be from hypoxia)

10. TREAT BURN WOUND
    Maintain irrigation of eye wounds
    Stabilize other injuries (fractures, etc.)
    For patients being transferred to burn center, cover with clean dry sheet
    For all other burn patients, cleanse gently with soap and water or saline

5. REVIEW FOR MAJOR TRAUMA

Assess for head or spinal trauma, blunt and penetrating injuries and stabilize

Triage criteria	Consider admission to hospital	Consider transfer to burn center
Age	<5 or >60	<5 or >60
Airway or inhalation injury	Present	Severe
Electrical injury	Present	Present
Significant associated injury or pre-existing disease	Present	Present
Burns of face, hands, feet or perineum	Present	Present
Suspected child abuse	Present	Present
Burned area 2° and 3°	>15%	>20%
Burned area 3° only	>2%	>10%

*These guidelines should be modified by the judgment and experience of the responsible physician

Source: Courtesy of Burn Foundation, Philadelphia, Pennsylvania.

11. TETANUS PROPHYLAXIS

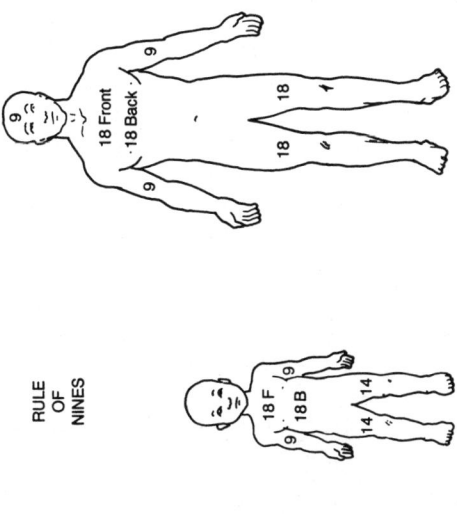

RULE OF NINES

The Burn Foundation has developed and distributed a wall chart to assist emergency room personnel in burn care (Exhibit 10–1). A burn referral checklist accompanies the wall chart to ensure adequate communication between the transferring and receiving institutions (Exhibit 10-2).

If patient transfer is anticipated, no topical agent should be applied to the burn so that evaluation of extent and depth can be done on the patient's arrival to the receiving institution. A permeable, nonadherent dressing such as Xeroflo® or Adaptic® that permits egress of serum and exudate is a comfortable dressing for the child en route and does not mask the appearance of the wound.

The greatest reduction in mortality over the last 15 years has been achieved in the infant-toddler age group. This improved survival of burned children is attributed to their being treated according to pediatric principles in institutions devoted exclusively to care of pediatric patients.[3]

During the initial evaluation, one member of the trauma team must provide progress reports to the child's primary caretakers, the parents or guardians. Their greatest fear is that their child may be dying, and naturally they will want to be with their child. Even though attention is focused on the child's condition, the parents' condition must not be neglected. Parents may suffer guilt regardless of how the accident occurred. They are concerned that the child is in pain and may be frightened by the emergency department environment and the multitude of strangers that surround the child. They must not be treated as interlopers in a high-technology environment when the reason for the technology is their child.

DETERMINING THE BURN EXTENT AND DEPTH

Extent

Accurate determination of the extent of burn injury is one of the factors in determining the severity of injury. The two methods largely in use are the rule of nines and the Lund and Browder chart. A third method, the palmar method, estimates the palm of the burned individual as 1 percent of the individual's total body surface area and is useful only in evaluating minor burns. The rule of nines divides the body surface into areas representing multiples of 9 percent: the head and each upper extremity is 9 percent, each lower extremity is 18 percent, the trunk is 36 percent, and the remaining 1 percent is assigned to the perineum. This method is quick and easy for determining burn extent in the adult, but it is useless in determining burn extent in the child. The rule of nines does not allow for the relatively larger surface area of the head of the child and the proportionately smaller surface area of the lower extremities, which changes with age.

The age-related Lund and Browder (Exhibit 10-3) method is the only method for determining accurate extent of burn injury in the child. In this method, the burn is sketched on an anterior and posterior view, the age factor is circled, areas of burn are recorded, and the extent of the total body surface area burned is computed.

It is always good practice to recalculate the extent of burn injury because extent determines the total amount of fluid therapy. Another way to check the accuracy of

Exhibit 10-2 Burn Referral Checklist

BURN FOUNDATION
BURN REFERRAL CHECKLIST

(Use this form to collect essential information when preparing to refer a burn patient)

NAME _____ AGE _____ WT. _____
DATE/TIME OF BURN _____ %BSA _____
TYPE OF BURN: (circle)   FLAME   SCALD   ELEC.   CHEM.   CONTACT
SPECIAL AREAS AFFECTED: RESP.   FACE   HANDS   FEET   PERIN.
CIRCUMFERENTIAL AREAS: THORAX ARMS: L R   LEGS: L R
CAUSE OF INJURY _____

ACCOMPANYING TRAUMA _____
PMH _____ ALLERGIES _____

INITIAL MANAGEMENT (complete as applicable)

A) INHALATION INJURY:

ETT # _____ NASAL _____ O_2 THERAPY _____
CARBOXYHEMOGLOBIN (PURPLE TOP ON ICE) _____
ABG _____ CXR _____

B) FLUID MANAGEMENT:

IV LINES: PERIPH# _____ CVC# _____ (CONFIRMED BY CXR _____)
IV FLUIDS _____ cc/hr.   UO _____ cc/hr.
FOLEY # _____ NPO _____
LAB STUDIES _____

C) OTHER

VS:T _____ P _____ RR _____ BP _____
NGT # _____ NGT TO SUCTION _____
TETANUS TOXOID _____ HYPERTET _____
IV ANALGESIA _____
ACCEPTING BURN CENTER _____
CONTACT PERSON/PHONE _____
MODE OF TRANSPORT _____ BURN TEAM ETA _____

Source: Courtesy of Burn Foundation, Philadelphia, Pennsylvania.

---

calculations is to sketch in the unburned area on another chart; the sum of the two must equal 100 percent. Burn size is frequently overestimated. Any discrepancy between the initial evaluation of the extent of burn injury and the actual total body surface burned may have significant effects on clinical management.[4]

Exhibit 10-3 Lund and Browder Chart To Determine the Percentage of Total Body Surface Area Burned

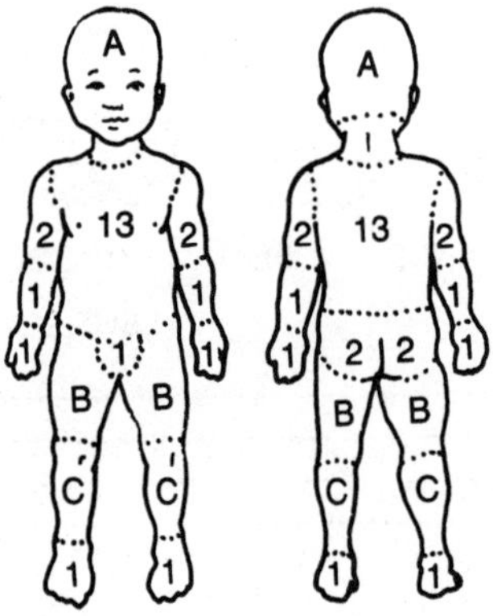

% BURN BY AREAS

AREA	%2	%3
HEAD		
NECK		
UPPER ARM		
FOREARM		
ANTERIOR TRUNK		
POSTERIOR TRUNK		
GENITALS		
BUTTOCKS		
THIGHS		
LEGS		
FEET		
HANDS		
TOTALS		

RELATIVE PERCENTAGES OF AREA AFFECTED BY GROWTH			
AREA	AGE 0	1	5
A = ½ of head	9½	8½	6½
B = ½ of One Thigh	2¾	3¼	4
C = ½ of One Leg	2½	2½	2¾

WEIGHT _____ HEIGHT _____
SURFACE AREA _____
TYPE OF BURN _____
COMMENT _____

Source: Reprinted from *Surgery, Gynecology and Obstetrics*, Vol. 79, p. 356, © 1947, by permission of *Surgery, Gynecology and Obstetrics*.

Fluid Resuscitation

The immediate effect of a major thermal injury of more than 20 percent of the total body surface area is an increase in capillary permeability and a loss of capillary integrity not only at the site of injury but also throughout the entire body. The exact cause for these changes in vascular permeability is unknown, but the release of histamines, kinins, and prostaglandins and serotonin edema results in shifts of protein-rich plasma fluid from the intravascular space to the interstitial space, decreasing colloid osmotic pressure. Simultaneously, an electrolyte imbalance results because changes in cell permeability and a defective ion pump allow extracellular (intravascular and interstitial) sodium to accumulate intracellularly and intracellular potassium to accumulate extracellularly. Fluid is also lost through the burn wound. With this massive shift, plasma becomes unavailable as circulating volume to perfuse vital organs; therefore, the major threat to survival is circulatory collapse from hypovolemia, which is known as burn shock.[5]

Aggressive fluid resuscitation immediately after the burn injury with adequate volume and sodium is essential for patient survival. Ringer's lactate is the fluid of choice because it is similar in composition to the fluid being lost. Seizures in the early postburn period occur as a result of hyponatremia when electrolyte-free solution is used. Of all infants with burns, 15 percent are hypoglycemic; therefore, serum glucose levels must be monitored closely in this age group.

The calculation of replacement fluid volumes used by the receiving institution should be considered by the burn trauma team. The concept of multiples in pediatric fluid maintenance is useful in discussing fluid requirements with emergency room personnel who are unaccustomed to burn resuscitation. For example, a 15 percent burn injury requires 1.5 times maintenance; a 20 percent burn injury requires 2 times maintenance; and for burns greater than 30 percent a burn formula works well.[6]

There are a number of formulas available that determine the various combinations of colloid and crystalloid solutions on the basis of the type and amount of colloid necessary (Table 10-1). Crystalloid solutions provide early expansion of depleted plasma and extracellular volume and return of cardiac output toward normal; after 24 hours, colloid maintains plasma volume without increasing edema. Burn formulas cannot consider all severity factors, so that they serve only as a guide to initiate therapy. These formulas account for fluid loss due to burn injury only. Maintenance fluids and other third-space losses (from intra-abdominal injuries, long bone fractures, and so forth) must be added to these to maintain adequate intravascular volume.[7]

Available formulas are inappropriate for the child with a burn of less than 20 percent of the total body surface area because the replacement volume is less than maintenance requirements. Physiologic fluid therapy is therefore the method of treatment for small burns.[8] An alternate approach is to provide hydration orally to maintain urine output of 1.5 mL/kg/hour; if the child is unable to drink, intravenous fluids at 1.5 to 2 times maintenance requirement are given. A good rule of thumb is to insert a heparin lock in any child with a burn less than 20 percent at time of admission so that intravenous access is immediately available if an ileus develops or if the child refuses to drink.

The existing formulas to determine fluid requirements are based on the child's weight and the extent of the burn. An essential factor in fluid resuscitation is the time of burn injury. When calculating the rate of administration over 24 hours, the time of burn injury is the starting point, not the time of the patient's arrival at the hospital. This is especially important when the child is transported from another institution. Half the 24-hour fluid requirement is given during the first 8 hours postburn; if there is a delay in obtaining

Table 10-1 Formulas for Fluid Resuscitation

Formula	First 24 Hours	Second 24 Hours
Parkland*	4 mL of Ringer's lactate per kilogram of body weight per percent of body surface burned	5% dextrose in 50 percent normal saline, 5 percent albumin (as indicated)
Duke*	3 mL of Ringer's lactate per kilogram of body weight per percent of body surface burned, plus one-half ampule of sodium bicarbonate per liter of replacement fluid	Ringer's lactate plus sodium bicarbonate plus 5 percent albumin (3 to 5 g/kg plus 1 g per percent of body surface burned)
Hypertonic lactated saline (HLS)	2 mL of HLS per kilogram of body weight per percent of body surface burned	0.6 mL HLS per kilogram of body weight per percent of body surface burned, plus oral Haldane's solution to replace calculated insensible fluid loss

*Give half the calculated volume over the first 8 hours and the other half over the next 16 hours.

venous access or in administering appropriate amounts of fluid, this deficit must be compensated for during the first 8 hours.

Massive edema is expected, even in unburned areas. The child's head may swell to twice its size, the eyes will swell shut, and the scrotum will increase significantly in size. This phenomenon is not an indication of a mistake in fluid therapy or that the child's condition is worsening.

Management of fluid resuscitation during the emergent phase is aimed at establishing adequate vascular volume and tissue perfusion by titrating fluids to maintain urinary output at 0.5 to 1.0 mL/kg/hour. Urine output is the most sensitive indicator of cardiac output in children. Vital signs, sensorium, urine specific gravity, and peripheral capillary refill are the parameters monitored to determine underresuscitation or overresuscitation. Trends (such as the average urine output for three to four consecutive hours) rather than a single sign are evaluated before altering the infusion rate. If urine output decreases, the infusion rate should be increased. Diuretics deplete an already depleted volume and are reserved for specific situations.

Capillary integrity begins to return at about 24 hours and is complete at about 2 to 3 weeks after burn injury; at 48 hours, a brisk diuresis signifies mobilization and reabsorption of fluid from the capillary bed. Clinical parameters within normal limits plus normal electrolytes and a decreasing hematocrit indicate a successful resuscitation.

Depth

Depth is dependent on the temperature of the burning agent and the duration of exposure. Burn injury is classified as partial-thickness or full-thickness injury (Table 10-2).

Table 10-2 Classification of Burn Injuries on the Basis of Depth

Type of Burn	Depth of Injury	Appearance
Partial-thickness		
Superficial	Involves epidermis and upper layers of dermis.	Red and wet; with or without blisters.
Deep	Involves entire epidermis with destruction of dermal papillae. Skin appendages (sweat glands, hair follicles) are intact.	Red or white; large blisters; blanches with pressure; soft and elastic.
Full-thickness	Involves epidermis, all dermal appendages, and epithelial elements; subcutaneous fat, muscle, and bone may be involved.	Red, white, tan, black (charred), or brown; small or absent blisters; does not blanch; inelastic; may appear to be sunken; thrombosed vessels may be visible.

In a partial-thickness injury part of the skin is damaged, but enough epithelial elements remain to provide new coverage (Figure 10-1). Superficial partial-thickness injuries heal within 3 to 10 days without scarring. Deep partial-thickness burns heal in 2 to 3 weeks, often with scarring. Although these wounds are initially smooth, soft, and flat, they can develop scars up to 3 months after they heal. Full-thickness injury denotes that all dermal appendages are destroyed. Wound closure can only be achieved by means of autografting.

It is difficult initially to determine the depth of injury in the child because of the thinness of the skin. The usual characteristics of color, texture, and sensation may or may not be present, especially in scald injuries. The burn wound is usually a combination of depths. Reassessment during the first week provides a more accurate determination of depth.

Compartment Syndrome

The inelastic eschar of a full-thickness, circumferential burn of an extremity acts as a tourniquet. This eschar envelops bone, muscle, nerves, and blood vessels as burn edema develops in this closed space. The pressure, if unrelieved, squeezes vessels and thereby reduces or eliminates blood supply to the extremity. Clinical assessment of blood flow is done by taking hourly doppler readings through windows cut in the burn dressing or by direct transcutaneous compartment pressure readings. Escharotomy is performed to release the constricting eschar and to restore blood flow. Escharotomy is done surgically with a scalpel or chemically with an enzymatic agent. Circumferential third-degree burns of the chest diminish chest expansion and interfere with normal or assisted ventilation; escharotomies relieve the constriction of the unyielding eschar and subcutaneous edema.

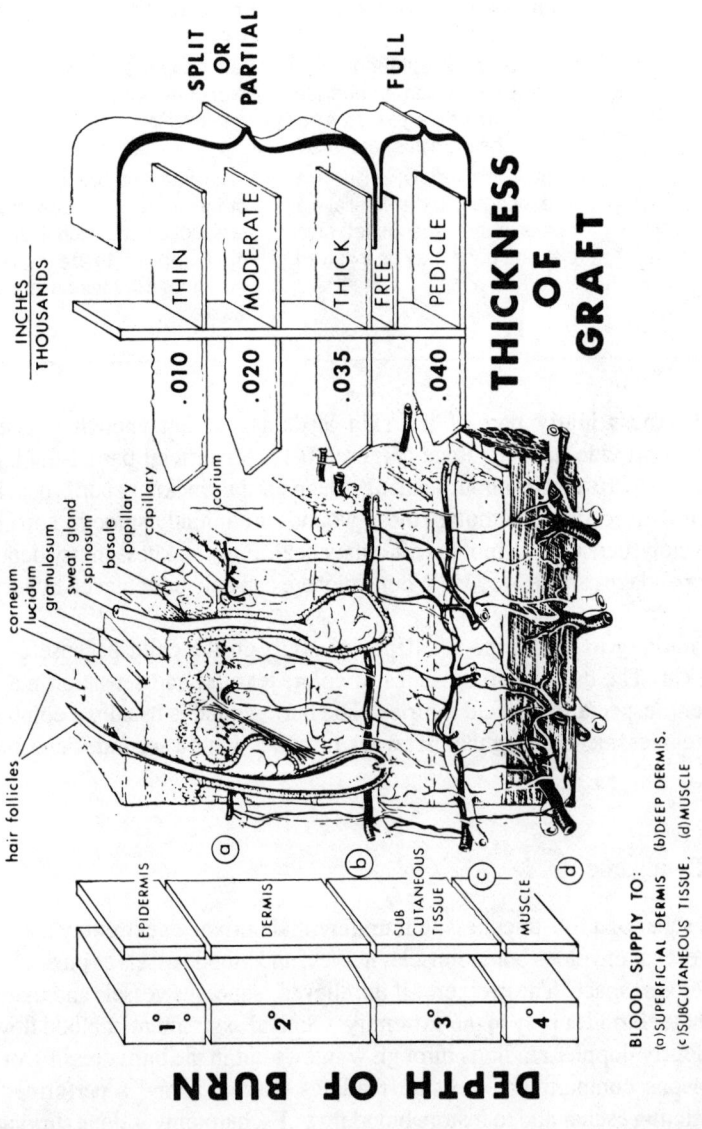

Figure 10-1 Cross-Section of Skin Depicting Blood Supply, Depth of Burn, and Relative Thickness of Skin Grafts. *Source:* Reprinted from *Burns: A Team Approach* by C.P. Artz, J.A. Moncrief, and B.A. Pruitt, p. 434, with permission of W.B. Saunders Company © 1979.

CARE OF BURN WOUND

The objectives of wound care are to heal the wound, to prepare the wound for grafting, to prevent infection, and to provide patient comfort. Daily or more frequent dressing with a topical antibacterial controls bacteria until epithelialization or eschar separation is performed. Silver sulfadiazine (Silvadene®) is the most popular topical antibacterial in use because it is a broad-spectrum agent and comfortable to apply. Closed dressings allow the child to be held and wheeled to the playroom, which are priorities in pediatric care.

Burn redressings are painful, and analgesics such as morphine sulfate (0.1 mg/kg) are given intravenously before the dressing change. All burn patients fear and dread this aspect of burn care. Older children can verbalize their anxieties; younger ones cannot. An experienced, confident nurse can make the difference during this especially stressful part of burn care. Spreading cream on the gauze and not on the child with a sterile gloved hand or tongue blade eliminates the pain of pressure on exquisitely tender exposed nerve endings. Opening all supplies before removing the soiled dressing decreases the length of wound exposure to air, which is known to cause pain. Encouraging the child to assist in dressing removal allows control of pain because the child knows how hard to pull the dressing. Generally, if bleeding occurs, pain occurs.

Hydrotherapy in the form of whirlpool tubbing appears to be on the decline. Most institutions use a regular or adapted shower for bathing patients or a plinth over a regular tub.[9] The noise of the whirlpool motor and the gushing water currents are sometimes frightening to children. Simple wound cleansing with the warm water of the bath dilutes and reduces the bacterial population and facilitates dressing removal.[10] Children are less frightened by this method of dressing change because it is similar to their routine daily bath. Allowing parents to be present and to participate when they are ready to review the wounds aids in alleviating fear and anxiety. Parents are told what to expect and are reminded that distraught looks and tears will upset their child. Parents are assured leaving the room to avoid showing their distress will not be interpreted as failure. It is always helpful to point out the healing of the wound, such as the appearance of epithelial buds and islands, so that parents see improvement and understand the rationale for daily redressing.

The child who sustains an immersion scald accidentally or through abuse is the exception to the above. Weeks or months may elapse before the fear of the bathtub is overcome. Blotting the wound with wet gauze is an alternative to the bath in this situation.

As with any experience, understanding the rationale for the dressing change, having some control in timing, participating in the process, and having questions answered honestly increase cooperation and alleviate fear in the child.

For full-thickness injury, daily dressing in conjunction with frequent tangential excision of eschar under anesthesia is done to prepare the wound for grafting. Parents frequently volunteer to donate their skin for wound coverage. They must understand that this is not feasible because autografting (with the child's own skin) and isografting (with skin from an identical twin) are the only permanent skin grafts.

Many different synthetic and biologic dressings are available for temporary coverage of burn wounds until autografting is done. A number of topical antibacterials are available, and each has specific advantages and disadvantages. Burn wound protocols vary among institutions, but the underlying principle is the same: to decrease the size of the wound, to improve survival, and to lessen morbidity.

HYPERMETABOLISM

Hypermetabolism is in direct proportion to the size of the burn injury up to 50 percent of the total body surface area; there is no further change in metabolic rate beyond this percentage. The hypermetabolic state in burn injury is mediated through the hypothalamic-pituitary response to the presence of prostaglandins. This response is an autonomic efferent signal expressed as catecholamine excretion, which causes an increased release of catabolic hormones, an increased rate of gluconeogenesis and lipolysis, a decrease in protein synthesis, and transient impaired secretion of the anabolic hormone insulin. Because of the relatively small muscle mass and body fat of the child, protein and caloric malnutrition resulting in marked weight loss, negative nitrogen balance, and altered immunologic function is a nutritional emergency. Caloric expenditure and protein catabolism are greater and more sustained in burn injury than in any other physiologic stress state. This increased metabolic rate may be as much as 2 to 3 times greater than normal to meet energy demands for wound healing of partial-thickness burns and graft donor sites, vascularization of grafts, increased oxygen consumption due to pain and anxiety, and the body's attempt to maintain temperature. Complications of sepsis and pulmonary injury, if present, add to the already stressed hyperdynamic state of the child with burns. Research is being undertaken to discover a method whereby the metabolic rate will decrease but wound healing and host immunity remain unaltered.

Evaporative water loss with resultant surface cooling and subsequent increased metabolic rate to maintain temperature was thought to be the cause of the hypermetabolic response in burns. Studies have demonstrated that that metabolic rate remains elevated when evaporative water loss is blocked, however.[11]

Aggressive nutritional support to counteract the hypermetabolic response to burn injury is one of the major factors contributing to the improved survival rate of all patients with thermal injury over the last two decades. Recovery from the adynamic ileus that develops after burn injury usually occurs at 48 to 72 hours. Nutritional replacement begins through the enteral route with continuous drip feedings, or night feedings if the child will not eat during the day. A formula to calculate caloric needs for burned children on the basis of body surface area estimates 1800 Kcal/m^2/day for maintenance plus 2200 Kcal/m^2/day for thermal injury.[12] The recently developed Curreri Junior formula (Table 10-3) more accurately describes the nutritional needs of the pediatric burn patient with small injuries (2 percent to 50 percent of total body surface area).[13] Other clinicians estimate protein and caloric requirements at 2 to 2.5 times the recommended daily allowances according to age.

Table 10-3 The Curreri Junior Formula for Postburn Hypermetabolism

Age (years)	Caloric Requirements
0–1	Basal calories plus 15 Kcal per percent of body surface burned
1–3	Basal calories plus 25 Kcal per percent of body surface burned
3–15	Basal calories plus 40 Kcal per percent of body surface burned

Source: Reprinted from *Journal of Trauma* with permission of Williams & Wilkins Company, in press. © by Williams & Wilkins Company.

OTHER PHYSIOLOGIC ALTERATIONS

In addition to the body's response to stress and shock, burn injury produces other specific changes. Immediately after the burn there is a precipitous decrease in cardiac output. Depending on the size of the burn, this may be 50 percent to 70 percent of normal vascular volume. This is due in part to increased blood viscosity, metabolic acidosis, and increased total peripheral vascular resistance.

The normal cardiac output to the kidneys (20 percent to 25 percent) is reduced to 10 percent. Loss of fluid from the vascular space causes renal vasoconstriction. The decreased renal blood flow reduces the glomerular filtration rate. Hemochromagens (myoglobin from damaged muscle and hemoglobin from heat-damaged red blood cells) can plug renal tubules, causing acute tubular necrosis. The renin-angiotensin-aldosterone system is activated to stimulate release of the antidiuretic hormone, causing retention of sodium and water. Activation of this system may be the etiologic factor for postburn hypertension in 30 percent of children with extensive burns.[14]

Loss of potassium ion during the first 24 to 48 hours after burn injury occurs as a result of tissue necrosis and hemolysis of red blood cells. Potassium replacement over the next few days is necessary to counter losses through urine, gastric suction, and diarrhea.

Red blood cell loss is proportional to the depth and extent of burn injury. A deep burn of 50 percent of total body surface area can hemolyze up to 15 percent of red blood cells at the burn site during the first 12 hours, releasing hemoglobin and causing hemoglobinuria. Thrombosis of blood in capillaries at the burn site, delayed hemolysis from heat damage, a decreased blood cell survival time, and a generalized suppression of cell production all contribute to anemia that is evident days to weeks after burn injury. In spite of these mechanisms, an elevated hematocrit is seen initially because the volume of red blood cells is great relative to plasma volume.

INHALATION INJURY

Smoke inhalation influences the child's ability to survive cutaneous burns and approximately doubles the mortality rate for a burn of any size. Therefore, excellent pulmonary care is essential for a child with smoke inhalation without associated burns if the child is conscious on arrival to the emergency department. With pulmonary care, death from smoke inhalation is rare in such cases.[15]

Of all children injured in a fire, 30 percent sustain some form of inhalation injury. Because of their inability to climb over crib rails, to open doors, and to walk down steps, children are frequently trapped in smoke-filled areas for an extended period of time, which increases the likelihood of pulmonary injury. Indirect clues to the presence of these injuries are (1) burns of the face and neck, (2) singed nasal or eyebrow hairs, (3) sooty sputum, (4) hoarseness in voice or cry, and (5) wheezing, rales, or cough. The difficulty in diagnosis arises because these signs and symptoms may or may not be present initially. During the immediate postburn period, the status of the respiratory tract must be continually evaluated.

Carbon Monoxide Poisoning

Carbon monoxide is a by-product of combustion and is found wherever there is smoke. Carbon monoxide poisoning is the most frequent immediate cause of fire-related deaths. The carbon monoxide molecule has an affinity for hemoglobin that is 250 times greater than that of oxygen. Tissue hypoxia occurs as carboxyhemoglobin displaces and reduces the oxygen-carrying capacity of hemoglobin.[16] The only indication of the presumptive diagnosis of carbon monoxide poisoning is the history of entrapment in an enclosed or poorly ventilated smoke-filled area. Specific carboxyhemoglobin levels and related symptoms are given in Table 10-4. Carboxyhemoglobin levels greater than 50 percent cause irreversible central nervous system damage unless prompt treatment is provided.

Management is aimed at restoring adequate oxygenation with 100 percent oxygen humidified with cool mist. With high-flow oxygen therapy delivered by tight mask or endotracheal tube (while serum carboxyhemoglobin level is determined in the laboratory), carboxyhemoglobin levels are reduced by approximately 50 percent in the first 20 minutes of treatment. In room air, one or more hours are required to reduce carboxyhemoglobin to normal levels; in a hyperbaric chamber it takes less than 30 minutes. The inability to gain access to the patient for other treatments and the possibility of vomiting and aspiration during decompression are major disadvantages to the use of hyperbaric oxygen.

Children who awaken in a mist tent after rescue from a smoke-filled room are often terrified because of the similarities of mist and smoke. Delivery to the hospital with the use of an oxyshield is less frightening.

Table 10-4 Carboxyhemoglobin Levels and Related Symptoms of Carbon Monoxide Poisoning from Smoke Inhalation

Carboxyhemoglobin Level (percent)	Symptoms
0 to 8	Asymptomatic
9 to 20	Slight drowsiness, but easily arousable
20 to 40	Headache, nausea, vomiting, and confusion
40 to 60	Severe confusion, ataxia, hallucinations, coma, death

Thermal Injury

Burns of the face, neck, and mucosa of the mouth and nasopharynx produce stridor, tachypnea, and wheezing because burn edema develops in the first 18 to 24 hours. One millimeter of edema or secretions causes a 26 percent reduction of air flow in an adult's trachea (14 mm in diameter). The same amount of edema causes a 55 percent reduction of air flow in a child's trachea (6 mm in diameter). Thus the child's airway is at greater risk for compromise than the adult's.[17] Mucosal burns are an indication for prophylactic endotracheal intubation before progressive edema precludes intubation and makes tracheostomy the only alternative. Tracheostomy near burns gives organisms and debris from the wound an entrance point into the respiratory system.

It is difficult to tape an endotracheal tube to a burned face. Tracheostomy tape looped around the tube instead of adhesive tape allows loosening as edema increases and tightening as edema subsides (Figure 10-2). A card taped to the head of the bed indicating the number on the endotracheal tube at the level of the canine tooth is a good way to check that the tube is where it is supposed to be.

Smoke Poisoning

Combustion of certain products releases toxic chemical irritants, causing both upper and lower airway injury. Burning upholstery produces hydrogen cyanide gas, which

Figure 10-2 Two Methods of Tying Tracheostomy Tape around an Endotracheal Tube To Secure the Tube in the Child with Facial Burns.

inhibits cellular respiration. Breath-holding and laryngospasm are protective mechanisms against excessive exposure to toxic irritants in the conscious patient. Prehospital personnel are urged to perform cardiopulmonary resuscitation on the scene to increase the patient's chances for survival.

In the unconscious patient, chemical irritation causes more severe lower airway injury. Bronchiolitis, atelectasis, pulmonary edema, and sloughing of tracheobronchial mucosa occur as late as 48 to 72 hours after injury.

Assessment

History is the most important factor in determining inhalation injury in the child who is too young or too frightened to talk. The information from emergency medical technicians and fire fighters is invaluable in predicting impending problems. Where the child was found (for example, on a stairway or in a closed closet), the condition of others taken to a different hospital (whether they were intubated or released), and the alertness of the child at the scene are important pieces of information that should not be missed in assessing children injured in house fires. Initial chest roentgenograms and arterial blood gases may be initially normal and serve as good baseline data. Fiberoptic bronchoscopy in adults detects reddened mucosa, which indicates the presence but not the severity of injury. Reddened mucosa is meaningless in a screaming child, and this procedure may precipitate laryngospasm in a child younger than 5 years old. Reassessment of pulmonary status cannot be overemphasized.

Treatment

Vigorous pulmonary toilet, close monitoring of vital signs, measurement of arterial blood gases, and auscultation for breath sounds are the routine aspects of treatment for inhalation injury. Increased mortality is associated with the use of steroids and prophylactic antibiotics.

ELECTRICAL BURNS

The most serious injury sustained by the older child is direct electric current injury from high-tension wires around railroad stations and power stations. The entrance wound is charred and finely demarcated, and the exit wound has an explosive appearance. These wounds are only the "tip of the iceberg," however, and mask underlying progressive damage. The visible burn wound on the skin provides no clue as to the amount of underlying damage because of the unpredictable nature of the course of the electric current. Electricity follows the path of least resistance but generates the greatest amount of heat in bone, which is the most resistant tissue. Nerve, blood, and muscle are the least resistant tissues to electric current, and tendon and fat have moderate resistance. Skin resistance is variable depending on thickness and moisture. Greater systemic effects occur with thin, wet skin and prolonged exposure.[18]

Children who sustain electrical burns require cardiopulmonary resuscitation at the scene and intubation to deliver 100 percent oxygen. Burn resuscitation formulas based on the amount of the total body surface area burned are not useful for direct electrical injuries because the damage is far greater than what is seen. The electrical burn has been likened to a crush injury, with severe muscle necrosis initially and subsequent thrombosis of vessels. Thrombosis causes further muscle damage, with release of myoglobin and hemoglobin manifested as dark, tea-colored urine. Fluid therapy is directed at flushing the kidneys of these products to avoid acute tubular necrosis. Mannitol (0.5 to 1.0 g/kg) is given as a bolus and then as a drip at 0.5 mg/kg/hour to maintain urine output at 1 to 2 mL/kg/hour. If myoglobinuria persists for more than 6 hours, amputation of the affected extremity may be required.[19]

Treatment of the burn wound is early, with frequent excision of necrotic tissue. Mafenide acetate (Sulfamylon®) is the preferred topical antibacterial because of its deeper penetration and effectiveness against clostridial infection. Hourly peripheral pulse readings by ultrasonic flowmeter are helpful in determining the development of compartment syndrome and the need for immediate escharotomy. Amputations are common with these injuries. Neurological changes, secondary hemorrhage, sepsis, and cataracts are just a few of the complications that arise weeks to months after the initial injury.

Electrical burns of the lip involving the commissure are a common pediatric injury that is not limited to the young child who sucks on frayed electrical cords. This injury is most often seen in the preschool to preadolescent group; the child places the female end of an extension cord into the mouth so that both hands can be used as leverage to disconnect an appliance from an extension cord. Arc and contact burns result as electrolyte-rich saliva contacts exposed wires. Low-voltage electricity burns can cause ventricular fibrillation, but systemic effects are rare. The burn is a small area of local necrosis with swelling and pain. As the eschar of this full-thickness injury begins to separate in 10 to 21 days, hemorrhage may occur from the labial arteries. Instructing parents to control bleeding by direct pressure and in wound care in conjunction with close outpatient follow-up is a safe and cost-effective method of management for these injuries.[20]

CHEMICAL BURNS

Chemical burns account for less than 1 percent of pediatric burn admissions. Chemical burns differ from thermal burns in the length of time during which tissue destruction occurs. With thermal injury tissue damage ceases with removal of the heat source; with chemical injury tissue damage continues until the burning agent is inactivated or diluted. These burns are full-thickness injuries, although they appear to be superficial with a tan discoloration on intact, dry skin in the first few days after the injury.

Precious time can be wasted in searching for a neutralizing agent that, if found, can cause a reaction that creates further damage. The immediate treatment for a chemical burn is copious lavage with water to dilute and remove the chemical. Irrigation should be done under a flowing tap for small burns or under a shower for more diffuse burns and should last for 2 to 12 hours. Alkali burns require longer irrigation. To determine the need for further irrigation, it is helpful to check the surface of the wound with litmus paper; a pH greater than 7 indicates alkalinity; if there is doubt concerning the acidity or basicity of the burning agent, irrigation should continue.[21]

NOTES

1. D. Trunkey and S. Parks, "Burns in Children," *Current Problems in Pediatrics* 6(1976):3.
2. James A. O'Neill, Jr., "Burns," in Kenneth J. Welch, Judson G. Randolph, Mark M. Lavitch, James A. O'Neill, Jr., and Marc I. Row, eds., *Pediatric Surgery* (Chicago: Year Book Medical Publishers, 1986), 221.
3. Hugo F. Carvajal and Donald Parks, "Survival Statistics of Burned Children," *Journal of Burn Care and Rehabilitation* 3(1982):84.
4. Brenda L. Berkebile, I. William Goldfarb, and Harvey Slater, "Comparison of Burn Size Estimates between Prehospital Reports and Burn Center Evaluations," *Journal of Burn Care and Rehabilitation* 7(1986):411.
5. M. Costa Arturson, "The Pathophysiology of Severe Thermal Injury," *Journal of Burn Care and Rehabilitation* 6(1985):131.
6. Stuart J. Hulnick, "Burn Resuscitation" (lecture given at St. Christopher's Hospital for Children, Philadelphia, 8 October 1985).
7. John J. McAuliffe and J.A.J. Martyn, "The Burn-Injured Child: Principles of Early Management and Care," *Resident and Staff Physician* 32(1986):33.
8. James A. O'Neill, Jr., "Fluid Resuscitation in the Burned Child—A Reappraisal," *Journal of Pediatric Surgery* 17(1982):607.
9. Gary Purdue, "Reflections on Modern Burn Care," *Journal of Burn Care and Rehabilitation* 5(1984):60.
10. C.A. Jones, I. Feller, and K.E. Richards, "Nursing Care of the Burned Child," in William Carl Bailey, ed., *Pediatric Burns* (Chicago: Year Book Medical Publishers, 1979), 67.
11. Fred T. Caldwell, B.H. Bowser, and J.H. Crabtree, "The Effect of Occlusive Dressings on the Energy Requirements of Burned Children," *Annals of Surgery* 193(1981):587.
12. Marsha Hildreth and Hugo F. Carvajal, "Caloric Requirements in Burned Children," *Journal of Burn Care and Rehabilitation* 3(1982):78.
13. Timothy Day et al., "Nutritional Requirements of the Burned Child," *Proceedings of the American Burn Association* 18(1986):86.
14. Martin B. Popp, Daniel L. Friedberg, and Bruce G. MacMillian, "Clinical Characteristics of Hypertension in Burned Children," *Annals of Surgery* 191(1980):476.
15. David M. Heimbach, "Smoke Inhalation: Current Concepts," in T.L. Wachtel, Virginia Kahn, and Hugh A. Frank, eds., *Current Topics in Burn Care* (Rockville, Md.: Aspen Publishers, Inc., 1983), 31.
16. Manu H. Desai, "Inhalation Injuries in Burned Victims," *Critical Care Quarterly* 3(1984):3.
17. William Carl Bailey, "Overview and Insights," *Journal of Burn Care and Rehabilitation* 3(1982):100.
18. Curtis P. Artz, "Electrical Injury," in C.P. Artz, J.A. Moncrief, and G.A. Pruitt, eds., *Burns: A Team Approach* (Philadelphia: W.B. Saunders Co., 1979), 352.
19. Hal Bingham, "Electrical Burns," *Clinics in Plastic Surgery* 13(1986):79.
20. Joann G. D'Italia and Stuart J. Hulnick, "Outpatient Management of Electrical Burns of the Lip," *Journal of Burn Care and Rehabilitation* 5(1984):465.
21. Stuart J. Hulnick, personal communication, 25 March 1987.

Chapter 11

Pediatric Poisoning

Frances T. Gill

Poisonings are one of the most common medical emergencies involving the pediatric population. Emergency care providers must be able to react swiftly and effectively when dealing with these patients. According to recent statistics, there are approximately two million cases of human exposure to poisons annually in the United States. Of this predicted total number 39.1 percent are reported to be in children between the ages of 1 and 2 years, and 63.4 percent are in children younger than 6 years of age. Children are at risk because they are natural explorers with little sense of danger. Statistically, males 1 to 5 years of age are involved in toxic ingestions most frequently. During the adolescent and adult years, exposures in females increase to 18.1 percent more than in males.

Accidental poisonings in children account for 89.9 percent of all toxic exposures, ingestions accounting for 79.2 percent of this number. Intentional incidents due to drug abuse or suicide attempts are responsible for 8.2 percent. Anaphylactic reactions to food or drugs are linked to 1.3 percent of the total percentage. Professionals dealing with poisoned patients should be aware of the increasing incidence of poisonings related to child abuse. What may appear to be accidental may in reality be an intentional poisoning inflicted by an adult on an unsuspecting child.

Poisonings may be acute or chronic. Acute poisonings occur after a single episode of exposure to a toxin and account for 98.5 percent of available statistical data. Chronic poisoning is often more difficult to pinpoint and is characterized by a slow, insidious change in clinical status that is due to a gradual rise in accumulation of toxic substances in the system. Chronic poisonings are a result of repeated exposures or a prolonged single exposure to a toxin for more than 8 hours. A single substance was responsible for chronic poisoning in the vast majority of reported cases (93.3 percent), and a small number (1.3 percent) were attributable to exposure to two or more toxic substances.

The substances most frequently involved in poisoning episodes for all age groups are

- pharmaceuticals (39.7 percent)
- cleaning substances (9.5 percent)
- plants (8.3 percent)

- personal care products (5.8 percent)
- insect or snake venom (3.4 percent)
- insecticides (2.9 percent).

NONTOXIC INGESTIONS

Often, the poisoned child presenting to the emergency department has ingested a substance that is considered nontoxic. A nontoxic ingestion is defined as the consumption of a nonedible product that usually does not produce symptoms (Exhibit 11-1).[1] For proper identification of a nontoxic ingestion, the detailed history must include

- substance ingested
- components of the substance
- amount ingested

Exhibit 11-1 Substances Commonly Consumed by Children in Nontoxic Ingestions

Abrasives	Indelible markers
Adhesives	Ink
Antacids	Laxatives
Baby care products	Lipstick
Bath oil	Matches
Bleach	Mineral oil
Bubble bath	Mylar balloon paint
Bubble solution	Newspaper
Calamine lotion	Paint (latex)
Candles	Pencils
Chalk	Perfume
Cigarettes and cigars	Petroleum jelly
Clay	Phenolphthalein laxatives
Contraceptive pills	Putty (less than 2 oz.)
Corticosteroids	Rat poison (warfarin)
Cosmetics	Rubber cement
Crayons	Shampoos
Dehumidifying packets	Shaving cream
Deodorizers	Soap
Detergent (phosphate)	Suntan lotion
Fabric softeners	Sweetening agents
Fish-bowl additives	Teething rings
Glues and paste	Thermometers (mercury)
Grease	Toothpaste
Hair care products (dye, spray)	Toy pistol caps
Hand lotion	Vitamins (without iron)
Hydrogen peroxide (3%)	

Source: Adapted by permission of *Pediatrics*, Vol. 54, page 338, copyright 1974.

- absence of clinical symptoms
- absence of "signal word" on the container (such as DANGER, CAUTION, or POISON)

Proper diagnosis of a nontoxic ingestion avoids aggressive, invasive treatment, but further investigation is still warranted. There must be an established means of follow-up assessment. This episode may signify a home environment that is not adequately secure or supervised. In the older child it may signal a suicidal gesture that warrants further medical and psychiatric evaluation.

HISTORY OF POISONING

The most important factor in dealing with a patient who is poisoned is obtaining a full history of the event. This is a challenging assignment for the care provider because the history is often available from an unreliable, unclear source who is enveloped in a crisis situation. Taking the history may begin on the patient's arrival to the emergency department but also may be in the form of a telephone call to a poison control center for immediate advice. It is imperative for the care provider to be calm, clear, concise, and focused during data collection. It is best to approach the history-taking process in a systematic manner.

1. *WHO?* Include the patient's name, age, weight, correct address, and telephone number in the event that follow-up care is needed. Record the name of the parent or guardian who is bringing the child to the health care facility. Document past medical history, current medications being used, and allergy information.
2. *WHAT?* Record the name of the poison, if available. Instruct the family to bring containers of the substance to the hospital. Obtain the name of the product, expiration date, strength, and manufacturer's data on contents and possible treatment for ingestions or exposures. Are there "signal words" on the container? If the substance is unknown, quiz the family about any drug or toxic substances that may be in the home or the surrounding environment. If needed, send someone to the home to search for possible clues. Encourage the family members to think of others who came in contact with the patient and who may have had medications with them. Investigate street names and composition of illegal drugs.
3. *HOW MUCH?* Determine the size of the container and how much of the substance was in it before the incident. Was this the original container? Count pills or measure liquid medications and calculate doses that should be missing according to the pharmacy label and patient history of compliance to the prescription regimen. Contact the appropriate pharmacy as needed for further information. Was there any evidence of substance on the patient's clothing or in the surrounding environment? Is there any possibility that the substance was shared with other children? With caustic liquids, assess the oral cavity, mucosa, skin, and eyes for evidence of

splash injury. Is there any chance that more than one substance was involved?
4. *WHEN?* How much time has elapsed since the exposure? Has there been an unexplained change in the child's level of consciousness? When did these symptoms first become evident, and have they increased or decreased since the time of this event?
5. *WHY?* Was this an accidental or intentional incident? Does this child have a past history of pica? Has this ever occurred before? Was there supervision at the time of the incident? Who was the primary caregiver? Often it will be appropriate to question the family and child separately. Data should include changes in the family structure or school problems. The interview of adolescent females should include the possibility of pregnancy, the date of the last normal menstrual period, and current sexual activity and birth control methods in use.
6. *PREHOSPITAL CARE?* Was there any treatment given at home or by prehospital care providers? Were there any clues noted in the environment? Include the use of home remedies (milk, water, syrup of ipecac). Did vomiting occur? How much? What did the emesis look like? Were there pill particles or other foreign substances evident? Was a specimen brought with the patient?

With these data in hand, a plan can be formulated to deliver the most effective emergency care. Patients who have experienced an exposure to poison should be treated as critical emergencies until a life-threatening toxic event is completely ruled out. The local poison control center should be contacted immediately to provide guidelines for optimal patient management.

EMERGENCY MANAGEMENT

After the history is obtained, the care provider is often able to determine the level of emergency intervention that is needed. A rapid, thorough head-to-toe assessment, full vital signs, and Glasgow Coma Scale score enhance the verbal data. The patient should be fully undressed. If the history indicates the possible ingestion of a caustic liquid, the clothing should be examined for evidence of spills. Clothing should also be closely examined if the use of illegal substances is suspected. The eyes, skin, and mucous membranes should be assessed for areas of burns, irritation, or obvious signs of injury. Odors on the clothing, skin surfaces, and breath can offer valuable clues to the toxic substance.

Initial stabilization of the poisoned patient must be prioritized on the basis of the ABCs of resuscitation (airway, breathing, and circulation). An adequate airway is established and maintained throughout the resuscitative stage of emergency care. The airway is examined for possible burns, irritation, and edema. The lung fields are carefully auscultated for evidence of rales, rhonchi, wheezes, or decreased breath sounds. A chest roentgenogram is needed if the toxic substance is corrosive or if aspiration is suspected. Cool, misted oxygen given at 35 percent by blow-by may be adequate for support. If more aggressive measures are necessary, arterial blood gases may be measured to determine whether the patient is experiencing respiratory compromise. Specific toxic episodes may cause variable degrees of respiratory or metabolic alkalosis of acidosis, which require ventilatory support. Proper equipment for endotracheal or orotracheal intubation should be readily accessible. Suction must be at hand to protect the airway from possible emesis and aspiration.

Full vital signs are documented, and the patient is placed on a cardiorespiratory monitor to detect changes in heart rate and rhythm. A 12-lead electrocardiogram is obtained and evaluated. Blood pressure is assessed every 5 minutes until it is stable. Orthostatic blood pressure changes can occur with toxic ingestions, so that baseline readings with the patient lying, sitting, and standing should be obtained and reassessed as indicated. Alteration in temperature is also a risk, and changes attributable to an environmental exposure or a pharmaceutical effect must be differentiated. The central nervous system is assessed by general observation of the patient's affect, speech, gait, and ability to follow commands and answer simple age-appropriate questions. In the young child, the parent is the most important source of history of the child's typical behavior.

A large-bore intravenous line is inserted, and 0.9 percent normal saline or Ringer's lactate is administered at a rate equal to or greater than maintenance, according to physician order. In severe hypotension, the use of pneumatic antishock trousers has been suggested to provide a rapid fluid challenge to the patient. This measure is currently under evaluation for its effectiveness.[2,3]

Blood samples are sent for toxicology screen, alcohol levels, serum electrolytes, complete blood cell count, prothrombin time, partial thromboplastin time, and blood type and cross-match as indicated. Urine is obtained, examined for changes in color and clarity, and sent for routine analysis, toxicology screening, and pregnancy testing when applicable. Abdominal roentgenograms show radiopaque material such as iron, enteric-coated pills, and chloral hydrate in the gastrointestinal tract.

Gut Decontamination

The next important consideration in the management of the poisoned patient is decontamination of the gut. Dilution and demulcent therapy are the initial first aid for caustic or corrosive ingestions. Dilution with water or milk is indicated for soaps, detergents, and household cleaning agents. Demulcents such as egg whites, butter, or ice cream are indicated when the ingested substance causes mucosal irritation. Depending on certain factors, emesis may be contraindicated in situations such as

- a child younger than 6 months of age
- nontoxic ingestion
- coma, seizures, altered level of consciousness, or potential change in neurologic status within 20 minutes
- compromised gag reflex

- respiratory distress
- ingestion of a strong acid, alkali, pure petroleum distillate, turpentine, camphor, strychnine, or sharp foreign body.

When the history is clear and emesis is indicated, syrup of ipecac is the safe, effective emetic of choice. The appropriate dose is given by mouth as follows: in children 9 to 12 months of age, 10 mL; in children 1 year of age and older, 15 mL; in adolescents, 30 mL. This medication should be followed by at least 120 mL of clear, colorless fluid by mouth. Warm water is effective, and vomiting occurs in most patients within 15 minutes. Colored fluids should not be administered because they may distort the appearance of gastric contents being visually examined for foreign substances. If the child does not vomit within 15 to 20 minutes, the dose of syrup of ipecac is repeated once and fluids and activity encouraged as indicated. If it is deemed safer to keep the child at rest, the patient is positioned upright or on the left side to prevent possible aspiration of vomitus.

Gastric Lavage

In the patient who has not vomited after the second dose of syrup of ipecac or in whom inducement of vomiting is contraindicated, a nasogastric or orogastric tube should be inserted to begin effective gastric evacuation and appropriate lavage. The following guidelines should be followed.

1. Select the largest possible tube to capture pill particles.
2. Avoid trauma to the nose or mouth during tube insertion. Obtain a history of existing anatomical abnormalities before tube placement.
3. Measure the tube from the tip of the patient's ear to the nose to the xyphoid process. Mark the end point with a piece of tape.
4. Fully explain the procedure to the patient and family. Restrain the patient as needed, and position him or her upright or on the left side with the head flexed on the chest.
5. Lubricate the tube with water-soluble jelly or cold water.
6. Have suction readily available before tube insertion.
7. After passing the tube, check its proper placement by inserting 15 to 30 mL of air and auscultating at the area of the stomach. A "whoosh" should be heard. Aspirate and save the undiluted gastric contents for laboratory analysis for toxic substances. Lavage with isotonic solutions of normal saline, instilling 30 to 50 mL at a time to a total volume of 1 to 2 L or until the gastric contents are clear. Examine the aspirant for evidence of pill particles, foreign substances, or blood, and document findings. Avoid the use of sterile water for lavage because of the dangers of water intoxication and inducing disturbances in fluid and electrolyte balance.

It is estimated that less than 50 percent of toxins are eliminated from the gut during initial emesis or lavage. Activated charcoal is the adsorption agent that will bind toxic substances, decrease further absorption, and enhance excretion. Charcoal binds to syrup of ipecac and specific antidotes, so that proper timing of administration and indications for use must be thoroughly evaluated. Before administration of activated charcoal, it should be established that vomiting has subsided. The child can be given a small amount of clear fluid by mouth as a trial, if clinically indicated. The usual dose of activated charcoal is 1 g/kg and should be given early in the treatment course. The charcoal is mixed with water to form a slurry and given by mouth or nasogastric tube. Cherry or cola flavoring can be added without adverse reaction. Because of the appearance and texture of the mixture, children often refuse to drink it. It is therefore imperative to explain the importance of this therapy to the child and family and to set a time limit of 10 to 15 minutes for completion of administration. If this is not tolerated, the dose should be given by nasogastric tube.

After completion of the dose, a saline cathartic agent is administered to enhance the excretion of the poison or charcoal-poison complex. One of the following agents may be used in the appropriate dose: 20 percent magnesium sulfate, 250 mg/kg; 25 percent sodium sulfate, 250 mg/kg every 4 hours; or magnesium citrate, 4 mL/kg. Some new, premixed charcoal products contain sorbitol as the cathartic agent. When this preparation is used, no other cathartic agent is needed.

After assessment of adequate bowel sounds, the same dose of cathartic can be repeated every 1 to 2 hours until initial excretion of the charcoal is evident in the stools. Stimulant or oil cathartics are not recommended because they cause prolonged stooling and actually precipitate increased systemic absorption of lipid-soluble toxins, increasing the risk of aspiration and lipoid pneumonia.

Certain drugs are instituted for treatment of specific poisons. Table 11-1 lists several examples.

Table 11-1 Examples of Drugs Given to Counteract Toxic Effects of Ingested Substances

Drug and Dosage	Uses	Precautions
Apomorphine, 0.07 to 0.1 mg/kg subcutaneously (one dose only)	Inducement of emesis when rapid onset is indicated.	Not used in pediatrics. May suppress central nervous and respiratory system function. Keep narcotic antagonist at bedside.
Naloxone (Narcan®), 10 μg/kg to a total of 10 mg/kg intravenously	Specific antidote for narcotic overdoses.	Short half-life; may need to repeat. Restrain patient before administration.
N-Acetylcysteine (Mucomyst®), 140 mg/kg of 20% solution orally. Four hours later give 70 mg/kg every 4 hours for 17 doses (3 days).	Specific antidote for hepatotoxic acetaminophen ingestions.	Do not give activated charcoal in single acetaminophen ingestion.

Diuresis

Diuresis to promote increased glomerular filtration and decreased absorption of toxins is indicated for substances that are primarily excreted through the renal system. Before this treatment is instituted, the patient should be assessed for the following[4]:

- adequate kidney function
- cardiorespiratory stability
- stable vital signs (blood pressure > 90 mmHg systolic)
- blood levels of the toxin near the lethal range
- coma reaction that is expected to last 3 days or longer.

Adequate fluids are administered to increase significantly the urine output. Diuretic agents such as furosemide (Lasix®, 1 mg/kg) are administered to enhance excretion, but osmotic diuretics such as mannitol or urea are deemed more effective in reducing toxin absorption. A 20 percent solution of mannitol is given in an initial dose of 250 to 500 mg/kg and is maintained at 10 percent. A 50 percent solution of urea is administered at 1 mL/kg/hour over 4 hours and is maintained at the same concentration. An indwelling urinary catheter is needed to monitor urine output, which should be a minimum of 5 mL/kg/hour; the goal of diuretic therapy is 6 to 9 mL/kg/hour.[5] Strict intake and output data and urine specific gravity are recorded. Special attention must be given to fluid, electrolyte, and acid-base balance along with serum and urine osmolality and central venous pressure readings.[6]

Methods to alter urine pH may be beneficial in specific poisonings. Weak acid ingestions respond to urine alkalinization by intravenous administration of sodium bicarbonate at 3 to 5 mEq/kg to maintain the urine pH at 8.0.[7] Weak bases are treated with acidification measures such as ammonium chloride at 75 mg/kg per dose (by nasogastric tube) in four divided doses to maintain the urine pH at 4.5 to 5.5.[8]

SPECIFIC TOXINS

Although there are thousands of products that can be responsible for possible poisonings in the pediatric population, a few common ones are outlined in this section. All care providers are encouraged to contact a poison control center early in the treatment course of a poisoned patient. The poisondex reference system available at most poison control centers will provide detailed information about each particular substance along with the appropriate treatment guidelines.

Salicylates

Aspirin and over-the-counter medications containing salicylates are widely used and are often responsible for serious overdoses. Legislation limiting baby aspirin containers to 36 1.25-g tablets with child-proof packaging, along with recent warnings against aspirin use in varicella and viral illness, has decreased the incidences of these toxic episodes. Often, an uninformed parent will administer a proper dose of aspirin along with a cold remedy and other agents containing salicylates and expose the child to an accidental poisoning. Children presenting to the emergency department with a possible salicylate overdose need rapid clinical assessment, gut decontamination, and laboratory analysis of blood, urine, and emesis (Table 11-2).

Acetaminophen

Products containing acetaminophen are popular for their analgesic and antipyretic effects. There are currently more than three hundred products available. Because of their accessibility, acetaminophen-containing drugs are among the top five substances implicated in accidental ingestions and among the top ten in intentional overdoses. Many over-the-counter drugs contain a mixture of pharmaceutical agents; to ensure proper emergency management, care providers must examine container labels to determine whether acetaminophen is included in the ingested substance (Table 11-3).

It is important for care providers to understand the four clinical stages of acute acetaminophen overdose.

1. Stage 1 (first 24 hours): malaise, vomiting, pallor, diaphoresis, anorexia.
2. Stage 2 (24 to 48 hours; the latency phase): patient experiences a sense of well-being. Blood studies begin to show changes related to liver function tests, clotting factors, and serum glucose levels.
3. Stage 3 (72 to 96 hours): liver necrosis is evidenced by clinical signs.
4. Stage 4 (96 hours to 2 weeks): gradual or complete resolution of hepatic symptoms with treatment. If antidotes were not instituted and liver damage is irreversible, 2 percent to 4 percent of patients will experience hepatic failure.

Ethyl Alcohol

Ethyl alcohol is a component of many household products (such as mouthwash, colognes, and deodorants), and intoxications can occur when these materials are accidentally or intentionally ingested or when excessive amounts of alcoholic beverages are consumed. A blood level of 3.8 mL/kg is considered lethal. Absorption is rapid, and symptoms are classic. The characteristic odor of alcohol gives the health care provider the clue for appropriate management, but concomitant ingestions or trauma should not be arbitrarily ruled out (Table 11-4).

Iron

Poisoning with preparations containing iron are a common and potentially fatal occurrence in the pediatric population. Popular iron-fortified children's vitamins or candy look-alike ferrous sulfate tablets intended for adults are the major causes of intoxication. Elemental iron is considered toxic in doses of 50 mg/kg or more and lethal at 180 mg/kg (Table 11-5).[9]

Table 11-2 Salicylate Poisoning

System	Findings	Laboratory Values	Management
Respiratory	Respiratory alkalosis Hyperpnea Tachypnea	Increased blood pH Decreased arterial carbon dioxide pressure Decreased blood bicarbonate level	Maintain patent airway; support with oxygen; analyze arterial blood gases; draw blood for toxicology screen.
Cardiac	Hypotension Hypovolemia Tachycardia		Establish intravenous access; apply cardiac monitor; establish and analyze 12-lead electrocardiogram; record vital signs with orthostatic readings; maintain blood pressure with volume or drug infusion as ordered by physician.
Central nervous	Agitation Coma Delirium Hyperactivity Lethargy Seizures Sleeplessness Tinnitus	Decreased glucose levels in cerebrospinal fluid	Assess neurologic status; use Glasgow Coma Scale; provide safe environment.
Renal	Renal failure Sodium retention Tubular damage Water retention	Sodium levels may be normal	Record accurate hourly intake and output. Document urine specific gravity with each void.
Gastrointestinal	Decreased intestinal motility Diarrhea Bleeding Nausea Vomiting		Assess bowel sounds; hematest emesis and stools.
Hematologic	Bruising Decreased platelet aggregation Petechiae	Decreased level of clotting factor VIII Decreased platelet count Prolonged bleeding time	Observe for signs of bleeding; provide pressure at puncture sites; provide patient teaching to decrease bleeding potential (e.g., no toothbrushes).
Metabolic	Hyperpyrexia Increased metabolic rate Ketosis Metabolic acidosis Metabolic alkalosis	Hyperglycemia Hypoglycemia Hypokalemia Metabolic acidosis Decreased blood pH Decreased arterial carbon dioxide pressure	Monitor urine pH and maintain at 7.0; correct blood glucose level appropriately; monitor body temperature and treat accordingly; correct electrolyte balance as needed.

Pediatric Poisoning 183

Table 11-2 continued

System	Findings	Laboratory Values	Management
		Decreased blood bicarbonate level	
		Metabolic alkalosis	
		Increased blood pH	
		Increased arterial carbon dioxide pressure	
		Increased blood bicarbonate level	

Table 11-3 Acetaminophen Poisoning

System	Findings	Laboratory Values	Management
Respiratory			Maintain patent airway; support with oxygen; observe for signs of bronchospasm if using N-acetylcysteine (Mucomyst®) as antidote; draw blood for toxicology screen.
Cardiac	Myocardial changes ST segment abnormalities T wave flattening Pericarditis		Establish intravenous access; apply cardiac monitor; establish and analyze 12-lead electrocardiogram; record full vital signs.
Central nervous	Stupor Confusion		Assess neurologic status; use Glasgow Coma Scale; provide safe environment.
Renal	Decreased urine output Renal failure	Decreased blood urea nitrogen level	Record hourly urine output with specific gravity readings; document strict intake and output.
Gastrointestinal	Anorexia Nausea Vomiting	Increased liver enzyme levels Increased bilirubin	Induce vomiting with syrup of ipecac or perform gastric lavage as indicated; do not give activated charcoal in single acetaminophen ingestions. In multiple ingestions it may be used but must be removed by nasogastric tube before administration of specific antidote (N-acetylcysteine).

continues

Table 11-3 continued

System	Findings	Laboratory Values	Management
Hematologic	Coagulation abnormalities Nosebleeds Petechiae	Prolonged partial thromboplastin time (PTT)	Observe for signs of bleeding; administer vitamin K for prolonged PTT as ordered; draw blood for acetaminophen level 4 hours after ingestion; repeat at 8 hours if level is elevated.
Metabolic	Hypoglycemia	Decreased serum glucose level	Correct blood glucose level appropriately; maintain fluid and electrolyte balance.
Hepatic	Jaundice Liver necrosis Right upper quadrant pain	Transient, increased liver enzyme levels	Continue strict antidote regimen with N-acetylcysteine as ordered.

There are four clinical stages of iron poisoning.

1. Stage 1 (6 to 12 hours after ingestion): gastrointestinal symptoms with guaiac-positive stools and emesis, tachypnea, tachycardia, diaphoresis, pallor, cyanosis, shock, coma.
2. Stage 2 (6 to 12 hours and 48 hours after ingestion): clinical improvement.
3. Stage 3 (12 to 48 hours after ingestion): seizures, disorientation, multisystem failures.
4. Stage 4 (several weeks after ingestion): cirrhosis and pyloric or duodenal stenosis.

Tricyclic Antidepressants

Increased accessibility of tricyclic antidepressants as a result of their wide use for treatment of depression and enuresis presents a significant health problem for the pediatric population. A dose of 10 to 20 mg/kg causes serious side effects, and 35 to 50 mg/kg is deemed a fatal dose. Symptoms are usually evident within 4 hours of ingestion, and effects peak within 12 to 24 hours. These drugs create an anticholinergic effect in the overdosed patient (Table 11-6).

Household Products

Young children, who are actively investigating their environment, often out of curiosity ingest a household product. Most of these incidents are nontoxic episodes, but there is a significant risk of a dangerous event.

Cosmetics, cleaning products, bleach, and solvents are the products involved in most ingestions. Burning and irritation of the skin, oral mucosa, esophagus, or gastroin-

Table 11-4 Ethyl Alcohol Poisoning

System	Findings	Laboratory Values	Management
Respiratory	Respiratory distress	Increased blood ethanol levels (150 to 300 mg/dL causes symptoms of intoxication; more than 400 mg/dL may be fatal)	Maintain patent airway; assess gag reflex; have suction available; assess tidal volume (normal, 10 to 15 mL/kg); support with oxygen as needed; draw blood for toxicology screen and ethyl alcohol level (do not use alcohol to prepare the skin for injections).
Cardiac			Establish intravenous access; apply cardiac monitor.
Central nervous	Loss of deep tendon reflexes Ataxia Dilated pupils Loss of inhibition Stupor Slurred speech Seizures Coma		Assess neurologic status; use Glasgow Coma Scale; provide safe environment; treat seizures with diazepam (0.1 to 0.3 mg/kg by slow intravenous push) as ordered; naloxone may reverse depressant effect of ethyl alcohol.
Renal	Increased urine output		Record accurate intake and output; maintain fluid and electrolyte balance.
Gastrointestinal	Nausea Vomiting Abdominal pain Dehydration		Induce vomiting with syrup of ipecac or perform gastric lavage as indicated; administer activated charcoal and a cathartic as ordered.
Metabolic	Hypothermia Hypoglycemia Metabolic acidosis	Decreased blood glucose level Decreased blood pH, arterial carbon dioxide pressure, and blood bicarbonate levels	Maintain adequate body temperature; administer glucose intravenously for blood glucose level less than 60 mg/dL, as ordered; administer thiamine (100 mg intramuscularly) for chronic alcoholics.

testinal tract occurs. Strong cleaning agents and drain openers can cause serious burns, and their containers usually display special product labeling to alert the consumer. In the event of ingestion, the original containers must be thoroughly examined and the data reported to the poison control center (Table 11-7).

Table 11-5 Iron Poisoning

System	Findings	Laboratory Values	Management
Respiratory	Pallor Cyanosis Tachypnea Pneumonitis		Maintain patent airway; support with oxygen; evaluate breath sounds; examine chest roentgenogram; draw blood for appropriate laboratory tests.
Cardiac	Tachycardia Hypotension Circulatory collapse		Establish intravenous access; apply cardiac monitor; establish and analyze 12-lead electrocardiogram; record vital signs with orthostatic readings; maintain adequate blood pressure with volume or drug infusion as ordered by physician.
Central nervous	Lethargy Restlessness Confusion Seizures Shock Coma		Assess neurologic status; use Glasgow Coma Scale; provide safe environment.
Gastrointestinal	Nausea Vomiting Abdominal pain Guaiac-positive emesis and stool Late pyloric or duodenal stenosis		Induce vomiting with syrup of ipecac or perform gastric lavage as indicated; hold activated charcoal (may obstruct endoscopy); administer saline cathartic as ordered; evaluate abdominal roentgenograms before and after treatment (iron tablets are radiopaque).
Hematologic	Decreased plasma volume Leukocytosis Coagulopathy	Increased serum iron level Increased total iron binding capacity (if serum iron level exceeds total iron binding capacity, free iron is present systemically); white blood cell count greater than 15,000/mm^3	
Metabolic	Hyperglycemia Diaphoresis Hyperpyrexia Metabolic acidosis (rosé-colored urine with test dose of	Blood glucose level more than 150 mg/dL Decreased blood pH, arterial carbon dioxide pressure, blood bicarbonate levels	Correct hyperglycemia as ordered; administer oral sodium bicarbonate as ordered to convert iron to less absorbable salt; maintain adequate body

Table 11-5 continued

System	Findings	Laboratory Values	Management
	deferoxamine indicates that iron is present)		temperature; administer antidote as ordered: deferoxamine, 10 to 15 mg/kg/hour. intravenously (maximum dosage, 360 mg/kg to 6 g total in 24 hours).
Hepatic	Cirrhosis Liver failure Liver necrosis (2 to 4 days after ingestion)	Elevated liver function tests	

Table 11-6 Tricyclic Antidepressant Poisoning

System	Findings	Laboratory Values	Management
Respiratory	Respiratory depression		Maintain patent airway; support with oxygen; analyze arterial blood gases; draw blood for toxicology screen.
Cardiac	Tachycardia Ventricular dysrhythmia Initial hypertension then hypotension		Establish intravenous access; apply cardiac monitor; establish and analyze 12-lead electrocardiogram; treat dysrhythmias as ordered; maintain adequate blood pressure with volume or drug infusions as ordered.
Central nervous	Ataxia Anxiety Delirium Lethargy Myoclonus Hallucinations Dilated pupils (react to light) Coma		Assess neurologic status; use Glasgow Coma Scale; provide safe environment; treat seizures with diazepam (0.1 to 0.3 mg/kg by slow intravenous push) as ordered.
Renal	Urine retention		Record accurate intake and output; record hourly output as indicated.
Gastrointestinal	Decreased gastric motility		Induction of emesis is not indicated when patient exhibits symptoms of overdose due to rapid neurologic changes. Drug slows gastric motility and

continues

188 PEDIATRIC TRAUMA NURSING

Table 11-6 continued

System	Findings	Laboratory Values	Management
			is delayed in stomach. Administer activated charcoal and saline cathartic; prepare antidote per physician order: physostigmine (Antilirium®), 0.5 mg by slow intravenous push (may repeat every 5 minutes to maximum dose of 2 mg).
Metabolic	Hypothermia Hyperthermia Metabolic acidosis	Decreased blood pH Decreased arterial carbon dioxide pressure Decreased blood bicarbonate level	Maintain adequate body temperature; correct metabolic acidosis per physician order; maintain fluid and electrolyte balance.

Table 11-7 Household Product Poisoning

System	Findings	Laboratory Values	Management
Respiratory	Cough Nasopharyngeal irritation from vapors Pulmonary edema		Maintain patent airway; support with oxygen as needed; assess airway for burns, edema; set up for chest roentgenography.
Gastrointestinal	Nausea Vomiting Oral or esophageal burns		Assess gag reflex; have suction readily available; do not induce vomiting; assess gastrointestinal tract for burns, edema; administer dilution/demulcent therapy as indicated; maintain fluid and electrolyte balance.
Skin	Local irritation Erythema Burns		Flush skin with copious amounts of water; use aseptic technique in caring for skin to prevent infection.
Eyes	Severe irritation		Irrigate eyes with copious amounts of free-flowing fluid (normal saline, Ringer's lactate, Dacriose®); obtain full ophthalmic examination as indicated; explain probable need for follow-up care.

Caustics and Corrosives

Caustics and corrosives are a significant hazard, and there are long-term ramifications of ingestion. Common caustic products include metal cleaners, toilet bowl cleaners, hair dye, batteries, Clinitest tablets, drain cleaners, electric dishwasher products, bleach, and ammonia. These products are accessible in most homes (Table 11-8).

Lead

Lead poisoning, or plumbism, is a significant health problem for the pediatric age group. Characteristically, children aged 1 to 5 years with a history of pica are at the greatest risk. Children of families living in low-income housing or in homes built in the 1940s that have lead-based paint and plumbing are also at high risk for lead poisoning. Often, the normal activities of toddlers, including crawling and teething on various objects, increase the incidence of lead intoxication.

Lead is ingested and absorbed through the gastrointestinal tract or lungs. It is normally excreted by the kidney, but in large amounts it is deposited in the bones, blood, kidney, mucous tissues, and brain (Table 11-9).

POISONING PREVENTION

In recent years, mortality and morbidity statistics of children involved in poisoning episodes have decreased significantly. Numerous factors are responsible for this decline. Poison control centers are the most effective information resource for treatment of exposure to potential toxins. The first poison control center was established in 1953 in Chicago through the efforts of the local government and the medical community. This was a central system for collection of data on specific substances and appropriate toxicology information. There are presently more than 600 centers nationwide.

Poison control centers are staffed by clinical toxicologists, emergency and general practice physicians, nurses, and other personnel specifically trained in the treatment of potential poisonings. They provide numerous services to the public as well as to the medical community:

- comprehensive, current poison information
- information about treatment modalities
- links with appropriate treatment sites
- educational programs
- ongoing data collection
- toll-free 24-hour telephone service
- access to appropriate patient transport
- research
- assistance in emergency medical service poison system development.

The American Association of Poison Control Centers (AAPCC) collects ongoing data on poison exposures from around the country. The AAPCC has also developed standards

Table 11-8 Poisoning with Caustics and Corrosives

System	Findings	Laboratory Values	Management
Respiratory	Respiratory distress Laryngeal burns or edema Airway obstruction Pulmonary edema		Maintain patent airway; support with oxygen; have suction readily available; set up for chest and lateral neck roentgenography.
Gastrointestinal	Oral mucosa, esophageal, or stomach burns Gastrointestinal perforation or stricture Drooling Difficulty swallowing		Assess gag reflex; have suction readily available; do not induce vomiting or perform gastric lavage; do not give activated charcoal or saline cathartic; check for guaiac in stools; prepare for possible esophagoscopy.
Skin	Burns Erythema Blisters		Flush skin with copious amounts of water (skin must not have a soapy feeling at the end of irrigation; if this persists, continue flushing); use sterile or aseptic technique when caring for skin to prevent infection.
Eyes	Burns Blindness		Flush eyes with copious, free-flowing fluid (normal saline, Ringer's lactate, Dacriose®); obtain full ophthalmic examination as indicated; explain probable need for follow-up care.

of care for poison control centers and has established certification criteria. The American Academy of Clinical Toxicology and the American Academy of Pediatrics are active in poisoning prevention education and legislative issues. Legislation has mandated positive changes in the consumer market. In 1970, the Poison Prevention Packaging Act was passed and requires child-proof packaging on products posing a toxic risk to children. The Consumer Product Safety Commission's statistics show a significant decline in exposure to regulated products since that time.

Poisoning prevention education is a vital part of treating the patient involved in a toxic incident. Since 1961, there has been an annual Poison Prevention Week sponsored by the medical community, consumer groups, industry, local governments, and the news media. The purpose is to alert the public to the dangers of poisoning in children and to provide guidelines for aggressive prevention.

Table 11-9 Lead Poisoning

System	Findings	Laboratory Values	Management
Respiratory			Maintain patent airway; hyperventilate (if there are signs of increased intracranial pressure); document full vital signs.
Central nervous	Ataxia Headache Insomnia Irritability Cerebral edema Increased intracranial pressure Malaise Decreased deep tendon reflexes Seizures Coma	Spinal tap may be contraindicated (lead level less than 25 μg/dL is normal in children)	Assess neurologic status; establish intravenous access (administer fluids carefully because of central nervous system status); control seizures with diazepam (0.1 to 0.3 mg/kg by slow intravenous push) per physician order; provide safe environment; for lead levels greater than 50 to 60 μg/dL start chelation therapy as ordered: dimercaprol (3 to 5 mg/kg per dose) and Calcium EDTA (50 to 75 mg/kg/day)—refer to *Physicians' Desk Reference* for ongoing therapy.
Renal	Aminoaciduria Glycosuria Phosphaturia Fanconi's syndrome	Urine with high levels of amino acids, glucose, phosphate	Record accurate intake and output; maintain adequate urine output (1 to 2 mL/kg/hour).
Gastrointestinal	Anorexia Colic Constipation Vomiting	Roentgenogram shows gastrointestinal lead flecks or lead lines in long bones	In recent ingestion, induce vomiting with syrup of ipecac or perform gastric lavage as indicated; administer activated charcoal and saline cathartic as ordered; if abdominal roentgenogram shows lead flecks, administer a cleansing enema.

NOTES

1. Regine Aronow, *American Academy of Pediatrics Handbook of Common Poisonings in Children*, 2d ed. (Chicago: 1983).
2. J. Barber and S. Budassi, *Emergency Nursing Principles and Practice* (St. Louis: C.V. Mosby Co., 1981).

3. Lewis R. Goldfrank et al., *Goldfrank's Toxicologic Emergencies*, 3d ed. (Norwalk, Conn.: Appleton-Century-Crofts, 1986).

4. Steven Ludwig et al., *Textbook of Pediatric Emergency Medicine* (Baltimore, Md.: Williams & Wilkins, 1983).

5. Thom Mayer et al., *Emergency Management of Pediatric Trauma* (Philadelphia: W.B. Saunders Co., 1985).

6. M. Newton et al., "General Treatments of Household Poisonings," *Journal of Emergency Nursing* 13 (1987):12–15.

7. M. Newton et al., "Specific Treatments of Poisoning by Household Products and Medications," *Journal of Emergency Nursing* 13(1987):16–26.

8. D. Pascoe and M. Grossman, *Quick Reference to Pediatric Emergencies*, 3d ed. (Philadelphia: J.B. Lippincott Co., 1984).

9. Ibid.

Chapter 12
Submersion Injuries

Deborah P. Henderson

Only a few minutes of submersion may cause death or serious disability in human beings. This may seem to be remarkable in view of the fact that the first 9 months of human life are spent in a liquid medium. When an infant is born, however, the lungs change from a fluid-filled to a gas-filled organ, and submersion thereafter becomes a life-threatening event.

A large number of submersion injuries occur in children: drowning is the second leading cause of accidental death in children.[1] There are about 7,000 drowning deaths yearly in the United States and about 150,000 worldwide.[2] The number of deaths by drowning is only an indication of the risk of submersion injury; they represent less than one-tenth of all submersion incidents.[3] Some of the epidemiology of submersion injury is as follows:

1. Forty percent of drowning deaths occur in children younger than 4 years of age, and 20 percent of drownings are in individuals 5 to 20 years old. Alcohol is frequently a factor in incidents in teenagers.[4]
2. Drowning occurs more often in fresh water (80 percent) than in salt water: residential pools, ponds, and lakes are the most common sites of submersion injuries.[5]
3. Two-thirds of swimming pool drowning deaths occur in children younger than 3 years of age; the combination of curiosity, mobility, and inability to swim puts this age group at high risk for submersion injuries.[6]
4. Drowning is three times more common in males than in females[7] and three times more common in blacks than in whites; the highest rate is among Native Americans.[8]
5. The peak time for submersion injuries is during the summer months, on weekends, between 4 and 6 P.M.[9]

The pathophysiologic processes in drowning are asphyxia and hypoxemia, which lead to respiratory and metabolic acidosis and organ failure.[10] Hypothermia and cardiac effects may play a role in any drowning, especially in cold water drownings.[11] Although medical treatment for submersion injuries has improved in the last 10 years as a result of advancements in resuscitation procedures and increased understanding of the pathophysiology of submersion injuries, prevention remains the most important factor in lowering mortality and morbidity.

TERMINOLOGY AND CAUSES OF SUBMERSION INJURIES

There have been many attempts to categorize types of submersion incidents and injuries. A review of the literature shows several terms to be in common but inconsistent use (Exhibit 12-1). Injuries resulting from submersion incidents have many factors in common, and there is wide variation in the use of the various terms. To avoid confusion, only two general terms for these injuries will be used in this chapter: "drowning," to mean death resulting from a submersion incident, and "submersion injury," a general term to include all injuries resulting from submersion in a liquid medium.

The chief causes of submersion incidents include one or more of the following:

- inability to swim and exhaustion
- substance abuse, usually alcohol (especially in older children)
- traumatic incidents including traffic accidents, diving or surfing accidents, rough play, falls, and assaults
- suicide attempts, mainly in the adolescent age group
- cardiac rhythm disturbances (mostly in the adult population, rarely in children)
- hyperventilation, which eliminates the respiratory drive during breathholding (a cause in underwater swimmers attempting to prolong submersion times[12])
- scuba diving accidents
- child abuse, most often bathtub or pail submersions of young children
- epilepsy or other previous medical illness.

Other factors contributing to the high incidence of submersion injuries in children include

- lack of effective safety barriers for pools
- improper supervision of children
- disobedience
- poor pool design.

FRESH WATER, SALT WATER, AND COLD WATER INJURY

Submersion injuries occur in many different locations: in swimming pools, lakes, ponds, canals, oceans, marshes, bathtubs, hottubs, toilets, buckets, and even dog bowls. The two most common immersion fluids are fresh and salt water. It was originally believed that there were significant variations in the effects of these fluids because of the difference in osmolality, but studies have shown that there is little to distinguish the two.

Exhibit 12-1 Commonly Used Terminology in Submersion Injury

Drowning	Death by submersion.
Near drowning	Survival for a period of time after suffocation by submersion.
Secondary drowning	Death occurring well after, and as a result of, the submersion incident, also used to mean pulmonary complications from the submersion injury.
Postimmersion syndrome	Complications resulting from the submersion incident.
Wet drowning	Drowning with fluid filling the lungs.
Dry drowning	Drowning with laryngospasm maintained until death or rescue, preventing fluid from entering the lungs.
Sudden immersion syndrome	Death from cardiac rhythm disturbance resulting from sudden immersion in very cold water.

In most cases, patients do not aspirate sufficient fluid to cause life-threatening changes either in blood volume or electrolytes.[13]

The initial insult in submersion injuries is damage to the lungs from (1) loss or destruction of surfactant, (2) damage to the alveolar basement membrane, and (3) pulmonary edema.[14,15] The severity of submersion injuries in children is largely dependent on the length of time before initiation of ventilation and correction of hypoxia and acidosis, although cold water may alter the clinical course.

Cold water has been found to have a protective effect on some submersion injuries, especially in children; the mechanism for this continues to be debated.[16,17] One proposed explanation is that the cold water causes reflex apnea, slowing of the rate of metabolism and the shunting of blood from the peripheral circulation while maintaining flow to heart and brain tissue. This has been referred to as the "dive reflex,"[18,19] and the response is thought by some investigators to be stronger in children than in adults.[20]

Hypothermia occurs rapidly in pediatric patients submerged in cool or cold water because of their relatively large body surface area, lack of protective body fat, and small size.[21] This is compounded by the fact that children lose heat quickly by radiation, evaporation, and conduction and that water is thirty-two times as conductive as air. In addition, vigorous activity such as struggling during a submersion incident accelerates heat loss.

THE SUBMERSION INCIDENT

The course of the submersion incident may vary, but it generally begins with panic and breathholding and a subsequent period of violent struggling. During this period of frantic activity, as the urge to breathe becomes uncontrollable and the carbon dioxide level increases, reflex gasping occurs and some fluid may be aspirated. Aspiration of even a small amount of fluid may cause laryngospasm and result in severe hypoxia. A large volume of fluid may also be swallowed into the stomach. As hypoxia continues, cerebral depression ensues, and, unless rescue occurs, cardiac arrest becomes the terminal event. In 80 percent to 90 percent of drownings, fluid fills the airways when laryngospasm relaxes secondary to hypoxia and loss of consciousness; in 10 percent to 20 percent, the reflex laryngospasm persists, occluding the airway and causing suffocation without allowing entrance of fluid into the lungs, even when the child becomes unconscious.[22]

PREHOSPITAL CARE OF SUBMERSION INJURIES

Immediate and appropriate prehospital care is the most critical intervention for patients with submersion injuries; effective field resuscitation is crucial to survival.[23] Because emergency department management often begins with supervision of prehospital care providers, protocols addressing field treatment of these patients are necessary for base hospitals directing care.

There is controversy about some of the issues in the field treatment of submersion injuries. It is universally agreed, however, that the primary goals of prehospital care are to ensure an adequate airway and to restore ventilation and perfusion. Early notification of base hospital personnel by prehospital care providers allows for medical management on the scene, time for preparation of equipment, and early contact of specialists.

Rescue

Airway management of the nonbreathing patient found in a pool or other large body of water begins during rescue in the water. The rescuer maintains spinal immobilization with a flotation board or other flat object if trauma is suspected (which is rare in the preadolescent age group), opens the airway by means of the jaw thrust maneuver, ensures airway patency, and ventilates the patient until removal from the water is possible.[24] The "sniffing" position should be used for positioning the airway in children. Mouth-to-mouth breathing is used for large children and mouth-to-mouth and nose breathing for smaller ones. Obstructed airway techniques may be attempted, if necessary, but chest compressions are not considered useful while the patient is still in the water.

Removal from the Water

After removal of the patient from the water, with spinal immobilization if trauma is suspected, more advanced life support can be initiated. Some authorities recommend a brief attempt to drain fluid from the lungs in salt water submersion injuries,[25,26] but it is generally agreed that continued attempts to remove aspirated fluid from the lungs are of dubious value and may cause more harm than benefit when ventilation of the patient is delayed.[27,28] The use of the Heimlich maneuver[29] may induce vomiting with the attendant risk of aspiration. The primary consideration is rapid restoration of ventilation.

Basic Life Support

Basic life support procedures are important in the initial resuscitation of patients with submersion injuries. If the chest is not rising with attempted ventilation, obstructed airway maneuvers are used. Persistent occlusion of the airway mandates the continued use of obstructed airway techniques until the airway is cleared. If respiration continues to be absent or compromised, continued ventilatory assistance is necessary. High-flow oxygen should be administered to the person providing rescue breathing because this increases the amount of oxygen available to the patient. Rescuers should be directed to use a bag-valve-mask device with high-flow oxygen if they are able to do so effectively. Endotracheal intubation is the treatment of choice for field management of the airway when the patient's mental status or gag reflex is significantly impaired and should be performed when protocols allow. This may be a lifesaving intervention in areas where transport times to emergency care facilities are lengthy. Esophageal airways and powered breathing devices are not used for children younger than 16 years of age.

When the patient is in cardiac as well as respiratory arrest, chest compressions are initiated by means of the American Heart Association's basic life support procedures.[30] Prehospital care providers should be directed to transport the patient rapidly to the nearest emergency facility that is appropriate for care.

Venous Access

Obtaining venous access, when necessary, may be difficult in the child with a submersion injury because of vasoconstriction and shock. The value of attempting to insert intravenous lines in the prehospital setting is questionable for pediatric patients when an emergency care facility is nearby. In general, personnel should be directed to make these attempts en route; delaying transport for repeated attempts to obtain intravenous access is pointless. Intraosseous infusion, although not a widely accepted field procedure, is a rapid and effective means of access in children younger than 4 years of age; most drugs used for resuscitation can be given by this route.[31] When the patient is intubated, some medications may be given endotracheally.

Pharmacological management of the patient in both respiratory and cardiac arrest from a submersion injury follows standard American Heart Association advanced cardiac life support protocols.

Hypothermia

In the prehospital setting, passive warming is used for hypothermia patients. All wet clothing should be removed, if possible, and the patient should be dried to prevent further cooling. Warm, dry covers should be used to wrap the patient, who should be maintained in a warm environment surrounded by coverings to prevent further heat loss. Active warming should take place in an acute care facility. Patients with lengthy submersion in ice water should be moved gently, because rough handling may precipitate ventricular fibrillation in patients with severe hypothermia (less than 32°C).[32] Cardiopulmonary resuscitation should be initiated only when it is certain that the patient is pulseless; the pulse should be taken for one full minute.

In all cases, patients with submersion injuries should be considered salvageable until proved otherwise because patients submerged for up to 40 minutes in cold water have been resuscitated without long-term adverse effects.[33–35] Resuscitation is continued under base hospital direction until an emergency care facility is reached. Most patients, even the most seriously injured, arrive in the emergency department with signs of life.

EMERGENCY DEPARTMENT CARE

All patients with submersion injuries, even those who are not believed to be seriously injured, must be transported to an emergency facility. It is rarely possible to obtain an accurate report of the submersion incident, and there are many variables that may alter the outcome of these injuries. Expert evaluation is therefore essential.

Frequent, continued, and accurate systems assessment is fundamental to the recognition of improvement or deterioration of the patient's condition. Signs and symptoms depend on factors such as the length and type of the submersion incident, the age and size of the patient, and the temperature and type of immersion fluid.

Assessment should include a general picture of the submersion incident and a brief medical history. When the patient is severely injured, only a brief history is obtained at first; the full history must be deferred until a later time. It is useful to attempt to determine the water temperature and the length of submersion. If cardiopulmonary resuscitation was required, it may be helpful to know (1) the length of time elapsed before this procedure was initiated, (2) the length of time the procedure was in progress, and (3) if the procedure was performed by a trained provider.

Spectator reports are often inaccurate; there is sometimes confusion between the length of time that the child was submerged and the length of time that the child was in the water. Any accounts obtained should be considered approximate rather than accurate information. Other general information that should be obtained whenever possible can be remembered by the mnemonic AMPLE (Exhibit 12-2).

Respiratory Assessment

Respiratory status is always the most crucial consideration for patients with submersion injuries. Oxygen (100 percent) should be given to all patients suspected of submersion injuries during the resuscitation phase, regardless of the age of the patient or type of incident. The reason for this is simple: every patient with a submersion injury is considered hypoxic until proved otherwise. Because survival of the seriously injured patient depends primarily on control of the airway and ventilation, initial efforts should be directed toward ensuring airway patency and adequate ventilation.

Observation

General signs of respiratory distress in children include rapid breathing (tachypnea), deep breathing (hyperpnea), and shallow breathing (hypopnea). Blood-tinged and frothy sputum indicates serious pulmonary injury, and periodic breathing, or breathing with apneic spells, indicates severe hypoxia affecting the central nervous system. Nonspecific signs of respiratory distress include anxiety, restlessness, combativeness, altered level of consciousness, and abnormal skin color (mottling, duskiness, or cyanosis).

Exhibit 12-2 Information To Obtain when Taking the Medical History (Mnemonic AMPLE)

A	Allergies
M	Medications
P	Previous history of illness
L	Last meal (time)
E	Events preceding the injury

Rate

Children younger than 6 or 7 years of age are abdominal breathers; respiratory rates are best obtained by watching the rise and fall of the abdomen rather than the chest. Respiratory rates should be counted for one full minute for accuracy. Normal respiratory rates by age groups are listed in Table 12-1.

Depth

In the patient with a submersion injury, depth of respiration may be limited by gastric distention from swallowed air or water; this should be recognized early. Later, the depth of respiration may be limited by lack of compliance in the lungs as a result of the injury. The possibility of chest wall injury should be considered if trauma is involved.

Effort

Respiratory effort should also be evaluated. There are two special considerations in the assessment of the pediatric patient. (1) Children younger than 3 months of age are obligatory nose breathers; nasal flaring is an indication of increased respiratory effort in this age group. (2) The chest wall is more pliable in children than in adults, and the muscles of the chest wall are less well developed; children therefore show supraclavicular, sternal, and intercostal retractions with increased respiratory effort.

Table 12-1 Vital Signs by Age

Age	Pulse (beats/min)	Respiratory Rate (per minute)	Systolic Blood Pressure (mmHg)
Newborn	140 to 160	30 to 50	50 to 70
0 to 6 months	120 to 140	25 to 35	70 to 95
7 months to 2 years	110 to 130	20 to 30	80 to 100
2 to 6 years	80 to 120	16 to 24	80 to 100
7 to 10 years	70 to 90	16 to 20	80 to 110
10 to 16 years	70 to 90	12 to 18	90 to 120

Source: Reprinted from *Prehospital Care of Pediatric Emergencies* by J.S. Seidel and D.P. Henderson, with permission of Los Angeles Pediatric Society.

Auscultation

Aspiration of fluid is likely not only from the submersion incident but from aspiration of vomitus, which may occur either in the course of the submersion incident or during resuscitative efforts. Rales, rhonchi, or wheezing within the first hour or two after the incident are more often an indication of aspiration of submersion fluid or vomitus than pulmonary edema secondary to the injury. Stridor is likely to be due to foreign body aspiration. A normal chest examination does not rule out serious pulmonary problems, but does provide a good baseline by which to monitor pulmonary changes.

Circulatory Assessment

Circulation and perfusion in children is assessed by heart rate, skin signs, blood pressure, and capillary refill. Core temperature assessment is also essential in submersion injuries.

Heart Rate

Heart rates vary greatly among different age groups (see Table 12-1). The short, thick necks of children younger than 1 year of age make the carotid pulse difficult to assess; the brachial or femoral pulse is easily obtainable in most nonhypotensive pediatric patients. When in doubt, an apical pulse is the most accurate. The child's pulse should be taken for at least one full minute because it may vary considerably within a short time period and because hypothermic patients may be severely bradycardic. Cardiac rhythm disturbances are rare in children and are usually resolved with correction of hypoxia and acidosis.

Skin Signs

Skin signs are important in assessing a patient for shock. In children, shock is at first well compensated for by an increase in heart rate and peripheral vasoconstriction. A child may not appear to be severely ill while in this state. Deterioration after this period of compensated shock may be rapid; early recognition is therefore essential. A high suspicion of shock should be maintained when one or more of the following is present:

- a well-documented history of lengthy submersion
- abnormal heart rate or respiratory rate
- abnormal skin signs, such as mottling or blanching
- any signs or symptoms of difficult breathing
- changes in mental status such as restlessness, anxiety, or combativeness.

Capillary Refill

Capillary refill is one of the best methods of assessing perfusion in the pediatric patient. An easy method is to exert pressure on a peripheral skin surface for several seconds. Commonly the child's finger tip is used for this evaluation, but the kneecap also affords an easily accessible and visible area. When the pressure is released, the amount of time needed for the skin color to return to normal is estimated; return of color in more than 2 seconds denotes decreased perfusion in the normothermic patient. Hypothermia causes peripheral vasoconstriction and makes this test less useful.

Blood Pressure

Emergency department staff should have a general knowledge of normal values for blood pressures as well as pulse and respiratory rates for pediatric patients (see Table 12-1) to evaluate these parameters properly. As a general rule, a systolic blood pressure less than 60 to 70 mmHg is considered hypotensive in the pediatric patient. In obtaining an accurate blood pressure reading, the correct size of the cuff is one-half to two-thirds the distance between the child's elbow and shoulder. A smaller cuff gives a high reading, and a larger cuff gives a low reading. Frequent serial assessments are the best method of monitoring the progress of the patient in the acute phase.

Temperature

Core temperature should be taken, preferably rectally. Most thermometers begin at 35°C, or 94°F; because hypothermia is considered 35°C or less, a more sensitive device to assess core temperature, such as the one used for cooling blankets, should be used.[36] Inexpensive glass thermometers that include low-temperature readings (to 27.8°C) are available from hospital supply houses. Temperature should be assessed every 10 to 15 minutes as warming takes place.

Neurological Assessment

The effects of hypoxia on the central nervous system, even with short submersion times, can be devastating. A baseline assessment of level of consciousness should be made on the patient's presentation in the emergency department and reevaluated at frequent intervals. Modified versions of the Glasgow Coma Scale are available for assessment of pediatric patients, along with other scales and scores. Most of these have been extensively described and debated, and as yet no ideal scoring mechanism that is accurate, easy to use, and suitable for preverbal patients has been found.

The simplest method of assessment currently used is AVPU, which is easily remembered and quickly performed and gives a good general idea of the patient's condition (Exhibit 12-3). More sophisticated evaluation is done as the patient progresses through the hospital system, but the use of AVPU gives sufficient information for use in initial evaluation. Good assessment and documentation allows early identification of serious injury and deterioration or improvement in the patient's condition. Specialized care,

---

Exhibit 12-3 AVPU Method of Neurological Assessment

A	Alert
V	Responds to verbal stimuli
P	Responds to painful stimuli
U	Unresponsive

such as cerebral resuscitation measures, may be considered for the severely injured child and should be started immediately.

There has been concern recently that, as resuscitation becomes more effective, there will be a decrease in the number of deaths from submersion injury and an increase in the number of patients with permanent serious neurologic damage. For this reason, classification tools and other assessment methods have been used in attempts to predict outcomes. The use of ABC as a mnemonic has been suggested. This method of classification, which bears some resemblance to the motor assessment of the Glasgow Coma Scale, was specifically devised for submersion injuries (Exhibit 12-4).[37]

Neurological assessment may help give a clear picture of injury severity; in the ABC method, patients classified as C-1, C-2, and C-3 had the poorest outcome.[38] Other proposed predictors of poor outcome include a Glasgow Coma Scale score of 5 or less, the need for continued cardiopulmonary resuscitation in the emergency department, and arrival in the emergency department with fixed and dilated pupils.[39-42] Conversely, studies have shown that the presence of spontaneous respiration after resuscitation is associated with a more favorable neurologic prognosis.[43,44]

Despite repeated attempts to link assessment directly to prognosis, there are as yet no absolute predictors. Although there may be some questions about the value of resuscitation procedures, energies should still be directed to full resuscitation of all patients.[45]

Suspected Child Abuse

Child abuse should be suspected when the history of the submersion incident told by the child or the family is inconsistent or when the injuries of the child appear to be unusual or more severe than might be expected. Evaluation for suspected child abuse requires sensitive and skillful exploration, preferably by experienced staff. Whenever possible, the patient should be admitted to gain time to perform a thorough evaluation of both the patient and the family. Reporting of suspected child abuse is mandatory in most states; standard reporting procedures should be followed.

MANAGEMENT OF SUBMERSION INJURIES

Emergency department management of submersion injuries is directed, even during the assessment phase, to the treatment of hypoxia and acidosis, which are the most common causes of end organ failure. Central nervous system injury resulting from

Exhibit 12-4 ABC Method of Classifying Neurologic Outcome in Submersion Injury

A	Alert
B	Blunted consciousness
C	Comatose
C-1	Decorticate; flexion response to pain; Cheyne-Stokes respiration
C-2	Decerebrate; extension response to pain; central hyperventilation
C-3	Flaccid, no response to pain, cluster breathing

hypoxia may be significant, and measures to reduce or prevent cerebral edema must be taken. Electrolyte or hemodynamic changes are unlikely to occur with aspiration of less than 22 mL of fluid per kilogram of body weight, and only 15 percent of submersion injury patients or fewer aspirate such a large volume.[46,47] Observed abnormalities are usually transient and rarely significant. Patients are treated virtually identically during initial resuscitation, regardless of whether the immersion fluid is fresh or salt water. Pulmonary edema may develop later but is rarely present on initial presentation. As in other types of trauma, management follows the ABCs.

Airway and Breathing

The primary focus in caring for submersion injuries in pediatric patients is unquestionably and invariably maintenance of the airway and ventilation. When trauma is present or suspected (such as in diving accidents), spinal immobilization should be maintained. A stiff collar is effective for the cervical spine, but it must fit correctly to protect the airway. Sandbags (or plastic intravenous line bags) and tape are often the best means of immobilizing the spine; this equipment has the advantage of being readily available both in the prehospital setting and in the acute care facility.

Standard airway techniques are used, as in the prehospital phase, with the child's head in the "sniffing" position. The patient should be suctioned by tonsillar suction and given oxygen by nasal cannula at 6 L/min or by mask at 10 L/min. If assisted ventilation is required, a bag-valve-mask device with 100 percent oxygen may be used until intubation is possible. Great care must be taken to avoid overinflation of the lungs of children, which carries the risk of pneumothorax; the lungs should be inflated only until the chest begins to rise.

Intubation is necessary for definitive management of the airway in (1) nonbreathing patients, (2) patients whose arterial carbon dioxide pressure is more than 50 mmHg or whose arterial oxygen pressure is less than 50 mmHg while on maximum oxygen concentration, and (3) patients who are unable to clear secretions.[48] Uncuffed endotracheal tubes are used in children younger than 8 years of age; the diameter of the tube should be approximately the same as the diameter of the child's little finger. Because the narrowest point of the airway in pediatric patients is at the cricoid cartilage, difficulties in intubation are encountered at that point rather than at the glottic opening, as in adults.

In emergency intubations, the patient may have to be paralyzed with an agent such as succinylcholine. For this procedure, the patient should be hyperventilated for 1 minute with 100 percent oxygen, and then a dose of succinylcholine of 1 to 2 mg/kg should be given intravenously. Atropine (0.02 mg/kg intravenously) is also given unless the heart rate is greater than 200 beats/min. Along with succinylcholine, the patient is given pancuronium (0.02 mg/kg intravenously) to prevent fasciculation and lidocaine (1 mg/kg).

Circulation

If the patient shows no spontaneous cardiac activity on arrival in the emergency department, cardiac compressions are initiated; if cardiopulmonary resuscitation is in progress, it is continued. Monitoring of the heart rate and assessment of the rhythm are necessary, and a 12-lead electrocardiogram should be used for accuracy. The most common cardiac rhythm disturbances in children with serious submersion injuries are severe bradycardia or asystole due to hypoxemia; ventricular fibrillation may be present in hypothermia patients. The standard advanced cardiac life support drugs are used for treatment of cardiac rhythm disturbances.

Patients who are experiencing mild hypothermia (33° to 35°C) should be kept covered as much as possible, and warming lights should be used if available. Passive warming—keeping the patient covered with blankets to prevent heat escape—may be sufficient for these patients. Severe hypothermia requires more aggressive measures (Table 12-2).

Arterial blood gases are measured for all patients with significant injury as early as possible to determine the degree of hypoxemia and acidosis. Use of sodium bicarbonate for correction of metabolic acidosis should be based on blood gas analysis.[49] A chest roentgenogram is necessary to determine the amount of aspiration and should be obtained when the patient is sufficiently stable to allow this procedure. The first chest film may be normal; some patients develop pulmonary edema after a few hours, however, and this first film will be useful for comparison.

Shock

When shock is present or suspected, two intravenous lines should be started immediately. All patients with serious submersion injuries should have at least one intravenous line inserted with a large-bore needle. Any peripheral vein may be cannulated, which-

Table 12-2 Treatment of Hypothermia in Submersion Injury

Degree of Hypothermia	Temperature	Warming Method	Treatment
Mild	33° to 35°C (91.4° to 95.0°F)	Passive external	Prevent active movement; conserve body heat with coverings; maintain patient in warm environment.
Moderate	30° to 32°C (86.0° to 86.6°F)	Active external	Use passive external warming methods as well as warmed blankets; apply warm soaks to trunk; use heat lamp; warm slowly (+1°F per hour).
Severe	<30°C (<86°F)	Active internal (core warming)	Use active external warming methods plus others such as heated humidified air; warmed intravenous fluids; gastric, colonic, or peritoneal lavage; peritoneal dialysis. The most severe cases may require mediastinal lavage or cardiac bypass.

ever is most readily available. For insertion of a central line, the internal jugular vein is used preferentially. The lungs of children rise higher in the thoracic cavity than in adults, and attempts to insert an intravenous line in the subclavian vein carry significant risk of pneumothorax. Normal saline is the intravenous solution of choice; 20 mL/kg is given rapidly. The same amount may be given again immediately if perfusion does not improve.

When shock persists after two infusions of 20 mL/kg, the ABCs of resuscitation should be reassessed and the possibility of hemorrhage considered, especially when trauma is known to be involved or is suspected. If blood loss is confirmed, a plasma extender, O^- blood, type-specific blood, or typed and cross-matched blood is given, depending on the urgency of the situation. When hemorrhage has been eliminated as a cause of shock, other possibilities to be considered include severe acidosis, continuing hypoxemia, drug or alcohol abuse, and, in the trauma victim, tension pneumothorax, cardiac tamponade, and head injury.

Disability

When there is evidence of altered level of consciousness or progressive neurologic damage, the patient should be hyperventilated to decrease cerebral edema. The aim is to keep the arterial carbon dioxide pressure at about 25 to 30 torr, which decreases cerebral blood flow and lowers intracranial pressure.[50] If the patient is conscious and breathing well, 100 percent oxygen should be given throughout the stay in the emergency department. The head of the bed may be elevated 30° if there is no spinal injury or shock, and the amount of fluid given should be closely monitored.

Gastric Distention

The stomach may be filled with air and water, which are often swallowed as the child fights against the submersion. Air may also be forced into the stomach during resuscitation by rescuers' efforts at ventilation. A nasogastric tube should be inserted as soon as possible to empty gastric contents, allowing full expansion of the lungs and preventing aspiration. This procedure should be performed after intubation in the unconscious patient. When substance abuse is a consideration in the submersion incident, a toxicology screen should be requested for suctioned stomach contents.

Urine Output

Urine output is a good indicator of renal function because the kidneys are sensitive to hypoxia and may show signs of damage at an early stage. Children should normally have a minimum output of 1 to 2 mL/kg/hour. An appropriate size of Foley catheter should be inserted if the patient is unconscious. Urine output should be measured serially every 15 to 20 minutes during the first few hours. After admission to the hospital, a routine urinalysis is usually ordered; urine may be tested by dipstick in the emergency department for more rapid assessment. Proteinuria and microscopic hematuria may be present at first; these often disappear spontaneously.

Laboratory Procedures

Blood should be obtained for laboratory analysis while the intravenous line is being inserted, when possible. The standard laboratory tests in submersion injuries include (1) hemoglobin and hematocrit, (2) complete blood cell count, (3) serum electrolytes, (4) blood urea nitrogen, (5) creatinine, (6) serum amylase, and (7) urinalysis. Typing and cross-matching of two to four units of blood should be included if the patient is in shock or when significant trauma is present. If drug abuse is suspected, a toxicology screen may be ordered for blood, urine, and stomach contents. Many laboratory findings may be normal during resuscitation, except when hypoxia is protracted or severe and when trauma or drug abuse plays a role in the injury.

SEVERE HYPOTHERMIA

In cases of severe hypothermia ventricular fibrillation is easily induced by rough handling, so that unnecessary resuscitation procedures should be avoided.[51] The hypothermic heart does not respond well to electrical stimulation; if fibrillation occurs, defibrillation may not be effective until the patient is warmer. Standard advanced cardiac life support drugs may be used, but with caution: the delayed metabolism of hypothermia patients prevents effective drug utilization until rewarming, at which point drugs given during resuscitation may take rapid effect.

Warming of the severely hypothermic patient should proceed slowly (see Table 12-2). The life-threatening phenomenon known as "rewarming shock" or "afterdrop" must be avoided. This occurs with peripheral vasodilation, which sends stagnant, cold, and acidotic peripheral blood into the central circulation. The core temperature and the blood pH lower precipitously, increasing the risk of ventricular fibrillation. When used exclusively, peripheral warming has been identified as a cause of afterdrop and may have disastrous results.[52] There is little agreement about the treatment of severe hypothermia, but recent literature suggests that severely hypothermic patients (with a core temperature of 32°C or less) should be actively warmed.

Continuous evaluation of core temperature of hypothermia patients is necessary. The wisest course for all patients is to obtain accurate temperature readings and to continue resuscitative efforts until metabolic and thermal imbalances have been corrected. The patient's temperature should reach at least 35°C before death is pronounced. This is often stated more succinctly: "No patient should be pronounced dead until warm and dead."

ADMISSION TO THE HOSPITAL

Some patients may be asymptomatic on arrival in the emergency department, but all patients, regardless of clinical presentation, should be kept in the hospital for observation for a period of 12 to 24 hours because the onset of pulmonary edema, which is a major complication of submersion injury, may be delayed for several hours.[53]

The patient with a severe submersion injury requires a continued high level of care and close observation in an intensive care unit. Pulmonary, neurologic, and renal complications are most prevalent in the postresuscitation phase.

Pulmonary Complications

All patients should have continued oxygen and other ventilatory support if necessary. If the patient shows any early signs of pulmonary complications (respiratory distress, abnormal chest roentgenogram, or abnormal arterial blood gases), continuous attention must be paid to ventilation and perfusion. An arterial line may be helpful to monitor blood pressure, to obtain serial blood gases, and to obtain blood for other laboratory tests.

Damage to the lungs and some lack of lung compliance is almost inevitable; the severity depends on the length of the submersion incident. Positive airway pressure should be provided if ventilation continues to be inadequate. Intubation is the most effective means of providing positive airway pressure to reduce hypoxemia caused by intrapulmonary shunting and permits access to the bronchopulmonary tree for removal of secretions. Oxygen tension should be maintained at 60 to 90 mmHg. Continuous positive airway pressure at 5 to 15 mmH$_2$O is used for spontaneously breathing patients; positive end-expiratory pressure is used when mechanical support is necessary. Continued mechanical ventilation is necessary for nonbreathing patients.

Although pneumonia is always a possible complication, antibiotics are seldom necessary in the first few days of hospitalization; their use should be based on signs of clinical deterioration and laboratory analysis of sputum.[54]

Neurologic Complications

With successful resuscitation, the severity of central nervous system dysfunction becomes the major determinant of outcome. If there is a history of lengthy submersion or altered level of consciousness (or both), the patient must be observed for signs of increasing intracranial pressure. Various therapeutic modalities for patients with anoxic brain insults have been attempted, with varying results.[55] These therapies are directed toward maintaining intracranial pressure at 20 mmHg or less and commonly include intracranial pressure monitoring, hyperventilation, restriction of fluids to half the daily requirement, use of osmotic and loop diuretics (mannitol or furosemide), and maintenance of controlled hypothermia (30° to 32°C). Barbiturates to induce coma, paralytic agents, and steroids have also been used.[56] Some of these therapies have not been effective and are not recommended.[57,58] Steroids, which were once commonly used in submersion injuries for cerebral edema or to combat aspiration pneumonitis, are rarely considered useful today,[59] and there continue to be questions about the use of controlled hypothermia.[60,61] Hyperventilation to maintain arterial carbon dioxide pressure at 25 to 35 mmHg and restriction of fluids to maintain urine flow at 0.5 to 1.0 mL/kg are still used extensively.[62] The decision to use any type of therapy must be carefully weighed against the possible complications because there is little evidence of consistently improved outcomes in severe submersion injuries.[63]

Renal Complications

Hypoxemia and hypotension may lead to acute tubular necrosis and renal failure within 24 to 48 hours. This may be due to hemolysis and hemoglobinuria in the fresh

Exhibit 12-5 Submersion Injury Prevention Strategies

1. Required fencing and locks for all public and private pools.
2. Development of standards for safe pool design.
3. Accessible rescue and resuscitation equipment near private and public pools.
4. Compulsory rescue and first aid training for pool owners.
5. Warning signs and flags in hazardous water areas.
6. Public education about the dangers of consumption of alcohol and swimming.
7. Education of parents in child supervision and pool and bathtub safety issues.
8. Public education in water rescue and basic life support.

water aspiration patient[64] or to myoglobinuria secondary to muscle trauma, hypoperfusion, acidosis, and hypoxia.[65] Dialysis may be considered if renal failure occurs.

PREVENTION

Drowning is preventable. Several factors contribute to the incidence of submersion injuries[66]; individual and community efforts should be directed to their control. Some recommendations for prevention of submersion injuries are listed in Exhibit 12-5. In addition to these, training in resuscitation of pediatric patients with submersion injuries should be provided for prehospital care providers and specific triage and transfer protocols included in the emergency care system.

Drownings and submersion injuries are particularly tragic because they are almost always preventable and because such a large number occur in children. Despite some progress in improving outcomes for these patients, it has been shown that patients arriving in the emergency department with cardiopulmonary resuscitation in progress continue to have a poor prognosis. For this reason, personnel caring for these patients must understand that the patient's condition on rescue or arrival rather than failure of their efforts and of treatment modalities may be the cause of a poor outcome. The most important point to remember is that treatment of serious submersion injuries must be initiated rapidly and continued aggressively to ensure an optimal outcome.

NOTES

1. James P. Orlowski, "Drowning, Near-Drowning and Ice-Water Submersions," *Pediatric Clinics of North America* 34(1987):76.
2. Jerrold A. Kram and Kenneth W. Kizer, "Submersion Injury," *Emergency Medicine Clinics of North America* 2(1984):545.
3. Stanley H. Schuman et al., "Risk of Drowning: An Iceberg Phenomenon," *Journal of the American College of Emergency Physicians* 6(1977):139.
4. Kram and Kizer, "Submersion Injury," 546.
5. Centers for Disease Control, "Aquatic Deaths and Injuries—United States," *Morbidity and Mortality Weekly Report* 31:31 (13 August 1982):417.
6. Orlowski, "Drowning, Near-Drowning, and Ice-Water Submersions," 75.
7. D.A. Spyker, "Submersion Injury: Epidemiology, Prevention, and Management," *Pediatric Clinics of North America* 32(1985):114.

8. Joseph S. Redding, "Drowning and Near Drowning," *Postgraduate Medicine* 74(1983):96.
9. Orlowski, "Drowning, Near-Drowning, and Ice-Water Submersions," 76.
10. Kram and Kizer, "Submersion Injury," 547.
11. Vernon D. Plueckhahn, "Alcohol and Accidental Drowning: A 25-Year Study," *Medical Journal of Australia* 141(1984):25.
12. Ricardo Gonzalez-Rothi, "Near Drowning: Consensus and Controversies in Pulmonary and Cerebral Resuscitation," *Heart and Lung* 5(1987):475.
13. F. Segarra and R.A. Redding, "Modern Concepts About Drowning," *Canadian Medical Association Journal* 110(1974):1059.
14. Redding, "Drowning and Near Drowning," 88.
15. Samuel T. Giammona and Jerome H. Modell, "Drowning by Total Immersion," *American Journal of the Diseases of Children* 114(1967):622.
16. J.S. Hayward et al., "Temperature Effect on the Human Dive Response in Relation to Cold Water Near-Drowning," *American Physiological Society* 22(1984):205.
17. Orlowski, "Drowning, Near-Drowning, and Ice-Water Submersions," 76.
18. Gonzalez-Rothi, "Near Drowning," 474.
19. Brett A. Gooden, "Drowning and the Diving Reflex in Man," *Medical Journal of Australia* 2(1972):584.
20. A.W. Conn, J.F. Edmonds, and G.A. Barker, "Near-Drowning in Cold Fresh Water: Current Treatment Regimen," *Canadian Anaesthetists' Society Journal* 25(1978):259.
21. Ibid.
22. Thomas G. Martin, "Neardrowning and Cold Water Immersion," *Annals of Emergency Medicine* 13(1984):263.
23. Jerome H. Modell, Shirley A. Graves, and Alan Ketover, "Clinical Course of 91 Consecutive Near-Drowning Victims," *Chest* 70(1976):236.
24. American Heart Association, "Standards and Guidelines for Cardiopulmonary Resuscitation and Emergency Cardiac Care," *Journal of the American Medical Association* 255(1986):2841–3044.
25. Robert Knopp, "Near Drowning," *Journal of the American College of Emergency Physicians* 7(1978):252.
26. M. Lawrence Podolsky, "Saving the Near-Drowning Victim: An Update," *ER Reports* 1 (24 November 1980):133.
27. Redding, "Drowning and Near Drowning," 88.
28. Joseph P. Ornato, "The Resuscitation of Near-Drowning Victims," *Journal of the American Medical Association* 256(1986):76.
29. Henry J. Heimlich, "Subdiaphragmatic Pressure to Expel Water from the Lungs of Drowning Persons," *Annals of Emergency Medicine* 10(1981):476.
30. American Heart Association, "Standards and Guidelines for Cardiopulmonary Resuscitation and Emergency Cardiac Care," 2841–3044.
31. James S. Seidel and Deborah P. Henderson, *Prehospital Care of Pediatric Emergencies* (Los Angeles: Los Angeles Pediatric Society, 1987).
32. Martin, "Neardrowning and Cold Water Immersion," 267.
33. Harald Siebke et al., "Survival After 40 Minutes' Submersion without Cerebral Sequelae," *Lancet* (7 June 1975):1275.
34. J.K. Sims and Mike Penick, "How Much CPR is Enough CPR?" *Journal of the American College of Emergency Physicians* 7(1978):218.
35. Tone Dahl Kvittingen and Arne Naess, "Recovery from Drowning in Fresh Water," *British Medical Journal* (May 18, 1963):1316.
36. Martin, "Neardrowning and Cold Water Immersion," 268.

37. Jerome H. Modell, S.A. Graves, and E.J. Kuck, "Near-Drowning: Correlation of Level of Consciousness and Survival," *Canadian Anaesthetists' Society Journal* 27(1980):211.
38. Ibid., 214.
39. J. Michael Dean and Neal D. Kaufman, "Prognostic Indicators in Pediatric Near-Drowning: The Glasgow Coma Scale," *Critical Care Medicine* 9(1981):539.
40. Ralph C. Frates, "Analysis of Predictive Factors in the Assessment of Warm-Water Near-Drowning in Children," *American Journal of the Diseases of Children* 135(1981):1006.
41. Timothy C. Frewen et al., "Cerebral Resuscitation Therapy in Pediatric Near-Drowning," *The Journal of Pediatrics* 106(1985):616.
42. Bradley Peterson, "Morbidity of Childhood Near-Drowning," *Pediatrics* 59(1977):369.
43. Gonzalez-Rothi, "Near Drowning," 479.
44. Wayne C. Jacobsen et al., "Correlation of Spontaneous Respiration and Neurologic Damage in Near-Drowning," *Critical Care Medicine* 11(1983):488.
45. Dean and Kaufman, "Prognostic Indicators in Pediatric Near-Drowning," 538.
46. Martin, "Neardrowning and Cold Water Immersion," 264.
47. Jerome H. Modell and Joseph H. Davis, "Electrolyte Changes in Human Drowning Victims," *Anesthesiology* 30(1968):420.
48. Kram and Kizer, "Submersion Injury," 549.
49. American Heart Association, "Standards and Guidelines for Cardiopulmonary Resuscitation and Emergency Cardiac Care," 2841–3044.
50. Brian H. Hoff, "Multisystem Failure: A Review with Special Reference to Drowning," *Critical Care Medicine* 7(1979):313.
51. Orlowski, "Drowning, Near-Drowning, and Ice-Water Submersions," 89.
52. James B. Reuler, "Hypothermia: Pathophysiology, Clinical Settings, and Management," *Annals of Internal Medicine* 89(1978):524.
53. Redding, "Drowning and Near Drowning," 85.
54. Gonzalez-Rothi, "Near Drowning," 476.
55. Ashok P. Sarnaik et al., "Intracranial Pressure and Cerebral Perfusion Pressure in Near Drowning," *Critical Care Medicine* 13(1985):224.
56. A.W. Conn, J.F. Edmonds, and G.A. Barker, "Cerebral Resuscitation in Near-Drowning," *Pediatric Clinics of North America* 3(1979):698.
57. Gonzalez-Rothi, "Near Drowning," 479.
58. Ornato, "The Resuscitation of Near-Drowning Victims," 77.
59. Modell, Graves, and Ketover, "Clinical Course of 91 Consecutive Near-Drowning Victims," 238.
60. Jerome H. Modell, "Biology of Drowning," *Annual Review of Medicine* 29(1978):7.
61. Frank D. Allman et al., "Outcome Following Cardiopulmonary Resuscitation in Severe Pediatric Near-Drowning," *American Journal of Diseases of Children* 140(1986):575.
62. Spyker, "Submersion Injury," 123.
63. Gonzalez-Rothi, "Near Drowning," 480.
64. Knopp, "Near Drowning," 251.
65. Hoff, "Multisystem Failure," 315.
66. John Pearn and James Nixon, "Prevention of Childhood Drowning Accidents," *Medical Journal of Australia* 1(1977):616.

Chapter 13
Child Abuse

Margaret Farmer Keil

Child abuse is a complex public health problem with medical, nursing, social, and legal ramifications. One of the many challenges of this problem is distinguishing accidental from inflicted trauma. This chapter focuses on the diagnosis of abuse, the objective findings in typical cases of physical abuse,[1] the precipitating factors involved in abuse, and nursing interventions for working with abusive families. Specific management of the physical injuries resulting from abuse are discussed throughout this book.

HISTORICAL BACKGROUND

Child abuse has been sanctioned for many centuries. It occurs in all populations, cultures, socioeconomic levels, and religions. In certain ancient cultures, the sacrifice of children to please the god of their household was a common, accepted practice. Children who were born with a birth defect, or unwanted female children, were deliberately killed or abandoned by their parents. Children who were mentally retarded, seriously ill, or had seizures or other neurologic defects were often thought to be possessed; these children were frequently subjected to various kinds of torture in the belief that evil spirits would thereby be forced out of their bodies.

In contemporary societies, many people hold the notion that physical and emotional abuse is important to the education of children. Parents and other caretakers believe that berating or beating a child is necessary to "knock some sense" into him or her or perhaps to help "teach the child a lesson." Culture also has a significant effect on childrearing practices, the value placed on children, and issues of parental and child rights.

In the United States, concern about abused children began with the famous case of Maryellen in 1874. Maryellen was an 8-year-old girl who was routinely beaten, starved, imprisoned, and kept in rags by her adoptive parents. Neighbors attempted to intervene on her behalf, but none of the institutions contacted could help her. Finally, out of desperation, they contacted the Society for the Prevention of Cruelty to Animals, which intervened on behalf of the child and removed her from the home. Later that year, the New York Society for the Prevention of Cruelty to Children was organized. A few years later in 1904, the National Child Labor Committee was formed to crusade against the child labor conditions that prevailed at that time.[2]

Child abuse gained national medical attention in 1962 when Dr. C. Henry Kempe and his associates reported in the *Journal of the American Medical Association* that abuse was a frequent and unsuspected cause of permanent injury or death in children and coined the term "battered child syndrome."[3] Before Kempe's report, Dr. John Caffey, a radiologist, noted in 1946 an association between subdural hematomas and long bone fractures. In 1955, Dr. P.V. Wooley and Dr. W.A. Evans, two radiologists, attributed the findings of Caffey to intentionally inflicted trauma.[4]

In 1963, Dr. Vincent J. Fontana proposed a more broadly defined "maltreatment syndrome," which indicated that the battered child phenomenon is the last phase of the maltreatment spectrum. Fontana reported that the maltreated child often "presents without obvious signs of being battered but with multiple evidence of emotional and, at times, nutritional deprivation, neglect and abuse."[5]

By June 1967, every state had adopted laws that either required or recommended physicians and certain others to report suspected cases of child abuse to appropriate law enforcement or welfare authorities and provided legal protection for reporting persons.

DEFINITION OF CHILD ABUSE AND NEGLECT

Child abuse can be defined on several levels. A legal definition is supplied by each state's laws. An institutional-operational definition is used in a hospital, school, or other organization. A personal definition is established on the basis of an individual's background and experience. Today's definition of child maltreatment encompasses a wide spectrum of commissions and omissions by parents and guardians. The legal definition of abuse enacted by Congress in 1974 in Public Law 93-247 states "Child abuse and neglect means the physical or mental injury, sexual abuse, negligent treatment, or maltreatment of a child under the age of 18 by a person who is responsible for the child's welfare under circumstances which indicate that the child's health or welfare is harmed or threatened thereby."[6]

TYPES OF ABUSE

Physical abuse is also known as nonaccidental trauma. It includes any injuries inflicted by a caretaker, such as bruises, hematomas, fractures, dislocations, burns, central nervous system injury, abdominal injury, and bizarre types of injuries.

Nutritional deprivation is also known as failure to thrive. It is defined as an underweight, malnourished condition with no identifiable organic cause.

Sexual abuse is defined as sexual exploitation of a child younger than 18 years of age by an adult caretaker. It includes incest, sexual intercourse, sodomy, oral-genital contact, molestation (fondling, masturbation, or exposure), and exploitation (pornography or prostitution).

Intentional drugging or poisoning occurs when a parent or caretaker gives a child a prescription medication that is harmful and not intended for children (for example, sustained doses of a depressant to keep the child quiet). Addicted mothers who continue their drug use during pregnancy may have infants born suffering withdrawal symptoms and possibly permanent sequelae. In the child with repeated "accidental" poisonings, suspicion of abuse should be aroused.

Neglect is generally defined as a condition in which the adult caretaker responsible for the child either deliberately or by inattentiveness allows the child to suffer or fails to provide one or more of the elements generally deemed essential for the development of a child's physical, intellectual or emotional capacities. Physical neglect occurs when food, shelter, and clothing needs are neglected. Emotional neglect is when a child is denied the nurturing qualities necessary for sound personality development. Medical neglect is when usual and accepted minimum levels of preventive, diagnostic, or therapeutic medical services are not provided. Educational neglect occurs when a caretaker fails to ensure that the child receives education as provided by state laws.

Emotional abuse is defined as severe verbal abuse, constant belittling, continual scapegoating, or rejection of a child by a caretaker.[7]

INCIDENCE OF ABUSE

The true incidence of child abuse is unknown for a number of reasons. Incomplete reporting is the major one and may be due to the lack of a uniformly accepted definition of abuse, frequent failures in diagnosing abuse, an unwillingness to report identified abuse, or the absence of child abuse as a listing in the International Classification of Disease.

From the data available on child abuse, it is known that

- most cases involve children younger than 3 years of age (this age group is considered at highest risk and in danger of death)
- abuse is most likely to be reported in low-income and minority groups[8]
- children of both sexes are equally physically abused
- sexual abuse is reported to occur more frequently in girls than in boys
- abuse occurs in every geographic area, on all socioeconomic levels, and in all ethnic groups.[9]

Statistics

Exhibit 13-1 lists data from the National Study on Child Neglect and Abuse Reporting in 1981. From this study, several generalizations can be made. Hundreds of thousands of children are physically abused in the United States every year. Tens of thousands of American children every year suffer major inflicted physical injuries and are at risk for fatality and permanent disability. Children younger than 7 years of age are at the greatest risk for fatality. Most families involved in child maltreatment are white. Although certain families with economic stress are over-represented, most families reported for child abuse are not experiencing economic difficulty.[10] Some investigators hold that

Exhibit 13-1 1981 National Study on Child Abuse and Neglect Reporting

Total case reports	850,980
Physical abuse reports (45 percent)	382,941
"Major" physical injury (4 percent)	34,039
Average age of reported children	7.2 years
Average age of case fatalities	3.3 years
Cases reported by medical personnel (11 percent)	93,608
Families with economic problems	44 percent
Ethnic distribution of maltreated children	
White	68 percent
Black	22 percent
Hispanic	8 percent
Other	2 percent

Source: Adapted from *National Study on Child Neglect and Abuse Reporting,* with permission of American Humane Association, © 1981.

poverty-level groups may have an increased incidence of abuse as a result of a greater number of situational crises and the decreased availability of resources.[11]

It is generally estimated that 10 percent of injuries to children younger than 5 years of age who are seen in an emergency department are the result of inflicted trauma.[12] To conceptualize, it is helpful to use the "iceberg theory"; that is, there are more actual than known cases of abuse, with the most serious cases hospitalized, the least serious cases treated on an outpatient basis, and most incidents never identified.

Morbidity and Mortality

Reports of morbidity statistics for cases of child abuse vary, but some general trends are apparent. Of children who are abused and not reported, 30 percent to 50 percent will be severely abused again, 15 percent to 20 percent will be battered again even with supervision, and an estimated 15 percent will be left with some type of neurologic deficit.[13] Mortality statistics for the total population of child abuse are generally reported to range from 2 percent to 11 percent.[14]

Reporting

Individual state laws determine who is obligated to report suspected cases of abuse, where reports are filed, and what legal protection is afforded the reporter. Failure to report suspected child abuse or neglect may result in civil or criminal penalties. Physicians are required to report in every state; nurses, teachers, day care workers, social workers, and police officers are required to report in many states.

Kauffman and Neill state

Although nurses are unaccustomed to the use of reporting as a prevention and treatment approach, reporting is essential for the safety of the child and to initiate delivery of services to the family. Legal involvement is recognized as an integral component of the multidisciplinary and community approach to child abuse. Judge Delaney writes: "Inherent in family law is the delicate balance between what is exclusively a matter within the family and what is a concern to society. In the area of family, the court's true role is to define and protect the rights and enforce the responsibilities of the parent, of the child and of the community."[15]

The safety of the child is of paramount importance. Reporting provides the basis for legal intervention on behalf of the child. Failure to report suspected cases of abuse places the child at risk for additional abuse and even death. Reporting should not be done as a punitive measure or out of anger or frustration. If this occurs, it will be more difficult for the parent to understand that reporting is an intervention to provide services to the "dysfunctional" family. It is also important for the reporter to remember that he or she is not required to prove that abuse or neglect has occurred but that, on the basis of the history and physical examination, there is reason to believe or reasonable cause to suspect that abuse has occurred.

ETIOLOGY AND PRECIPITATING FACTORS

Child abuse and neglect can be viewed as a symptom of family dysfunction that may be due to a number of factors, including

- history of abuse in the parent's childhood
- family stress factors, such as divorce, separation, alcoholism, drug addiction, teenage pregnancy, mental retardation, recurring mental illness, unemployment, financial distress, or a new family member
- poor parental coping mechanisms, impulse control, and self-image
- high demand for the child to perform to gratify the parents
- social isolation.

In less than 5 percent of reported cases of abuse is the parent identified as psychotic or sociopathic. Race, ethnic origin, sex, income, religion, education, and social status do not determine child abuse.

The abuser is a related caretaker in 90 percent of cases, a maternal boyfriend in 5 percent of cases, a babysitter in 4 percent, and a sibling in 1 percent. Because mothers usually spend more time with their children than fathers, they are more likely to be involved in abuse. If the father is unemployed, however, the gender difference is not present.[16]

Factors such as alcohol and drug addiction have not been shown to have a major effect on the etiology of child abuse. Nevertheless, it stands to reason that a caretaker who is impaired by the effects of alcohol or drugs may not be as attentive to the child's needs or activities, which could result in neglect, failure to prevent an accidental injury, or failure to respond appropriately if an accident occurs.

The most significant factor identified in the literature is that the basic pattern of childrearing is poor in abusive families. In many cases, the parents were abused as children and therefore had poor role models.

Although a specific abusive personality has not been defined by investigators in psychiatry or psychology, some general characteristics of parents who are considered at "high risk" for abuse are

- a history of abuse in one parent's own childhood
- unrealistic and inappropriate performance expectations of the child
- low self-esteem, emotional immaturity, and dependency
- unrealistic expectations of the child's growth and development
- expectations of the child to fulfill parents' needs, or "role reversal"
- youth, loneliness, isolation, or lack of social support systems
- poor impulse control or aggressive behavior
- unwillingness to assume the responsibilities of parenting
- choosing an abusive partner or partners.[17]

Abuse is the result of a distorted relationship between a parent and child. Frequently, one child is singled out by the parent as being different, bad, or even evil. Some characteristics of the child at risk for abuse are

- unplanned, unwanted, or illegitimate
- premature, or the result of a difficult pregnancy or delivery
- handicapped, including developmental disabilities, mental retardation, cerebral palsy, epilepsy, autism, and the like
- "difficult": colicky, hyperactive, hard to feed, low sensory threshold, "won't mind," and so forth
- "different": congenital abnormality, unpleasant personality, reminiscent of abusive person from parent's past, and so forth
- rebellious adolescent who is asserting independence and becoming sexually active.[18]

The combination of a potentially abusive parent and an at-risk child confronted with a situational trigger frequently results in abuse. A triggering event can be a crisis, either major or minor, that the parent perceives as unmanageable. Examples include the following.

- The child gets sick (vomits), "messes his pants," "won't listen," refuses to eat, or cries constantly.
- The family has financial problems (such as a job loss) or social problems (such as a fight or a recent illness).

- The family endures environmental stress (for example, eviction, moving, crowded living conditions, poverty, crime, or disconnected utilities).[19]

CLINICAL PRESENTATION OF THE ABUSED CHILD

How can the nurse recognize abuse? It is a difficult task at times to differentiate among a "normal" childhood injury, "normal" parental behavior, and abuse. It is of critical importance to remember that a reason to suspect or believe that abuse has occurred is all that is necessary to file on behalf of the child and that guilt need not be established by the health care provider.

Suspicion is the prerequisite for successful diagnosis of child abuse or neglect. One study showed that 6 percent of one hundred sixty pediatric patients with multiple trauma and neurologic injuries were child abuse cases; child abuse was the third most common single cause of injury in that series.[20] In many institutions where ill or injured children are treated, the nurse is often the first professional to encounter the child. It is usually the responsibility of the nurse to screen information from the caretaker related to the chief complaint, to perform a rapid physical assessment, and to assign a triage priority and destination to the patient. During the initial phase of entry into the health care system, the nurse should keep in mind the possibility of abuse because it is such a frequent occurrence and have an awareness of what clues to look for in the history and physical examination.

In a "building-block" approach to diagnosis, data from the physical examination, history, laboratory, and observed pattern of parent-child interaction can be utilized to develop a level of suspicion necessary for filing a report.[21] It is the child welfare worker's role to investigate the report and to substantiate the findings.

The following injury histories are suggestive of child abuse and are essential components of the "building-block" approach to diagnosis.

Unexplained Injury

In this situation, the parents are reluctant or unwilling to elaborate on how the child's injury may have occurred. Frequently heard expressions include "I just found him that way" and "I don't know how it could have happened but maybe she just fell." When pressed for details, the parents may become evasive, defensive, or even hostile. These explanations and expressions are self-incriminating because normally parents know exactly when, where, and how their child was injured and are completely willing to discuss the event in detail.[22]

Discrepant History

The parents may offer conflicting histories of the injury, or the history may change with regard to dates, times, or causes with subsequent tellings. Other discrepancies in the history relate to the child's developmental age. For example, a story in which a

4-month-old infant supposedly climbed out of a crib and fell is obviously suspicious because an infant is not developmentally capable of the actions described by the parent.

Another typical contradiction is seen when the history offered and the physical findings do not concur. An example of this is the child who allegedly "just fell off the bed" yet is covered with bruises. In some instances the parent may claim that the child fell a few hours ago, but on physical examination the "date" of the bruises does not concur. Another example of a discrepant history is when a parent states that the child bruises easily but when blood studies do not show any abnormalities in the child's clotting capabilities and the child does not develop any new bruises during the hospital stay.[23]

Alleged Self-Inflicted Injury

Children rarely deliberately injure themselves seriously. Parents may offer a history that implies that the child is masochistic or hurt himself or herself during a "temper tantrum." These implications are almost always false. Histories of a child younger than 6 months of age with a self-inflicted accident or injury are highly suspicious.[24]

Alleged Third Party Inflicted Injury

When the parents blame their child's injury on someone else (a babysitter, neighbor, or sibling), the health care provider should be suspicious. The alleged abuser should be interviewed separately as soon as possible for confirmation of suspicions. In some instances such stories may be confirmed, but often the parent will not be able to name the alleged third party, or the person is named but is "unreachable."[25]

Delay in Seeking Medical Care

Normally when significant accidental trauma occurs, parents seek immediate medical attention for their child. When there is a significant delay in seeking medical care, the parent either did not understand the seriousness of the injury or is avoiding the possible discovery of the nature of the injury. One study of abused children reported that 40 percent of the children were not brought to the hospital until the morning after the injury and that another 40 percent were not brought in until 1 to 4 days after the injury had occurred.[26]

In addition to a delay in seeking medical care, the timing of the injury itself is an important consideration. In general, "accidents" occurring between the hours of midnight and 6 A.M. are suspicious because children are normally asleep during these hours.

Parental Reaction

When a child is accidentally injured, parents normally react with anxiety, concern, or guilt that they somehow did not prevent the injury. Typical parental reactions to an injury inflicted through child abuse include detachment, depression, hostility, or defensiveness. These behaviors should raise suspicion about the nature of the injury.

Another parental reaction that suggests child abuse occurs when the possibility of child abuse is raised with the parent. In general, when parents are confronted with the differential diagnosis of abuse or neglect but are not responsible for inflicting the injury and are not negligent in seeking care, they react with either surprise or irritation. The reaction of an abusive parent may be hostility, extreme defensiveness, or intimidation.[27]

Parental Focus of Concern

When a child is injured, it is expected that the parents' chief concern is the child's physical and emotional status. If the parents are indifferent or apathetic toward the child and are primarily preoccupied with their own needs, as when they complain about being tired or hungry or about the inconvenience of the hospital visit, concern should be raised regarding the nature of the parent-child relationship.[28]

History of Previous Trauma

It is important to elicit a careful history of any previous trauma to the child. This includes a review of the child's previous medical records to verify the reliability of the parent as a historian as well as to establish any pattern of multiple injuries over a period of time. In addition, information regarding a history of suspected abuse or neglect can be elicited.

If available, medical records of any siblings should be reviewed for patterns of injuries or neglect. The frequent use of multiple hospitals or emergency rooms makes it difficult for the nurse to gather information but is a common behavior in abusive families.

Parental Mental Status

An assessment of parental mental status is an essential component of every child health encounter. It is important to document strange behavior, any inappropriate or bizarre statements made by the parent, or the presence of alcohol on a parent's breath. Such findings do not necessarily indicate abuse, but they should raise concern about the ability of the parent to provide a safe environment for the child or to react appropriately if any injury occurs.[29]

Child Health History

A careful review of the child's health history provides invaluable background information in the "building-block" approach to the diagnosis of child abuse. Some of the areas that should be assessed include

- birth history (planned pregnancy, any problems with labor or delivery, congenital abnormality)

- childhood illnesses, operations, and diseases
- allergies, immunization status, and primary health care source
- family health history (hereditary diseases, history of abuse)
- nutritional history (food allergies, problems with weight gain)
- developmental milestones achieved
- cultural remedies used for treatment of illness.

Psychosocial History

This information typically is best elicited by the hospital social worker or protective services case worker. Nevertheless, basic information regarding who lives in the home, environmental conditions, caretaker roles, support systems, financial status, recent stressors, and discipline techniques should be included in the evaluation of any child with a serious injury or illness.

History of the Injury

The history of the injury should be as detailed as possible. Specific information should be elicited about the events before and after the incident as well as about the nature of the incident itself. When possible, it is important to interview the child and any witnesses separately to discern if any discrepancies exist that could raise suspicion about the etiology of the injury.

Sometimes when a parent or child is asked about the circumstances related to the injury, they will identify the "trigger" or related crisis that precipitated the incident. Often, injured children feel that they are to blame and somehow deserved the "punishment" or injury because they were "bad."[30]

CHARACTERISTIC PHYSICAL FINDINGS IN CHILD ABUSE

Cutaneous Injuries

Injuries to the skin are the most common physical manifestation of inflicted injuries in childhood. They can be categorized as bruises, burns, welts, lacerations, and bite marks. Characteristics such as location, pattern, presence of multiple lesions of different ages, and failure of new bruises to appear after hospitalization help distinguish inflicted skin injuries from accidental ones.

Bruises

All children at one time or another get their share of minor and not so minor bruises. Usually these ecchymoses are located over bony prominences (such as the shins, knees, elbows, hands, chin, and forehead). Suspicious bruises include those on infants, bruises over soft surfaces (such as the cheeks, neck, abdomen, back, buttocks, and thighs), and bruises with a characteristic shape or pattern.[31]

The determination of the approximate age of a bruise is important in the context of the history of the injury. Table 13-1 lists the color changes of a typical bruise with time.

If a parent reports that the alleged injury occurred on the previous day and if the bruises are blue-green in color, there is a discrepancy between the history and the physical findings. Often in abuse cases, the child presents with bruises in multiple phases of healing and in suspicious locations. Many black children and children of mediterranean descent normally have bluish discolorations over the lower back and buttocks, which are commonly referred to as mongolian spots; these birthmarks should not be mistaken for signs of abuse.

Some bruises have a characteristic shape or pattern that raise suspicions about their etiology. Examples include

- grab marks—oval ecchymoses with indistinct borders that may appear in a pattern suggestive of violent grabbing
- pinch marks—linear or slightly crescentic bruises usually 1 to 2 cm in length
- slap marks—complete or incomplete hand prints
- belt marks—broad, linear ecchymoses
- loop marks—elliptic ecchymoses typically resulting from an injury inflicted with electric cords, ropes, and the like
- comb marks—multiple, parallel, linear abrasions and bruises resulting from a comb dragged across the skin
- circumferential marks—bruises encircling the ankles, wrists, neck, or sides of the mouth that indicate the use of restraint or an attempt to choke.[32]

Burns

It is estimated that 10 percent of child abuse cases admitted to the hospital are burns of a nonaccidental origin. Three typical types of burn injuries are hot water, splash, and branding injuries.

Hot water immersion is the type of burn seen when a part (or parts) of the child's body is immersed in hot water. One example is the confluent "stocking glove" appearance of

Table 13-1 Color Changes in Cutaneous Contusions

Age of the Bruise (days)	Color
0 to 2	Colorless, but swollen and tender
0 to 5	Red, blue
5 to 7	Green
7 to 10	Yellow
10 to 14	Brown
14 to 28	Colorless

Source: Adapted by permission of *Pediatrics,* Vol. 60, page 750, copyright 1977.

an extremity when it has been immersed in hot water for a period of time. Another example is the "dunking" burn frequently seen in toddlers. In this situation, the toddler is dunked buttocks first into a tub of hot water as a discipline measure after a toileting accident. The burn is confluent on the buttocks; often the central area is spared as the result of contact with the cooler surface of the tub. The intertriginous folds are usually spared, and the burn ends near the waist with a mark indicating the depth of the water. Depending on the position of the child, the perineum, genitalia, and parts of the legs may also be burned.

Splash burns are caused by hot liquids (water, coffee, tea, oil, and so forth) thrown at or poured onto the child. This type of burn is frequently caused accidentally, so that the history of the injury is important in determining the etiology. The burns that result from this are large confluent areas of second- to third-degree burns with smaller burns scattered around the area.

Branding is a burn that occurs when a solid hot object is pressed against the skin. Commonly seen examples include burns from electric range heating elements, cigarettes, clothes irons, curling irons, heating grates, and the like. The resulting burn may be amorphous or may take the form of the object. Sometimes infected insect bites or superficial puncture wounds are mistaken for cigarette burns if they are not carefully diagnosed.[33]

Bite Marks

Human bite marks are another frequently seen type of nonaccidental soft tissue trauma in children. Two common forms are linear puncture wounds on fingers and curvilinear to circular ecchymoses on any body part. Children often bite one another, and individual tooth characteristics (such as arch, width, and intercanine distance) can be determined by forensic odontologic techniques.[34]

Head Injuries

Shaken Infant Syndrome

The recognition that subdural hematomas may result from pathogenic shaking of infants was an important discovery, previously unrecognized due to a lack of external findings. Subdural hematomas, which were almost always traumatic in origin, were most common in children younger than 24 months of age, with a peak incidence at about 6 months. The infants at highest risk for this syndrome are males (in whom the incidence is twice as high as in females) who are of low birth weight or premature.[35]

The child often presents with vague or nonspecific symptoms such as lethargy, decreased appetite, and irritability or with signs of increased intracranial pressure (vomiting, seizures, stupor, or coma). The physical finding of retinal hemorrhage is strongly suggestive of the whiplash origin of the injury. Other diagnostic tests to confirm this type of injury include a spinal or subdural tap (to detect blood) and computerized tomography (CT). In addition, the child may present with associated skin bruises (grab marks on the chest, shoulder, arms, or head) or a long bone fracture.

Skull Fractures

Skull fractures may occur accidentally, as from falls or motor vehicle accidents, or as a result of inflicted trauma. As always, a careful history helps determine the cause of the injury. Falls from small heights (less than 3 feet) rarely result in skull fractures (approximately 1 percent of the time or less), and intracranial complications are infrequent.[36]

Three types of skull fractures commonly seen in physically abused children are multiple, depressed, and basilar fractures. Multiple fractures can be caused by a single traumatic event, but if fractures are in various stages of healing, suspicion is warranted. Depressed fractures are usually caused by impact with a blunt object, not by a fall. Basilar fractures typically present with periorbital ecchymoses (raccoon eyes), ecchymoses over the mastoid bone (Battle's sign), hemotympanum, cerebrospinal fluid otorrhea, or rhinorrhea.

Scalp Injuries

Scalp injuries secondary to trauma include bruises, lacerations, abrasions, edema, and hair loss (traumatic alopecia). These injuries are the result of the child being beaten on the head with either a hand or a solid object or of violent hair pulling.[37]

Skeletal Injuries

In child abuse cases, skeletal injuries (most commonly fractures) rank second in frequency only to cutaneous injuries. In determining whether a specific fracture was inflicted, the pattern of bony injury and an estimation of the "age" of the fracture should be compared to the history of the injury.

A broad estimation of the age of the fracture can be made by a radiologist. Fracture ages can be generally categorized into the following time intervals: (1) 0 to 10 days, (2) 10 days to 2 months (3) 2 to 6 months, and (4) older than 6 months. Gross discrepancies with the history of the injury can be discerned, but fine discrepancies cannot.[38]

In general, fractures that indicate a high probability of child abuse include

- multiple fractures of different ages, which are indicative of repeated abuse
- metaphyseal fractures of long bones caused by violent torsion or traction of the extremity, especially when seen in infants and toddlers
- spiral fractures caused by powerful twisting forces on an extremity, especially when seen in infants and toddlers; typical sites are the tibia, femur, radius, and humerus
- bilateral rib fractures, which occur when the chest is strongly crushed between two hands; this is occasionally seen in the shaken infant syndrome.[39]

Abdominal Injuries

Visceral injuries rank second only to head trauma as the leading cause of mortality due to child abuse. In many instances of intra-abdominal injuries there are no external signs of trauma. Many cases are diagnosed only at post-mortem examination. Frequently, the child is brought to the hospital many hours or even days after the injury, when complications (shock and infection) are well advanced. The history of abdominal injuries is usually given as a fall from a height onto a flat surface or a fall down a flight of stairs. Such falls rarely produce intra-abdominal visceral damage of the type seen in nonaccidental trauma because most documented cases are blunt trauma resulting in tears, rupture, or hematomas of the viscera.[40]

Inflicted abdominal injuries most often seen in child abuse cases include

- ruptured liver or spleen
- intestinal perforation
- intramuscular hematoma of the duodenum or proximal jejunum
- ruptured blood vessel
- pancreatic injury (pancreatic pseudocyst)
- kidney injury.

Sexual Abuse

It is beyond the scope of this chapter to address fully the topic of sexual abuse. Sexual abuse is considered the most obscure form of child abuse because the child rarely presents with physical signs or symptoms. Rather, the child typically exhibits emotional disturbances or behavioral symptoms as a result of sexual abuse that may not be readily apparent.

The physical signs and symptoms of possible sexual abuse in children include any trauma to the genital, urinary, or rectal area, which may be indicated by the presence of any of the following:

- bruising, pain, swelling, bleeding, lacerations, or tears
- discharges that indicate inflammation or infection
- venereal disease (trichomoniasis, gonorrhea, syphilis, or chlamydiosis)
- pregnancy, particularly in the young adolescent.[41]

Emotional manifestations of sexual abuse are listed in Exhibit 13-2. Many of these physical and emotional signs and symptoms may be indicative of various diseases, injuries, or other problems. Their presence, however, should always alert the nurse to the possibility of sexual abuse.

DIAGNOSTIC TESTS AND PROCEDURES

Hematologic Studies

The hematologic workup of a child suspected of being abused should include a hematogram and coagulogram to rule out bleeding disorders or the presence of anemia. This is crucial information in cases involving bruises to rule out an organic pathology.

Exhibit 13-2 Emotional Manifestations of Child Sexual Abuse

1. Infants and Toddlers
   - Irritability
   - Feeding difficulty
   - Sleep disturbances
   - Altered levels of activity
2. School-Aged Children
   - Behavioral problems
   - Anxieties
   - Sleep disturbances
   - Frightening dreams
   - Withdrawn attitude
3. Adolescents
   - Fright and confusion
   - Guilt feelings
   - Anger and acting out
   - Depressive affect

Source: Reprinted from *Pediatric Annals,* Vol. 13, No. 10, p. 755, with permission of Charles B. Slack, Inc., © October 1984.

Skeletal Series

In children younger than 6 years of age who are suspected of being abused, a total body roentgenogram is necessary to identify fractures, to look for evidence of multiple fractures of different ages, and to rule out pre-existing bone disease (osteogenesis imperfecta).

Toxicology Screen

In suspected cases of child abuse, it is important to screen for the presence of exogenous poisons or overdoses of commonly used therapeutic medications (such as aspirin, barbiturates, and cough medication).

Miscellaneous Tests and Procedures

In children with suspected head injuries, a CT scan is required to rule out the presence of contusions, subdural and epidural hematomas, or fractures. In cases of suspected abdominal trauma, an amylase level is measured to rule out pancreatic injury and a urinalysis is helpful to screen for renal trauma. In children suspected of being sexually abused, the same protocols should be followed as in adult rape cases.

Developmental Assessment

Plotting the child's physical growth measurements (height, weight, and head circumference) on the nationally standardized charts for sex and age provides important information in the evaluation of a child for possible abuse. If the child is well below the fifth percentile for height and weight or is significantly off the curve, suspicion should be raised about the adequacy of care that the child receives at home. For various reasons (prematurity, cystic fibrosis, congenital heart defect, renal disease, and so forth), some children are below the fifth percentile but demonstrate a generally positive direction in their growth curve. Previous medical records are helpful in distinguishing any gross fluctuations in the child's physical growth.

A child who shows a gross delay in achievement of developmental milestones according to such standards as the Denver Developmental Screening Test warrants further investigation. It is also important to document the child's physical and developmental status at the time of admission to the hospital to look for any significant changes that may occur during hospitalization. This information can be crucial later in identifying any discrepancies in the parents' history. An example is when the parent labels the child a "difficult feeder" or "slow" in his or her development but when the child shows significant growth and development while hospitalized.

Photographs

In cases of abuse with physical manifestations (such as a general wasted appearance, skin markings, limb deformities, and the like), color photographs help document findings for law enforcement agencies and courts. State child protection statutes, hospital policies and procedures, and hospital legal consultants can be of assistance in dealing with consent and confidentiality issues.[42]

CASE MANAGEMENT

Because child abuse is a complex problem, input from several disciplines is necessary for effective management. The University of Colorado Health Sciences Center in Denver was one of the first to use a multidisciplinary team approach to discuss the difficult diagnostic and therapeutic problems of abused children and their families. Since then, many different forms of a team approach have been developed depending on the needs and purposes of the institution. In general, most multidisciplinary teams consist of a physician, a social worker, a coordinator (often a nurse), a psychologist, a developmental specialist, a lawyer, a public health nurse, a protective services social worker, and a law enforcement representative.

The Child Protection Team at the University of Colorado reports several advantages to the team approach, which include a decreased incidence of subsequent abuse, serious injury, and death; fewer errors in decision making about appropriate interventions for the child and family; increased case finding and reporting within the community; improved interagency cooperation; and improved court hearings, preparation of expert witnesses, and testimony.[43]

The general priorities of management of the child suspected of being abused include the following.

1. Protect the child (and possibly the siblings) from further abuse or neglect. When appropriate, this may indicate hospitalization.
2. Provide treatment for the child's physical injuries, general health deficits, and emotional needs.
3. Document carefully all physical, diagnostic, developmental, and subjective findings, and estimate the probability that an injury has been inflicted. These entries will become the database for future civil or criminal court testimony.
4. When appropriate, initiate sociolegal interventions such as filing a report to child protective services or law enforcement authorities. If there is a reasonable probability that the parent is likely to attempt to flee with the child, emergency custody can be obtained with a court order.
5. Support, educate, and initiate referrals to help rehabilitate the parents to enable the child to return to a safe, healthy environment if possible. Frequent therapies utilized include parent aides, homemaker services, Parents Anonymous groups, telephone hotlines, crisis nurseries, psychotherapy, marital counseling, vocational rehabilitation, childrearing counseling, play therapy, therapeutic preschool or day care, child protective services, home visits, and temporary foster homes.
6. Ensure that appropriate follow-up is planned for the child and family. This should include primary health care, social services intervention, visiting nurse appointments, and medical follow-up visits for specific injuries for which the child was treated.[44]

NURSING INTERVENTIONS WITH ABUSIVE FAMILIES

When a child is hospitalized for injuries suggestive of abuse, the nurse is generally viewed as the least threatening and therefore most approachable member of the health care team. In general, nurses are thought of as helping professionals and therefore have the advantage of gaining quick acceptance by families.

To be effective in establishing a therapeutic relationship with the child and the family, the nurse must first examine her or his own feelings toward both the abusive parent and the abused child. It is important for the nurse to realize that she or he will experience various emotional responses while caring for an abused or neglected child. This is a normal process, and nurses should take care not to label these feelings but only to be aware of them and their potential effect on care delivered.

With an awareness of the feelings elicited when caring for an abused child and family and an understanding of the factors outlined at the beginning of this chapter, the nurse can coordinate an individual plan of care. A written nursing care plan helps define short- and long-term goals for the child and the family, ensure consistency among various staff caring for the child, and evaluate progress.

When caring for the hospitalized abused child and family, the roles of the nurse can be summarized by the following directives.

1. Listen

    Listening conveys the nurse's concern about the parent and the child as human beings. It is not necessary for the nurse to agree with the parent or child, but listening assists them in clarifying their feelings. Many abusive parents are socially isolated and have poor self-esteem, so that someone who shows an interest by taking time to listen can help foster their sense of self-worth.

2. Teach

    Because abusive parents often have feelings of failure and inadequacy coupled with unrealistic expectations, it is important for the nurse to plan any teaching carefully. The child's hospitalization also provides an opportunity for the nurse to teach any basics of child care that the parent does not know.

3. Set Limits

    On the child's admission to the hospital, all hospital rules and regulations, particularly the visiting policies, should be clearly explained so that the family has the opportunity to respond appropriately. It is also important to set limits of acceptable behavior for the parents and the child and to include these in the nursing care plan.

4. Act As a Role Model

    One of the most significant functions of the nurse in working with the abusive family is acting as a role model. During the child's hospital stay, the nurse has many opportunities to demonstrate, by example, positive ways of interacting with the child. The parents will observe how the nurse communicates with their child and techniques that the nurse uses when discipline is necessary. In addition, the nurse has the opportunity to show the benefits of positive reinforcement and appropriate developmental activities on the child's behavior. The parents will also observe how the nurse vents his or her frustration and manages difficult situations.

5. Document

    Documentation of evidence is vital in child abuse cases because records help substantiate the reasonable cause that provides the basis for legal intervention on behalf of the child. Admissible medical records in court include medical history, nursing history, daily charting, and results of diagnostic tests and procedures. Documentation of the observed parent-child interactions is primarily the nurse's responsibility. These entries should be objective, accurate, and timely. The nurse should include in the documentation who initiates the parent-child interaction observed, how the parent handles the child (discipline techniques and comfort measures), a description of any behavioral patterns, and the frequency of calls or visits of family members. The nurse must be careful to describe and report objectively, separating out any emotional response when charting.[45]

6. Ensure Prevention and Early Detection

Because nurses interact with families in a number of settings (such as the school, home, clinic, emergency department, hospital, and so forth), they are in an ideal position to identify signs and symptoms of children at risk for abuse. The nurse can initiate appropriate referrals to provide necessary support, whether financial, social, or educational, that the family may be lacking.

In addition to the individual care that a nurse gives to the abused child and family, there are opportunities for the nurse to intervene through community efforts for the prevention of child abuse. For example, participation in the local chapter of the National Committee for the Prevention of Child Abuse or promotion of local school programs that address parenting issues are two ways in which a nurse can address environmental factors. Nurses can increase their effectiveness in this area by being aware of legislative issues that affect child and youth services because resources are limited and because prevention programs are often at risk of not being funded.

Finally, the nursing role in identifying families at risk for violence needs to be defined further through promotion of and participation in research. It has frequently been left to other disciplines to conduct research in this area. A nursing perspective would appropriately emphasize the healthy aspects of the families experiencing violence, an approach that is well supported by research on actual cases.[46] Through research, nurses can also identify more effective types of interventions in cases of child abuse.

NOTES

1. Jacqueline Campbell, *Nursing Care of Victims of Family Violence* (Reston, Va.: Reston Publications, 1984), 123.

2. Vincent J. Fontana, *Somewhere a Child Is Crying: Maltreatment—Causes and Prevention* (New York: New American Library, Inc., 1973), 11.

3. C. Henry Kempe et al., "The Battered Child Syndrome," *Journal of the American Medical Association* 181(1962):17.

4. Robert M. Reece and Michael A. Grodin, "Recognition of Non-Accidental Injury," *Pediatric Clinics of North America* 32(1985):47.

5. Vincent J. Fontana, *The Maltreated Child: The Maltreatment Syndrome in Children* (Springfield, Ill.: Charles C Thomas, 1971), 4.

6. R.L. Mindlen, "Child Abuse and Neglect: The Role of the Pediatrician and the Academy," *Pediatrics* 54(1974):393.

7. American Humane Association, *National Study on Child Abuse and Neglect Reporting* (Denver: American Humane Association, 1983).

8. David F. Gil, *Violence Against Children: Physical Child Abuse in the United States* (Cambridge, Mass.: Harvard Univ. Press, 1970), 136, 138.

9. Donalda Parkes and Carmella Sylvestre-Simon, "The Care of the Abused and Neglected Child," in American Association of Critical Care Nursing, *Critical Care Nursing of Children* (Philadelphia: W.B. Saunders Co., 1981), 320.

10. David L. Kerns, "Child Abuse," in Thomas Mayer, ed., *Emergency Management of Pediatric Trauma* (Philadelphia: W.B. Saunders Co., 1985), 421.

11. Barton C. Schmitt, "The Battered Child Syndrome," in Robert Touloukian, ed., *Pediatric Trauma* (New York: John Wiley & Sons, 1978), 181.

12. J.C. Holter and S.B. Friedman, "Child Abuse: Early Case Finding in the Emergency Department," *Pediatrics* 42(1968):128.

13. Parkes and Sylvestre-Simon, "The Care of the Abused and Neglected Child," 320.

14. Ibid.

15. Carole K. Kauffman and Mary Kathleen Neill, "The Abusive Parent," in Suzanne Hall, ed., *High-Risk Parenting: Nursing Assessment and Strategies for the Family at Risk* (Philadelphia: J.B. Lippincott Co., 1979), 228.

16. Schmitt, "The Battered Child Syndrome," 181.

17. Parkes and Sylvestre-Simon, "The Care of the Abused and Neglected Child," 321.

18. Ibid.

19. Ibid., 321–22.

20. Reece and Grodin, "Recognition of Non-Accidental Injury," 42.

21. Stephen Ludwig, Information reported at Child Abuse Conference, Lancaster, Penn., 28 October 1986.

22. Schmitt, "The Battered Child Syndrome," 182.

23. Ibid.

24. Ibid.

25. Ibid.

26. Kerns, "Child Abuse," 423.

27. Ibid.

28. Ibid.

29. Ibid.

30. Ibid.

31. Ibid., 424.

32. Ibid., 424–25.

33. Ibid., 427.

34. Ibid., 422.

35. Reece and Grodin, "Recognition of Non-Accidental Injury," 47–48.

36. Kerns, "Child Abuse," 428.

37. Ibid., 427.

38. Ibid., 428–29.

39. Ibid., 429–30.

40. Reece and Grodin, "Recognition of Non-Accidental Injury," 50.

41. Carolyn V. Fore and Sharon S. Holmes, "Sexual Abuse of Children," *Nursing Clinics of North America* 19(1984):331.

42. Parkes and Sylvestre-Simon, "The Care of the Abused and Neglected Child," 325.

43. Richard D. Krugman, "The Multidisciplinary Treatment of Abusive and Neglectful Families," *Pediatric Annals* 13(1984):761–62.
44. Parkes and Sylvestre-Simon, "The Care of the Abused and Neglected Child," 325–27.
45. Ibid., 123–24.
46. Campbell, *Nursing Care of Victims of Family Violence*, 7.

Chapter 14

Emotional Support of the Injured Child and Family

Tracy Kelly

Nurses who accept the challenge of caring for a pediatric trauma patient call on their sharp assessment skills and knowledge of acute interventions in providing the care necessary to overcome the devastating results of physical injury. While doing so, nurses must also be aware of the psychological impact of trauma to provide the consistent emotional care and support that is vital to the patient. When the trauma patient is a child, the challenges are even greater. The nurse must recognize the developmental stage of the child and how this affects stress and emotional recovery. The child's needs are unlike those of the adult, who through life experiences has adopted coping behaviors and strategies for dealing with difficult situations. The child, on the other hand, is vulnerable to the fears of continued bodily injury and the psychological impact of even brief separation from parents. Most young children are incapable of understanding the emotional stresses of a devastating injury. The nurse who cares for the pediatric trauma patient must be clearly aware of these special considerations and know how to handle them.

The child is an integral part of the total family system, and along with the unique needs of the child come the needs of family members. Caring for the family may indeed be more challenging than caring for the patient. The physical needs of families are different with each patient and among family members. All families establish their own emotional, cultural, and social wellness. Trauma to any child tests the wellness of the entire family. The nurse involved in caring for the child and family faces the challenge of helping maintain emotional health and facilitating the recovery of the wellness that has been lost.

DEVELOPMENTAL CONSIDERATIONS

Accidents resulting in trauma occur at any age. Children are particularly vulnerable to trauma because of their small size, their exploration of the world about them, and their immature physical development. The nature of accidents and mechanisms of injury are unique in the pediatric age group, as has been discussed in the preceding chapters. The interventions necessary to care for the child are as unique as the injuries themselves.

The challenge of caring competently for the pediatric patient begins with the nurse's ability to assess cognitive, behavioral, and developmental needs of children. Factors that must be considered in this assessment include

- the developmental age of the child
- the child's cognitive understanding and ability to comprehend threats in the environment
- previous life experiences, such as hospitalization
- the ability of the child to communicate effectively.

All these factors can and do contribute to the child's ability to cope with the stressful experience of hospitalization.

Infants

The developmental task of infancy has been identified as establishing a sense of trust while combating mistrust. This task is carried out slowly as parents feed, clothe, warm, and protect the infant. This bonding may begin as early as the first few hours after birth. Studies have shown that the period immediately after delivery is the most sensitive period of bonding and that separation of parent and child at this point may play a significant part in later psychosocial adjustment for both parent and child.[1,2] As the bond between parent and child becomes stronger, the infant develops a sense of protection and security.

This task of developing a sense of trust is jeopardized during hospitalization, when painful procedures are common and parental protection is difficult, if not impossible, to maintain. The immediate needs of hospitalized trauma patients mandate swift, decisive medical intervention, which allows little chance for a father or mother to provide the child protection from harm or assurance of safe surroundings. The environment of a busy emergency room or intensive care unit and the interventions necessary to treat the child practically guarantee a stress response in the child. Nevertheless, reactions to stress in the child who is hospitalized are more directly related to the separation from the parents and less so to the actual medical procedures being performed. In fact, infants have a tremendous capacity to withstand many types of stress as long as they are accompanied by their parents.

Toddlers

When the infant becomes a toddler, he or she has established a foundation for trust and is now concerned with developing a sense of autonomy while overcoming shame and doubt. The child is now more developmentally mature and has discovered both abilities and limitations. Physical growth has allowed mobility. The toddler develops autonomy independently yet needs protection from the accidents that independence may make possible as a result of a lack of discriminating abilities.

Cognitively the child is still immature. Language has not yet been mastered, although others' demands are comprehended. This can be frustrating for the toddlers because they must comply with the requests of others but cannot enunciate their own needs. The toddler's thinking is concrete and literal. Toddlers do not understand the relationship between cause and effect or intervals of time. Because of this cognitive immaturity, toddlers are constantly struggling to understand events around them but are impeded by their lack of understanding of the relationship between events. This can lead to fears and frustrations that are difficult to allay. The toddler who is hospitalized because of a traumatic accident is confronted with real fears and anxieties but does not have the cognitive skills to control emotional responses. Consequently, the health care team is often confronted with a scared, crying youngster fighting to be free from the restraints necessary for his or her own protection.

Interventions by the nurse incorporate an understanding of variables that explain the often combative behavior of the toddler. Explanations must be basic and clear. Efforts should be aimed at alleviating the fears of the child. Most important, the security of parental protection must be maintained. Parents should be invited and encouraged to room with the toddler. Objects of security such as blankets or stuffed animals should be near the child. Parents' participation in alleviating stress, such as identifying objects of comfort and recognizing ways of soothing the child, should be encouraged by the nurse.

Preschoolers

The preschooler is much like the toddler but has an emerging sense of self and improved language skills. The preschooler begins to tolerate short periods away from parents to search out the environment but returns for needed attention and recognition of achievements.

The reasoning of the preschool-aged child is more creative than that of the toddler but is not exact. The child often substitutes fantasy for reality, and magical thinking is common. This is helpful to a child who is trying to cope with the stress of hospitalization. Play therapy is a useful tool for health providers in explaining the many complex instruments used in the hospital. The child will often initiate this play as he or she attempts to associate past events with the reason for hospitalization. Magical games and fantasies may also be helpful in providing emotional care to the preschooler. These interventions are effective but cannot substitute for a basic explanation of exactly what will happen to the child during the course of the hospitalization. Explanations should be given slowly so as not to confuse the child and immediately before interventions. Long-term planning is not helpful because the child still has no ability to understand time and cannot differentiate hours from days.

School-Aged Children

The years between 7 and 12 are years of tremendous growth and development, both physically and cognitively. Concepts and ideas that were incomprehensible several years earlier are now understood. The school-aged child interacts with friends outside of the immediate family, marking a formal end to the child's isolation from surroundings beyond the family unit. Peer groups, personal friendships, and cultural activities dominate the life of a school child. The task of developing self-worth and social acceptance is recognized and mastered. Social morality and abiding by rules are tested by the child's participation in team sports. The young child acquires a positive sense of self by succeeding in school and at play. The development of moral judgment takes place, and right and wrong are the basis for the decisions that the child makes independently.

Along with an advancing developmental maturity comes cognitive understanding. This time can be termed the concrete operational period because the child now has the capacity to comprehend the concept of the past, periods of waiting and cause and effect. The child thinks in relative terms, is less egocentric than in earlier years, and appreciates the needs and views of others as legitimate.

The result of all these tasks and achievements is a sense of belonging and acceptance. One of the most delicate aspects of caring for the pediatric trauma patient during these years is considering the potentially irreversible nature of the psychological damage that may result from misunderstanding events or treatment of the trauma. It is imperative that the health team members be astutely aware of the special concerns of the child at this sensitive age and the natural challenge to developing a strong sense of accomplishment that the child experiences. Preventing communication of fault and blame to the child during this time is a crucial aspect of giving appropriate care to the young trauma patient.

Adolescents

Perhaps the most difficult age group to understand and to provide supportive care to is adolescents. Adolescents are much like adults in their patterns and abilities to cope; they are able to reason abstractly, to present logical arguments, to organize thoughts, and to anticipate possibilities. Adolescents can take general principles and apply them to specific situations. They can utilize alternative means of communicating if language is impaired, trying symbols or signs to make points. Unlike the adult, however, the adolescent has yet to form a strong sense of identity. While striving to acquire a comfortable view of themselves, adolescents are often awkward with their emerging self-image.

The stress created by hospitalization of the adolescent is of considerable proportion. Disruption in normal socialization occurs, and often the youth must revert to the dependency and care of parents. The mental strain of immobility and lack of autonomy are overwhelming to the young adult. Attention to these factors is of utmost importance in providing appropriate emotional care. Privacy must be maintained at all costs. Respect for personal space and decision making must be maintained throughout the recovery time. Attention to these details minimizes the effects of confinement and disruption during hospitalization.

NURSING ROLES IN THE CARE OF THE INJURED CHILD

Nurses caring for pediatric trauma patients must be aware of the phases of maturity to assess accurately the coping strategies of the child. Each phase of development challenges the child with tasks to be mastered. Successful mastery ensures satisfaction and a positive sense of self. Failure to master goals places the child at risk of frustration and doubt, slowing the process of maturity.

Throughout each phase of development, the child needs guidance and support. In most cases this support comes from the family; sometimes peers are a source. In the event of hospitalization for trauma, when parent and child are separated physically and emotionally, developmental support is diverted and the task of developmental maturity is often halted. In the most severe cases, children show regressive behavior such as wetting the bed or throwing "temper tantrums." At other times alteration in the child's usual behavior, such as inability to sleep, change in eating habits, unwillingness to engage in play, may be seen. These are signs of stress that the child exhibits while struggling to cope with the hospitalization.

Given the complicating issue of developmental phases in children, the child's typical response to sudden and severe trauma can be generalized as three interconnected phases: (1) a period of helplessness and panic, when the child's outward affect may fluctuate from angry outbursts to quiet dependency; (2) a phase of denial, when an attempt is made to avoid the reality of the trauma; and (3) a phase of intrusiveness, when thoughts are uncontrolled and often center on the accident itself. Nightmares and fantasies occur, and rest is commonly disturbed. Hostility may be a common reaction at this point. Play therapy may be an effective means for the child to work through some of the emotional outbursts in a safe setting.[3] Recognizing these stages of reactions to trauma may be helpful to the nurse by marking the child's adjustment to confinement; the nurse can direct play therapy to help the child work through each phase.

The nurse's role in the care of a child with multiple injuries is difficult because it demands an acute and sensitive recognition of the frailties of children. In addition, the nurse must intervene in a manner that allows the child to employ his or her own coping strategies yet supports the child's autonomy and striving sense of self. Goals that meet the immediate needs of the hospitalized child include the following[4,5]:

- to prevent separation from parents and peers
- to decrease fear of bodily injury
- to minimize pain
- to reduce loss of control
- to promote positive coping
- to decrease the ambiguity of the event.

THE FAMILY SYSTEM

One of the unique aspects of caring for the family of a trauma patient is minimizing the disruption of the family unit. Each family member has his or her own role in the family system. The parents' role is, in many ways, defined by their ability to care for and protect their children. Children learn their place in the family by the rules and roles that parents establish for them. In the case of trauma, accidental or otherwise, parents are expected to maintain the family unit under the most arduous of circumstances. Unlike the family of a chronically ill child or a child who is admitted to the hospital for planned surgery, the family who is disrupted in their daily tasks and roles by a sudden traumatic accident is unable to mobilize quickly the resources that a scheduled hospitalization requires. They are then faced with the task of reestablishing the roles they once had or altering them permanently.

Nurses are in a position to observe this disruption of the family unit and can intervene by providing resources and supports to families when necessary. The nurse begins by gathering information about the unique aspects of each family—its social make up, particular habits and behaviors, usual pattern of responding to a crisis, and cultural idiosyncracies. Together with this information and knowledge of reactions to the critical care environment, the nurse gathers an accurate assessment of family needs. Once an assessment is completed, the nurse provides crisis intervention to the family while providing physical care to the child. Finally, the nurse evaluates care by considering outcomes and reviewing the family's responses to interventions. This process is cyclic, and the nurse repeats all the steps again and again as he or she strives to provide optimal support to the family.

Assessing Family Needs

The assessment phase of the nursing process is often the most difficult for the nurse because it must encompass all the observations and questions that collectively lead to a better understanding of the needs of each individual family. Pertinent information to gather includes

- the nature of the accident
- initial treatment by family members (if they were in attendance at the time of the accident)
- other crises dealt with by the family
- supportive resources available to the family
- common parental responses to the hospitalization of a child.

Parental Response to Trauma

The stress response to trauma in parents and their reactions to the unexpected hospitalization of their child vary widely. Several factors influence parental response. Societal expectations of their role in protecting their children is one such factor. When a traumatic injury occurs, the implication is sometimes that neglect is a causal factor in the events leading to the accident. Parents therefore often react to a traumatic accident with guilt. This intense response is a consequence of the "assault on the identities that parents have of themselves as protectors and providers for their children."[6] Further, this reaction may have an impact on the entire family unit, causing disruption in their daily functioning.

The extent of injury influences parents' expectations of their child's prognosis and ultimate recovery, but any injury necessitating hospitalization is considered significant and can alter the way in which parents view themselves as guardians and protectors of their child.

Time is another factor in the response of parents to the sudden accidental death of their child; the response is conceptualized as three separate stages.[7] The immediate reaction is one of shock, numbness, and disbelief. Emotional outbursts are common at this time, interspersed with periods of quiet immobility and inability to carry out daily functions. The second stage begins when the reality of the child's death is accepted. Intense grief is evident at this point. Parents experience loneliness and sadness about the loss of their child. It is during this period that guilt may overpower the grieving parent. The third stage involves reorganization, when the family resumes the tasks of everyday living. These stages, although suggestive of the response of parents to the death of their child, may also be seen in parents of a child who is traumatically injured and faces a long period of recovery.

Nurses engaged in the care of children who have sustained traumatic injury must be acutely aware of how the hospital surroundings affect parents. The hospital environment, including all areas that a parent may visit, is often both foreign and frightening. Daily family life, with few exceptions, does not include busy emergency rooms, sterile surgical recovery units, or crowded intensive care units. It is imperative that nurses appreciate the response of parents to this environment because this response greatly influences subsequent nursing interventions. Several studies illustrate parental stress responses to hospitalization and personal needs arising from emergency medical care.[8-12] Although most of these studies were conducted in intensive care units, their conclusions can be applied to all areas of the hospital.

For example, one study sought to determine the immediate needs of family members during the first 72 hours after admission of their child to the hospital. The study concluded that information, more than any other one element, was vital in reducing anxiety and satisfying immediate needs of family members.[13] Specifically, "family members want foremost to be informed of their relative's condition, to be kept informed as honestly as possible, to have the chance to speak with the doctor, and to know that their relative is receiving the best care possible."[14] The nurse, however, must be able to make accurate judgments about what information is to be given, the manner in which it should be presented, and the appropriate environment for the exchange. Who will give the information is also another important decision for the nurse to make. Parents sometimes are intimidated by the physician, and nurses can be rushed in providing information if they are needed at the bedside. Social workers, who are available in most hospitals 24 hours a day, may indeed be the best individuals to provide information in clear, comprehensible language. A quiet family room with a social worker who has unrestricted time can reduce much of the parents' anxiety. Some trauma systems require that in order to receive accreditation as a trauma center, the hospital must provide social services on a 24-hour basis and a separate area for family support within the acute resuscitation area. Pastoral care should also be available for families for which such services would be helpful.

Carter and Miles devised an instrument that measures the stimulators of stress arising from the physical and psychosocial dimensions of the pediatric intensive care unit.[15] Again, although this study was conducted in a pediatric intensive care unit, its conclusions are of value to nurses working in all areas of the hospital. The dimensions identified that create stress to parents include parental role deprivation; the child's behavior, emotion, and appearance; the sights and sounds of the environment; medical and nursing procedures; and staff behavior and communication. The investigators concluded that the most significant stress stimulus is the perceived alteration in their role as parents.[16] The participants of the study pointed out the following stressors:

- separation from the child for long periods
- not being able to take care of the child themselves
- not being able to visit the child when they wanted
- not being able to hold the child
- being unable to protect the child from pain.[17]

In a follow-up article, the investigators surmised that "interruption in the parent-child relationship may be more stressful than physical aspects of the [intensive care unit] environment."[18]

This stress factor is crucial for the nurse to understand when intervening in the period immediately after the patient's admission to the hospital. Parents experience a great need to be close to their child. Nurses must respond to this need with a plan for family involvement in care. The nurse can immediately help parents to retrieve their role by asking them for needed information about the child's usual response to a crisis; only parents will have this information. It is the role of the nurse to engage the family in the activity of gathering necessary information to plan care. Emphasis should be placed on explaining to parents the value of their knowledge and how this knowledge will be used in helping the child. In this way, the parents recognize their unique role in the care of their child.

PLANNING CARE

Anticipating family response to the crisis of hospitalization becomes the major task in planning appropriate intervention.[19] Pediatric trauma centers must be ready to provide immediate emotional intervention for all family members. Cultural idiosyncrasies regarding health care delivery and language barriers can cause difficulties to health care providers and can slow the provision of supportive measures to family members. "Lack of knowledge about cultural beliefs can create misunderstandings of human behaviors and prevent the establishment of helping relationships between nurse and patient."[20] One tool that hospitals use to avoid this problem is language and culture banks, whereby a translator can be on the scene almost immediately to facilitate explaining or interpreting cultural idiosyncrasies.

Once a thorough, precise assessment has been made and a plan of nursing care has been formulated, intervention can begin. As with all phases of the nursing process, however, the steps often overlap. Crisis intervention may be the first encounter with family members, but the components of the nursing process that precede this step should be included as intervention is being provided.

There are four interventions for emotional support that are included in the care provided to family members of children hospitalized for trauma: (1) providing needed information, (2) promoting parental involvement, (3) facilitating problem solving, and (4) providing humanistic care.

Providing Needed Information

During acute resuscitation of critically injured children, the parents have lost all control over the ultimate outcome of their child. This is an unanticipated situation for them and one that may generate a sense of powerlessness. One of the most effective ways to give parents a renewed sense of power is providing information. A vivid and honest description of exactly what is taking place with their child is extremely important. Information should be much more than a passing "we are doing all that we can." Instead, nurses should give exact details, such as by saying "Your child is being cared for in a room just behind these double doors. There are two pediatric surgeons examining him to determine the full extent of his injuries. There is an anesthesiologist who specializes in caring for children and who is making sure that your child's breathing is being watched and is assisting, if necessary. There are also nurses who are specially trained to take care of children just like your child. They will let you know the very minute when it is possible for you to come in to be with your child." Although this may seem like too much information for a family under stress to absorb, hearing this gives them a sense that the hospital and staff recognize that their child is important and are making the child their priority.

Once the initial resuscitation period is over, information about the hospital setting should be provided to families. Details should be brief but should include information about the physical surroundings, the rules of the unit, visiting hours, personnel and their roles, and hospital accommodations for parents. This information can be given in various forms. Written material is helpful because the parents are likely to forget some of the information given verbally. All information must be given in clear language, particularly during the initial resuscitation period when medical terminology and acronyms can be easily misunderstood.

Promoting Parental Involvement

As has been discussed, the greatest threat to parents during emergency hospitalization of their child is the alteration in their role as parents. In the resuscitation phase, trauma patients are physically removed from parents so that emergency aid can be provided. On reunion, the child may be surrounded with catheters and monitors, an appearance that may frighten the parents and instill a sense of powerlessness. A natural tendency of parents is to remove themselves further from the child, stepping away from the bed to allow the nurse to provide technical care. This movement is indicative of the parents' sense of role deprivation and loss of control over the child's welfare.[21]

It is of paramount importance during this initial contact with parents that the nurse immediately reassure parents of their unique role in relation to the child. Serving as a role model, the nurse touches and talks to the child and addresses the child by name. The nurse encourages parents to do the same, showing them where to touch safely. While doing so the nurse tries to bolster the self-confidence of the parents with words of encouragement and by acknowledging the positive response of the child. The nurse must be especially certain to address the parents in terms of their role, such as by saying "You are Sammy's parents, and you know best how to calm and soothe him." It is through these techniques that the nurse fosters the reestablishment of parental role during hospitalization. Incorporation of parents as active members of the health care team by encouraging them to participate in the care of the child can reduce parental anxiety and minimize psychological trauma to the child.[22] Commitment to parent involvement in caring for the child must be widely accepted and encouraged in all areas of the hospital.

Facilitating Problem Solving

The shock of accidental trauma makes even simple decisions arduous, and family members are asked to make very tough decisions under the most extreme conditions: "Should I consent to surgery? What are the risks to my child? Should I stay the night? Who will care for my other children? Whom should I notify?" In the most tragic cases, parents may be asked to consent to an autopsy, or give permission to donate vital organs.

Frequently, family members are unaware of their options or of the consequences of each decision that they make. Nurses are in a key position to help family members to solve problems. Because of their professional experience, nurses are aware of what decisions must be made now and what decisions can wait until later, what the outcomes are of certain choices, and who should be consulted. This is not to suggest that decisions are made by the nurse and offered to parents because that would further compromise their role as parents. Rather, nurses can support decisions made independently by parents or clarify points to help parents understand better what they may expect. Often, parents are fearful of making one choice and are hesitant and unable to articulate their wants fully. Nurses must be aware of this verbal and nonverbal behavior to avoid misunderstandings later. Other health care members can be valuable supports during the difficult periods of decision making. Notifying social work services or the clergy may be the most appropriate action on the part of the nurse.

Sometimes it is necessary to include a multidisciplinary team in a formal meeting with family members to make decisions or explain treatments.[23] Pertinent team members include the nurse caring for the child (the primary nurse), the medical staff, and other support staff such as social workers or members of the clergy. A family meeting can be crucial in establishing and maintaining an open, trusting exchange between family members and health team members.

Providing Humanistic Care

Throughout all stages of physical and emotional care to the child and family, one element must be ever present: humanistic nursing care. Humanistic care is exhibited by technical competence, respect for the injured, and honest concern for the emotional well-being of the child and family.

The development of a mutually trusting relationship begins with the first encounter between nurse and family. This is a crucial meeting because it sets the tone for many encounters to follow, and it should convey deep concern and understanding of the family's plight while communicating to the family a high degree of competence in nursing skill and practice. Ideally this introduction should take place away from the bedside, but in many cases this is not possible.

There are several basic concepts to consider in humanizing the environment in which injured children receive care.[24] One of the parents' greatest concerns is whether the child is in pain. Parents must be shown signs that the child is comfortable and be told how pain is being controlled. Another common concern is the altered behavior of their child. An explanation of normal childhood reactions to hospitalization is helpful in allaying this concern. Nurses, because of their experience with and knowledge of trauma recovery, can verbalize anticipatory outcomes for families by providing general time frames for and clues to improvement. Neurologic changes in the child such as eye tracking and responding appropriately to commands are signs of improvement. It is important that the family be able to detect these positive signs as well.

The nurse's task in providing emotional support to the injured child and family is to blend physical competence with emotional intervention, conveying confidence and personal concern to both. By using the techniques offered here and studying the developmental growth of children, nurses can successfully meet this challenge.

NOTES

1. Susan B. Goodman-Campbell and Paul M. Taylor, "Bonding and Attachment: Theoretical Issues," *Seminars in Perinatology* 3(1979):3–13.

2. M.H. Klaus and J.H. Kennell, *Maternal-Infant Bonding* (St. Louis: C.V. Mosby Co., 1976).

3. Irwin M. Marcus, "Emotional and Psychological Implications of Trauma in Children," in Randall E. Marcus, ed., *Trauma in Children* (Rockville, Md.: Aspen Publishers, Inc., 1986), 245–58.

4. Donna L. Wong, "Childhood Trauma: Its Developmental Aspects and Nursing Interventions," *Critical Care Quarterly* 3(1982):47–59.

5. Cecilia Fergunson, "Childhood Coping: Adaptive Behavior During Intensive Care Hospitalization," *Critical Care Quarterly* 6(1984):81–93.

6. Marcus, "Emotional and Psychological Implications of Trauma in Children," 247.

7. Margaret S. Miles and Kay Perry, "Parental Responses to Sudden Accidental Death of a Child," *Critical Care Quarterly* 8(1985):73–84.

8. Melba C. Carter and Margaret S. Miles, "Parental Environmental Stress in Pediatric Intensive Care Units," *Dimensions of Critical Care Nursing* 4(1985):180–88.

9. Margaret S. Miles and Melba C. Carter, "Sources of Parental Stress in Pediatric Intensive Care Units," *Children's Health Care* 11(1982):65–69.

10. Melba C. Carter and Margaret S. Miles, "Parental Stressor Scale: Pediatric ICU," *Nursing Research* 31(1982):121.

11. Linda Daley, "The Perceived Immediate Needs of Families with Relatives in the Intensive Care Setting," *Heart and Lung* 13(1984):231–37.

12. Tamara W. Eberly et al., "Parental Stress after the Unexpected Admission of a Child to the Intensive Care Unit," *Critical Care Quarterly* 8(1985):57–65.
13. Daley, "The Perceived Immediate Needs of Families with Relatives in the Intensive Care Setting," 231–37.
14. Ibid., 234.
15. Carter and Miles, "Parental Stressor Scale," 121.
16. Eberly et al., "Parental Stress after the Unexpected Admission of a Child to the Intensive Care Unit," 57–65.
17. Miles and Carter, "Sources of Parental Stress in Pediatric Intensive Care Units," 68.
18. Carter and Miles, "Parental Environmental Stress in Pediatric Intensive Care Units," 181.
19. Marion E. Broome, "Working with the Family of a Critically Ill Child," *Heart and Lung* 14(1985):370.
20. Colette R. York and Jaynelle F. Stichler, "Cultural Grief Expressions Following Infant Death," *Dimensions of Critical Care Nursing* 4(1985):126.
21. Janet Rennick, "Reestablishing the Parental Role in a Pediatric Intensive Care Unit," *Journal of Pediatric Nursing* 1(1986):40–44.
22. Marlynn D. Pass and Cleo M. Pass, "Anticipatory Guidance for Parents of Hospitalized Children," *Journal of Pediatric Nursing* 2(1987):250–58.
23. J.H. Atkinson, Nancy Stewart, and Daniel Gardner, "The Family Meeting in Critical Care Settings," *Journal of Trauma* 20(1980):43–46.
24. Eleanor A. Hedenkamp, "Humanizing the Intensive Care Unit for Children," *Critical Care Quarterly* 3(1980):82–91.

Chapter 15

Injury Prevention in Children

Karin Bannerot Braithwaite

There has been a tremendous shift in the focus of care for pediatric trauma patients. Today's health professionals no longer treat just the immediate injury; they are now making a concerted effort to understand the precipitating factors that contribute to the occurrence of childhood trauma and are taking steps toward the prevention of injury through anticipatory guidance.

This chapter examines pediatric behavior as it relates to the risk of injury in infants, toddlers, preschoolers, school-aged children, and adolescents. The cognitive and psychosocial theories of Jean Piaget and Erik Erikson provide valuable insights into the behavior of these groups. Care planning education should be based on key psychological, motor, and social developmental needs. By using these elements, the nurse provides optimal, holistic care for the patient and family.

An important part of treating pediatric trauma takes place before injury ever occurs. It is essential that adult caretakers learn various safety skills to prevent trauma in their children. Therefore, selected topics for educating patients and parents in trauma prevention are outlined in this chapter.

INFANTS

Jean Piaget's theories are mostly concerned with a child's cognitive and perceptual growth. He describes infancy (from birth to 18 months of age) as the sensorimotor period and stresses two important cognitive processes that occur during this time.[1,2] First, the infant attains object permanence. The newborn is initially unable to understand that, even though an object is taken from view, it still exists. As the child matures, so do the cognitive processes. The infant soon learns that objects do not disappear when they are out of sight. The second cognitive process is the basic ability to understand cause and effect. The infant learns that a seemingly random action has purpose and consistently produces a desired effect.[3] An infant demonstrates these two processes, for example, by protesting when a parent leaves the room (separation anxiety) and learns that crying is likely to bring the parent back and to elicit comfort.

The implications of these new levels of understanding can be grave. A child who has mastered object permanence may deliberately seek hidden items such as medication bottles in cabinets or brightly colored containers of cleaning fluids. A child who knows that pulling a string causes toys to come closer may pull a lamp cord and inadvertently send it crashing down on his or her head. Teaching parents anticipatory guidance therefore begins with even the youngest child.

Erikson describes a child's first developmental task as acquiring a sense of trust while overcoming a sense of mistrust.[4] The infant's well-being depends entirely on the caretaker's ability to provide a safe, hazard-free environment. It is through the parent's reliability that the infant learns to trust.

The major milestones of infancy are often marked by what motor skills the child has attained. By 4 to 6 months, an infant begins rolling over. This means that they can fall off changing tables or beds. Caretakers should always keep one hand on the infant while bathing, diapering, or dressing is taking place.

Infants have strong sucking reflexes and experience the world through oral sensations. The child has a natural tendency to place objects in the mouth, especially as the pincer grasp becomes refined by 9 months of age. Mechanical suffocation from aspirated objects is the leading cause of death in children 6 to 12 months old.[5] Care must be exercised to protect the infant from choking on buttons, toy beads, and small bits of food.

Within 12 to 18 months the child begins to walk, which increases the likelihood of injury related to falls. According to one study, 77 percent of all infants 5 to 15 months of age use infant walkers.[6] The type and severity of injuries associated with such walkers outweighs their acclaimed benefit of assisting early ambulation. Injuries usually occur when the child in the walker tips over, falls down stairs, or traps the fingers in the x-frame models.[7] The child should be allowed safe in-house walking areas and should never be left unattended. Use of stair gates and high door locks prevents most injuries by falls. Infant walkers must comply with current federal safety standards.

Play is an important part of every child's social development. It is a means of communication and facilitates emotional growth. The toys recommended for infants up to 18 months old should produce safe sensory stimulation for vision, hearing, and touch.[8] Some suggestions of age-appropriate toys are listed in Exhibit 15-1.

Burns from hot liquid spills, sun exposure, and fire are common sources of injury during infancy. Bath water temperature should be checked before placing a child in a tub. The delicate skin of a baby is susceptible to heat and sunburn, so that the use of sunscreens is recommended when the child is outside. Baby clothing and bedding should be flame retardant. Finally, smoke detectors are an essential part of home safety and should be installed on every level of the house.

Motor vehicles are also a leading cause of injury and death in infants and young children. Each year, 5,000 children younger than 15 years of age die in automobile accidents,[9] and approximately 200,000 are hospitalized with injuries sustained in traffic accidents.[10] Car seats provide the best protection for infants in moving vehicles. Forty-nine states have mandatory child-passenger safety laws.[11] Information about car seat styles, sizes, and costs is given in Exhibit 15-2.

Exhibit 15-1 Safe Toys and Play Activities

Infants (birth to 18 months)
Wooden blocks and stacking toys
Metal pots and pans
Rattles, teething rings
Push and pull toys
Mobiles out of reach (suspended, bright, moving objects)
Soft, colorful dolls and animals
Musical toys

Toddlers (18 to 30 months)
Books with easily turned pages
Large crawl-into boxes
Stuffed animals (without glass or button decorations)
Simple puzzles, shape boards
Crayons, nontoxic finger paint
Nonbreakable plastic hammer boards
Filling and emptying toys (trucks)

Preschoolers (3 to 5 years)
Nontoxic modeling clays
Housekeeping and adult activity imitating toys
Drawing, scribbling materials
Puppets, doll houses
Dress-up clothes
Jungle gym sets
Tricycles

School-aged children (6 to 12 years)
Reading and writing materials
Jump ropes, bicycles, playground toys
Simple science experiments
Puzzles, mental games
Building toys
Collection and hobby materials
Drama, play-acting games

Adolescents (12 to 18 years)
Board games, crafts
Organized sports
Theater outings
Supervised parties, roller-skating, ice-skating
Cooking, carpentry lessons
Community activities, youth groups
Volunteer work

Sources: Adapted from *Pediatric Clinics of North America*, Vol. 32, No. 1, pp. 127–139, W.B. Saunders Company, © February 1985; and from *Journal of Pediatric Nursing*, Vol. 1, No. 4, pp. 260–270, Grune & Stratton, Inc., © August 1986.

In summary, the most likely causes of injury to the infant are falls, suffocation, infant walkers, burns, and motor vehicle accidents. Improper use of equipment, inexperience of young parents or caregivers, and a lack of knowledge related to emergency care contributes to an increased level of risk to the child. Infant caretakers should review the following areas:

- car seat safety
- babysitter education
- proper use of infant walkers and cribs
- age-appropriate toys
- safe parenting skills

Exhibit 15-2 Guide to Car Safety Restraints for Infants and Toddlers

Infant Seat (birth to approximately 20 pounds; rear-facing only)

Name of Seat	Manufacturer/Distributor	Approximate Cost
Century 570	Century	$25 to $30
Cuddle Shuttle®	Collier-Keyworth	$45 to $55
Infant Carrier	Ford	$40

Convertible Safety Seat (birth to approximately 40 pounds; infants, rear-facing; toddlers, forward-facing)

Name of Seat	Manufacturer/Distributor	Approximate Cost
Century 100, 200, 300, and 400XL	Century	$45 to $100
Fisher-Price®	Fisher-Price	$75 to $80
One Step®	Evenflo	$50
Plush Wee Care 614 or 620®	Strolee	$49 to $85
Wee Care 609, 610, and 618®	Strolee	$35 to $69
Pride Ride 825, 827, 830-1, 832, 835, and 837®	Pride-Trimble	$50 to $70

Toddler Seat (20 to 43 pounds; forward-facing)

Name of Seat	Manufacturer/Distributor	Approximate Cost
Babob 2	Z.B. Sales, Inc.	$129
SafeGuard®	Evenflo	$30

Source: Courtesy of American Academy of Pediatrics, January 1986.

- feeding and bottle precautions
- protective clothing
- initiating cardiopulmonary resuscitation and making use of emergency resources.

TODDLERS

The toddler (18 months to 3 years of age) makes rapid gains in language, physical coordination, and socialization skills. During this developmental stage the child becomes less dependent and more interactive in behavior.

Piaget's theory holds that the child is in transition from the sensorimotor to the preoperational period, where he or she remains until approximately age 7.[12] Piaget subdivides the preoperational period into two phases: preconceptual (2 to 4 years) and intuitive (4 to 7 years).[13] The child's thought processes become more sophisticated, and knowledge is based on the use of symbols.[14] In the early years, a preoperational child reasons egocentrically and illogically. This, combined with the toddler's magical thinking, places the child at risk for various injuries.

The toddler views himself or herself as the center of a world controlled by his or her actions, opinions, and thoughts. Having no sense of danger, toddlers may repeatedly place themselves in hazardous situations. Because they have a poorly developed sense of reason, they do not internalize rules or parental restrictions. For example, the 3-year-old has a predilection for climbing on furniture, and playing in water. Because the child does not intend to fall off a sofa or to drown in a pool, he or she feels safe from injury.

The toddler's strong drive to be independent and lack of impulse control is challenging to parents. To support the child's need to be more self-reliant, caretakers should provide consistent and clearly defined instructions for safe behaviors. Elaborate, lengthy discussions on the "whys" of rules are inappropriate for toddlers.

Concomitant with the rapid growth of cognitive skills, the toddler makes tremendous progress in motor development. The child climbs, is energetic, and moves quickly.[15] Because they are inquisitive, children at this age enjoy taking things apart. Their curiosity can lead to electrocution burns or poisoning by the ingestion of medications and house plants.

Toddlers mimic the actions of playmates and adults. Imitation assists children in the transition from sensorimotor functioning to higher levels of reasoning and behavior.[16] Therefore, adults must set good examples and continually repeat safety rules to toddlers. It is during this stage of development that caretakers can begin to teach the child about injury prevention.

Stairways should be free of clutter, and safety gates should be placed where they are needed to prevent falls. Cabinet doors can be fitted with child-proof catches. All windows should have screens in place. Space heaters, fireplaces, and furnaces must have protective guards. Finally, inexpensive caps are available to place over electrical outlets.

As with the infant, play is an important part of the toddler's development. During play, toddlers exercise, learn to manage their bodies, improve physical skills, test their emotional limits, and learn about themselves in relation to a large world. In essence, play is the communication of a child, and toys must be constructed to withstand a toddler's rugged play.

In warm weather, social activities outside must be carefully monitored. YMCAs and swimming clubs offer classes to introduce young children to water play. Children should never be left unattended near water. Near-drowning is the second most common cause of death in infants and children[17]; approximately 40 percent of near-drownings occur in children younger than 4 years of age.[18]

Motor vehicles are a leading cause of death in the toddler population. It is estimated that up to 90 percent of these fatalities are preventable through the use of proper restraints.[19] Car seats are essential but are often not used because toddlers are difficult to keep confined. Lap seat belts are not safe for children who weigh less than 40 pounds (because of the risk of abdominal injury), and shoulder straps are not recommended for children less than 55 inches tall (because of the risk of neck injuries).[20]

Overall, the most common injuries seen in toddlers include falls, cuts and lacerations, burns, ingestions, drownings, and motor vehicle accidents. Caretakers of toddlers should be educated in the following areas:

- home safety
- play area safety

- how to set limits and enforce rules
- prevention of drowning and fire injury
- car seat use
- use of the local poison control center phone number.

PRESCHOOLERS

The preschooler (3 to 5 years old), in Piaget's terms, is becoming intuitive. This means that young children are able to separate disparate objects and events into a system of simple classification.[21] The child becomes inquisitive and asks a lot of "why" questions. The preschooler uses mental symbols to think and engages in symbolic play to develop language skills.[22]

The thought processes are still egocentric, and the child has difficulty separating reality from fantasy. For example, a 4-year-old burn patient is likely to believe that he or she caused the fire because of a nightmare about a house in flames or because of a wish to "burn up" a new baby sibling out of jealousy.

Preschoolers' thought processes are prelogical, which means that they do not fully understand cause and effect relationships. Like the older toddler, they cannot generalize from concrete experiences.[23] The 3- to 5-year-old does not learn from past injuries; therefore, safety teaching must be stated clearly and repeated often. In this age group energy levels are high, curiosity abounds, and more of the child's activities are undertaken farther away from the parents. It is easy for a child to forget a parent's rules during activities.

The preschooler has been described as the "hurrying child" and "lightning fast."[24] Motor skills such as jumping, throwing objects, and peddling tricycles are developing. Even though the child displays much enthusiasm for these activities, the quality of performance may be poor. Falls and cuts are common. The incidence of multiple trauma secondary to being struck by a motor vehicle is high in this group.

Inside, the preschooler is often underfoot. In 1979, of 4,429 fatal injuries to children younger than 5 years of age, 52 percent were in and around the home.[25] One of every twelve children younger than 6 years required hospital treatment for fall injuries, mostly in the home environment.[26] Caretakers must find appropriate indoor activities and include children in safe household tasks.

Socially, the preschooler spends more time with other children than with adults. Caretakers should be familiar with play areas, noting the type and durability of playground equipment. Supervision of play without constant interruption is the parent's best strategy for developmentally appropriate injury prevention for preschoolers.

The 3- to 5-year-old has the highest incidence of burn injuries.[27] Most of these injuries occur in kitchens and are caused by scalds or contact with stoves, ovens, or irons. Children should be taught the potential dangers of these appliances, not to play with matches, and what to do in case of a fire. An important part of preventive education includes planning and practicing fire drills. Children must learn that, no matter how frightened they are, a burning house is never a safe place in which to hide and that their parents may not be able to help them escape. This teaching can significantly reduce the number of deaths in house fires.

Firearm injury and death statistics are on the rise; children are often injured as the result of adult carelessness. Loaded guns should never be handled in front of a child, and preferably guns should not be in the home environment.[28] It may be difficult for a child to distinguish between realistic toy guns and the loaded handgun of an adult. A child cannot be responsible for knowing the difference.

Because preschool-aged children spend increasing amounts of time outside, caretakers should teach them to remember their address and telephone number and the basics of pedestrian safety, including how to refuse rides with strangers and how to cross streets. Caretakers of preschoolers should review the following:

- proper use of recreational toys
- how to maintain a safe home environment
- use of syrup of ipecac
- fire, gun, and water safety
- basic self-protection measures
- traffic and road safety.

SCHOOL-AGED CHILDREN

This period of development is often referred to as middle childhood (6 to 12 years of age). School-aged children become competent in a number of areas: they are more independent, they take increased responsibility for their safety, and they learn the consequences of their behavior. On the other hand, 6- to 12-year-olds are adventuresome and daring. They are easily distracted and often succumb to peer pressure.

Cognitively, the child is in transition from preoperational to operational thinking. By age 7 the child is more reflective, by age 10 the child thinks in a matter-of-fact manner, and by age 12 the child begins to think abstractly. The rate of development of cognitive processes varies; therefore, injuries related to poor judgment can occur at any age.

It is well known that children are greatly influenced by television. They may imitate the heroic feats of admired characters. The following example from a recent emergency department admission illustrates this. A 7-year-old Hispanic male was admitted with multiple stab wounds to the chest and abdomen. His uncle stated that the patient taped steak knives to his body and jumped off a dresser to imitate his favorite cartoon idol, 'He-Man'.[29] This child was unable to separate reality from fantasy, and in the excitement of play he seriously injured himself.

A child's ability to formulate moral judgments and to follow rules develops gradually from age 5 to 12.[30] Initially, rules are seen as external forces created and upheld by adults. Gradually concrete thought develops, and the child masters rule formation. School-aged children try to convince adults that they understand instructions that they often do not. The caretaker must evaluate the child's comprehension of safety issues by more than verbal feedback. The child's actions and past history of obedience are key indicators to safe behavior. It is important that children participate in rule formation. With input, they are more likely to listen to reason and to abide by established guidelines. The attitudes of this period strongly influence the more rebellious time of adolescence.

The period from 7 to 12 years of age is marked by the development of both gross and fine motor skills and an awareness of peer relationships. Learning to ride a bicycle is a major accomplishment at this time. School-aged children tend to be clumsy, and hand-eye coordination is often poor. Fractured bones and head trauma are common because children may attempt daring, careless stunts to prove their worth or to gain acceptance in a peer group.

Bicycle injuries are the leading cause of severe injury in this age group. Most accidents are the result of adults violating traffic laws,[31] children riding oversized bicycles,[32] and falls resulting in abdominal trauma from the new "all-terrain" style bicycle handlebars. The use of helmets is one way to reduce the occurrence of serious head trauma, but it may be difficult to get children to wear proper protective equipment.

School-aged children are also likely to be injured as pedestrians. A parent's misunderstanding or unreal expectation of a child's ability to cope with complex traffic environments can have fatal consequences.[33] Children may not understand traffic signals, and they have poor visual and auditory perception. Because of their small stature, children are difficult for drivers to see. If children are out at night, it is recommended that they wear bright or reflective clothing.

It is the adult's responsibility to locate and encourage appropriate activities for the school-aged child. Groups such as the Boy Scouts and Girl Scouts, school clubs, organized sports, and summer camps provide excellent diversional activities. Many of these also offer health and safety education. Participation in such activities assists the school-aged child to meet intellectual, emotional, and physical needs in a safe and structured environment.

The school-aged child should learn about the hazards of careless behavior. As they mature, children need to assume responsibility for their own and their peer's safety. Praise from adults serves as a positive reinforcement for safe behavior. Caretakers of children in this age group should be educated in the following areas:

- teaching the child to say "no" to peer pressure
- encouraging structured activities with friends
- teaching the proper use of household tools and equipment
- teaching how and when to call the police or fire rescue
- teaching rules of traffic and bicycle safety
- establishing guidelines for safety near water.

ADOLESCENTS

Adolescence (12 to 18 years of age) is marked by dramatic physical and emotional changes. The transition from childhood to young adulthood is often difficult, but with appropriate support it can be a time of self-discovery. Injury prevention becomes a shared responsibility between the adolescent and adult.

Piaget's final stage of cognitive development places the adolescent in the period of formal operation.[34] According to Eldridge, the adolescent's mind is at the point of greatest ability to acquire and utilize knowledge.[35] The 12- to 18-year-old thinks in an abstract, analytical manner and understands causality. At this level of cognitive function, the adolescent is able to take responsibility for learning and following safe rules of behavior.

At the same time that the thought processes are maturing, there is a return to egocentrism. The adolescent believes that everyone should come to terms with only his or her own idealistic schemes.[36] It is this self-centered thinking that causes teens to criticize adults and to challenge established rules. Their rebellious feelings may lead to reckless behavior, which in turn may cause serious injury.

According to Erikson, the adolescent must overcome role confusion and master identity formation.[37] The term "identity diffusion" describes what happens in a teenager's psychosocial development if a sense of identity does not form. Adolescents frequently berate themselves and have difficulty overcoming feelings of inadequacy. Teens falsely assume that society sees only their flaws. The inability to form a positive role identity and a sense of self-importance may contribute to depression and explain the increasing number of deaths in adolescents by substance abuse and suicide.

The number of adolescent injuries related to violent behavior is on the rise. As the child gets older, lethal weapons such as knives and firearms replace traditional objects (such as fists) to ventilate angry feelings. Homicide and suicide by firearms is now a leading cause of death in adolescence.[38] During the early 1980s, nearly 60 percent of homicides and 50 percent of suicides in this age group were caused by handguns.[39] Prevention of such injury is difficult, but the rate of suicide should be decreased by eliminating handguns from the environment of adolescents.[40]

Parents must provide firm guidance and support for their teenager. They are in ideal positions to recognize subtle changes in behavior or depression that can, if unheeded, lead to death. Some of the symptoms of depression include

- abrupt mood changes
- aggressive behavior
- school phobia and decreased social contacts
- self-effacing remarks
- lethargy and lack of interest in activities
- frequent questions about or thoughts of death
- change in sleeping or eating patterns
- suicide attempts.

Good communication between parent and child is essential in the early diagnosis of suicidal tendencies. If listening does not improve a problematic situation, parents should consult professional counselors. Any suicide attempt must be taken seriously. Factors that may precipitate a suicide attempt by the adolescent include

- anger or frustration
- desire to escape from bad situations or punishment
- desire to join a deceased loved one
- unresolved grief
- psychotic episode, possibly related to drugs or alcohol
- perception of worthlessness leading to a cry for help.

Suicide prevention begins with the recognition of these warning signs of emotional disturbance or instability. Adults can reduce the frequency of teenage suicide by active listening and by following up on concerns of the troubled child.

The adolescent experiences rapid physical growth during puberty. One of every fourteen teenagers required hospital treatment for athletic injury in 1980.[41] A number of factors contribute to the high incidence of sports-related injuries in the 12- to 18-year-old age group. The epiphyses of the skeletal system have not yet closed, and the extremities are poorly protected by stabilizing musculature. Coordination is poor because of the rapid and uneven physical development of the extremities. Finally, teenagers participate in vigorous activities and contact sports such as football and rugby.

Motor vehicle–related injuries (with the child as a car occupant, on a bicycle, or as a pedestrian) are the single leading cause of death in adolescents and young adults.[42] A major social and motor milestone for teenagers is learning to drive. Although they are able to think analytically, their emotional response to crisis situations may be less than optimal. Coupled with feelings of infallibility, alcohol consumption, or drug ingestion, the adolescent's risk of injury is increased in or around motor vehicles.[43]

Once believed to be an important part of accident prevention, the value of driver's education classes in high school is now being disputed.[44,45] The courses increase the total number of teen drivers[46] and yet may inadequately prepare them for safe driving. It is suggested instead that teens enroll in driving courses offered through major insurance companies.

Socially, adolescents seek both support and acceptance from their peer group. To promote positive role-identity formation, adults must appreciate the teenager's attempts to be independent. The peer group can be used to promote self-esteem in teenagers. Organized activities that allow for creative mental and physical expression should be encouraged.

Along with motor vehicle accidents, suicide, and sports-related injuries, common causes of injury to the 12- to 18-year-old age group include drownings, burns, falls, and poisonings by solids, liquids, and gases.[47] Injury prevention and education goes beyond the sphere of the child, parent, and health care provider. Government legislation must also address the issues of safety regulations from infancy to adolescence. Seat belt laws, toy safety standards, public drug and alcohol education, physical fitness information, handgun control, and fire prevention standards are just a few of the many government interventions that provide for a more hazard-free community. The community agencies listed in Exhibit 15-3 provide valuable opportunities for adolescents to affiliate with adults as counselors and support persons.

Exhibit 15-3 Community Agencies That Are Potential Candidates for Participation in Injury Prevention Programs

Medical Organizations
American Academy of Pediatrics
American Association of Poison Control Centers
Schools of medicine
Community clinics

Allied Health Organizations
Hospital associations
Pharmacist associations
Nursing associations
Paramedic associations

Voluntary Organizations
Red Cross
Spinal Cord Injury Association
Sports injury associations
National Safety Council

Consumer Agencies
Consumer Product Safety Commission
YMCA and YWCA
Mothers' groups

Media
Newspapers
Radio and television broadcasting stations

Public Health Agencies
Maternal and child health agencies
Environmental health agencies
Food and Drug Administration
Vital statistics agencies
Health education agencies
Schools of public health
Boards of health

Public Safety Organizations
Highway Patrol and State Police
Local law enforcement agencies
Fire and rescue services

Educational Organizations
Public and private schools
Head-Start programs
Women-Infant Care programs
Parent-Teacher Association

Business Organizations
Insurance companies
Sporting goods manufacturers

Advocacy Groups
Children's lobby

Source: Adapted from *Pediatric Clinics of North America*, Vol. 32, No. 1, pp. 251–265, with permission of W.B. Saunders Company, © February 1985.

CONCLUSION

Injury prevention begins with the pediatric nurse's awareness of the various developmental needs and skills of children. It requires a commitment to family education, anticipatory guidance, and an understanding of the learning process. Ultimately, health care professionals have made valuable contributions to a safer environment and a healthier population of children.

NOTES

1. Herbert Ginsberg and Sylvia Opper, *Piaget's Theory of Intellectual Development* (Englewood Cliffs, N.J.: Prentice-Hall, 1979), 26–68.
2. Barry S. Zuckerman and John C. Duby, "Developmental Approach to Injury Prevention," *Pediatric Clinics of North America* 32 (1985):17–29.

3. Ibid., 21.
4. Erik Erikson, *Childhood and Society*, 2d ed. (New York: W.W. Norton and Co., Inc., 1963), 249.
5. M.P. Chow et al., *Handbook of Pediatric Primary Care* (New York: John Wiley & Sons, 1979), 335–61.
6. C.A. Kavanaugh and L. Banco, "The Infant Walker: A Previously Unrecognized Health Hazard," *American Journal of Diseases of Children* 136(1982):205–206.
7. Joseph Greensher and Howard C. Mofenson, "Injuries at Play," *Pediatric Clinics of North America* 32 (1985):127–39.
8. Ibid., 130.
9. J.S. O'Shea, E.W. Collins, and C.B. Butler, "Pediatric Accident Prevention," *Clinical Pediatrics* 21(1982):192–198.
10. R.C. Raphaely et al., "Management of Severe Pediatric Head Trauma," in J.P. Orlowski, ed., *Symposium on Pediatric Intensive Care* (Philadelphia: W.B. Saunders Co., 1980), 715–27.
11. C. Hurley, ed., *National Safety Council, Policy Update Beginning 1983* (available from Office of Federal Affairs, 1705 DeSales St., N.W., Washington, D.C. 20036).
12. Barry J. Wadsworth, *Piaget's Theory of Cognitive Development*, 2d ed. (New York: Longman, Inc., 1979), 69.
13. Karen L. Freiberg, *Human Development: A Life-Span Approach*, 2d ed. (Monterey, Calif.: Wadsworth, Inc., 1983), 204.
14. Zuckerman and Duby, "Developmental Approach," 22.
15. Chow et al., *Handbook*, 340.
16. Ginsberg and Opper, *Piaget's Theory*, 62.
17. Frederick P. Rivara, "Traumatic Deaths of Children in the United States: Currently Available Prevention Strategies," *Pediatric Clinics of North America* 75(1985):456–62.
18. Mary Fran Hazinski, *Nursing Care of the Critically Ill Child* (St. Louis: C.V. Mosby Co., 1984), 313.
19. Rivara, "Traumatic Deaths," 457.
20. "Car Safety Restraints for Children," *Consumer Reports* 42, no. 6(1977):153.
21. Freiberg, *Human Development*, 204.
22. Ginsberg and Opper, *Piaget's Theory*, 76–78.
23. Zuckerman and Duby, "Developmental Approach," 22.
24. Greensher and Mofenson, "Injuries at Play," 131.
25. National Safety Council, *Accident Facts, 1983 Edition* (Chicago: National Safety Council, 1983), 8, 80.
26. Bernard Guyer and Susan G. Gallagher, "An Approach to the Epidemiology of Childhood Injury," *Pediatric Clinics of North America* 32(1985):5–15.
27. Ibid., 11.
28. Chow et al., *Handbook*, 345.
29. Trauma Registry, St. Christopher's Hospital for Children, February 1987.
30. Ginsberg and Opper, *Piaget's Theory*, 96–99.
31. J.A. Paulson, "Accidental Injuries," in R.E. Behrman and V.C. Vaughn, eds., *Nelson's Textbook of Pediatrics* (Philadelphia: W.B. Saunders Co., 1983), 261.
32. J.S. O'Shea et al., "Pediatric Accident Prevention," *Clinical Pediatrics* 21(1982):290.
33. Zuckerman and Duby, "Developmental Approach," 25.
34. Jean Piaget, *The Psychology of Intelligence* (Towata, N.J.: Littlefield, Adams & Co., 1976), 148.
35. Theresa M. Eldridge, "Accident Prevention," in Jane A. Fox, ed., *Primary Health Care of the Young* (New York: McGraw-Hill Book Co., 1981), 158.
36. Freiberg, *Human Development*, 335.

37. Erikson, *Childhood and Society*, 261.
38. Katherine K. Christoffel and Tom Christoffel, "Handguns as a Pediatric Problem," *Pediatrics Emergency Care* 2(1986):75–81.
39. Rivara, "Traumatic Deaths," 461.
40. Ibid., 461.
41. Guyer and Gallagher, "An Approach," 12.
42. Joel L. Bass, Susan S. Gallagher, and Kishor Mehta, "Injuries to Adolescents and Young Adults," *Pediatric Clinics of North America* 32(1985):31–39.
43. Zuckerman and Duby, "Developmental Approach," 26.
44. L.S. Robertson, "Crash Involvement of Teen Drivers when Driver Education is Eliminated from High School," *American Journal of Public Health* 70(1980):599–603.
45. Lance A. Chilton, "Potential Benefit vs. Risks of Current Attempts in Health Education During Adolescence," *Journal of Pediatrics* 90(1977):163.
46. Bass, Gallagher, and Mehta, "Injuries to Adolescents," 38.
47. Ibid., 24.

Index

A

Abdominal injury
 blunt, 102
 diagnosis and treatment
  hollow organ injuries, 109
  solid organ injuries, 107-109
 due to child abuse, 223-224
 initial assessment and management, 105
 penetrating, 102, 105
 physical examination, 106-107
 solid and hollow organ trauma, 105-109
  hemorrhage, 106
  liver, 103t, 105, 108t
  pancreas, 106
  spleen, 104t, 105, 108t
Acetaminophen poisoning, 181, 183t-184t
N-Acetylcysteine, 179t
Advanced Cardiac Life Support, 6
Advanced Trauma Life Support
 courses, 6
 patient assessment and stabilization, 9
Aerophagia, 14
Air transport, 143-144
Airway, 10-13
 anatomy, 10, *11*
 primary assessment, 10-11
  in head-injured child, 56-57
 stabilization, 11-13
  cervical immobilization, 11-12
  intubation, 12-13, 13t
  mask-assisted ventilation, 12
  oral airway, 12
  oxygen administration, 11-12
Ambulance transport, 143
Amnesia, 47
Amputation, 137-138
 treatment, 138
 types, 137-138
Anesthesiologist, role of, 26
Ankle fracture, 135
Anorectal injuries, 109
Aortic rupture, 99-100
Apomorphine, 179t
Asphyxia, 94
Assessment and stabilization, 10-22. *See also* Neurological assessment
 airway, 10-3. *See also* Airway
 breathing, 14-15, 15t, 16t
 circulation, 15-18, 17t, 18t. *See also* Circulation
 complete physical examination, 21-22
 diagnostic tests, 21-22
 disability, 18-20, 19t, *20*
 exposure, 20
Automobile accidents, 245, 248, 253

B

Barbiturate coma, 63-64

Page numbers in *italics* indicate figures and exhibits; those followed by "t" indicate tables.

Battered child syndrome. *See* Child abuse
Battle's sign, 15
Bicycle injuries, 251
Bite injuries
  due to child abuse, 222
  facial, 71
Bladder injuries, 115
Bowel injuries, 109
Breathing
  assessment and stabilization, 14-15, 15t, 16t
  ataxic, 56
  in head-injured child, 56-57
Bronchial injuries, 98-99
Brown-Séquard syndrome, 80, *81*
Bruises, due to child abuse, 220-221, 221t
Bryant's skin traction, 123
Burns, 28, 154-172
  associated physiologic alterations, 167
  chemical, 171-172
  compartment syndrome and, 163
  determining depth, 162-163, 163t, *164*
  determining extent, 158-159, *160*
  due to child abuse, 221-222
  electrical, 170-171
  escharotomy, 163
  etiology, 154
  fluid resuscitation, 160-162, 162t
  hypermetabolism and, 166, 167t
  incidence, 154
  inhalation injury, 167-170. *See also* Inhalation injury
  initial evaluation and triage, 154-158, *156-157*
  prevention, 245, 249-250
  referral checklist, 158, *159*
  wound care, 165-166

C

Caloric reflex, 53, *54*
Capillary refill time, as indicator of shock, 15-16
Caput succedaneum, 44
Car safety restraints, *247*
Carbon monoxide poisoning, 154, 168, 168t
Cardiac tamponade, 100
Carpal fracture, 131
Catheterization, urethral, 110

Caustic product poisonings, 189, 190t
Central cord syndrome, 80, *81*
Cephalohematoma, 43-44
Cerebral perfusion pressure, 38
Charcoal, activated, 178-179
Chemical burns, 171-172
Chest trauma, 91-101
  assessment, 91-92
  bronchial injuries, 98-99
  chest wall injuries, 92-95
    flail chest, 93-94
    pulmonary contusion, 94-95
    rib fractures, 92-93
    sternal fractures, 93
    traumatic asphyxia, 94
  diaphragm injuries, 95-96
  esophageal injuries, 99
  injuries to heart and great vessels, 99-101
    aortic rupture, 99-100
    cardiac tamponade, 100
    hemothorax, 100-101
  pneumothorax, 96-97
  tracheal injuries, 98
Child abuse, 211-229
  case management, 226-227
  characteristic physical findings, 220-224
    abdominal injuries, 223-224
    anorectal injuries, 109
    bites, 222
    bruises, 220-221, 221t
    burns, 221-222
    fractures, 120
    genital injuries, 116
    scalp injuries, 223
    sexual abuse, 224
    shaken infant syndrome, 222
    skeletal injuries, 223
    skull fractures, 223
    submersion injury, 202
  clinical presentation of abused child, 217-220
  definitions, 212
  diagnostic tests/procedures, 224-226
    developmental assessment, 226
    hematologic studies, 224
    photographs, 226
    skeletal series, 225
    toxicology screen, 225
  emotional manifestations, 224, *225*

etiology and precipitating factors, 215-217
historical background, 211-212
incidence, 213-215
  morbidity and mortality, 214
  reporting, 214-215
  statistics, 213-214, *214*
indicators of abuse
  alleged self-inflicted injury, 218
  alleged third party inflicted injury, 218
  child health history, 219-220
  delay in seeking medical care, 218
  discrepant history, 217-218
  history of injury, 220
  history of previous trauma, 219
  parental focus of concern, 219
  parental mental status, 219
  parental reaction, 218-219
  psychosocial history, 220
  unexplained injury, 217
nursing interventions for families, 227-229
types, 212-213
Cimetidine, 58-59
Circulation
  assessment, 16, 57
  child's blood volume, 15
  indicators of shock, 15
  stabilization, 17t, 17-18, 18t
  use of pneumatic antishock trousers, 16, 27
Clavicular fracture, 122, 129
Coma, barbiturate, 63-64
Commitment, 3-4
Compartment syndrome, 138-140
  burns and, 163
  complications, 140
  diagnosis, 139-140
  symptoms, 139
  treatment, 140
Competence, 6-7
Computerized tomography, 53, 55
Concussion, 47-48
Contusion
  cerebral, 48
  pulmonary, 94-95
Cooperation, 4-6
Corneal injury, 74
Corneal reflex, 53
Corpus cavernosum fracture, 116

Corrosive product poisonings, 189, 190t
Cricothyrotomy, 13
Crush injuries, 136-137
  classification, 136
  diagnosis, 136-137
  treatment, 137
Cullen's sign, 107
Cushing's triad, 57
Cyst, leptomeningeal, 44, *44*

D

Deep vein thrombosis, 86-87
Dental injuries, 75-76
Dexamethasone, 58
Diaphragm injuries, 95-96
Diazepam, 19, 60
Disability
  assessment, 18-19, 19t
  stabilization, 19-20, *20*
Diuresis, for poisonings, 180
Doll's-eye reflex, 53, *54*
Drowning. *See* Submersion injuries
Drugs, cardiovascular, 31t

E

E cylinder, 148-149
Edema
  in burn patients, 162
  cerebral, 41-42
Elbow
  fractures, 130
  "nursemaid's" (pulled), 130-131
Electrical burns, 170-171
Emergency medical services system, 5
Emergency room nurse, role of, 31
Emotional support of child and family, 232-242
  developmental considerations, 232-235
    adolescents, 235
    infants, 233
    preschoolers, 234
    school-aged children, 234-235
    toddlers, 233-234
  family system, 236-239
    assessing needs, 237
    parental response to trauma, 237-239
    nurses' roles, 235-236

planning care, 239-242
  facilitating problem solving, 241
  promoting parental involvement, 240-241
  providing humanistic care, 241-242
  providing information, 240
Emphysema, subcutaneous, 97
Escharotomy, 163
Esophageal injuries, 99
Ethyl alcohol poisoning, 181, 185t
Exposure, assessment and stabilization, 20

F

Facial trauma, 68-77
  anesthesia for, 70
  complications of, 76-77
  dental injuries, 75-76
  etiology, 69
  factors unique to children, 68
  fractures, 71-74
    management principles, 71-72
    mandibular, 72
    mid-face, 72-73
    nasal, 72
    orbital, 73
    postoperative management, 73-74
    zygomatic complex, 73
  laryngeal trauma, 70
  ocular injuries, 74-75
  soft tissue injuries, 70-71
    bites, 71
    lacerations, 71
  treatment principles, 69-70
Family of patient, 236-239. *See also* Emotional support of child and family
  assessing needs, 237
  involvement in child's care, 240-241
  parental response to trauma, 237-239
  sensitivity to, 10
Femoral fracture, 122-123, 134-135
Fibular fracture, 135
Fingers
  amputation, 132
  crush injuries, 132
  fractures, 131-132
Flail chest, 93-94
Fluid resuscitation
  for burn patients, 160-162, 162t
  in head-injured child, 57-58
  for hypovolemic shock, 17, 18t, 27
  maintenance requirements, 17, 18t
Foot fracture, 135
Fractures, 120-121, 127-136
  ankle, 135
  birth, 122-123
  carpal, 131
  clavicle, 122, 129
  complete vs. incomplete, 129
  corpus cavernosum, 116
  due to child abuse, 223
  elbow, 130-131
  epiphyseal plate, 123, 124t
  face, 71-74
  femur, 122-123, 134-135
  fibula, 135
  foot, 135
  fracture resistance of bones, 119-120
  greenstick, 129
  hand, 131-132
  healing, 123
  humerus, 122, 130
    proximal, 129-130
  knee, 135
  lower extremity, 133-136
  metacarpal, 132
  open vs. closed, 127
  pelvis, 133-134
  phalangeal, 132
  radius, 131
  rib, 92-93
  scapula, 129
  simple vs. comminuted, 127
  skull, 44-47
  spine, 123, 132-133
  stabilization, 127
  sternum, 93
  tibia, 135
  ulna, 131
  upper extremity, 129-132
  wrist, 131
Furosemide, 58

G

Gag reflex, 53
Genitourinary trauma, 110-116
  bladder injuries, 115

complications, 110
diagnostic tests, 110-111
genital injuries, 116
hematuria, 110, 112, 114
initial evaluation, 110-111
renal injuries, 111-114, *113*. See also Renal injuries
signs and symptoms, 110, *111*
ureteral injuries, 114-115
urethral catheterization, 110
urethral injuries, 115-116
Glasgow Coma Scale, 18-19, 19t, 51, 176, 201
"Golden hour", 147
Greenstick fracture, 129
Grey-Turner's sign, 110
Gunshot wounds
  abdominal, 102, 105
  prevention, 250, 252

H

Hamman's sign, 99
Hand injuries
  fractures, 131-132
  specialized care for, 132
Head injury, 36-66
  due to child abuse, 222-223
  epidemiology, 36
  increased intracranial pressure, 56-65. See also Increased intracranial pressure
  neurological assessment, 51-56. See also Neurological assessment
  pathophysiologic principles, 36-38
    cerebral perfusion pressure, 38
    Monro-Kellie doctrine, 36-37
    volume-pressure curve, *37*, 37-38
  recovery from, 65-66
  stabilization protocol, 19-20, *20*
  types, 38-51
    amnesia, 47
    cerebral edema, 41-42
    closed head, 47-51
    concussion, 47
    contusions, 48
    epidural hematomas, 48-49, 49t
    herniation, 39-41, *40*
    intracranial hematomas, 48

pediatric concussion syndrome, 47-48
posttraumatic hyperemia, 39
primary and secondary brain injury, 38-39
scalp hematomas, *43*, 43-44
scalp lacerations, *42*, 42-43
skull fractures, 44-47
subdural hematomas, 50-51
Helicopter transport, 143-144
Hematomas
  cephalohematoma, 43-44
  epidural, 48-49, 49t
  intracranial, 48
  subdural, 50-51
  subgaleal, 43
Hematuria, 110, 112, 114
Hemorrhage
  abdominal, 106
  musculoskeletal trauma and, 121
Hemothorax, 14-15, 100-101
Hepatic injury, 103t, 105, 108, 108t, 112
Hernia, diaphragmatic, 96
Herniation, 39-41, *40*
  tonsilar, 41
  transtentorial, 41
  uncal, 39-40
History taking, 55-56
Household product poisonings, 184-185, 188t
Humeral fracture, 122, 129-130, *130*
Hydrotherapy, for burns, 165
Hyperbaric oxygen therapy
  for carbon monoxide poisoning, 168
  for compartment syndrome, 140
  for crush injuries, 137
Hyperemia, posttraumatic, 39
Hypermetabolism, in burn patients, 166, 167t
Hyperventilation, 59
Hypothermia
  assessment and stabilization, 20
  burns and, 155
  due to cold water submersion, 195, 197-198, 204, 204t, 206
  induced, for increased intracranial pressure, 64-65

I

Increased intracranial pressure, 56-65

initial assessment and management, 56-59
  airway and ventilation, 56-57
  circulatory support, 57
  drugs, 58-59
  fluid balance, 58
  tissue perfusion, 57
  urine output, 58
secondary assessment and management, 59-63
  arterial line, 60
  hyperventilation, 59
  intracranial pressure monitoring, 60-61, *62*
  neuromuscular blockade, 59-60
  osmotic therapy, 61-63
  respiratory care, 60
  skin care, 60
unresponsive, 63-65
  barbiturate coma, 63-64
  hypothermia, 64-65
Inhalation injury, 167-170
  assessment, 170
  carbon monoxide poisoning, 168, 168t
  incidence, 168
  smoke poisoning, 169-170
  thermal injury, 169, *169*
  treatment, 170
Intubation, 12-13
  endotracheal tube sizes, 12, 13t
  in head-injured child, 56-57
  sedation for, 13, 13t, 56
  tube placement, 12
Ipecac, syrup of, 178
Iron poisoning, 181, 184, 186t-187t

K

Kehr's sign, 106
Kidney injuries. *See* Renal injuries
Knee injuries, 135

L

Lacerations
  diaphragmatic, 96
  facial, 71
  scalp, 42-43
Laparotomy, indications for, *23*

Laryngeal trauma, 70
Lasix. *See* Furosemide
Lavage
  gastric, 178-179
  peritoneal, 22, 107-108
Lead poisoning, 189, 191t
Legg-Calvé-Perthes disease, 134
Leptomeningeal cyst, 44, *44*
Liver injury, 103t, 105, 108, 108t, 112

M

Magnetic resonance imaging, 55
Mandibular fracture, 72
Mannitol, 61-63
Medication nurse, role of, 30-31, 31t
Metacarpal fracture, 132
Metatarsal fracture, 135
Mid-face fractures, 72-73
Monro-Kellie doctrine, 36-37
Morphine sulfate, 60
Motor strength evaluation, 126, *126*
Motor vehicle accidents, 245, 248, 253
Musculoskeletal trauma, 119-140. *See also* Fractures
  blood loss, 121
  comparison of injury types, 120-121
  diagnosis, 121-122
  due to child abuse, 223
  evaluation, 125-127, *126*, 127t
  management, 127-140
    amputation and limb salvage, 137-138
    compartment syndrome, 138-140
    crush injuries, 136-137
    fractures, 127-136
    management of multisystem injury, 123, 125-127
  mechanisms of injury, 119-120
Myoglobinuria, 137

N

Nail injuries, 132
Naloxone, 179t
Nasal fracture, 72
Nasogastric tube, 15, 16t
Nembutal. *See* Pentobarbital
Nerve function evaluation, 126, 127t
Neurological assessment, 51-56

diagnostic tests, 53, 55
Glasgow Coma Scale, 18-19, 19t, 51
history, 55-56
of key cranial nerves, 51-53
  caloric reflex, 53, *54*
  corneal reflex, 53
  doll's-eye reflex, 53, *54*
  gag reflex, 53
  pupil responses, 51-53, *52*
  startle reflex, 53
of patient with submersion injury, 201-202, *201-202*
Neurovascular assessment flow sheet, 126, *128*
Nursing diagnoses
  alteration in family process, 88
  decreased cardiac output, 85-86
  impaired gas exchange, 86-87
  impaired temperature regulation, related to poikilothermia, 87
  impaired verbal communication, 87-88
  ineffective breathing pattern, related to neurologic innervation, 84-85
  potential for injury, related to vertebral instability, 82-84
  powerlessness, 88
Nutritional deprivation, 212. *See also* Child abuse
Nutritional therapy, for burn patients, 166, 167t

O

Ocular trauma, 74-75
Orbital fracture, 73
Orthopedic injuries. *See* Fractures; Musculoskeletal trauma
Osmotic therapy, 61-63
Oxygen tank, 148-149

P

Pancreatic injury, 106
Pancuronium bromide, 56, 59-60
Paralytic ileus, 112
Pavulon. *See* Pancuronium bromide
Pediatric concussion syndrome, 47-48
Pediatric trauma team, 22-34
  continuum of care, 34-35

goals of injury management, 125
inner core team, 25-31
  airway team, 26
  medical team: left, 29-30
  medical team: right, 26-29
  nursing support team, 30-31, 31t
  surgical coordinator, 25-26
outer core team, 31-34
  central supply technician, 34
  emergency room attending physician, 32
  lab technician, 33
  nursing administrator liaison, 31-32
  operating room trauma nurse, 33
  radiology technician, 34
  security, 34
  social worker, 32-33
team interactions, 23-25, *24*
"Pelvic crunch" sign, 133
Pelvic fracture, 133-134
Pennsylvania Trauma Systems Foundation, 5
Pentobarbital, 63
Peritoneal lavage, 22, 107-108
Phalangeal fracture, 132
"Platinum half hour", 147
Pneumatic antishock trousers, 16, 27
  for femoral fracture, 134
  for pelvic fracture, 133
Pneumothorax, 14-15, 96-97
  open, 97
  subcutaneous emphysema, 97
  tension, 97
Poikilothermia, 87
Poisonings, 173-191
  acute vs. chronic, 173
  emergency management, 176-180
    activated charcoal, 178-179
    assessment and stabilization, 176-177
    diuresis, 180
    gastric lavage, 178-179
    gut decontamination, 177-178
    specific antidotes, 179t
    syrup of ipecac, 178
  frequently involved substances, 173-174
  history taking, 175-176
  incidence, 173
  nontoxic ingestions, *174*, 174-175
  poison control centers, 189-190
  prevention, 189-190

specific toxins, 180-189
  acetaminophen, 181, 183t-184t
  carbon monoxide, 154, 168, 168t
  caustics and corrosives, 189, 190t
  ethyl alcohol, 181, 185t
  household products, 184-185, 188t
  iron, 181, 184, 186t-187t
  lead, 189, 191t
  salicylates, 180-181, 182t-183t
  smoke, 169-170
  tricyclic antidepressants, 184, 187t-188t
Preventing injuries, 244-254
  in adolescents, 251-254
  age-appropriate toys, *246*
  burns, 245, 249-250
  car safety restraints, *247*
  gunshot wounds, 250, 252
  in infants, 244-247
  motor vehicle accidents, 245, 248, 253
  participation by community agencies, *254*
  poisoning, 189-190
  in preschoolers, 249-250
  in school-aged children, 250-251
  spinal cord injury, 79-80, *80*
  submersion injury, 208, *208*
  suicide attempts, 252-253
  in toddlers, 247-249
Pulmonary embolism, in spinal cord-injured patient, 86-87
Pulses, evaluation of, 126, *126*
Pupil responses, 51-53, *52*

R

Raccoon eyes, 15
Radial fracture, 131
Regionalization of care, 1-7
  benefits, 1
  education, 6
  essential elements, 3-7
    commitment, 3-4
    competence, 6-7
    cooperation, 4-6
  evaluation, 7
  improving care, 7
  rationale, 2-3
    level of expertise, 2-3
    preparedness, 2

  resource availability, 2
Renal injuries, 111-114, *113*
  classification, 112-113, *113*
  diagnosis, 112
  management, 113-114
  mechanism, 112
  pre-existing anomalies, 112
Respiratory distress, 14-15
Respiratory therapist, role of, 26
Rib fracture, 92-93
Rule of nines, 158

S

Salicylate poisoning, 180-181, 182t-183t
Scalp
  hematomas, *43*, 43-44
  injuries due to child abuse, 223
  lacerations, 42-43
  layers of, *42*
Scapular fracture, 129
Seat belt sign, 107
Sedation
  for hyperventilation, 59-60
  for intubation, 13, 13t, 56
Seizures, posttraumatic, 19
Sepsis, postsplenectomy, 109
Sexual abuse, 116, 212, 224. *See also* Child abuse
Shaken infant syndrome, 222
Shock
  hypovolemic
    fluid resuscitation for, 17, 18t
    indicators of, 15
    monitoring protocol, 19, *20*
    use of pneumatic antishock trousers, 16, 27
  submersion injury and, 204-205
Skull fractures, 44-47
  basilar, 46-47
  depressed, 45
  diastatic, 45
  due to child abuse, 223
  linear, 45
Smoke inhalation. *See* Inhalation injury
Social worker, role of, 32-33
Soft tissue injuries, facial, 70-71
Spinal cord injury, 79-89
  age incidence, 79

assessment and management, 81-82
Brown-Séquard syndrome, 80, *81*
causes, 79
central cord syndrome, 80, *81*
complete vs. incomplete, 80-81
nursing diagnoses, 82-89
   alteration in family process, 88
   decreased cardiac output, 85-86
   impaired gas exchange, 86-87
   impaired temperature regulation, 87
   impaired verbal communication, 87-88
   ineffective breathing pattern, 84-85
   potential for injury, 82-84
   powerlessness, 89
prevention, 79-80, *80*
Spinal fracture, 123, 132-133
Splenic injury, 104t, 105, 108t, 108-109
Sports injuries, 253
   dental, 76
   facial, 69
   musculoskeletal, 120
   ocular, 74
Stabilization of patient. *See* Assessment and stabilization
Startle reflex, 53
Status epilepticus, 19
Sternal fracture, 93
Stomach injuries, 109
Submersion injuries, 193-208
   causes, 194
   complications, 206-208
      neurologic, 207
      pulmonary, 207
      renal, 207-208
   course of incident, 195-196
   emergency department care, 198-202
      circulatory assessment, 200-201
      history taking, 198, *199*
      neurological assessment, 201-202, *201-202*
      respiratory assessment, 198-200
      suspected child abuse, 202
      vital signs by age, 199t
   epidemiology, 193
   fresh water, salt water, and cold water injury, 194-195
   hospital admission, 206
   incidence, 193
   management, 202-206
      airway and breathing, 203
      circulation, 203-204
      disability, 205
      gastric distention, 205
      hypothermia, 204, 204t, 206
      lab procedures, 206
      shock, 204-205
      urine output, 205
   prehospital care, 196-198
      basic life support, 196-197
      hypothermia, 197-198
      removal from water, 196
      rescue, 196
      venous access, 197
   prevention, 208, *208*
   terminology, 194, *195*
Suicide prevention, 252-253
Sympathetic ophthalmia, 75

T

Testicular injuries, 116
Thermal injuries. *See* Burns
Thiopental, 63
   use in head-injured child, 56
Thomas half-ring splint, 134
Thoracentesis, needle, 15
Thoracostomy tube sizes, 15t
Tibial fracture, 135
Tissue perfusion, assessment and management, 57
Toys, age-appropriate, *246*
Tracheal injuries, 98
Tracheostomy, 13
Transport of patients, 5, 143-152
   decision to transport, 146-147
   documentation, *150-151*, 152
   equipment needs, 144, *145*
   initiating transport call, 147
   management and stabilization en route, 148-149
   medication and supply needs, 144, *145-146*
   modes of transport, 143-144
   parental concerns, 152
   preparing child, 147-148
   safety and risk factors, 149, 152
   security, 34
Trauma resuscitation bay, 24. *See also*

Pediatric trauma team
Tricyclic antidepressant poisoning, 184, 187t-188t

U

Ulnar fracture, 131
Ureteral injuries, 114-115
Urethra
　catheterization, 110
　injuries, 115-116

V

Valium. *See* Diazepam
Volkmann's ischemia, 131, 140
Volume-pressure curve, *37*, 37-38

W

Waddell's triad, 120
Wrist fracture, 131

About the Editor

Connie Joy is currently the director of Emergency, Trauma, and Maternal/Child Health Nursing, and the administrator for the state accredited trauma program at Brandywine Hospital and Trauma Center, Caln Township, Pennsylvania. In addition, she is the director of the Sky FlightCare Aeromedical Helicopter Program, which is a regional flight program serving eastern Pennsylvania, based at Brandywine Hospital. Previous to this, Connie spent ten years at The Children's Hospital of Philadelphia. Her experiences include both staff and supervisory positions in the Pediatric Intensive Care Unit, as a staff member of the Emergency Transport Team, a clinical nurse specialist in the Emergency Department, and most recently, as the trauma nurse coordinator. She was instrumental in the establishment of Children's Hospital of Philadelphia as the first fully accredited Pediatric Trauma Center in the state of Pennsylvania. Her educational background includes graduate work completed in the area of trauma nursing, with a master of science degree in nursing from Widener University, Chester, Pennsylvania. She is certified in emergency nursing from the Emergency Nurses Association, and is a frequent speaker at local and national conferences in the areas of trauma nursing and trauma program administration.

**NO LONGER THE PROPERTY
OF THE
UNIVERSITY OF R. I. LIBRARY**

Springer
*Berlin
Heidelberg
New York
Hongkong
London
Mailand
Paris
Tokio*

Engineering

http://www.springer.de/engine/

Anas N. Al-Rabadi

Reversible Logic Synthesis